RELIGION, POLITICS, AND SOCIETY IN SIXTEENTH-CENTURY ENGLAND

RELIGION, POLITICS, AND SOCIETY IN SIXTEENTH-CENTURY ENGLAND

edited by
IAN W. ARCHER
with SIMON ADAMS, G.W. BERNARD,
MARK GREENGRASS, PAUL E.J. HAMMER,
AND FIONA KISBY

CAMDEN FIFTH SERIES
Volume 22

CAMBRIDGE
UNIVERSITY PRESS

FOR THE ROYAL HISTORICAL SOCIETY
University College London, Queen Street, London WC1 6BT
2003

Published by the Press Syndicate of the University of Cambridge
The Edinburgh Building, Cambridge CB2 2RU, United Kingdom
40 West 20th Street, New York, NY 10011–4211, USA
477 Williamstown Road, Port Melbourne, VIC 3207, Australia
Ruiz de Alarcón 13, 28014 Madrid, Spain
Dock House, The Waterfront, Cape Town 8001, South Africa

First published 2003

A catalogue record for this book is available from the British Library

Library of Congress Cataloging-in-Publication Data applied for

ISBN 0 521 81867 2 hardback

SUBSCRIPTIONS. The serial publications of the Royal Historical Society, *Royal Historical Society Transactions* (ISSN 0080–4401) and Camden Fifth Series (ISSN 0960–1163), volumes may be purchased together on annual subscription. The 2003 subscription price which includes print and electronic access (but not VAT) is £67 (US$108 in the USA, Canada and Mexico) and includes Camden Fifth Series, volumes 22 and 23 (published in July and December) and Transactions Sixth Series, volume 13 (published in December). Japanese prices are available from Kinokuniya Company Ltd, P.O. Box 55, Chitose, Tokyo 156, Japan. EU subscribers (outside the UK) who are not registered for VAT should add VAT at their country's rate. VAT registered subscribers should provide their VAT registration number. Prices include delivery by air.

Subscription orders, which must be accompanied by payment, may be sent to a bookseller, subscription agent or direct to the publisher: Cambridge University Press, The Edinburgh Building, Shaftesbury Road, Cambridge CB2 2RU, UK; or in the USA, Canada and Mexico; Cambridge University Press, Journals Fulfillment Department, 100 Brook Hill Drive, West Nyack, New York, 10994–2133, USA.

SINGLE VOLUMES AND BACK VOLUMES. A list of Royal Historical Society volumes available from Cambridge University Press may be obtained from the Humanities Marketing Department at the address above.

Printed and bound in the United Kingdom by Butler & Tanner Ltd, Frome and London

CONTENTS

NOTES ON CONTRIBUTORS

Simon Adams is Senior Lecturer in History at the University of Strathclyde. His publications include *Household Accounts of Robert Dudley, Earl of Leicester* (Cambridge, 1995) and *Leicester and the Court: Essays on Elizabethan Politics* (Manchester, 2002). *Elizabeth I* (Yale English Monarchs Series) and *The Road to Nonsuch: England and the Netherlands 1575–1585* are in progress.

Ian Archer is Fellow and Tutor in Modern History at Keble College, Oxford. He is the author of *The Pursuit of Stability: Social Relations in Elizabethan London* (Cambridge, 1991), *The History of the Haberdashers' Company* (Chichester, 1991), and articles on various aspects of the social and political history of early modern London. He is currently working on aspects of charitable provision in early modern London. He is also General Editor of the Royal Historical Society bibliographies on British and Irish history.

George Bernard is a Reader in the Department of History at the University of Southampton. His publications include *The Power of the Early Tudor Nobility: A Study of the Fourth and Fifth Earls of Shrewsbury* (Brighton, 1984) and *Power and Politics in Tudor England* (Aldershot, 2000).

Mark Greengrass has a personal chair in history at the University of Sheffield and is currently Director of the University's Humanities Research Institute. His recent publications include (with Keith Cameron and Penny Roberts) *The Adventure of Religious Pluralism in Early Modern France* (Oxford, 2000). He is currently completing a book on the attempts at reforming French institutions and society in the wars of religion under the title: *Governing Passions: the Reformation of the French Kingdom, 1576–1586*.

Paul Hammer is a lecturer in history at the University of St Andrews. He is the author of *The Polarisation of Elizabethan Politics: the Political Career of Robert Devereux, 2nd Earl of Essex, 1585–1597* (Cambridge, 1999) and the forthcoming *Elizabeth's Wars: War, Society and Politics in Tudor England, 1544–1604*, as well as numerous articles on Elizabethan political culture. He is currently working on a book about the fall of the Earl of Essex.

Fiona Kisby completed a Ph.D. in 1996, and then held a British Academy post-doctoral research fellowship at Royal Holloway College, University of London. She is a Fellow of the Royal Historical Society, and has published several articles on the early Tudor court and the cultural life of late medieval towns in music and history journals. She currently teaches history, Latin, and music at Queenswood School, Hertfordshire.

ABBREVIATIONS

AGS	Archivo General de Simancas
APC	*Acts of the Privy Council of England*, 32 vols (London, 1890–1907)
AR	F. Grose and T. Astle (eds), *The Antiquarian Repertory*, 4 vols (London, 1807–1809)
Beza	Hippolyte Aubert *et al.* (eds), *Correspondance de Théodore de Bèze*, 23 vols published (Geneva, 1960–2001)
BNF	Bibliothèque Nationale de France
Briefe Johann Casimir	Friedrich von Bezold (ed.), *Briefe des Pfalzgraven Johann Casimir mit verwandten Schriftstücken*, 3 vols (Munich, 1882–1903)
BRO	Berkshire Record Office
BL	British Library
Bodl.	Bodleian Library
CLRO	Corporation of London Records Office
CoA	College of Arms
CPR	*Calendar of the Patent Rolls, Edward VI, Philip and Mary, and Elizabeth* (in progress, London 1924–)
CQJ	J.G. Nichols (ed.), *The Chronicle of Queen Jane and of Two Years of Queen Mary*, Camden Society, old series, 48 (1850)
Cramer, 'Malliet'	L. Cramer, 'La mission du conseiller Jean Malliet en Angleterre 1582–1583', *Bulletin de la Société d'Histoire et d'Archaeologie de Genève*, 3 (1911), pp. 385–404
Cramer, *Seigneurie*	L. Cramer, *La Seigneurie de Genève et la Maison de Savoie de 1559 à 1603*, 4 vols (Geneva and Paris, 1912–1950)
CSPD	*Calendar of State Papers, Domestic Series, of the Reigns of Edward VI, Mary, Elizabeth* (in progress, London, 1856–)
CSPIre.	*Calendar of State Papers, Relating to Ireland*, 11 vols (London, 1860–1912)
CSPF	*Calendar of State Papers, Foreign Series, Elizabeth I*, 23 vols (London 1863–1950)
CSPSc.	*Calendar of the State Papers Relating to Scotland and Mary Queen of Scots*, 13 vols in 14 (Edinburgh, 1898–1969)

CSPSp.	*Calendar of Letters and State Papers [...] Preserved in the Archives of Simancas*, 15 vols in 20 (London, 1862–1954)
Devereux	W.B. Devereux, *Lives and Letters of the Devereux, Earls of Essex, in the Reigns of Elizabeth, James I and Charles I, 1540–1646*, 2 vols (London, 1853)
DNB	L. Stephen and S. Lee (eds), *Dictionary of National Biography*, 22 vols (London, 1885–1900, 1908–1909 edn)
EC	D. Starkey (ed.), *The English Court: From the Wars of the Roses to the Civil War* (London, 1992)
EHR	*English Historical Review*
Henri	Michel François *et al.* (eds), *Lettres de Henri III roi de France*, 5 vols published (Paris, 1959–2000)
HC	H. Ellis (ed.), *Hall's Chronicle: Containing the History of England, during the Reign of Henry the Fourth [...] to the End of the Reign of Henry VIII [...]* (London, 1908)
HJ	*Historical Journal*
HMC	Historical Manuscripts Commission
HMCS	*A Calendar of the Manuscripts of the Most Hon. The Marquis of Salisbury, KG, &c, Preserved at Hatfield House, Hertfordshire*, 24 vols (London, 1883–1976)
HO	Society of Antiquaries, *A Collection of Ordinances and Regulations for the Government of the Royal Household* (London, 1790)
HoP, 1509–1558	S.T. Bindoff (ed.), *The History of Parliament: The House of Commons, 1509–1558*, 3 vols (London, 1982)
HoP, 1558–1603	P.W. Hasler (ed.), *The History of Parliament: The House of Commons, 1558–1603*, 3 vols (London, 1981)
KGP	F. Kisby, '"When the King Goeth a Procession": chapel ceremonies and services, the ritual year and religious reforms at the early-Tudor court, 1485–1547', *Journal of British Studies*, 40 (2001), pp. 44–74
L&A	R.B. Wernham (ed.), *List and Analysis of State Papers, Foreign Series, Elizabeth I, Preserved in the Public Record Office*, 6 vols (London, 1964–1994)
Leicester Accounts	S. Adams (ed.), *Household Accounts and Disbursement Books of Robert Dudley, Earl of Leicester, 1558–1561, 1584–1586*, Camden Society, fifth series, 6 (1995)

LP	J.S. Brewer *et al.* (eds), *Letters and Papers, Foreign and Domestic, of the Reign of Henry VIII*, 21 vols and addenda (London, 1862–1932)
LRC	W. Ullman (ed.), *Liber Regie Capelle: a Manuscript in the Biblioteca Publica, Evora*, Henry Bradshaw Society, 92 (London, 1961)
Machyn's Diary	J.G. Nichols (ed.), *The Diary of Henry Machyn [...] A.D. 1550 to A.D. 1563*, Camden Society, old series, 42 (1848)
OBG	D. Starkey, 'Henry VIII's old blue gown: the English court under the Lancastrians and Yorkists', *The Court Historian*, 4 (1999), pp. 1–29
PH	Pièces Historiques
PRO	Public Records Office
SP	State Papers
STC	A.W. Pollard and G.R. Redgrave (eds), *A Short-Title Catalogue of Books Printed in England, Scotland and Ireland, and of English Books Printed Abroad, 1475–1640*, revised by W.A. Jackson, F.S. Ferguson, and K.F. Pantzer, 3 vols (London, 1976–1991)
TRHS	*Transactions of the Royal Historical Society*
TRP	P.L. Hughes and J.F. Larkin (eds), *Tudor Royal Proclamations*, 3 vols (London, 1964–1969)
UC	*Correspondence of Sir Henry Unton, Knt, Ambassador from Queen Elizabeth to Henry IV, King of France, in the Years MDXCI and MDXCII* (London, 1847)
UCL	University College London
VCH	*The Victoria History of the Counties of England* (continuing series, London and elsewhere, 1900–)
Wriothesley's Chronicle	W.D. Hamilton (ed.), *Wriothesley's Chronicle*, Camden Society, second series, 2 vols, 116 (1875), 126 (1877)

RELIGIOUS CEREMONIAL AT THE TUDOR COURT: EXTRACTS FROM ROYAL HOUSEHOLD REGULATIONS

Edited by Fiona Kisby

ACKNOWLEDGMENTS

I wish to thank Andrea Clarke, John Guy, David Loades, Charles Littleton, Shelagh Mitchell, Glenn Richardson, David Starkey, and Richard Yorke for their expert advice during preparation of this edition. I am grateful to Andrew Wathey for originally drawing my attention to British Library, Additional MS 71009. Extracts from the manuscript are reproduced by kind permission of the British Library.

I would like to dedicate this piece to the memory of Michael Taylor, an inspiration.

EDITORIAL PRACTICE

The following extracts have been edited according to the guidelines suggested in R.F. Hunnisett, *Editing Records for Publication*, British Records Association, 4 (London, 1977). Punctuation and capitals have been modernized; abbreviations have been silently expanded, and otiose abbreviations have not been shown. The thorn has been rendered as 'th' or 'i'. For the sake of consistency, the ampersand, used only by the scribe of item (iii), has been spelt out. The modernization of spelling has been limited to the correction of scribal inconsistencies in the use of 'i' and 'j', 'u' and 'v', 'c' and 't'.

INTRODUCTION

Physical characteristics of the manuscript

British Library, Additional MS 71009 is a paper manuscript consisting of 114 leaves (300 × 210 mm) of which thirteen are completely blank. On the very first leaf, a list of contents occurs, together with other information on the probable authorship of the MS. This is probably in the hand of John Anstis (1669–1744), bibliophile and Garter King of Arms (1719). On the inside of the vellum cover is written 'Ex libris John Anstis' and no other marks of ownership are apparent.[1] From henceforward this source will be referred to as the Anstis MS.

The text in the Anstis MS consists of twenty-nine items appearing in three sections separated by blank leaves (Appendix). Sections 1 and 2 contain twenty-eight items, some of which are undated and concern ceremonial, both sacred and secular, at the court of unidentified kings (probably, on the basis of internal evidence, Henry VII and his son); dated items, relating to the reigns of Edward IV, Henry VIII, Edward VI, and Mary, are also present. Section 3 contains item (xxix), a mid-sixteenth-century copy of accounts of the Royal Collectors in Norfolk, 1346. Sections 1 and 2 are written on paper incorporating a pot with flower watermark, in use c. 1545. Section 3 begins on a new quire (from which the first two leaves have been torn) compiled from paper with a later pot with flower watermark, dated c. 1553–1554. The entire MS has been foliated in a modern hand; section 1 has no older foliation and sections 2 and 3 each bear separate contemporary foliations. Watermark evidence and textual analysis (discussed below) suggests that sections 1 and 2 are closely related, but section 3 appears to be unconnected. As the entire source is contained within a seventeenth-century binding, it is possible that the third section was, perhaps for reasons of preservation, bound in with the other two when they were acquired by Anstis during the earlier part of his lifetime.[2] Doubtless he was interested in the first two sections because they contained material on the Order of the Garter, the English order of knighthood of which he was an early historian.[3]

---

[1] L. Campbell, *A Catalogue of MSS in the College of Arms Collections* (London, 1988), p. 468. For Anstis's hand see College of Arms, MS Officers of Arms. For a similar list of contents in a MS formerly owned by Anstis see BL, Additional MS 71001, fos iv–v.

[2] As no marks of previous ownership are apparent, it is unlikely that Anstis acquired the MS ready-bound.

[3] D'A. Boulton, *The Knights of the Crown: The Monarchical Orders of Knighthood in Later Medieval Europe 1325–1520* (Woodbridge, 1987), pp. 96–166, 101; J. Anstis, *The Register of the*

Four anonymous mid-sixteenth-century secretary hands are present in sections 1 and 2 of the MS (Appendix). All hands are neat and errors in the text are minimal.[4] Scribe A consistently prefers 'gentleman ussher'; the descender of the 'es' abbreviation in 'kynges' always points to the left; the base of the 't' in 'the', 'that' etc. is distinct and curved. Also apparent is a preference for the use of marks of abbreviation in positions where they are either unnecessary or ambiguous (e.g. the horizontal stroke over 'on' and '-men'; the extension of the last stroke of every final 'n' with an ascending or descending left-pointing flourish). Scribe B uses virtually no otiose signs of abbreviation and prefers 'Gentilman ussher' with a distinctive initial reminiscent of a modern upper-case 'G' crowned with a curved 'c'-shaped flourish. The descender of the abbreviated form of 'kynges' invariably points to the right and the initial 't' of 'the', 'that' etc. has no base curve and the stem of the letter is usually formed with a long leftwards stroke beginning half-way along the length of the word. A distinctive approach stroke is used to form the bow of the first letter of 'and', and long descenders are often attached to the letters 's' and 'f'. Scribe C uses a hand distinguished by the use of a thickened, straight ascender of the letter 'd' which is slanted to the left at an angle of almost 45 degrees from the base line. Scribe D uses a small, compact hand; usually the looped ascender of the final 'd' of 'and' has a pronounced slant to the left towards the base line, often touching the head of the adjacent 'n'. In the formation of the looped ascender of the final letter of 'and', the scribe's quill invariably leaves the paper at approximately the height of the head of the 'n', and rarely touches the base line. This contrasts with the 'and' of scribe A, which invariably contains an upright 'd' with a looped ascender that terminates at the base of the writing line.

Contents, provenance, and dating

A catalogue entry for this source made when it was acquired by the British Library in 1992 suggested that it is a 'book of ceremonies at the court of Henry VIII etc. by John Norris, Gentleman Usher; mid-sixteenth century, 1554'.[5] No signatures appear in the MS, and this description almost certainly derives from one appearing in the 1939 Catalogue of Bernard Quaritch Ltd, a typed extract of which has been

---

Most Noble Order of the Garter [...], 2 vols (London, 1724). The MS contains a passage written by the Black Rod, one of the officers of the Order (fos 6v–7, see below), and a description of ceremonies on the feast of St George, the patron saint of the Order (fo. 26).

[4] Occasional interlinear insertions, deletions, or dittographical mistakes occur.

[5] British Library, MSS Students' Room, *Catalogue of Recent Additions, 1992–*.

inserted inside the manuscript's vellum cover on two loose leaves. The Quaritch cataloguer probably made the ascription on the basis of information given by Anstis, who prefaced his aforementioned table of contents: 'This noble Book of Ceremony was wrote by the Usher of the Order of the Garter, that is the Black Rod as appears in the first leafe, and as I take it from p. 22 [fo. 31] by John Norris who had that office given him 1 May Pat 1 Mar p. 4 m. 27'.[6] Thus, three pieces of information are given about this source: (a) that the MS contains ceremonials 'at the time of Henry VIII etc.'; (b) that it was 'wrote by' a gentleman usher at court who also held the office of Usher of the Order of the Garter or Black Rod; (c) that, according to evidence on fo. 31, the particular officer in question was an individual named John Norris. Analysis of the contents of the Anstis MS verifies that Norris was indeed almost certainly the one most closely associated with this source. He probably originally brought all the items of sections 1 and 2 together and may even have composed some of them; and this may have been done soon after the death of Mary Tudor in 1558.

Assuming that the third section of the MS is unrelated, then the 'book of ceremony' referred to consists of only the items appearing in sections 1 and 2. The text on fo. 31 cited by Anstis as proof that Norris composed this book is not, by itself, convincing evidence, for it merely describes, in the third person, the role of an individual of that name in the preparations for the marriage of Philip and Mary in 1554.[7] However, other evidence from elsewhere in the source can be adduced in support of the Norris identification. The very first item, (i), is a passage in the first person in which the author describes himself as a gentleman usher daily waiter, who served a king as a member of the Outer Chamber, and who also became usher of the Order of the Garter.[8] The Usher of the Garter, otherwise known as Black Rod, was one of the five offices of the Order and had the privilege of keeping all the doors where any council, including Parliament, was held. During Tudor times the office was usually awarded to one who held a prominent position at court, and the succession in the first half of the sixteenth century was William Compton (1513–), Henry Norris (1526–), Anthony Knyvet (1536–), Philip Hoby (1543–) and John Norris (1554–).[9] Compton and Henry Norris served as Henry VIII's groom of the stool, the principal royal body

[6] Fo. 1; see *CPR [...] Philip and Mary*, 4 vols (London, 1937–1939), I, p. 112.
[7] '[...] there was prepared by John Norres gent ussher (who had all the doinges for that mariage [...]) in the cathedral church [...]'.
[8] BL, Additional MS 71009, fo. 6v.
[9] A. Wagner, *The Heralds of England* (London, 1967), p. 150; M. Bond and D. Beamish, *The Gentleman Usher of the Black Rod* (London, 1981); *LP*, I.i, p. 1662 (10); *LP*, IV.ii, p. 2599 (23); *LP*, XI, p. 943 (2); *LP*, XVIII.ii, p. 449 (12); *CPR [...] Philip and Mary*, I, p. 112.

servant, and chief officer of the Privy Chamber.[10] Owing largely to the labours of David Starkey, the development of this sub-department of the royal household under the early Tudors and its relationship to the other departments of Hall and Outer Chamber is well known.[11] Knyvet and Hoby were also associated with the Privy Chamber, and served there as gentleman ushers in the 1520s–1540s.[12] Only John Norris (c. 1502–1577) was associated with the Outer Chamber of a king for a significant part of his royal career. A member of a family who had served at court since the reign of Henry VI, he was the brother of the aforementioned Henry.[13] He served as gentleman usher daily waiter of the Outer Chamber of Henry VIII from around 1536, and continued in that office until he was appointed gentleman usher of Mary's Privy Chamber by 1554.[14] He remained in royal service until his death in 1577.

Thus, John Norris's close association with the Anstis MS and his role as author of item (i) is confirmed, for he is the only Tudor courtier whose biographical profile fits the first-person description. If this is the case, then what survives as the 'noble book of ceremony' is not, however, holograph, because comparison of the hand and orthography of this item (and indeed all others in the MS) with Norris's own reveals no similarities.[15] As a gentleman usher of the Outer Chamber under

[10] PRO, LC9/50, fo. 206; *LP*, I.i, pp. 94 (27), 640, 1015; *ibid.*, II.i, p. 2735; *ibid.*, III.i, p. 51, *ibid.*, p. 80; *ibid.*, pp. 316, 610, 1035, 2074 (14); *ibid.*, IV.i, p. 297; *ibid.*, V, p. 1065; *EC*, pp. 78, 94; *HO*, p. 156.

[11] D. Starkey, 'Intimacy and innovation: the rise of the Privy Chamber, 1485–1547', in *EC*, pp. 71–119; see also D. Loades, *The Tudor Court* (London, 1987), pp. 46–52; *HO*, pp. 165–166.

[12] *LP*, II.i, p. 875; *ibid.*, II.ii, p. 1507; *ibid.*, III.ii, p. 1536; *ibid.*, III.i, p. 999; *ibid.*, III.ii, p. 1556; *HC*, pp. 631, 689; *HO*, pp. 154–155; *LP*, IV.ii, p. 2673 (20); *ibid.*, IV, p. 5243 (27); *ibid.*, V, p. 119 (43); *ibid.*, II.i, p. 2735; *ibid.*, XIV.i, p. 3 (2); A.G.W. Murray and E.F. Bosanquet, 'Excerpts from the ms of William Dunche', *The Genealogist*, new series, 30 (1914), pp. 18–28, 19; *LP*, XIV.i, pp. 3 (2); *ibid.*, p. 16, 220 (25).

[13] *DNB*, XIV, pp. 566–567; W. Dugdale, *The Baronage of England*, 2 vols (London, 1675), II, pp. 403–404; *CPR [...] Henry VI*, 6 vols (London, 1909), II, p. 37; III, pp. 92, 568.

[14] Before he received his formal court appointment, Norris was an unsalaried member (as groom of the Outer Chamber) of the King's wider affinity in the counties, c. 1520–1525; PRO, E36/130, fo. 231v; J. Guy, 'Wolsey and the Tudor polity', in S. Gunn and P.J. Lindley (eds), *Cardinal Wolsey* (Cambridge, 1991), pp. 54–75, 67. For his service at court see: BL, Royal MS 7 F. XIV, fo. 100 (1536, not 1516 as given in *LP*, II.i, p. 2735); *LP*, X, p. 392 (11); *ibid.*, XIV.i, p. 607; Murray and Bosanquet, 'Excerpts from the ms of William Dunch', p. 20; *LP*, XVII, p. 580; PRO, LC2/2, fo. 37; BL, Stowe MS 571, fo. 30; *CPR [...] Philip and Mary*, i. 200; PRO, LC2/3 prt 1, 86; PRO, LC2/4/1, fo. 18; PRO, E101/427/5, fo. 14v; PRO, LC9/50, fo. 206 (1509); PRO, LC2/2, fo. 37 (1547); *HoP, 1509–1558*, III, p. 19 incorrectly describes him as a member of the Privy (rather than the Outer) Chamber from 1536.

[15] M. St Clare Byrne (ed.), *The Lisle Letters*, 6 vols (London, 1981), I, pp. 118, 122; VI, pp. 2, 7–10, 18–19, 293.

Henry VIII and Edward VI and member of the *domus magnificencie* – the 'above-stairs' department of the royal household under the jurisdiction of the Lord Chamberlain whose servants were concerned with the public, formal aspects of kingship and royal body service – Norris would have performed a leading role in the organization of the ceremonial life of the court.[16] As a full-time 'daily waiter', he would have acted as the Lord Chamberlain's assistant and organized other servants on duty in the public rooms of the Outer Chamber – the great or guard chamber and the presence chamber. In this capacity he would have had little formal contact with the other sub-section of the chamberlain's department, the Privy Chamber. Neither would he have dealt in a formal capacity with the below-stairs household or *domus providencie* under the jurisdiction of the Lord Steward.[17] An earlier household ordinance of Edward IV, of c. 1471–1472, stipulated that an officer in Norris's position was 'to be cunyng, curteys and glad to receue [...] and direct euery man in serues [...], and to know all the custumes and cerimoniez used aboute the king and other astates', because 'he assigneth the yomen of crown and chambre, gromez and pagez, to [...] busynes inwarde and outewarde for the king'.[18] Court ordinances issued under both Henry VIII and his father also stated that gentlemen ushers ought to be familiar with the duties of those working under them or else they risked 'the kinges displeasure'.[19]

In item (i) Norris states that he had 'set forth' regulations concerning ceremonial at royal banquets, coronations, christenings, burials, marriages, the Order of the Garter, the receiving of ambassadors, and visits of the Emperor and the French and Spanish kings.[20] This he did because he considered it 'mette for a gentilman ussher to know all estates, bothe lordes and ladies' in order to 'place them in suche order as their estates requirethe'. He also stressed that, even though men in his office dealt primarily with the ceremonial life of the *domus magnificencie*, some familiarity with the duties of those working in the *domus providencie* was necessary because 'it appertayneth to a gentleman ussher to know the estate and order of the hole howse as the halle and all other officis [...]'.[21] The items that follow in the MS contain just such material as Norris claimed he had assembled – a fact which further strengthens the argument that sections 1 and 2 are closely related. As what survives

[16] D.A.L. Morgan, 'The house of policy: the political role of the late Plantagenet household, 1422–1485', in *EC*, p. 32.

[17] *Ibid.*, p. 33.

[18] A.R. Myers (ed.), *The Household of Edward IV: the Black Book and the Ordinance of 1478* (Manchester, 1959), pp. 114–115.

[19] *AR*, II, p. 192.

[20] BL, Additional MS 71009, fo. 6v.

[21] *Ibid.*

occurs in four anonymous hands, it must be a copy of such a compilation. The discussion below shows that Norris could have composed some of the texts himself from personal experience; some other passages were probably the work of older individuals as they are retrospective and refer to the late fifteenth-century court.

Taken together, the texts of items (i) to (xxviii) survey almost the entire court and preserve material on the principal occasions of estate and other significant events which occurred under the early Tudor monarchs before Elizabeth. After the aforementioned introductory passage, item (i) goes on to outline the organization of the officers below stairs including those of the cellar, the kitchen, bakehouse etc. The first half of the remaining texts are formal regulations explaining household organization and, in particular, guiding a gentleman usher through his duties (Appendix). Item (ii) describes the order of the King's Hall, where many of the officers of the *domus providencie* worked. Item (iii) moves into the realms of the *domus magnificencie*, and deals with the order and ceremonial of the Outer Chamber. It advises the gentleman usher on the organization of the whole chamber staff, and describes how he was to receive visitors, manage access to the King, and deal with other formal aspects of domestic ceremonial. Information on the usher's role as the King's chief attendant during his visits to the household chapel on special 'holy days' forms a large part of this section. The holy days are not listed but, using evidence from elsewhere, it is possible to deduce that they included Sundays, Christmas Day, Easter Day, Whitsunday, and forty-four other feasts in the calendar of the Sarum Use (the rite used in the English Chapel Royal).[22] Throughout this item, ceremonial norms were set as if a king, prince, and cardinal were present.[23] As it was only under Henry VII that three such individuals were simultaneously alive, this passage probably refers to practice under the first Tudor king.[24]

Item (iv) deals with the Recording of the Chamber, a prime responsibility of the gentleman usher; and item (v) outlines his role during the royal removings, a regular aspect of court life.[25] Items (vii) and (viii) deal with preparations to be made by an usher for court banquets, and item (viii) draws attention to his duties during the opening ceremonies

---

[22] They are identified in KGP. A brief reference to the chapel also occurs in item (ii), because its members were entitled to eat their 'bouche of court', along with other courtiers, in the hall.

[23] BL, Additional MS 71009, fos 12, 13, 14, 14v, 15, 17, 17v.

[24] Cardinal John Morton (1493–1500); Princes Arthur (1486–1502) and Henry (1491–1547). Under Henry VIII, Wolsey became Cardinal in 1515 and died in 1529, eight years before Edward VI was born.

[25] F. Kisby, 'Kingship and the royal itinerary: a study of the peripatetic household of the early Tudor kings, 1485–1547', *The Court Historian*, 4 (1999), pp. 29–39.

of Parliament.[26] Item (ix) provides additional information on the usher's responsibilities as royal attendant when the King participated in the liturgical ceremonial occurring on sixteen of the highest-ranking chapel holy days. The five days when the monarch took communion in the chapel are also listed. Only four of the five days specified match those documented in the accounts of the Treasurer of the Chamber for Henry VIII; neither do they correspond to what little is known of the communion times of earlier English kings.[27] However, given that communion was rarely taken five times a year in pre-Reformation times, and as the realities of household life rarely matched idealized situations prescribed by court ordinances, this mismatch may be unimportant and this passage may reflect ideal practice under Henry VIII. Finally, items (x) to (xii) describe the usher's role in the ceremonies at the royal baptisms, the status of a king's deputy in his dominions, and the order of the two main rooms of the Outer Chamber in which the gentleman ushers worked – the great chamber and chamber of presence.

This material is followed by items (xiii)–(xxii) which, in contrast to the preceding texts, are narrative accounts, written in the third person. They describe, with varying detail, the receiving of Anne of Cleves, the marriage of Mary and Philip, the coronations of Edward VI and Anne Boleyn, the burials of Henry VIII and Queen Jane and the performance of a service of thanksgiving in St Paul's cathedral by Cardinal Wolsey in 1527. Meetings occurring between Henry VIII and Francis I (1520 and 1532) and the Emperor Charles V (1520) are also mentioned. Some of these passages were probably written by an individual closely associated with the Outer Chamber, for the role of a gentleman usher is often highlighted and details of precedence are provided that would interest one who held that post.[28] In this respect John Norris is certainly a likely candidate, especially for the narratives concerning events in the last two decades of Henry VIII's reign.[29] At the end of section 2 of the source, like an appendix, appear miscellaneous items, including an oath of allegiance sworn by members of the chamber of Edward IV, table plans at banquets during the time of Henry VIII, a diagram of the stage in Winchester Cathedral where Mary and Philip married, and

---

[26] Item (vi) is an anomaly in this context because it is not a formal regulation but a narrative account. In item (vii), reference is made to members of the chapel who sang a 'wassail song' on Twelfth Night, a court tradition since at least the reign of Edward IV; F. Kisby, 'The royal household chapel in Early Tudor London, 1485–1547' (unpublished Ph.D. thesis, University of London, 1996), pp. 218–221.

[27] See edition note 47.

[28] e.g. in item (xvii).

[29] Given Norris's leading role in the preparation of lodgings in Calais used by Anne of Cleves before she came to England to marry Henry VIII, his authorship of item (xv) is likely; *Lisle Letters*, VI, pp. 5, 7–10; BL, Arundel MS 97, fo. 112; BL, Additional MS 71009, fo. 34.

an order outlining the organization of Mary's Privy Chamber. Given the responsibilities bestowed on Norris by the Privy Council for organizing the stage at Winchester for Mary's marriage, he may well have drawn the stage diagram.[30] The Privy Chamber order is written in the first person and was intended to provide 'abreffe what order was used in this tyme'.[31] Norris's membership, as a 'cheffe ussher', of Mary's Privy Chamber by 1554 also points to his authorship of this item.[32]

If the Anstis MS is a copy, in a number of hands, of material 'set forth' by John Norris from his own and other people's knowledge, the question arises as to what prompted the assembly of the original materials and when this was done. An important clue to its dating is contained in the passage describing Mary's Privy Chamber. As its author speaks of 'the quene that dede is', 1558, not 1554 as suggested in the British Library catalogue, must be a *terminus post quem* for the MS.[33] In fact, there was a reason for John Norris to have made such a compilation in that very year. Listed as a 'gentleman usher quarter waiter' at the coronation of Elizabeth, he was soon promoted to gentleman usher of the Privy Chamber.[34] On 20 November 1558, three days after Elizabeth's accession, Norris was summoned to court.[35] The purpose of his visit is not stated, but it has been suggested that he was asked to give advice on the organization of the new royal household.[36] Any documentation produced on that occasion may have formed the exemplar, now lost, from which sections 1 and 2 were copied. If this was the case, it was not, as will be shown below, the first time that an usher of the English court had been commissioned to produce ordinances on ceremonial for guidance at the beginning of a new regime.

In the light of this, the items copied into the Anstis MS form a handlist which reflects information passed down to John Norris from the courts of both Edward IV and Henry VII, the experience he obtained under Henry VIII and Edward VI, and the issues he dealt with in Mary's reign. The MS contains highly topical items and can be seen as a precedent book providing guidance for those matters concerning royal ceremonial and household organization which preoccupied the new Queen as an unmarried female monarch (only the

---

[30] *CQJ*, p. 134.

[31] BL, Additional MS 71009, fo. 6ov.

[32] *CQJ*, pp. 128–129.

[33] BL, Additional 71009, fo. 6ov. This dating explains why, in item (i), Norris spoke of meeting the French King, Spanish King, and Emperor as if they were three different individuals, for it was only after 1556 that this was true: Francis I of France, Emperor Charles V (1516–1556) and I of Spain (1519–1556), and Philip, husband of Mary and King of Spain (1556–1598).

[34] PRO, LC2/4/3, 105; *EC*, p. 157; PRO, E351/1795, fos 12, 32, 36.

[35] *APC*, VII, p. 4.

[36] *HoP, 1509–1558*, III, p. 20.

second in English history and significantly younger than her predecessor) only days after her accession.[37] For example, as Mary was the first queen regnant to set up a Privy Chamber, her successor's interest in this through the inclusion of item (xxiii) is not surprising.[38] Neither is the inclusion of item (viii) concerning the 'Ordre [...] of commyng of the king to the hollighoste Masse att Westmunster before a parlament'. Catholic legislation was not repealed until Spring 1559. Thus, during the opening ceremonies of Elizabeth's first Parliament, which began earlier that year on 23 January, a mass was performed, as it had been in her father and grandfather's days.[39]

Significance and context

Certain items in the Anstis MS reproduce or supplement well-known Tudor narratives occurring in the state papers, sixteenth-century chronicles, and sources preserved in the College of Arms and British Library.[40] Other items, such as the orders concerning the Privy Chamber and the great and presence chambers contain material that is not, so far, known to occur elsewhere. Similarly, most of the material on the household chapel of the Henrician kings in items (iii) and (ix) is found in no other source. In fact, the information therein provides a more complete and detailed picture of the schedule of services in the early Tudor Chapel Royal, and the monarchs' attendance at and involvement in them, than it has hitherto been possible to obtain from other sources.[41] Moreover, as chapel days attracted many visitors to court, and the ceremonies in which the King participated (with nobility attendant) provided regular public occasions for the re-articulation of

[37] J.E. Neale, *Queen Elizabeth* (London, 1934), p. 72.

[38] J. Murphy, 'The illusion of decline: the Privy Chamber, 1547–1558', in *EC*, pp. 119–147; P. Wright, 'A change in direction: the ramifications of a female household 1558–1603', in *EC*, pp. 147–172.

[39] H.S. Cobb, 'Descriptions of the State Opening of Parliament 1485–1601', in *idem* (ed.), *Parliamentary History: Libraries and Records* (London, 1981), pp. 17–24, esp. 20.

[40] See Appendix.

[41] Other chapel sources: *Constitutio Domus Regis*, c. 1136; edition in C. Johnson (ed. and transl.), *Dialogus De Scaccario [...]* (Oxford, 1983), pp. 129–135. *Le Ordenement del Hostel le Rei [...] a Westmunster* of 1279; edition in T.F. Tout, *Chapters in the Administrative History of Medieval England*, 6 vols (Manchester, 1937), II, pp. 158–163. *Household Ordinance of York* of 1318 and 1323; edition in T.F. Tout, *The Place of the Reign of Edward II in English History* (Manchester, 1936), pp. 244–248, 281–283. *Liber Regie Capelle* of 1449; edition in *LRC: Liber Niger Domus Regis Angliae* of c. 1471–1472; edition in Myers, *The Household of Edward IV*, pp. 76–195. *Eltham Ordinances* of January, 1526; edition in *HO*, pp. 137–207. *Old Cheque Book* of c. 1561–1744; new edition in A. Ashbee and J. Harley (eds), *The Cheque Books of the Chapel Royal* (Aldershot, 2000). Of these, only the *Liber Regie Capelle* documents the ritual and ceremonial of the Chapel liturgy; the others deal mostly with the organization and duties of Chapel officers.

the symbolic power relationships between ruler and ruled, these chapel texts are of prime importance not just for the religious history of the household, but also for the history of kingship in England before the Reformation.[42] The chapel material in these items has therefore been reproduced in its entirety in the following edition. That this information should be contained in a precedent book for gentleman ushers, rather than an ordinance specifically for the chapel, is not surprising, for, as stated above, it was only the usher who was familiar 'with all the [...] cerimoniez used aboute the king'.

The Anstis MS is one of three ordinances that describe ceremonial in the early Tudor household chapel. Of the remaining two, one survives as a volume of *Articles* issued in February 1526.[43] It briefly alludes to the responsibilities of ushers on holy days when the monarch attended the chapel and sat in his great closet.[44] But it does not provide, as does item (iii) of the Anstis MS, the vital clue concerning the source of royal offerings on these days which allows their identification during the reigns of both Henry VII and his son.[45] The other, the *Ryalle Book*, is (owing to the fact that the published version contains an oath of allegiance sworn to Henry VII) usually described as an ordinance of the first Tudor king.[46] It identifies the feasts of highest liturgical rank upon which special ceremonies, involving the king, occurred – the crown-wearings, wearing of the purple, and days of estate.[47] However, little detail concerning the involvement of the King and his attendant nobility in the ceremonial on these occasions is provided; only item (ix) of the Anstis MS (technically referring to Henry VIII) contains a comprehensive account of royal participation on these and other feast days.

The 1526 *Articles* contain clauses which indicate that the book is a reissue of a text written originally for the court of Henry VII, 1494–1501.[48] In conjunction with evidence from other royal accounts discussed elsewhere, this fact establishes the continuity of ceremonial traditions at the courts of Henry VII and his son.[49] The *Ryalle Book* further

---

[42] See KGP.

[43] *AR*, II, pp. 184–208 (BL, Additional MS 34319, fos. 2–21v); see also CoA, Arundel MS XVII/2, fos 1–22; BL, Additional MS 21116, fos 3–15v; CoA, MS M8 fos 3–21v; OBG, pp. 26–28.

[44] *AR*, II, pp. 188–189, 192–193, 196.

[45] See edition notes 11, 50.

[46] The edition in *AR*, I, pp. 296–341 (BL, Additional MS 38174) is most often cited; (oath 240; fos 47–47v). OBG, pp. 25–26.

[47] *AR*, I, pp. 296, 299, 323–330.

[48] D. Starkey, 'The King's Privy Chamber, 1485–1547' (unpublished Ph.D. thesis, University of Cambridge, 1973), pp. 18–22.

[49] Fully explained in KGP. It has formerly been thought that Henry VIII discontinued ceremonial traditions followed in his father's household; S. Thurley, *Royal Palaces of Tudor England* (London, 1993), pp. 196, 198.

supports this hypothesis because copies with the oath of allegiance sworn to both Henry VII and Henry VIII exist.[50] In fact, the *Ryalle Book* preserves older material too. Its first half contains recollections of ceremonial practices at the court of Henry VI made by an anonymous gentleman usher of the Outer Chamber at the request of a senior usher of Edward IV at the commencement of the Yorkist regime; and its second part contains formularies reflecting ceremonial practices under Edward IV.[51] Thus, what was used as one of the two authoritative guides to ceremonial in both Henrician households in fact transmits practice from earlier Lancastrian and Yorkist regimes. Indeed, another copy of the *Ryalle Book* (prefaced with short articles dated 31 December 1493) exists, which contains the oath of allegiance sworn to Edward IV.[52]

If the *Ryalle Book* provided guidance on court and chapel ceremonial for the new dynasty in the 1460s, and was then added to and used as an official text for yet another in the 1490s, then the Anstis MS performed a similar role several decades later.[53] Yet this time, the dynasty remained and the changes of the Reformation formed the divide across which the traditions of royal ceremonial were transmitted. That this was considered necessary, even during a period of doctrinal and liturgical reform, is not surprising if the function of ceremonial attached to religious practice at the English court is fully understood. As has been shown elsewhere, the ceremonial and ritual routine of the court was such that the chapel, through the monarch's regular attendance at and participation in its services, discharged important functions in relation to magnificent display, access to the sovereign, and the public face of the regime.[54] Thus, on the one hand, John Norris was, in the words of Edward Underhill, a 'ranke papist' who, in setting forth the chapel clauses in the Anstis MS upon the accession of Elizabeth, reminisced about the early Catholic ceremonies because he faced the subversion of the whole traditional order.[55] On the other, he produced a ceremonial template for a court whose queen recognized that, even in the face of religious reform, these basic functions of ceremonial could not be easily dispensed with, for, as David Starkey has argued, they

---

[50] Henry VII – *AR*, I, p. 340 (BL, Additional MS 38173, fos 47–47v). Henry VIII – CoA, MS M 8, fos 27v–56v, fo. 56v; see also BL, Additional MS 21116, fos 18–37v, fo. 37v.

[51] OBG, pp. 11–14, 19.

[52] BL, Harleian MS 4107, fos 100–33, fos 132v–33. CoA, MS Vincent 98, is a partial copy with the oath sworn to Edward IV.

[53] Interestingly, the Anstis MS and the *Ryalle Book* share similarities in content, form and structure, for both contain formularies combined with first-person accounts and an appendix containing oaths of allegiance.

[54] Discussed in KGP.

[55] *CQJ*, pp. 128–129.

'conditioned the Royal Supremacy' and the whole development of sixteenth-century English politics and religion.[56] In view of this argument, it is striking that many clauses in the chapel items in the Anstis MS are echoed closely in a gentleman usher's handbook from the early years of the reign of Charles I.[57] Although in this later source certain liturgical details have inevitably been modified, essential aspects of the ceremonies concerning the most important liturgical feasts which persisted in Protestant England remain unchanged.

[56] OBG, p. 2.
[57] BL, Sloane MS 1494; the relevant passages are cited in the notes to the edition; see also P.E. McCullough, *Sermons at Court: Politics and Religion in Elizabethan and Jacobean Preaching* (Cambridge, 1998), pp. 52–53, n. 6. For other seventeenth-century chapel ordinances see BL, Additional MS 34324, fo. 215 (1622); PRO, SP 16/182/32, fo. 47 (1631); PRO, LC5/180 (c. 1629–1631); San Marino, Huntington Library, Miscellaneous Box 1, folder 32 (c. 1633).

Inventory of British Library Additional MS 71009

Text	Folio	Scribe	Watermark[1]
List of contents in the hand of John Anstis	1–2		
fos 2v–6v incl., blank			
i. When I wase a gentleman ussher dely waiter [...]	6v	A	12825 (c. 1545)
ii. The order of a kynges halle	7v	A	
fos 8v–10 incl., blank			
iii. Here begynnyth thorder of a kinges chambre and how a gentilman ussher [...] shoulde behave hym selfe	10–17v	B	12825 (c. 1545)
iv. The recordinge of the chamber	17v–18v	B	
v. How the kinge and the quenes lodginges shalbe made at every tyme of the kinge and the quenes removinge	19–20	B	
vi. Ordre of service and ceremonies done to the L. Cardinall Wolsie att Powles apon All Hallon day [...] (10 Henry VIII)	21	C	
vii. At Schroftide or ani other time when the king dothe bankkate	21–21v	D	
viii. The ordre [...] of commyng of the king to the Hollighoste Masse att Westminster before a parlament	22	C	
ix. Apon Twelfe day the king doth offre [...]	22v–26	C	
x. The ceremonies at the christening of a prince or princesse	27–28v	C	
xi. The maner and ordre of the astate of a kynges deputy in any of his dominions	29–29v	C	
xii. The ordre of the greate chambre and chambre of presence	30	C	
xiii. The mariage of Quene Mary and Kyng Philip Prynce of Spayne apon St James day [...]	31–32	C	
xiv. How Kyng Henry VIII receaved Charles the V Emperor into Cantorbury on Wytsonday eve	33–33v	C	
xv. The receaving of the Lady Anne of Cleve into Caleis [...]	34	C	

[1] Item number in C.M. Briquet, *Les Filigranes*, 4 vols (Geneva, 1907); all versions of pot with flower.

Text		Folio	Scribe	Watermark
xvi.	The Frenche kynges commyng to Calleis	34v	C	
xvii.	How the Constable of Fraunce cam to conclude a peace after the Frenche kyng was delyvered	35–36	C	
xviii.	A declaration of the the intierment of the verteows pryncesse Quene Jane	37–44v	C	
xix.	The trew order concerning the administration of [...] ceremones abought the solempe interent of [...] Prince Henry the viiith [...]	45–50v	D	
xx.	The order concerning the creating of [...] noble men [...] before the coronacion of [...] King Edwarde the Sixte [...] xij day of Februarie [...] The nexte day being Sondaye the xxth of February theorder then of the coronacion	51–52 52–56	D	
xxi.	When the king went overse to mette with the Frenche king at Ginies the xth yeare of his rainge	56v– 57v	D	
xxii.	The cronasion of Quine Ane	57v–60	D	
xxiii.	The order of the quenes privy chamber	60– 60v	D	
xxiv.	King Edwarde the iiij the othes for all his servantes	60v–61	D	
xxv.	Trappers for horses at beriall of a king	61–61v	D	
xxvi.	For the bankate at Grynwige the vijth daye of Juli	61v– 65v	D	
xxvii.	Bankate at Grenwige [...]after the Frenche king wasse delivered [...] xiiij Novembre [...] xiiij yere [...] Harre the viij; bankat at Grenwiche the viij [...] Juli ix [...] Henrie the viii; bankat [...] King Harry the viij wasse wonte to make every Schorftide (seating plans)	66–68	D	
xxviii.	The stage at Wynchester in the church at the mariage of King Philipe and Quene Mare	68v	D	

fos 69–72v incl., blank

xxix.	Compotus Nicholai de Castello, Edmundi de Baconesthorpe, Willelmi atte Park [...] collectorum [...] 1346	73– 108v		12752 (1553– 54)

Notes

(viii) Refers to the performance of the Mass of the Holy Ghost in Westminster Abbey which formed part of the opening ceremonies of Parliament; D. Dean, 'Image and ritual in the Tudor Parliaments', in D. Hoak (ed.), *Tudor Political Culture* (Cambridge, 1995), pp. 253, 255.

(xiii) Another account in *CQJ*, pp. 167–170.

(xiv) The meeting of Henry VIII and Emperor Charles V during Whitsun week, 1520; J.J. Scarisbrick, *Henry VIII* (London, 1991), pp. 75–76.

(xviii) A closely-related copy of this text occurs in BL, Additional 45716 A, fos 83–94; G.W. Murray and E.F. Bosanquet, 'Excerpts from the ms of William Dunche [...]', *The Genealogist*, new series, 29 (1913), pp. 21–22, 94–101, 144–151; see also CoA, MS M6, fos 1–13; MS I.11, fo. 37.

(xv) See also *HC*, pp. 832–835.

(xvi) Refers to the meetings, in October 1532, of Henry VIII and Francis I in Boulogne and Calais; Scarisbrick, *Henry VIII*, pp. 306–307; J.G. Nichols (ed.), *The Chronicle of Calais*, Camden Society, 35 (London, 1846), pp. 41–44.

(xvii) Service of thanksgiving at St Paul's Cathedral performed by Cardinal Wolsey, 1 November, 1527, involving Henry VIII and Anne de Montmorency, Constable of France. Text states that festivities organized at Greenwich occurred afterwards on 'the morrow after all sowles day', rather than on 10 November as reported in other accounts; G. Cavendish, *The Life and Death of Cardinal Wolsey*, R.S. Sylvester (ed.), Early English Text Society, 243 (London, 1959), pp. 66–67; *HC*, pp. 734–735; C.E. McGee and J.C. Meagher, 'Preliminary checklist of Tudor and Stuart entertainments: 1485–1558', *Research Opportunities in Renaissance Drama*, 25 (1982), pp. 31–99, 86.

(xix) For other sources for burial narratives see J. Loach, 'The function of ceremonial in the reign of Henry VIII', *Past and Present*, 142 (1994), pp. 43–68, 46, 56–60.

(xx) For other accounts see BL, Egerton MS 3026; CoA, MS I7 and I.8; Leland, *Collectanea*, IV, pp. 310–333.

(xxi) Date should read 12 Henry VIII. Refers to the meeting of Henry VIII and Francis I at the Field of Cloth of Gold, between Guines and Ardres, 1520; J.G. Russell, *The Field of Cloth of Gold: Men and Manners in 1520* (London, 1969).

(xxii) Coronation of Anne Boleyn, 2 June 1553; refers to Shaxton, Burgh/Borough, and Bainton the Queen's almoner, Lord Chamberlain and Vice Chamberlain (fo. 58v; *LP*, VII.i, p. 589 (8); *ibid.*, VII, pp. 386, 162; *DNB*, XVII, p. 1391).

(xxiii) Mentions ten gentlemen of Mary's Privy Chamber ('risse, bassate, kempe, ligons, norrisse, erle, bridman, hadnall, crostofer and large'; also listed in PRO, E101/427/5, fo. 14 (1553); PRO, LC2/4/2, fo. 26 (1558)). Also mentions 'mistris clarensins', chief gentlewomen of Mary's Privy Chamber (PRO, LC5/49, 58, 103; PRO, LC2/4/2, fos 25v–26; *EC*, p. 140). This gentlewoman did not serve Elizabeth (PRO, LC2/4/3, 104–105) but, on Mary's death, joined the household of the Count and Countess of Feria; J. Rowley-Williams, 'Image and reality: the lives of aristocratic women in early Tudor England', (unpublished Ph.D. dissertation, University of Wales at Bangor, 1998), pp. 218–245.

(xxiv) Reproduces, with additional details, oaths sworn to Edward IV appearing in BL, Harley MS 4107, fo. 132v and CoA, MS Vincent 98.

(xxvi) Banquet on July 1517; some of this material occurs in BL, Additional MS 21110, fos 40–43v.

EXTRACTS FROM ROYAL HOUSEHOLD REGULATIONS

British Library, Additional MS 71009

Item (iii)

[fo. 10]

HERE BEGYNNYTH THORDER OF A KINGES CHAMBRE AND HOW A GENTILMAN USSHER OF THE SAME FOR THE TYME BEINGE SHOULDE BEHAVE HIM SELFE

Furste it is to be knowen that ther be foure gentilmen usshers dayly wayters which ben dayly in wages; and thei have alwaie a chamber within the courte allowed to them and their lyvery unto their chambre of bredd, ale, wyne, wex, white lightes and fewell and cariage. And ther be also eight quarter wayters of gentilmen usshers and every of them shall have by the daie for the tyme of their waitinge vijd. ob. and their lyverie for their servantes. And when thei record the chambre thei shall have to their lodginges breade, ale, wine and white lightes; but neither thei have a chamber allowed to them within the courte ne fewell allowed to them. And one of the foure gentilmen usshers dayly wayters that be allowed within the courte ought to be in the kinges chamber betwene vij and viij of the clock in the mornynge, and to see the departinge of the night watche. And then and there to take the view of the waiters for that daie which shoulde appere there presently at the hower aforesaid; that is to saie two yeomen usshers and xij or xiiij yeomen of the chamber that be for that daie waytinge with gromes and padges as thei be in the watche so to keape their daies waitinge. And ther to continew betwext vij of the clocke and viij at night at which tyme the night watche sholde come into the chamber. And that the foure gentilmen usshers quarter wayters for that presente quarter to be in the aforesaid house in the morninge to assiste the gentilmen ussher daily wayter aforesaid. And that then the gentilman ussher shall comand of one of the aforesaid yeomen usshers to keape the kinges dininge chamber dore wher

[fo. 10v]

the clothe of estate hangeth.[1] And also to sett a yoman to keape everie

---

[1] The presence chamber containing a throne, where the monarch also dined in state and received visitors. Together with the great or outer chamber and the privy chamber,

chamber dore that is wont to be kept. And the other yeoman usher to walke in the utter chamber where the aforesaide yeoman geveth their attendance and to se them to be in good order and good service. And that yeoman ussher shall resorte unto his fellow that kepethe the kinges chamber dore and to assiste him. And so one of them to assiste the other from tyme to tyme as it shall be requisite. And that the shall lett no manner servante passe into the kinges dininge[2] chamber onles he be a gentilman, the servante of[3] a duke, a marques, an erle or a baron at the least, or a gentilman beinge servant to one of the kinges counsaile. And that no strainger ne serving man nor no marchant nor marchante stranger be let into none of the aforesaid chambers without thadvise of gentilman ussher dayly wayter or in his absence to a quarter wayter. And if ther be any gentilman within the chamber that will speak with his servaunte he shall resorte to the utter chamber dore and there to speak with him. But it be a lord or on of the kinges counsaile which shall have but one servant to waite one them within the kinges chamber. And that none of the yeoman usshers, yeomen of the chamber, gromes ne pages depart out of the kinges chamber without speciall cause nee licence or comandmente of the lord chamberlaine or of the gentilman ussher; and that he tarye not out of the chamber lenger then his cause of necessitie shall requier. And if any of the aforesaid yeomen, gromes or pages departe out of the chamber without lysence of the lord chamberlayne or of the gentilman ussher ther presente for the tyme beinge or tary longer then the cause shall requier, then he so offendinge to be punyshed at the will and discretion of the lord chamberlayn by the enformation of the gentilman ussher. And the gentilman ussher shall over see and view from chamber to chamber

[fo. 11]

and from tyme to tyme that nothinge be out of good order ne lackinge that ought to be in a kinges chamber. And that the gentilman ussher departe not out of the kinges chamber untill the comynge of the lord chamberlayne. And then the gentilman usshers to enqiuer of hym that the kinges pleasure maie be knowen where him list to here his masse in his secrett closett or abrod in his chappell or in any other place.[4]

---

it formed the suite of rooms which, in the fifteenth century, replaced the older one-room chamber; *EC*, p. 73.

² Interlined.

³ 'of' repeated.

⁴ Distinguishes between the privy or secret closet near the privy chamber, where the King heard daily masses performed by his privy chaplains (personnel distinct from those in the chapel); and the great or holy day closet, the first-floor chamber in which the monarch sat when attending services in the public Chapel Royal.

And it is to be enquired also if any ambassadors or any other stranger shall resorte that daie to the courte for whos comynge any preparation shulde be made. And if any suche shall repaire and come to the courte then the lord chamberlain shall appointe a gentilman ussher which shall give his attendance upon them [...][5]

[fo. 14v]

And when the kinge is departed out of the chamber then the gentilman ussher that keapeth the doore shall comaunde a yeoman ussher to keape it; for when the kinge is in presence no man ought to keape it but a gentilman ussher.

And when it shall please the kinge to have masse in his chappell and resorte to his closset on a high daie or in any other holye daie[6] when such estate as be beforenamed shall happene to be presente – that is to saie the cardinall the prince and one, two or thre of the ambassadors of divers regions, nations or realmes – then the said lorde chamberlyne shall call to him all the gentilmen usshers and shall shew to theym what estates, strangers and ambassadors shall resorte to the courte.[7] And then the said gentilman ussher shall send warninge to all the noblemen wher ever they be, and also to all gentilmen the kinge servantes and shall comaund gromes of the chamber and messengers to goe for them and to geve them warning that they may resorte to the courte. And when it shall plese the king to go to his clossett, theis aforesaid noble men beinge present, then the gentilman ussher shall se that the sword be there present and shall delyver it to an erle, for none under the degree of an erle ought to beare the sworde in such a daie. Then the lorde chamberlayne shall

[fo. 15]

appointe the greatest estate then being presente to accompanie and goe arme in arme with the said ambassadors as ther be in honor befor the kinge till they come to the closett. And thei shall stand by the one

---

[5] The description of the usher's duties continues, but contains nothing relating to the chapel.

[6] The monarch sat in his great closet and heard services in the Chapel Royal only on holy days; see below, n. 11.

[7] 'And when [...] courte'. This clause reappears in a gentleman usher's handbook from the early years of Charles I's reign; BL, Sloane MS 1494, fo. 9.

syd of the closset till the kinge be in his travers.[8] And a gentilman usssher shall comand a yeoman ussher to set carpetes and cusshions to be put in the chappell and for every ambassador a severall[9] cusshion and to set the said carpetes and cusshions in suche stalles of the chappell as the gentilman ussher shall think convenieble and convenient and after as the strangers be in degre and estate of royalnee. And theis aforesaid well provided and soon as it ought to be then the gentilman ussher shall resorte to the closset and ther to geve his attendance to bringe them downe to the chappell when the lord chamberleyn shall see convenient tyme. Then shall the gentilman ussher appoint every of the strangers to his stall and to the place that is ordeynyd for hym. And so the gentilmen ussher shall geve his attendance on them to bringe them to the closset after masse. And that in lykewise to goe before the kinge from the closset and in lyke manner accompanied as thei were in comynge to the closset.[10]

And the gentilman ussher shall warne the gentilman that wayteth on the cardinall to have a cusshion ready for his lorde, and in lyke manner to warne the princes ussher to have a cusshion redy and to be put in such places of the closset as by the lord chamberlayne shall be thought convenient for them to knele at. And that a gentilman ussher command a yeoman ussher to have a cusshion and a carpet redy in the chappell for the kinges offeringe. And that the gentilman ussher have allwaie in a redynes with him the kynges offeringe as shall appertayne for that daie which is comonly for Sondayes and holy daies a noble in gowlde, for the kinge offereth but only golde on Sondaies and holy daies.[11] The which golde shall be taken to the greatest estate there being presente which shall kisse it and delyver it to the kinge when he hathe kissed the patente of the chalice knelinge one his knees which will receyve it of him and offer it.

[fo. 15v]

And that no gentilman ussher presume to keape the kinges travers but if he be one of the iiij dayly wayters.[12]

---

[8] A traverse or curtained area erected in the body of the chapel, in which the King sat when he participated in particular services; possibly also, in certain contexts, a curtain drawn over the entrance to the holy day closet.

[9] An individual, separate cushion.

[10] '[...] and in lyke manner [...] closset' repeated.

[11] One noble = 6s 8d (Myers, *Household of Edward IV*, p. 91; *LRC*, p. 7). These payments are recorded, in early Tudor times, in the accounts of the Treasurer of the Chamber (holy days listed in KGP).

[12] 'And that a gentilman ussher command [...] wayters'; clause reappears in BL, Sloane MS 1494, fo. 10.

Christemas daie[13]

Also it is to be knowen that the kinge offerith one Christemas daie xxs;[14] that is to saie on noble to be hadd out of the comptinghouse and to be delyvered by the treasorer of houshoulde and two nobles to be delyveryd from the treasorer of the kinges chamber for the tyme beinge. And every holy daie in the Christmas wieke the kinge offereth a noble, and on newyeres day but a noble, and that to be had from the treasurer of the chamber.

Twelff daie

And one the twelf daie the kinge offereth aurum, thus and myrre;[15] that is to saie the sergeant of the confessionarie shall bringe unto the gentilman ussher that keepeth the travers that daie a propre pece of yellow sarcenet to enclose therin v nobles of goulde, the which goulde shalbe had from the aforesaid tresorer of the chamber.[16] And the said sergeant of the confessionarye shall also delyver unto the said gentilman ussher the thus aforenamed in redde[17] sarcenet and the myrre in white sarcenet eche of them to the michelnes,[18] other the quantetie of a tennis ball or of a paris ball and bound with a thredd of sylk.

Candilmas daie

Be it also known the kinge offerith on the Purification of our Lady comonly callyd Candelmas day vij nobles which shall be hadd from the treasorer of the kinges[19] chamber.[20] And the byshop that in that daie halloweth the wax shall in his own person bringe the taper that is ordeyned for the kinge unto the closset, and then the gentilman ussher shall drawe the travers and the bysshope shall enter into it and with dew reverence shall delyver the taper yt is hallowed into the kinges hand. And the kinge shall receave it from the bysshop and shall delyver it unto the lorde chamberlayne which shall delyver the same taper unto a gentilman ussher, the which shall take it unto the most ancient erle

---

[13] This and other headings in item (iii) are marginated.

[14] An offering of only 13s 4d is recorded in the Henrician treasurers' accounts (PRO, E36/214, 223; BL, Additional MS 21481, fos 19, 174).

[15] The ephiphany offering of gold, myrrh, and frankincense, made in remembrance of the Magi, was an ancient ceremony performed at the English court since the early fourteenth century and continued under Charles I (Tout, *The Place of the Reign of Edward II*, p. 283; BL, Sloane MS 1494, fo. 111).

[16] A sum of 5 nobles (33s 4d) is recorded in the Henrician treasurers' accounts (PRO, E101/414/6, fo. 58; BL, Additional MS 21481, fos 112, 177v).

[17] 'grene' struck through; 'redde' interlined.

[18] Obsolete form of mickle + ness, meaning here greatness or size.

[19] Interlined.

[20] A sum of 7 nobles (46s 8d) is usually recorded in the Henrician treasurers' accounts (BL, Additional MS 59899, fo. 77v; BL, Additional MS 21481, fo. 179v).

and greatest of blode that is there presente at that daie the which shall beare the taper on the right hand of[21]

[fo. 16]

the kinge; and lyttle knowledge after the sword while he goeth in procession.

And after the procession done the gentilman ussher that keapeth the travers that daie shall receave the taper from the erle and shall put the aforesaid goulde unto the myddel taper that is ordayned for the kynge; that is to saie v nobles shall be put into the lengthe of the myddel[22] taper[23] and two nobles shall be put by the sydes of the second noble that is highest in the taper in the maner of a crosse.

And when the kinge is come into the chappell and the carpet and cusshion layd and spredd as thei ought to be, and when the kinge kneleth, than shall the said erle knele at the king right hand; and when the king hathe kyssed the patent of the chalis the erle shall kysse the taper and then delyver it unto the kinges handes and there the kinge shall offer it.

And when the offeringe is done then will the kinge resorte again unto his closet where the gentilman ussher shall draw the travers to geve the kinge the entery into his travers.

And after that the kinge is departed out of his chappell aforesaid then shall the yeoman ussher take the cusshions and carpet that was in the chappell for the kinges offeringe and shall beare it againe into the wardrobe of the beddes and ther to delyver it for their discharge.

And if that any ambassadors shall fortune to be present at that daie the lord chamberlayne shall call and shew to the gentilman ussher of what realmes and what estate or degree that[24] thei be of and what persons shall accompanie them. That groundly knowen, the gentilman ussher shall send a yeoman ussher to the clerke of the spiceri and to the sergeant of the chaundry to prepare tapers for them accordinge to their degree and estate and as it shalbe devisid by the lord chamberlayne and the gentilman ussher and shall also prepare carpetes and cusshions

---

[21] 'of' repeated.
[22] Interlined.
[23] 'Be it also known [...] taper'; clause reappears in BL, Sloane MS 1494, fo. 17.
[24] Interlined; followed by 'is that', struck through.

[fo. 16v]

to be put at the comandment of the gentilman ussher in places convenient for their syttinge and leavinge within the churche or chappell wher the kinge at that daie maie happ to be present.

And if it fortune the kinge to be that daie at Windesore and to here his mass in the colledge where he must nedely goo in procession with the knightes of the Garter at that tyme there beinge presente and in the robes of the Garter and in the Estate, then shall the knightes of the garter goo in procession before the kinge in order as they be in their stalls, some on the on syde and some on the other syde of the quier, and none shall goe in the mydde. And the ambassadors with thos parsons that shall accompany them shall goo in the myddes in lykwise as the king doeth, for the represent the estate of their maisters whether it be emperoure, kinge or duke. And the greatest estate or ambasssador shall goo last and hindmost of the ambassadors so that he that goeth hindmoste of the ambassador shall goo a lyttle knowledge before the firste of the Knightes of the Garter and in the myddest as the kinge doeth. And the kinge shall goo behinde after all his knightes and in the myddest.

Shrove Mondaie and Tuesdaie

And the gentilman usher on Mondaie at night or on Shroff Tewsdaie in the morninge shall resorte to the lorde chamberlayne to have knowledge of the kinges pleasure whether it may be his pleasure to have a plaie on Shroff Tewsdaie at night.[25] And if his pleasure be to have a plaie then the gentilman ussher shall comand a yeoman ussher to prepare a chamber and to strawe it and hang it as it besemeth for such a purpose and after the states that will be therat and also to geve warnynge to thofficers of houshoulde to prepare and make ready for a banket and a void[26] for the kinge as the custom is in such a nighte.[27]

---

[25] The last day of feasting before Lent began, when people were 'shrived' and went to confession; E.K. Chambers, *The Medieval Stage*, 4 vols (Oxford, 1923–1926), I, pp. 157–159. In the reign of Henry VIII some members of the chapel performed in Shrovetide plays; Kisby, 'The royal household chapel', pp. 218–228.

[26] A collation of wine and fruit eaten standing up while the dining table was cleared or 'voided' after a banquet; M. Girouard, *Life in an English Country House* (London, 1978), pp. 104–105.

[27] 'And the gentilman usher on Mondaie [...] nighte'; clause reappears in BL, Sloane MS, fo. 18.

[fo. 17]

And after this done the gentilman ussher shall comaunde the yeoman ussher on Shroff Twesdaie at night to gyve warninge to the warderobe of the beddes to change the cloth of estate, the chairs, the cusshions that be in the kynges dyninge chamber on Ashwednesdaie in the morninge. And that all thinges be pressed and ready in the tyme that the king shall goe to his clossett to here his masse and to take asshes in his chappell or in his clossett at his pleasure.[28]

Ashwednesdaie
On Ashwednesdaie the color of the cloth of estate, the chaire, the cosshins and the skaberd of the kinges sword that day shalbe blew. And the yeoman ussher on Ashewednesdaie be ready in the chapell with a carpet and a blew coshion for the kinge to kneale upon when he shall come thether to take asshes. And the gentilman ussher shall also comaund a yeoman ussher, if the chappell be ther presente, to warn the sergeant of the vestry, and if the chappell be nott ther then to warn the deane of the chappell and the clark of the closset,[29] to make ready the chappell, church or abbey where ever the king shall fortune to be that daie and to provide for a pulpitt. For thuse of the king is to have a sermon one Ashwednesdaie in his chappell. The gentilman ussher shall prepare a stoole and a cusshion to be ready within the kinges clossett; that if his pleasure be to sytt whale he hereth the sermon then to be put within the travers at his pleasure and comandement. And if the kinge will have a sermon on Wednesdaies and Frydaies in the Lent then lyke prepaire must be made therfore as is beforesaid. But on Sondaies in the Lente sermons must be hadd by custom of kinges.[30]

And if a Cardinall of this realme shall fortune to be presente at any or all of theis sermons then the gentilman ussher shall comande a yeoman ussher to prepare a stole and a coshion to be put in the

[28] On Ash Wednesday, the beginning of Lent, the Sarum rite (which by the late fifteenth century was used throughout lowland England and in the Chapel Royal) required ashes to be placed on the heads of the congregation before Mass, symbolizing penance; T. Bailey, *The Processions of Sarum and the Western Church* (Toronto, 1971), pp. 19–20.

[29] The dean was the head of the chapel and conducted its services on principal feast days; the sergeant of the vestry organised the vestrymen who guarded the chapel vestments, books and plate; the clerk of the closet ministered to the monarch in his great closet, and also organized the privy chaplains mentioned above. For biographies of chapel personnel, see F. Kisby, 'Officers and office-holding at the Early Tudor court: a study of the Chapel Royal, 1485–1547', *Royal Musical Association Research Chronicle*, 32 (1999), pp. 1–62.

[30] 'On Ashwednesdaie [...] kinges'; clause reappears in BL, Sloane MS 1494, fos 20–20v. For a list of early Tudor court preachers see Kisby, 'The royal household chapel', Appendix 4.

chappell for the saide cardinall; and the cardinalles gentilman ussher shall sett it before the mydle of the aulter and the cardinall shall sytt and his back to the aulter and his face to the people.

[fo. 17v]

And if a prince of this realme shall fortune to be present then the gentilman ussher shall prepare a stole and a coshion for hym within the kinges clossett, and all other dukes and lordes shall sytt in the chappell.

Also the gentilman ussher shall comaund a yeoman ussher and a yeoman of the chamber to keape all doores and galeris necessarie to be kepte, that the kinge ne the lordes be not trobled with preast of people, ne with noyse, ne with other incovenient causes but that he may here his sermon quietly. And the gentilman ussher shall also on Palmesondaie geve warninge to iiij or vj of the best knightes that daie beinge present in the courte to be ready to beare the canapie over the sacrament, the which the kinge almoner ought to beare that daie in procession if he be present that daie in the courte. And shall also warne iiij squiers for the body to be ready to beare torches abought the canapie.

As for thorder of Our Lady Daie in Lente, Palmesondaie, Tenable Wednesdaie,[31] Maundey Thursdaie, Good Frydaie, Ester Eve and Ester daie ben sufficiently declarid afore.

Item (ix)

[fo. 22v]

Apon Twelfe Day[32]
The king doth offre myrrhe, golde and frankensence. The myrrhe and the franckensence must be sent for to the sergeant of the confessionarie. And the golde, which is fyve nobilles, must be had from the tresaurer of the chambre. And the same golde must be wrapped in a smalle piece of red silk.

---

[31] On the evenings of Wednesday, Thursday, and Friday of Holy Week a special form of nocturns, matins, and lauds, called Tenebrae, was performed; H.J. Feasey, *Ancient English Holy Week Ceremonial* (London, 1893), pp. 84–94.
[32] This and other headings in item (ix) are emboldened.

Apon Asshe Wednysday

The king cometh to the closett and tarieth there til the asshes be hallowed. Then cometh he downe into the chappell and receavith asshes. (And a quarter wayter must be redy there to ley the quyssion). And when he hath don he goeth up agayne into his closett and there tarieth till masse be don. And that day the swerde before hym.

Apon Palme Sonday

When the king shall go a procession a gentleman ussher must warne sixe knightes to bere the canopie. And iiij squyers for the body to bere the torches and also to warne a yoman ussher to be redye with carpett and quission at the place where the king shall staye in the procession tyme. And assoone as the king is com to ley the carpett, and when the sacrament cometh, a gentleman ussher to ley the quission for the king to kneele apon. And when the king hath kneled iij tymes att Osanna, then take upp the carpett and quission and sende them both to the chappell dore till the king doth com. And as the king cometh by the crosse in the hall he leavith his palme there;[33] and att the plucking up of the cloth before the rode, lett the carpett and quisshion be layde agayne for the king to knele apon. That day the king doth offre the besant,[34] which is delyvered by a gentleman ussher to the noblist parsonage that is present. And he to geve it to the king.[35]

[fo. 23]

Apon Candelmasse day

A gentleman ussher must send to the jewelhouse for vij nobles and when the ghospell is don he must sett them like a crosse in the myddle of the kinges taper on that syde the face is of. That day the king goeth a procession, and the lorde chamberlayne of Englande doth carrie the kinges taper before him. And at the ghospell tyme the king doth holde it in his hande. And when the king goeth to offre it the lord chambrelayne aforesaid doth beare it before him (the face forwarde). And at the place he delyvereth it into the kinges hande to offre.

[33] On Palm Sunday those in the procession carried greenery in remembrance of Christ's triumphant entry into Jerusalem, when the crowd strewed the way with palms; Feasey, *Ancient English Holy Week*, pp. 53–84. Richard Grene, Sergeant of the Vestry by 1530, received palms for chapel decoration in the 1530s; Kisby, 'Officers and office-holding', s.v. 'Richard Grene'.

[34] The offering made by the kings of England at the sacrament.

[35] 'When the king shall go a procession [...] king'; see clause in BL, Sloane MS 1494, fo. 22.

Apon Wednisday in Palme weeke

The king goeth to his service att v of the clocke and either a bishop or else the amner[36] do attende apon the king to say service with hym. And a gentleman ussher must see in a redynesse a carpett and quission for the king to kneele apon when he shall receave discipline.[37] And all that day he hath the swerde borne before him.[38]

Apon Mawndie Thursday

The king goeth to Masse and the swerde before him, and likewise home. In the afternone at iij of the clock the king goeth to the chappell without swerde or mace and there a gentleman ussher must be redy with a quission on the right syde of the chappell for the king to kneele apon. That done, the king, the bisshop, the deane or subdeane[39] do washe the altares, and that while the chappell do syng certayne respons appoynted for the service. And the vice chambrelayne or a squier for the body shall holde the kinges capp. When he hath don in the chappell, he goeth up into his owne closett and then into the quenes closett with all the chappell synging before hym. After that is don the king goeth either into his closett or into the wardobe of the robes and there he makith hym redy; and so cometh

[fo. 23v]

downe into the hall and the chappell syngyng before hym. And before he goeth to his Mawndye his grace hearith a ghospell. And then the noble men and gentlemen makith them redie to serve the king. And after the ghospell the amner doth make his grace redie with his towell and apron. Then the gentlemen usshers must be abowt the king with perfumes.[40] The Maundy don, and the service, the king goeth to take discipline where a gentleman ussher must be redy with carpett and quission for him to kneele upon. Also the swerde must be in a redynes

---

[36] i.e. almoner.
[37] Penitential exercise in the form of flagellation, undertaken in commemoration of Christ's crucifixion; L. Gougaud, *Devotional and Ascetic Practices in the Middle Ages*, G. Bateman (transl.) (London, 1927), pp. 179–204.
[38] 'The king goeth [...] him'; clause reappears in BL, Sloane MS 1494, fo. 23.
[39] The dean's deputy; see Kisby, 'Officers and office-holding'.
[40] The pedilavium or maundy ceremony, where the monarch washed the feet of poor men and distributed alms. It was performed in remembrance of the Last Supper, when Jesus washed the feet of the apostles and it had occurred at the English court since the reign of Edward II. A detailed account of this service occurs in CoA, MS M.8, fos 26–26v (see also BL, Additional MS 21481, fo. 57); B. Robinson, *Silver Pennies and Linen Towels* (London, 1992), pp. 19–20, 25, 42–43, 57.

to be borne before the king from his closett to his lodging; and also torches if nede shall require.[41]

Apon Goodefryday
The king goeth to his closett att viij of the clock and no swerde before him in that forenoone. And there he herith a sermon. That done the chappell begynneth service. Then there must gentlemen usshers to see long carpettes layde overthwart before the high altare and also an other long carpett layd along for the kyng to creepe apon to the crosse where he offerith xxs.[42] And incontinent the gentleman usshers must be redye with iiij formes with carpettes on them to enclose the kyng whatt tyme he hallowith the ringes, and a gentleman ussher to be redy with a quission for the king to kneele apon with in the formes. When the kynge be hallowed, a gentleman ussher to be redy with a quission att the high altare for his grace to kneele upon. And ij noblemen appoynted to beare the basons with the hallowed ringes; and the residue of the usshers to take awaye the formes. Then the king goeth from the high altare into the vestrie where a stoole or carpett and ij quissions must be redy for his grace to kneele on what tyme he sayeth his service and handelith the sick men and weoman.[43] That don there must be in a redynes warned the eware with water to washe the kinges handes and also the sellar must be redye there to geve the king drinck. And while the king is in the vestrie about the syck, the quene cometh and crepith to the crosse and goeth her way. Then shall that carpett be half turned upp agayne and when the king hath don agaynst he cometh further a forme with

[fo. 24]

carpett and quisson must be redy agaynst the sepulchre for hym where att he kneelith till the service be don. Then goeth his grace up to the closett and there he herith an other sermon; after that he goeth home with out a swerde. Att after none he cometh to service with a blewe

[41] Comparable clause in BL, Sloane MS 1494, fos 24, 29v.

[42] The Passion from the Gospel of St John was read and a covered crucifix was brought into the chapel. It was unveiled and taken to an altar where it was adored by the clergy and people, who crept to the cross and kissed it. An offering of 20s is recorded in the Henrician treasurers' accounts (BL, Additional MS 59899, fo. 81v; BL, Additional MS 21481, fo. 152).

[43] Rings were offered by the monarch, which, by virtue of their consecration in his sacred hands, were thought to cure those suffering from epilepsy or muscular pains. The ceremony also occurred under Henry VI; *LRC*, pp. 62–63. It was closely related to the procedure, practised by English kings since the early twelfth century, known as 'touching for the King's Evil', which was thought to cure scrofula; M. Bloch, *The Royal Touch: Sacred Monarchy and Scrofula in England and France*, J.E. Anderson (transl.) (London, 1973).

swerde before hym. And when he hath receaved discipline in maner as before he goeth home and the blew swede before hym That daye the cloth of estate is blewe.

Apon Easter eve
The king goeth to the hallowing of the fonte and hath the best swerde before hym.[44]

Apon Easter day
In the morning the king goeth to the Resurrecion agaynst which tyme a gentleman ussher must warne for ix torches to wayte on the king to churche. And to warne vj gentlemen for to beare the canopie; and iiij esquires for the body with iiij torches to be abowt the sacrament at the procession. And when the procession is don a carpett must be redy for the king and quene to crepe to the crosse where the king offerith a noble. Then the carpett is taken awaye, and the crosse is sett one stepp lower for the lordes and ladies to crepe to. And a gentleman ussher to see afore hand that a place be made redye for the king and quene to kneele at the masse while, and to see torches redy and one torchett of white waxe for the king for the Resurrection, and to see the offeringes redye; that is to say one noble for creping to the crosse, and one noble for his howsell,[45] and xxs. to offre at high masse[46] (wherof one noble cometh from the compting howse, the rest from the jewell howse). And when soever the king shall take his rites or howsell, a gentleman ussher must warne the clerke of the closett and he to send to the eweie for the towelles and to the seller for

[fo. 24v]

wyne, and to the chawndlery for ij torches and ii torchettes. And the gentleman ussher to geve warning to the noblemen that be in the howse to be there, and to appoynt ij of the best of them to holde the towell, and ij next them to holde the torches and a gentleman ussher to lay the carpett and no quission and also to geve the towell to the lordes; and when the king hath don he to receave it agayne of them.

These are the dayes apon the which the king doth take his rites or

[44] On Holy Saturday a procession carried the Paschal candle to a place near the baptismal font. It was lit, as were other tapers in the church and, after readings from the Old Testament, the ceremony of blessing of new water in the font took place. See also BL, Sloane MS 1494, fo. 33.

[45] The 'housel' or communion.

[46] The King's Easter Day offerings of 20s (13s 4d under Henry VIII) were recorded in the Henrician treasurers' accounts (BL, Additional MS 59899, fo. 19v; BL, Additional MS 21481, fo. 152).

howsell: Easter day, Corpus Christi day, the Assumption of Oure lady, All hallon day and Christmasse day. And att every tyme the king layeth downe a noble.[47]

Apon Easter Munday [48]

These are the iiij offering dayes for the kyng: Easter day, Wittsonday, All hallonday and Christmas day[49]

Apon every of the aforesaid offering dayes the king doth offre xxs., which offering a gentleman ussher must sende for vjs. viijd. from the compting howse,[50] and a mark from the jewell howse, and delyver the same to the lorde stewarde if he be present; and in his absence to the treasaurer or to the comptroller to geve the king when he shall offre.

[fo. 25]

Apon Wytsonday

A bisshopp bringith holly water to the king and furthwith he goeth a procession. That don, the hympne Veni creator is solempnely song. That day the kyng offerith as is afforesaide.

Trinitie Sonday is the churche hollyday of the kinges howse, and that day the king goeth a procession and every sergeant officer in the howse carieth a banner at procession. That day the king offerith.[51]

Apon Corpus Christi day

The king goeth a procession and the sacrament is borne undre the canopie. And a gentleman ussher that day must warne vj knightes to beare the canopie and iiij squyers for the body to beare the torches. That day the king offerith.

[47] Paragraph indented. Offerings recorded in the treasurer's accounts indicate that it was only by 1531 that Henry VIII took communion on five feasts: Easter, Whitsun, Corpus Christi, All Hallows, and Christmas (BL, Additional MS 21481, fos 46, 58; PRO, E36/216, fo. 111v; PRO, E101/420/11, fo. 3v, 102v, 166; BL, Arundel MS 97, fos 12v, 20v, 43, 46). Henry VII probably took communion at Easter and Christmas, for this schedule was followed by Henry VIII until c. 1521; for details see KGP.

[48] No entry.

[49] Sentence indented like a heading.

[50] For Easter and Christmas offerings see above. The offering for All Hallows, recorded in the Henrician treasurers' accounts, was 13s 4d (BL, Additional MS 59899, fo. 68v; BL, Additional MS 21481, fo. 171). The Whitsun offering was 6s 8d (BL, Additional MS 59899, fo. 87; BL, Additional MS 21481, fo. 158).

[51] BL, Sloane MS 1494, fo. 84 'Trinity Sonday [...] is one of the kings patron dayes [...] wheresoever the king goeth to warre he hath the image of the trinite in his standard [...]'; see also LRC, p. 58. The offering, recorded by the Henrician treasurers, was 13s 4d; (BL, Additional MS 59899, fo. 87v; BL, Additional MS 21481, fo. 159).

Apon the Assumption of Oure Lady
The king takith his rites or howsell, goeth a procession and offerith.[52]

Apon All hallon day
The king takith his rites or howsell, goeth a procession and offerith as before. At evensong when the quyere begyneth dirige, the blewe swerde must be sent for to be borne before the king; and to see the blew cloth of estate to be hanged upp and to lett it hang All Sowllenday till afternoone.

[fo. 25v]

Apon Cristmas day
The king takith his rites or howsell, he goeth a procession and offerith as is aforesaide.

[fo. 26]

Apon Seynt Georges day or even
If it be fasting day, than there is a voyde servid. And then a gentleman ussher appoynt a lorde for the spice plate; a cuppberare and a gentleman ussher to beare the bolles and bring them to the cubberde. Then every one of the ordre in his degree cometh and servith the king of the voyde and a gentilman ussher to see them that shall beare the spice plate armed with the towelles abowt theire [...].[53] And the kinges spice plate to be covered, and one towell.

Apon St George's day
When the lordes do sitt att dinner in the presence of the king, the gentleman ussher that walketh the chambre shall appoynt first the wayters for the king as the sewer, the carver and cuppbearer, and then the sewer for the bourdes ende. And he to knowe the kinges pleasure who shall sytt att the bourdes ende. And if the king putt it to the discretion of the ussher then he to appoynt the best of the lordes of the Ordre that are present to sytt as there stalles be in ordre. And in like maner the residue to sytt att the syde table as theire stalles standeth and ij together to wash (after the king hath don) standing both before and after dynner. And one of the meanest lordes of the order to bring in water for the king.

---

[52] The offerings for the feasts of Corpus Christi and the Assumption of the Virgin, recorded in the Treasurer's accounts, was 6s 8d (BL, Additional MS, 59899, fos 87v, 96v; BL, Additional MS 21481, fos 159, 164).
[53] Blank.

Att Seint Georges Feast at Wyndesore

Likewise as before, saving that the lief tenauntes servantes shall do the service. And when they shall offre any helmett up, first the lief tenaunte shall offre for the king and after that for hymself; and so every lorde in his degree. After that shall they offre the banner and the swerde, and then the helmett; and when masse is done every lorde to offre in his degree. And then the quiere to say De profundis, and so att the chaptre howse dore to putt of theire robes.

Note. The first nyght the lordes come they go into the chaptrehowse and declare their comission.

A 'JOURNALL' OF MATTERS OF STATE HAPPENED FROM TIME TO TIME AS WELL WITHIN AND WITHOUT THE REALME FROM AND BEFORE THE DEATH OF KING EDW. THE 6TH UNTILL THE YERE 1562

CERTAYNE BRIFE NOTES OF THE CONTROVERSY BETWENE THE DUKES OF SOMERSET AND DUKE OF NOR[T]HUMBERLAND

Edited by Simon Adams, Ian W. Archer, and G.W. Bernard

ACKNOWLEDGMENTS

We are grateful to the British Library for its permission to reproduce the two texts. We have sought the counsel of numerous colleagues and would like to thank them for their advice. Andy Boyle, Christopher Challis, Cliff Davies, Joan Davies, Steven Gunn, Deborah Harkness, Henry James, Norman Jones, Diarmaid MacCulloch, Anthony Martin, Maggie Pelling, Rory Rapple, Richard Repp, Mark Stoyle, and David Trim have all offered invaluable assistance on knotty points. Malcolm Parkes offered advice on the transcription of the convocation articles of 1563. It was Andrew Malciewicz who first saw the significance of the 'Certayne brife notes', and our notes on the previously printed section draw heavily on his annotation, but with revisions and additions. We are grateful to Mr Malkiewicz and to the *English Historical Review* for permission. Ian Archer would also like to thank Denise Battisby and Danielle MacCallium for secretarial assistance.

EDITORIAL PRACTICE

The editing of the documents has followed the guidelines recommended by R.F. Hunnisett, *Editing Records for Publication* (London, 1977). Capitalization and punctuation have been modernized, elisions separated, and broken words joined. Deletions are indicated by letters being struck through. Standard abbreviations have been silently expanded, but something of the flavour of the idiosyncratic form of abbreviation of personal names and places used in the 'Journall' has been preserved to give a sense of the document.

INTRODUCTION

Two remarkable accounts of mid-sixteenth century politics are to be found among the papers of Robert Beale (1541–1601), now in the Yelverton manuscripts (Additional MSS 48000–48196) in the British Library. 'A "Journall" of Matters of State', as it was later described, covers political events from 1547 to 1552 (with occasional references to the earlier 1540s), and 1559 to 1562 (with occasional references to events in Mary's reign): it is published here for the first time. It was discovered by George Bernard in December 1978, following up a tantalizing, but only partially accurate, reference to a 'brief chronology of occurences in England, 1559 to 1562', in an early listing of the manuscripts.[1] Several historians have since drawn on it: Diarmaid MacCulloch in his analysis of Kett's Rebellion in 1981,[2] Norman Jones in his account of the 1560s,[3] Susan Doran in her analysis of the politics of marriage in the reign of Elizabeth,[4] and Greg Walker and Henry James in their assessment of the play *Gorboduc*.[5] The three editors here have all made extensive use of it for their own work: George Bernard in his exploration of the fall of Thomas Seymour,[6] and his account of Amy Robsart,[7] Simon Adams for valuable context for his edition of the accounts of Robert Dudley, Earl of Leicester,[8] and Ian Archer for its information on London.[9] But so rich and varied is the text that it deserves publication in full: there

---

[1] HMC, *Second Report, Appendix* (1871), p. 41. The text was also discovered independently at much the same time by Pam Wright, then a graduate student in the University of Birmingham.

[2] D. MacCulloch, 'Kett's Rebellion in context: a rejoinder', *Past and Present*, 93 (1981), pp. 171–172.

[3] N. Jones, *The Birth of the Elizabethan Age: England in the 1560s* (Oxford, 1993), pp. 15, 37, 42, 105, 124–128, 133–135, 138, 146, 202–203, 231–239.

[4] S. Doran, *Monarchy and Matrimony: The Courtships of Elizabeth I* (London, 1996), chs 2–3, and pp. 223, 225–226, 228–229; *idem*, 'Juno versus Diana: the treatment of Elizabeth I's marriage plans in plays and entertainments, 1561–1581', *HJ*, 38 (1995), pp. 257–274, 262–263.

[5] H. James and G. Walker, 'The politics of *Gorboduc*', *EHR*, 110 (1995), pp. 109–121, revised as 'Strategies of courtship: the marital politics of *Gorboduc*', in G. Walker, *The Politics of Performance in Early Renaissance Drama* (Cambridge, 1998), pp. 196–221.

[6] G.W. Bernard, 'The downfall of Sir Thomas Seymour', in *idem* (ed.), *The Tudor Nobility* (Manchester, 1992), pp. 212–240 (reprinted in *idem*, *Power and Politics in Tudor England* (Aldershot, 2000), pp. 134–160.

[7] *Idem*, 'Amy Robsart', in *idem*, *Power and Politics in Tudor England*, pp. 161–174.

[8] Simon Adams first referred to the document in M.J. Rodriguez-Salgado and S. Adams (eds), 'The Count of Feria's dispatch to Philip II of 14 November 1558', *Camden Miscellany XXVIII*, Camden Society, fourth series, 29 (Cambridge, 1984), p. 315.

[9] I.W. Archer, *The Pursuit of Stability: Social Relations in Elizabethan London* (Cambridge, 1991), p. 180.

remains much material for further investigation by scholars.

'Certayne brife notes of the controversy betwene the Dukes of Somerset and Duke of Northumberland', was discovered in the Yelverton papers and partially transcribed and edited by A.J.A. Malkiewicz, 'An eye-witness's account of the coup d'etat of October 1549', *English Historical Review*, 70 (1955), pp. 600–609. In 1976 Dale Hoak, in his study of the politics of Edward VI's reign, drew especially on the parts not published by Malkiewicz.[10] The full text, including Malkiewicz's transcription, slightly amended, is now edited here. There are uncanny parallels between this text and the 'Journall'.

Provenance

It can be shown that both accounts were originally in the possession of Thomas Norton (by 1532–1584), Remembrancer of the City of London and man of business.[11] Beale and Norton were well known to each other, Beale referring to Norton as 'honest, poore, playne Norton' in December 1581.[12] The occasion of that remark was Norton's imprisonment in the Tower, possibly for outspoken remarks in Parliament on the subject of the Anjou match.[13] When he died in on 10 March 1584, Thomas Wilkes was sent by the Privy Council to seize the papers in Norton's study, and a full inventory was produced. It survives in the Hatfield papers as 'A catalogue of all the bookes, papers and matters of state founde in Tho: Nortons studie and commited by Her Majestie to the charge of Thomas Wilkes, Clarke of the Counsell', and is endorsed April 1584. The catalogue lists the titles of seventy-three individual manuscripts. Item 10 is a 'Journall of matters of state happened from time to time as well within and without the realme from and before the death of king edw. the 6th untill the yere 1562', and item 30 'Certaine briefe notes of the controversie betweene the dukes of Somersett & Northumberland'.[14] These items were identified by Ian Archer and Simon Adams as respectively the texts in Additional MSS 48023 and 48126 printed here.

Comparison of this list with the British Library's Catalogue of the Yelverton manuscripts reveals that many of the other 'Norton Papers'

---

[10] D.L. Hoak, *The King's Council in the Reign of Edward VI* (Cambridge, 1976), ch. 6.

[11] M.A.R. Graves, *Thomas Norton the Parliament Man* (Oxford, 1994); P. Collinson, 'Puritans, men of business and parliaments', *Parliamentary History*, 7 (1982), pp. 187–211, reprinted in his *Elizabethan Essays* (London, 1994), pp. 59–86.

[12] BL, Additional MS 48039, fo. 48v.

[13] Collinson, 'Puritans, men of business, and parliaments', p. 198; idem, *Elizabethan Essays*, p. 74.

[14] Hatfield House, Cecil Papers, 140, fo. 51–v.

can be found in it as well.[15] This is not a particularly novel discovery for, although provenance escaped the compilers of the catalogue of the Yelverton manuscripts, Conyers Read had noted the existence of Norton material among them.[16] The most recent treatment of Beale's papers by Mark Taviner shows that fifty of the seventy-four items inventoried by Wilkes are identifiable in Beale's papers.[17] Precisely why Norton's papers were seized is unknown,[18] as are the circumstances under which they were transferred from Wilkes's custody to that of his colleague Beale, although it was some time after 1586.[19] We can only be thankful that they were, for otherwise they would probably have been destroyed along with the rest of the archive of the Privy Council in the Palace of Whitehall fire of 1619. The papers passed into the Yelverton family through Beale's daughter Margaret who married Sir Henry Yelverton of Easton Maudit, Attorney General and Chief Justice of Common Pleas. In 1697 they were summarily listed by E. Bernard, *Catalogi librorum manuscriptorum Angliae at Hiberniae* (II, pt 1 *sub* Henry, Viscount Longueville). In 1795 the papers were rescued from the extravagant and financially hard-pressed Henry Yelverton, third Earl of Sussex, by his cousin Sir Henry Gough Calthorpe, to whose London home they were transferred. In 1871 they were listed by the Historical Manuscripts Commission, 2nd report, appendix. The collection was then purchased by the British Museum from Brigadier Richard Hamilton-Anstruther-Gough-Calthorpe in 1953. A working catalogue of the Yelverton manuscripts was published by the British Library in 1994.[20]

Description

Both narratives are now found in different volumes of miscellaneous papers, bound at the end of the sixteenth or in the early seventeenth century.[21] The rationale behind the choice of the various papers in each

[15] The Yelverton manuscripts contain a large body of Beale's own papers and collections as well.

[16] C. Read, 'William Cecil and Elizabethan public relations', in S.T. Bindoff *et al.* (eds), *Elizabethan Government and Society* (London, 1961), p. 37. Graves, *Norton*, pp. 147–148 has a brief discussion of the Norton papers. Patrick Collinson noted the preservation of Norton's papers among Beale's in 'Puritans, men of business and parliaments', p. 77.

[17] M. Taviner, 'Robert Beale and the Elizabethan polity', (unpublished Ph.D. thesis, University of St Andrews, 2000), pp. 266, 271–279.

[18] Diarmaid MacCulloch has suggested to us that it may have been related to a Chancery case involving the estate of Cranmer's widow, then Mrs Scott, of which Norton had been a trustee; PRO, C3/217/30.

[19] Taviner, 'Robert Beale', p. 266.

[20] B. Schofield, 'The Yelverton manuscripts', *British Museum Quarterly*, 19 (1954), pp. 3–9; BL, *Catalogue of Yelverton Manuscripts*, I, pp. x–xii.

[21] For the contents, see *Yelverton Manuscripts*, I, pp. 80–88, 300–308.

volume is not clear. The narratives bear no immediate relationship to the other contents of either volume, though both volumes contain material from Thomas Norton's collection. The leaves of the 48023 measure 31½ inches by 20½ inches, and those of the 48126, 31 inches by 20½ inches.

The texts are neatly written in different secretary hands, clearly Elizabethan rather than mid-Tudor. Neither hand bears any resemblance to the hands of Thomas Norton or Robert Beale, nor to those of any likely authors. But that is not significant. The surviving manuscripts are best seen as fair copies written by a scribe or secretary (of the two texts, Add. MS 48023 fos 350–369v is the more professional, with a number of scribal flourishes, including the use of italic for Latin words and phrases). The 'Journall' reads almost like a dictated text. There are instructions from the narrator to the copyist on points to be followed up. The exotic orthography (sometimes gobbledegook), particularly of people and places overseas (Byturiges for Bourges, Marlecorne for Marlorat, Cicilius for Séchelles), hints at the difficulty the scribe had in rendering the unfamiliar sounds he was hearing, and at the subsequent struggles that he, or a copyist, had in deciphering hastily scribbled renditions of unfamiliar names and places.

Significance

'Certayne brife notes' is a coherent narrative dealing with political events in the first part of Edward VI's reign. The use of Ambrose Dudley's title of Earl of Warwick suggests that it cannot have been written before 1561.[22] The 'Journall' is more complex in form. The first pages, dealing with the years 1547 to 1552, read like the working notes of a would-be historian. The bulk of the text, treating the years 1559 to 1562, is much fuller, and from September 1561 is arranged in the form of a chronicle or diary with monthly entries (though with perplexing discursions that break the logical sequence). The monthly arrangement, and a shift from the past to the present tense ('the comen brute is'; fo. 362v) and even to the future tense ('the Baron des Addresses and his frindes wil be at Orleans'; fo. 368v), moreover suggest that possibly from as early as autumn 1561 or spring 1562, and more certainly in autumn 1562, the original author was compiling his text month by month, referring as he does in September 1562 to 'the xth of this present'; fo. 368v).[23] The inclusion of draft articles for the convocation

[22] See 'Brife Notes', n. 10.
[23] K. Waters, 'BL Add. MS 48023 fos 350–69v: a neglected source', (B.A. thesis, University College, London, 1998), p. 9.

of 1563 suggests that early 1563 is the most plausible date for its completion.

What the two texts have in common is their strong bias against the Dudleys: John Dudley, Earl of Warwick, later Duke of Northumberland, and his son Robert Dudley, later Earl of Leicester. They can be seen as promoting what has been called the 'black legend' about the Dudleys.[24] 'Certayne brife notes' deals with the years 1547 to 1550, and offers an interpretation of the hostility between Warwick and Somerset, a detailed narrative of the struggles between Somerset and his supporters with the lords of the council in London in early October 1549, and an account of the subsequent divisions between those councillors who had successfully brought Somerset down. Warwick is seen as the evil genius throughout. The 'Journall' likewise depicts Warwick as the arch-manipulator who drove a wedge between Somerset and his brother: 'he procured and mainteyned hatred betwene the bretherne, yt so he might the rather dyspatche one and at leingth the other, and in the ende rule alone him self' (fo. 350). But the 'Journall' also provides evidence of the deep distrust aroused by Northumberland's son, Lord Robert Dudley, about whom it is consistently negative. He is possibly guilty of colluding in the murder of his wife; he is seen scheming to make concessions to Catholics to secure Spanish support for his marriage to the Queen; he is accused of protecting murderous retainers from the rigours of the law; his brother is given a 'cut-price' peerage; his trade concessions arouse opposition in London.

But if the 'Journall' repeatedly attacks the Dudleys, its scope is much broader than the 'Certayne brife notes', and it is much more than an anti-Dudley tract. Well informed political gossip from the court is combined with reports of developments overseas and with more local information on what was happening in London. It is true that its dictated nature make for a disjointed account: there are inexplicable digressions (e.g. at fos 358v–359v, where the narrative breaks from 1561 to recall events in Calais in 1557–1558, the loans and benevolences of the 1540s, and a contrast in the effectiveness of defensive measures in 1545 and 1558), and treatment of episodes is unbalanced. But another feature is the author's appreciation of the interconnectedness of events. He understood the importance of developments in Scotland, Ireland, and France, and the implications of events in Germany and the Mediterranean theatre for the Protestant cause. The 'Journall' refers to a variety of printed materials which were evidently to be drawn upon

---

[24] Much particular detail may be confirmed from other sources, as the annotation here shows, but the negative portrayal of Warwick will remain a matter for controversy, and is not endorsed by the latest study, (D.M. Loades, *John Dudley, Duke of Northumberland* (Oxford, 1996)); though it has significantly influenced Hoak, *King's Council*, pp. 231–258.

in a fuller version of the narrative, and to which the author clearly had access. These include propaganda material relating to the reasons for the Queen's intervention in Scotland in 1560 and in France in 1562, and religious materials, including the Scottish confession of faith of 1560, Beza's oration at the Colloquy of Poissy in 1561, and the religious polemics over the burning of St Paul's in 1561.[25] The proximity of the author to Roger Ascham, the Queen's Latin secretary, Ralph Sadler, her agent in Scotland, and Gregory Raylton, Sadler's inward man, gave him access to key diplomatic materials.[26] Some of the information from France in 1562 is clearly derived from documents now in the state papers, suggesting that manuscript newsletters were circulating widely. There are indications that the author also had access to the reports of Christopher Mount, the Queen's agent in Germany.[27] He also had well-placed sources of information in the city of London: he offers fresh insights into the controversies caused by the repair of St Paul's after the lightning strike of 1561; the popularity among the citizens of the Swedish suit for the Queen's hand in marriage is several times reported; he records the Privy Council's bullying of the city over the price of silks in December 1561; there are details of divided counsels among the merchant adventurers (not otherwise known) over whether to accept the repayment of a loan from the Queen on the eve of a widely expected calling-down of the coinage; we learn of the unpopularity of Dudley's licence to export wool in 1561; there is evidence of hostility among the city merchants to Gresham, whose transactions the author followed closely, and who was himself another possible source of information. Much of the material presented in the 'Journall', however, comes from what was being widely reported.[28] The most frequent phrases in the account are 'some saied', 'a saying that', 'yt was thought', 'yt was bruted', 'the comen brute', 'reporte that', 'dyversitie of opinions whether [...]'. On some issues, such as the Hertford marriage, the 'Journall' makes it clear that there was a wide range of opinion, 'some saied they were maried, som that they were not' (fo. 361v). It is tantalizingly unclear as to the precise milieu within which such specu-lations occurred. Sometimes it seems quite general: 'it was thought by the people that [...] they wold attempte to prove the L[ady] Fraunces [...] a bastard' (fo. 361v). At the very least we have confirmation in the 'Journall' of the existence of an educated metropolitan public that was well informed about domestic and foreign politics. That should occasion

[25] 'Journall', nn. 60, 128, 142, 148, 294, 295.
[26] Ibid., nn. 43, 58, 61, 68, 235.
[27] Ibid., nn. 89, 261.
[28] Ibid., nn. 69, 112, 117, 128–131, 158, 177–180, 196.

little surprise given the government's dependence on mercantile contacts for much of its foreign intelligence.

The author of the 'Journall' writes from a decidedly Protestant position. There are several stories told to put Catholics in a bad light, such as the comparison of the efforts of Cranmer and Pole in national defence against possible French invasions in 1545 and 1557–1558 respectively. It is interesting that the prebendaries' plot still cast its shadow over reactions to Catholic activity in the early years of Elizabeth's reign, as our author records the involvement of several of the discredited clergy of 1561 in the earlier plotting. He is anxious about the future of the 'gospell' when Dudley is exposed as willing to trade religious concessions to Catholics in return for Spanish support for his bid to marry the Queen, and he fears that Philip will 'sett vppon the protestauntes' (fo. 356) once his hands are free from the Ottomans. He participates in the Protestant providentialist outlook on the world, which could see the burning of a portion of the Spanish navy in 1562 as 'a grete miracle of god that hindereth the papistes purposes' (fo. 369v). There are signs of the 'commonwealth' legacy, as the 'Journall' calls down 'a plage of god' (fo. 365v) on usurers, and uses reactions to Somerset's anti-enclosure policy as evidence of the prevalence of self-interest. The inclusion of a hitherto unknown set of articles of reform drawn up in preparation for the convocation of 1563 shows an interest in the projects for further reform that were circulating within the regime in the 1560s. In a particularly striking passage, the author shows familiarity with and sympathy for the resistance theories produced in Mary's reign, expressing scepticism that the actions of the lords of the congregation should be described as a rebellion, 'yf yt may be called rebellion to withstand that the prince will have don contrary to his lawes and his othe' (fo. 352v). But he shows a mixture of contempt and fear of the commons – the conservative rebels who besieged Exeter in 1549 were undermining hierarchy, 'every hick and Tom making him self a capiten' (fo. 356) – and deplores that 'many Coblers, Taylers and suche licke [were] made minesters which breade a grete sclaunder to the minestery' (fo. 357).

The very compilation of a 'Journall' by a relatively low-ranking member of the adminstration (see below, for a discussion of possible authorship) would in itself be valuable, as we have suggested, as a guide to just how much was known, and the range of contemporary reactions to well-known episodes.[29] But the value of the 'Journall' goes beyond that. For on a number of important issues it offers entirely fresh

---

[29] Cf. I.W. Archer, 'Popular politics in sixteenth- and early seventeenth-century London', in P. Griffiths and M. Jenner (eds), *Londinopolis: Essays in the Cultural and Social History of Early Modern London* (Manchester, 2000), pp. 26–46.

material. The account of the rivalry between the Seymour brothers in 1547–1549 complements that in 'Certayne brife notes', but gives key information on the controversies in parliament in 1547 over the confirmation of the letters patent establishing the protectorate and on the anxieties of the judges about the trial of Thomas Seymour, which lay behind the decision to proceed by attainder. That the Lady Mary and Sir Richard Southwell were suspected of complicity in Kett's Rebellion opens up new lines of investigation on the disturbances of 1549. The account of Amy Robsart's death shows that the charges against Sir Richard Verney later publicized in *Leicester's Commonwealth* were not new in the 1580s but circulated as rumours immediately after her death. The 'Journall' gives an eye-witness account of the first performance of *Gorboduc*, which differed in some critical details from the published version. We learn a great deal more about the controversies raised by a projected calling-down of the coinage in 1562, called off at the last minute in the face of popular anger and divided counsels at the centre. This is one of several episodes pointing to the malign backstairs influence of William, first Lord Paget. He is also seen as working against intervention in Scotland in 1560; he was involved in the negotiations between La Quadra and Dudley in 1561 which compromised the integrity of the Elizabethan settlement; and he offered to act as Dudley's agent in tax farming and proposing to him what appears to be an excise tax. This is to give him a far greater role than is apparent from other sources.

The 'Journall' is not always accurate, but sometimes its inaccuracies are telling in themselves. There is a consistent tendency to exaggerate the military success of the Huguenot forces during the French war of religion, which may indicate something of the way in which the war was being presented in England. There are numerous new angles on familiar episodes: the notion that the relaxation of treason legislation in 1547 was part of a bid for Scottish support, and the suggestion that Cecil may have been on the brink of resignation as the Queen dithered over the Newhaven expedition, are particularly arresting. Lacunae in the central government records are revealed, as the 'Journall' reports hitherto unnoticed initiatives such as a campaign against unlawful apparel in the winter of 1560–1561, the appointment of muster masters in the summer of 1562, and the work of a commission for finding horses in the capital in 1562. We gain additional fragments on the pattern of disease: the 'Journall' remarks on a smallpox epidemic in the winter of 1561, and on a 'newe dissease [...] of the cough' a year later. There is graphic confirmation of the vulnerability of people before the weather, the keenness with which price fluctuations were observed, and the sensitivity of prices to the government's monetary policy.

Authorship

The writer of the 'Certayne brife notes' describes himself 'as being than in the Duke of Somerset howse' (fo. 7). Mr Malkiewicz claimed that 'the particular information which he thus expressly claims to base on personal experience is exaggerated', but the writer's claim that John Dudley, Earl of Warwick, always lodged at Somerset's house before the downfall of Sir Thomas Seymour is echoed in the 'Journall', fo. 351v: 'Howe Warewick was lodged with Somersett in his howse for feare of his brother the Admerall'. The writer was almost certainly a clerk of some kind in Protector Somerset's household, but his identity remains elusive. Dr Sybil Jack suggested, given the prominence he plays in the early part of the account of Somerset's fall, that Thomas Fisher (1515/16–1577) might have been its author (see pp. 126 and 127 below), but that can be no more than suggestive speculation.

As for the 'Journall', we can discount either Norton or Beale as authors. Its survival among the papers collected by Robert Beale is purely coincidental, and it has no direct association with Beale, other than through his office as clerk of the Privy Council. Norton would hardly have described the performance of *Gorboduc* without making it clear that he had written it. In any case, the author provides clues as to his identity and Norton does not fit the bill. The author was, as we have seen, on familiar terms with Sir Ralph Sadler, Sadler's secretary, Gregory Raylton, and Roger Ascham. His strong Protestantism is obvious, and no less marked are his political views, especially a sympathy for the Duke of Somerset and a deep suspicion of the Duke of Northumberland and his son.

There is, however, a further specific personal reference which has encouraged Simon Adams to suggest an identity for the narrator. This is the reference to his oration during a visit of Roger Ascham to Tottenham in the summer of 1560. Tottenham was then the residence of the controversial Clerk of the Hanaper, John Hales (1516–1572), and his brother Stephen (d. 1574). Stephen Hales was a merchant tailor of London and a citizen of Coventry, who is identified as 'of Tottenham' in the pardon roll of 1559.[30] In two commissions to survey the lands of the Bishop of London, one of 4 October 1559 and another of 20 July 1560, John Hales is identified as of Tottenham High Cross.[31]

John Hales had been Sir Ralph Sadler's protégé in Henry's reign, holding with him the Clerkship of the Hanaper in survivorship since the late 1530s, and serving as deputy to Sadler as Master of the

---

[30] *CPR, 1558–1560*, p. 197.
[31] *Ibid.*, pp. 30, 422.

Wardrobe at Edward's coronation.[32] Stephen Hales may also have held an office in the Wardrobe, a point of importance because the manor of Tottenham was a perquisite of officers of the household.[33] The Hales brothers were trustees to a use for Sadler's son on 19 February 1560.[34] An even more precise reference to their association in the context of this 'Journall' is Hales's surrender of his interest in the Hanaper to Sadler in 1554 'understanding that Sadleyr had suffered very great losses through the fraud and craft of the duke of Northumberland'.[35] This may have been a politically correct statement to make during Mary's reign, for curiously Sadler does not appear to have held any resentment towards Lord Robert Dudley, with whom he was corresponding on very friendly terms in 1559–1561.[36] Yet Hales seems to have borne a continued suspicion of Dudley, and was surprised and very gratified when he later helped him in his disputes with Sadler over the Clerkship of the Hanaper, and consulted him over the statutes for his hospital.[37]

Given Hales's wider reputation for outspokenness and his radical views on matters economic, the attribution of the 'Journall' to him has numerous attractions. But at the same time it also raises a number of questions that demand consideration, in particular the relationship between its contents and the 'Hales Book': 'The declaration of the succession of the crown imperial of England' that Hales circulated in 1563. No adequate biographical treatment of Hales survives, particularly for the reign of Elizabeth, and what little there is, is chiefly concerned

[32] See A.J. Slavin, 'Sir Ralph Sadler and Master John Hales at the Hanaper: a sixteenth-century struggle for property and profit', *Bulletin of the Institute of Historical Research*, 38 (1965), pp. 31–47, and the references to Hales in *idem, Politics and Profit: A Study of Sir Ralph Sadler, 1507–1547* (Cambridge, 1966), pp. 169–171. PRO, LC2/3/2 shows Hales as deputy to Sadler at the Wardrobe.

[33] See the biography of Stephen Hales by W.J. Jones in *HoP, 1558–1603*. On Tottenham, see Allegra Woodworth, 'Purveyance for the royal household in the reign of Queen Elizabeth', *Proceedings of the American Philosophical Society*, new series 35 (1945), p. 62.

[34] *CPR, 1559–1560*, p. 380.

[35] *CPR, 1557–1558*, p. 191.

[36] Longleat, Dudley Papers, I, fos 92, 181, Sadler to Dudley, 4 December 1559, 24 January 1561.

[37] BL, Additional MS 32091, fo. 248, Hales to Leicester, 28 July 1571. He also took this occasion to recommend his proteges Robert and William Beale to Leicester. His brother was also in Leicester's orbit by this stage; see Longleat, Dudley Papers, II, fo. 133, Stephen Hales to Leicester, 5 March 1573. Leicester appears to have helped Hales during the 'Hales Book' affair in 1564; see Francis Newdigate to Cecil, 23 April 1564, Hatfield House, Cecil Papers 154, art. 54. Leicester's later relations with Hales are suggestive of his efforts to repair the enmities created in Edward's reign; see S. Adams, 'The Dudley clientele, 1553–1563', in Bernard, *Tudor Nobility*, p. 257. If the attribution of the 'Journall' to Hales is correct, it is revealing of how strong they were.

with what Walter Haddon described as the *Tempestas Halesiana*.[38] Two aspects of Hales's life are of direct relevance. He was briefly imprisoned after the fall of Somerset, but then in the winter of 1550–1551 went abroad and did not return to England until some point in 1559.[39] Secondly, after his arrest for the 'Hales Book' in April 1564, he spent most of the rest of his life under some form of house arrest. These 'interruptions' may explain why the 'Journall' says little about the period between Somerset's overthrow and the middle of 1559, and why it comes a sudden halt at the end of 1562. The first may also explain one apparent reservation about identifying Hales as the narrator – his statement that he had never seen Robert Dudley before September 1560. This seems incredible for someone in Hales's position, given Dudley's prominence, but in view of Hales's absence from England it is just possible.

Hales's arrest over the 'Declaration' was not simply for dabbling in succession politics. In advancing the claim of Lady Catherine Grey and her heirs by the Earl of Hertford, he brought up a number of complex issues. Firstly, he appears to have been the first person to employ the will of Henry VIII to bar Mary, Queen of Scots.[40] Secondly, to bar the Countess of Lennox (Lady Margaret Douglas), he brought up the issue of the possibly bigamous second marriage of her father, Archibald, Earl of Angus. Lastly, he was faced with certain difficulties with regard to Lady Catherine. There was her possible pre-contract to Lord Henry Herbert, but also the question of the possibly bigamous marriage of her grandfather Charles Brandon, Duke of Suffolk. Lastly, and most controversially, there was his involvement in preparing an appeal against the nullification of her marriage to the Earl of Hertford. It was to this end that he sent his protégé, Robert Beale, to seek further legal advice on the continent.[41] This attempt to reopen a matter Elizabeth wished closed clearly annoyed her as much as – if not more than – the 'Declaration' itself.

Of these issues, only the issue of the illegitimacy of Lady Margaret Douglas appears here clearly. On the question of Lady Catherine and Hertford the narrator is quite neutral – although noting their 'standing

---

[38] M. Levine, *The Early Elizabethan Succession Question 1558–1568* (Stanford CA, 1966) ch. 5 is the fullest. The entry in *HoP, 1558–1603* is minimal.

[39] According to C.H. Garret, *The Marian Exiles: A Study in the Origins of Elizabethan Puritanism* (Cambridge, 1938), p. 173, he had returned by 3 January, but she supplies no source. 'John Hales, Clarke of the Hanaper' received livery for Elizabeth's coronation; see the warrant filed in PRO, E101/429/5.

[40] One of the questions put to him in April 1564 was how he got hold of a copy of Henry's will; Levine, *Early Elizabethan Succession Question*, p. 70.

[41] The date usually assigned for Beale's journey is 1561, but given that Lady Catherine's pregnancy was not discovered until September of that year and the nullification proceedings took place in March 1562, it seems a bit early.

stiff' on the fact of their marriage. Nothing is said about the will of Henry VIII. Of no less importance than these questions, though, is a further issue, of relevance not just to the succession question but also the involvement of Hales and Norton in this 'Journall'. This is the entry on the performance of the *Tragedie of Porrex and Ferrex* [*Gorboduc*] at the Inner Temple at Christmas 1561. *Gorboduc* has been a regular subject of debate, and this entry has only added to it. For this reason some discussion of it is necessary.

According to the authorized edition of *Gorboduc* (1570), which also confirmed the identification of Thomas Norton and Thomas Sackville as the authors, 'this tragedie' was originally part of the Inner Temple Christmas revels and then 'shown' before the Queen on 18 January 1562. These dates are confirmed by entries in Henry Machyn's diary, which note the arrival of a Lord of Misrule at the Inner Temple on 27 December 1561 and grand revels there, and then, on 18 January, a play by the gentlemen of the Temple at the Queen's hall, Whitehall, followed by a great masque.[42] Modern scholarly interest in *Gorboduc* has been inspired in large part by what appear to be specific political allusions, notably the emphasis on native lines of succession and the appearance of a hostile Scot, the Duke of Albany, at the end. The assumption – understandably enough – has been that this was a direct reference to the succession question, and that the play as a whole was in written in support of Catherine Grey's claim against that of Mary, Queen of Scots.[43] This assumption, however, has posed some questions about the authors. Norton is straightforward enough; given that Earl of Hertford had been his pupil, and by his attacks on Mary in the Parliaments of 1571–1572, he would appear to be an obvious supporter of the Grey claim.[44] Sackville is more difficult, for these were not views he espoused elsewhere and throughout his life he was suspected of Catholic sympathies.

A new twist or twists were introduced by Marie Axton some twenty years ago. The first was the association of Lord Robert Dudley with the Inner Temple, and his prominence as the prince in the Christmas revels. The second was another masque variously titled *Pallas, Perseus and Andromeda* or *Pallaphilos*, which she reconstructed from Gerard Legh's *Accedens of Armory*.[45] Both this masque and *Gorboduc* were played together

[42] M. Axton, *The Queen's Two Bodies: Drama and the Elizabethan Succession* (London, 1977), pp. 40–41, and 'Robert Dudley and the Inner Temple revels', *HJ*, 13 (1970), p. 365, n. 2. The relevant section of Machyn's text is damaged (*Machyn's Diary*, pp. 273–274).

[43] See the case summarized in Levine, *Early Elizabethan Succession Question*, pp. 39–44, quoting Sir John Neale in particular.

[44] Graves also notes that Norton was receiving fees from Hertford for legal services between 1563 and 1572; Graves, *Norton*, p. 103.

[45] Axton, 'Inner Temple revels', pp. 365–374, and *idem*, *Queen's Two Bodies*, pp. 39–48.

at the Inner Temple, and Axton deduced, on the basis of Machyn's reference to both a play and a masque, that both were played again before the Queen on 18 January.[46] Equally, she assumed that Dudley was the means by which the court performance was arranged. The combination was important because *Pallaphilos* was a masque in favour of marriage. At the same time she did not dissent from the accepted view that *Gorboduc* itself was written in favour of the Grey claim, but argued that Dudley, who had shown his sympathy to Lady Catherine over her pregnancy the previous September, was now supporting it.[47]

In 1988 Simon Adams suggested that the description of *The Tragedie of Porrex and Ferrex* in the 'Journall' (which Axton had not seen) raised doubts about the assumption that *Gorboduc* was written to support the Grey claim.[48] Moreover, he also voiced further doubts about Dudley's involvement with the Grey claim at this point. Between 1561 and 1563 Elizabeth, Dudley, and Cecil were, in fact, united in their desire to avoid open discussion of the succession, whether in Parliament or elsewhere. For Elizabeth this was a consistent desire, for Dudley and Cecil the immediate motive was their involvement in the attempt to build good relations with Mary after her return to Scotland, in order to stabilize the Anglophile regime there. The easiest way to alienate her would be to challenge her claim, and therefore it was in everyone's interest to let sleeping dogs lie. Hales's public espousal of the Grey claim was distinctly unhelpful.[49]

Since then, the impact of the entry in the 'Journall' on the '*Gorboduc* question' has been discussed at length, directly in an article by Henry James and Greg Walker published in 1995, and another by Norman Jones and Paul Whitfield White the following year, and also in two books that appeared nearly simultaneously in 1996, Michael Graves's biography of Norton and Susan Doran's study of the Queen's courtships. Graves's assessment is to some extent negative, but no less valuable for that. Combining Axton's case for Dudley's role and the importance of *Pallaphilos* with the observations of the 'Journall', he sees the performances as a combined exercise in favour of the Dudley marriage, in which *Pallaphilos* was more important than *Gorboduc*.[50] More importantly, he is also at pains to uncouple Norton from a 'Grey faction'. He

---

[46] *Idem*, 'Inner Temple revels', p. 374.

[47] *Ibid.*, pp. 366–367.

[48] S. Adams, 'The release of Lord Darnley and the failure of the amity', in M. Lynch (ed.), *Mary Stewart: Queen in Three Kingdoms* (Oxford, 1988), pp. 150–151, n. 117.

[49] Simon Adams comments on Geoffrey Elton's and Susan Doran's assessment of Dudley's role in the parliament of 1563 in his 'The Eltonian legacy: politics', *TRHS*, sixth series, 7 (1997), pp. 258–260. This does not mean that Dudley and Cecil shared the same views on the succession (Dudley thought Mary had a stronger case) but they were allied on the timing.

[50] Graves, *Norton*, pp. 96–97.

considers that no significance can be attributed to Norton's membership of the committee to draft the petition on the succession and marriage in the Commons in 1563, but more importantly, that Norton was not among those investigated over the 'Hales Book' in 1564. Norton's only role in that affair was to assist the Privy Council's investigation.[51] Henry James and Greg Walker in their paper, Norman Jones and Paul Whitfield White in theirs, and Susan Doran in her book have all placed *Gorboduc* squarely in what Doran calls Dudley's 'campaign of courtship', together with several other works of the time advising marriage to a native rather than a foreigner. The civil war in the play was a warning of what would happen if Elizabeth rejected Dudley's suit.[52]

One of the assumptions in the association of *Gorboduc* with Dudley has been that it was written at his behest. Yet neither Norton nor Sackville was particularly close to him at this point or later, and they can hardly be placed in his stable of writers.[53] To the extent that *Gorboduc* was commissioned, it was the Inner Temple itself that was responsible, and Dudley was the recipient of the entertainment. Nor, although there is no clear evidence either way, need we necessarily assume that Dudley arranged the performance before the Queen. The more interesting question here, though, is whether Hales had been present himself at the Inner Temple performance, given the detail he recounts. In view of his suspicion of Dudley, it is easy to see how he might have read meanings into the play.

The more relevant issue is the light shed on Hales's relations with Norton and on Norton's later possession of the 'Journall'. One argument that can be dismissed is that Norton was the copyist, for there would have been no reason for Hales to describe his own play to him. Moreover, thanks to Graves' research, we can uncouple Hales's views on the succession and Norton's. Norton was not part of Hales's inner circle, while Thomas Dannett, who clearly was at least an acquaintance of Hales, was among those deeply involved in the 'Hales Book'.[54] However, Norton's involvement in the investigation may provide an answer. Did Norton obtain this (or have the original copied) during some examination of Hales's papers?

We can also dismiss any direct association between the 'Journall'

---

[51] *Ibid.*, pp. 97, 103–104.

[52] James and Walker, 'Politics of *Gorboduc*'; N. Jones and P.W. White, '*Gorboduc* and royal marriage politics: an Elizabethan playgoer's report of the premiere performance', *English Literary Renaissance*, 26 (1996), pp. 3–16; Doran, *Monarchy and Matrimony*, pp. 57–58.

[53] Another question that has not been posed or answered is who wrote *Pallaphilos*?

[54] Levine, *Early Elizabethan Succession Question*, pp. 72–75, 79. It might be noted that the strong suspicion of William, Lord Paget displayed in the 'Journall' was also shared by another key figure in the 'Hales Book' affair, Lord John Grey of Pirgo; see 'Journall', n. 109 below.

and the 'Declaration'. Although it touches on some of the succession issues, it ranges far more widely. The basic problem is that it is incomplete, there is a reasonably organized chronological narrative of Elizabeth's reign from mid-1559 to the end of 1562, but also a number of notes on the background to the fall of the Duke of Somerset. All we can suggest is that it might have been something Hales and an associate were working on and either abandoned or were forced to abandon by his arrest in April 1564.

The case for John Hales's authorship is highly suggestive. Although the evidence is largely circumstantial, it is stronger than for any other candidate who has been suggested.[55] It has convinced Simon Adams (on whose arguments the case rests) and Ian Archer; George Bernard remains agnostic. The case is put forward here as a challenge to future research.

---

[55] George Bernard has suggested that a circumstantial case might be made for the authorship of John Aylmer (c.1521–1594), later Bishop of London. An exile in Mary's reign (for which period there are very few entries), he was the tutor of Thomas Dannett the younger (?1543–1601), son of Thomas Dannet the elder (d. 1569), a Kentish gentleman who was possibly the 'Mr Dannett' referred to in fo. 353 (see 'Journall', n. 67), and a close friend of Roger Ascham, before whom the author of this text 'began an oration' justifying English foreign policy' (fo. 352v). Aylmer was apparently refused favour in these years by Robert Dudley whom he asked for the deanery of Durham. He was appointed Archdeacon of Lincoln in 1562 through the influence of Thomas Dannett *père* over his cousin, Secretary William Cecil; J. Strype, *Life and Acts of John Aylmer, Bishop of London* (London, 1701), pp. 7, 10, 17–18; *CPR, 1560–1563*, p. 298; P. Collinson, *The Elizabethan Puritan Movement* (London, 1967), p. 63. Henry James (in an unpublished paper) has made a circumstantial case for Armagil Waad (d. 1568), chief clerk of the council under Edward VI, and involved in commercial and diplomatic business under Elizabeth, including military preparations for the French expedition of 1562. He was one of twenty-eight gentlemen who gave a New Year's gift to the Queen in 1561/1562, the time of the first performance of *Gorboduc* described here. The account of Edward VI's reign, Henry James urges, must have been written by someone with access to important conciliar documents, and even an eye-witness account of a stormy council meeting. Waad also lived at Belsize, near Hampstead, and not far from Tottenham, mentioned in the text. But in common with other attempts at identification of the author, this can offer no more than degrees of circumstantial plausibility.

A 'JOURNALL' OF MATTERS OF STATE HAPPENED FROM TIME TO TIME AS WELL WITHIN AND WITHOUT THE REALME FROM AND BEFORE THE DEATH OF KING EDW. THE 6ᵀᴴ UNTILL THE YERE 1562

British Library, Additional MS 48023, fos 350–369v

[fo. 350]

The mariage betwene the two duckes at Shene. Howe Northumberland suspecteth he should have ben betraied there and therfore cam not thither.[1]

Howe Sir R. Moryson was sent ambassador to the emperor and Sir William Pickering to the Flemyshe king.[2]

Loocke for eyther of their lettres.

The second taking of the duke of Somersett and of Arundell. Palmer.[3]

---

[1] The marriage between John Dudley (c. 1528–1554), Lord Lisle, son of John Dudley (c. 1502–1553), then Earl of Warwick and later Duke of Northumberland, and Anne (d. 1588), daughter of Edward Seymour (c. 1500–1552), Duke of Somerset, formerly Lord Protector, and his second wife, Anne Stanhope (d. 1587) was celebrated at Sheen on 3 June 1550; *Wriothesley's Chronicle*, II, p. 41; J.G. Nichols (ed.), *Literary Remains of King Edward VI*, 2 vols, Roxburghe Club, 74 (1857), II, p. 273, n. 3. The imperial ambassador thought that the celebrations took place at Sion, but significantly noted that 'The earl of Warwick was not present'; *CSPSp., 1550–1552*, p. 98. The reconciliation between Warwick and Somerset – after Warwick's part in the conciliar protest against Somerset in October 1549 which led to Somerset's resignation as Lord Protector – may well have been provoked by the efforts of the Earl of Arundel and Earl of Southampton to exploit the fall of Somerset to destroy Warwick as well (see below, *Brife Notes*, pp. 134–136). The gradual reconciliation between Warwick and Somerset was warmer than self-interest alone would have dictated (*CSPSp., 1550–1552*, pp. 7–8, 14, 28, 63, 72, 97), but eventually Warwick and Somerset quarrelled, largely because of Somerset's renewed intriguing. On 26 June 1550, a few weeks after the wedding, Warwick was described by Richard Whalley as a 'faithful friend' of Somerset, but Warwick warned that the councillors thought that Somerset aspired again to have the same authority he had when Lord Protector (PRO, SP10/10/9). On Somerset's intriguing, see G.W. Bernard, *The Power of the Early Tudor Nobility: a Study of the Fourth and Fifth Earls of Shrewsbury* (Brighton, 1985), pp. 63–70.

[2] Sir Richard Morrison (by 1514–1556), pamphleteer and diplomat (*DNB*), was sent to the Emperor on 22 August 1550 (*CSPSp., 1550–1552*, p. 167); Sir William Pickering (1516/17–1575), courtier (*HoP, 1509–1558*, III, pp. 107–108), described as a creature of the Earl of Warwick, replaced Sir John Mason (1502/3–1566), diplomat and administrator, as ambassador to the French, not the Flemish, king in April 1551 (*CSPSp., 1550–1552*, p. 218).

[3] Somerset's intriguing culminated in his arrest in October 1551: *CSPSp., 1550–1552*, pp. 381–386, 392–393; *Wriothesley's Chronicle*, II, pp. 56–57; *Machyn's Diary*, p. 10; W.K. Jordan (ed.), *The Chronicle and Political Papers of Edward VI* (London, 1966), p. 89. Involved

That the duke should aspire to ———— wherof he was acquited but condempned of fellony, for that he was suspected to have gon aboutes to have killed Northumberland wherof he was ~~condep~~ condempned.[4]

The reioysing of the people when they hard he was acquyted thincking he had ben acquyted of all.[5]

The good will of the people to Somersett his execution.[6]

Fane saied yt was Pensehurst that hadd offended, which the duke ofte before required, but he would not departe with hytt because hyt was geven him in respecte of the taking of the Earle Huntley.[7]

Howe after yt was concluded by the counsell that the duke of Somersett should be protector and governor of the king, the earle of Warwick saied to the admirall, Sir Thomas Seymer that he should doe well to move in councell that his brother beinge protector he might be the kinge's governour, as thoughe that office had not ben graunted

in his downfall were Sir Thomas Arundell (c. 1502–1552), of Wardour Castle, Wiltshire, lawyer and administrator, and a committed Catholic, who was indicted (PRO, SP10/13/64) and also convicted of felony, but not of treason, and executed on 26 February 1552 (*Machyn's Diary*, p. 15; also *HoP, 1509–1558*, I, pp. 337–338) and Sir Thomas Palmer, military strategist in the Scottish campaigns of the 1540s, who survived, perhaps after making suit to the King (PRO, SP10/13/12).

[4] In fact Somerset was acquitted of treason (presumably the missing word) but found guilty of felony: he had brought men together for riot by malicious purposes, a crime under clause 3 of the statute 3 and 4 Edward VI c. 5 (J. Bellamy, *The Tudor Law of Treason: An Introduction* (London, 1979), pp. 244–245).

[5] Popular rejoicing was noted by others: *CSPSp.*, *1550–1552*, pp. 407–408; Jordan, *Chronicle of Edward VI*, pp. 99–100; *Wriothesley's Chronicle*, II, p. 63; *Machyn's Diary*, p. 12.

[6] For the mourning of the people at Somerset's execution, see *CSPSp.*, *1550–1552*, pp. 452–453; *Wriothesley's Chronicle*, II, p. 65. How far was this conventional; how far did it reflect popular support for the good duke's social policies?

[7] Sir Ralph Fane or Vane (by 1510–1552), of Hadlow, Kent, was a victim of the political intrigues of the royal minority. A courtier, diplomat, and soldier in the 1540s, he was knighted after the capture of Boulogne in 1544. At the Battle of Pinkie he captured George Gordon (1513–1562), fourth Earl of Huntly, but (according to the later grant), the earl was subsequently taken out of his hands by the King without recompense. Vane was then granted the manor of Penshurst, Kent, in July 1550 as a belated reward for his service on the Scottish borders in 1547;. *CPR, Edward VI, 1550–1553*, pp. 12–13; *APC*, III, p. 61. In September 1550 John Dudley, Earl of Warwick, later Duke of Northumberland, was granted the neighbouring manor of Tonbridge, Kent (*CPR, Edward VI, 1549–1551*, pp. 277–278); in March 1551 Vane attempted to assert rights to Posterne Park, part of that manor, bringing twenty-six or twenty-seven men on his own admission, 'viii or ix skore, and in such sorte as was leeke to have breede some great mischief, using him self with all very arrogantlie', according to counter-depositions, and meeting 'certein of my Lord of Warrewickes servantes' there. Vane was committed to the Tower until June, when he was released on condition that he did not trouble Warwick in his possession of Posterne Park (*APC*, III, pp. 244, 245–246, 296). Imprisoned again in October 1551, he was later executed in February 1552 for his alleged part in Somerset's conspiracy the previous year (*CSPSp.*, *1550–1552*, pp. 386, 389, 453; Jordan, *Chronicle of Edward VI*, pp. 88–89, 108; *APC*, III, pp. 391, 397, 478, 483, 484; PRO, SP11/13/57). For further remarks about Vane, see p. 60 below, and *HoP, 1509–1558*, III, p. 513.

when he knew certenly yt was determined before, and promised the admirall all his helpe and furtheraunce, and that yf he woulde yt, he would declare yt he meante as he saied. The admirall accordingly did move yt in the counsell which as sone as the ducke herde, he soudenly arose and spake not one worde, and so the councell was dissolved. After Warwick cam unto the duke and saied thus, yor grace may see this mans ambytion. After suche sorte he procured and mainteyned hatred betwene the bretherne, yt so he might the rather dyspatche one and at leingth the other, and in the ende rule alone him self.[8]

[fo. 350v]

The cause of the falling owte of the protector and the admyrall was the ambytion of the admirall and the envy he hadd that his brother should be more advaunced than he.[9]

Howe imediatly after King H. death, he began to make bandes and to kepe a grete howse, and howe he conferred with divers of the goverment of the realme, and condempned his brother because of his simplicitie.[10]

Howe being admirall he would not goe in person in the iorney againste Scottland.[11]

Howe his brother being in Scotlande he practysed to have had the goverment of the king, and howe at the returne, Wroth, Cheke and divers of the privey chamber were putt owte because they were suspected to further his ambytion.[12]

---

[8] This account of Warwick's sowing enmity between Somerset and his brother Thomas, Lord Seymour of Sudeley, is similar to that offered in the anonymous 'eye-witness's account; A.J.A. Malkiewicz, 'An eye-witness account of the coup d'etat of October 1549', *EHR*, 70 (1955), pp. 600–609; and see below, pp. 123–136. For a discussion, see Hoak, *King's Council*, pp. 231–234. Cf. also Paris, BNF, MS français, 15888, fo. 186v. For discussion of Thomas Seymour's wish to be governor of the King's person, and the constitutional background, see Bernard, 'Downfall of Sir Thomas Seymour', in *idem, The Tudor Nobility*, pp. 217–218, 236–237, nn. 49, 232, reprinted in *idem, Power and Politics*, pp. 138–139, 155–156, nn. 50, 151.

[9] For a discussion of the relationship between Somerset and Seymour, see Bernard, 'Downfall of Sir Thomas Seymour', in *idem, The Tudor Nobility*, pp. 212–240, and *idem, Power and Politics*, pp. 134–160.

[10] On Seymour's retaining see *ibid.*, in *The Tudor Nobility*, pp. 221–223, and *Power and Politics*, pp. 142–144; on his conferring see *ibid.*, in *The Tudor Nobility*, pp. 220–221, and *Power and Politics*, pp. 140–142.

[11] Seymour did not serve on the Scottish borders or in Scottish waters during the military campaign which led to Somerset's victory against the Scots at Pinkie in August 1547, despite holding the post of Lord Admiral. Nor did he serve on the Scottish borders during the campaign of 1548 which centred on the fortification of Haddington.

[12] Seymour believed that he should be governor of the King's person (see above). During Somerset's absence he intrigued against him, recruiting two members of the young King's Privy Chamber, John Cheke (1514–1557), sometime Regius Professor of Greek at Cambridge, and tutor to Prince Edward in the 1540s (*DNB*), and Thomas

Of the hatred betwene the quene and the duchesse of Somersett, and howe the duches hated the admirall, and contrary wyse, and howe the admirall sought the disheritaunce of her children and would have had the dukes children by his first wief to be his heyres.[13]

Howe the brethren were once pacyfied but the love continved not.

Howe the admirall made the acte of confirmacon of lettres patentes a grete mater against his brother surmysing that he would therby geve away Callies, and what sturre was in the parliament by that meanes.[14]

Howe the acte of repeale of capitall lawes was made partly to allure the Scottes and partly to wyn favor of the worlde nobylitie. And howe many honest men of the howse were against hytt so generall, because yt was thought a grete surety for the king in his nonage and howe the papistes accused the protestantes to be papistes, because they spake against hytt.[15]

Wroth (1518–1573), a long serving courtier in Edward's household (*HoP, 1509–1558*, III, pp. 667–678). Seymour attempted to persuade the young King to sign a letter on his behalf for the imminent parliament: it read 'Mi Lordes I prai yow fauor my Lord Admiral mine vncles sute which he wil make unto yow'. But on Cheke's advice Edward refused to sign it (PRO, SP10/6/26; 10/6/10; BL, Hatfield Microfilms M485/39, vol. 150, fo. 71v; S. Haynes, *A Collection of State Papers at Hatfield* (London, 1740), p. 74). Somerset rushed back from the Scottish borders on learning of his brother's plotting (Abbé de Vertot (ed.), *Ambassades de Messieurs de Noailles en Angleterre*, 5 vols (Leiden, 1763), I, pp. 129–131; cf. G. Burnet, *A History of the Reformation of the Church of England*, N. Pocock (ed.), 6 vols (Oxford, 1865), II, pp. 84, 114–116). If Cheke and Wroth were among those blamed, both evidently recovered their standing and continued to serve in the King's Privy Chamber.

[13] Seymour married Catherine Parr, Henry VIII's widow: there was ill-feeling between Catherine and Protector Somerset's second wife, Anne Stanhope; J. Hayward, *The Life and Raigne of King Edward the Sixth* (1630), p. 82; Vertot, *Ambassades*, I, p. 132; J.A. de Thou, *Histoire Universelle*, 11 vols (La Haye, 1740), I, p. 497, n. 4; G. Lefèvre-Pontalis (ed.), *Correspondance Politique de Odet de Selve* (Paris, 1888), no. 304, p. 287.

[14] No doubt in order to forestall Seymour's intrigues, Somerset asked Parliament in autumn 1547 to enact the letters patent of 12 March 1547 confirming Henry VIII's alleged oral appointment of him as Lord Protector and governor of the King's person; Nichols, *Literary Remains*, I, p. 120; *CPR, 1547–1548*, p. 217. Seymour opposed the bill, dissenting in the Lords on 14 December (*Lords' Journals*, I, pp. 295–299, 307, 313); there are hints that the bill had a troubled passage (see Bernard, 'Downfall of Sir Thomas Seymour', p. 219; idem, *Power and Politics*, pp. 141–142). Seymour was accused of boasting that 'I wyll make the blakiste parliament that euer was in England' (PRO, SP10/6/7 (10, 11); BL, Hatfield Microfilms, M485/39, vol. 150, fo. 61 (Haynes, *State Papers*, p. 85); BL, Harleian MS, 249 fo. 34 (5). The claim that these constitutional arrangements jeopardized the security of Calais is baffling.

[15] This refers to an 'Act for the repeal of certain statutes for treasons and felonies' (1 Edward VI c.12), which was amended in Parliament, repealing much of the legislation passed against treason in the reign of Henry VIII. The suggestion that the repeal was intended to win the support of the Scots and the nobility is intriguing. A bill was read four times in the Lords between 10 and 16 November, and a 'provisio annectenda' was read on 19 November. The bill was read in the Commons between 30 November and 12 December and received back in the Lords on 13 December. On 16 December, a

The admiralle's wyfe, Quene Katherine dieth.[16] Afterward as yt was supposed he made meanes to mary with the Lady Elizabeth.

The admirall is commytted to the Towre, laied to his charge howe he went aboutes the maryage of the Lady Elizabeth wherby he sought the crowne,[17] how he mainteyned rovers and had parte of the spoyle,[18] and howe he was of counsell with Sherington in coyning testornes his commyssion being reuoked, because he spacke for ~~Shence~~ Shering. to the counsell.[19]

[fo. 351]

Ande howe he had fortefied and vytayled the castell of Holte.[20] The examynacion of his treason by the lawe was commytted to Mountague, the kinge's sargeauntes and atturney, and to Goderick and Gosnall,

deputation of the Lords met representatives of the Commons to discuss the bill. Between 20 and 22 December 'nova billa' was read in the Lords and on 21 December this 'new bill' was read in the Commons (*Commons' Journals*, I, pp. 2, 4; *Lords' Journals*, I, pp. 296–297, 299, 307–308). In 1549, Edward Fiennes (1512–1585), Lord Clinton, would testify that Seymour sought to obtain 'a promyse that men shold not have had lybertye to a spokeyn any thing ayenst the quene [i.e. Catherine Parr, Henry VIII's widow, Seymour's wife]' (PRO, SP10/6/11; BL, Hatfield Microfilms, M485/39, vol. 150, fo. 113; Haynes, *State Papers*, p. 76).

[16] Catherine Parr gave birth to a daughter shortly before 27 August 1548; she died a few days later on 5 September 1548.

[17] Seymour was clearly interested in marrying Princess Elizabeth, Henry VIII's daughter by Anne Boleyn: he had flirted with her while Catherine was alive, and after her death, renewed his solicitations (BL, Hatfield Microfilms, M485/39 vol. 150, fos 44v, 74, 80–81, 83–88 [Haynes, *State Papers*, pp. 69, 93, 96–101]; PRO, SP10/6/16, 10/6/19, 10/6/22); cf. Bernard, 'Downfall of Sir Thomas Seymour', pp. 215–217; in *idem*, *Power and Politics*, pp. 136–138.

[18] Seymour was accusing of dealings with pirates, exploiting his office as Lord Admiral: see BL, Harleian MS 249, fos 37–38.

[19] Seymour asked Sir William Sharington (c.1495–1553), of Lacock, Wiltshire, Under-Treasurer of the mint at Bristol, whom in 1547 he had described as 'my friend', in a letter to Catherine (PRO, SP10/1/43), if he could coin money for him (PRO, SP10/1/43; SP10/6/13 (9); BL, Harleian MS 249, fo. 36v). Sharington was attainted in 1549 for unauthorized manufacture of testoons for personal gain (2 and 3 Edward VI, c. 17); presumably he had become involved in Seymour's plots when seeking high-placed friends to shelter him from the consequences of the discovery of his corruption. He was rehabilitated and pardoned on 5 November 1549 (PRO, SP10/9/48; C.E. Challis, *The Tudor Coinage* (Manchester, 1978), pp. 100–103; 3 and 4 Edward VI, c. 13; *HoP, 1509–1558*, III, pp. 302–304).

[20] On Holt Castle, Denbighshire, 'a goodly castel' at a key crossing point on the Dee and astride 'the gateway from north Wales to the south', see L.T. Smith (ed.), *The Itinerary of John Leland*, 5 vols (London, 1906–1908), III, p. 69; A. Palmer, 'The town of Holt, Denbighshire', *Archaeologia Cambrensis*, 66 (1907), pp. 313–314; R.R. Davies, *Lordship and Society in the Marches of Wales 1282–1400* (Oxford, 1978), pp. 56–58, 72. (We are grateful to Mr Henry James for this reference.) On Seymour's laying-in of victual at Holt see 2 & 3 Edward VI, c. 18; *APC*, II, p. 255.

which Goderick and Gosnall saied that his falte was not treason, but mespasion at the vttermost, yf yt could be proved that Sherington hadd don yt was layed to his charge, and the admirall should consent unto hytt, as yt was not proved that the commyssion was reuoked. Well, saied Mongtague, yf yow were fleshed as we be, yow would not stick at this matter. Goderick answered, if yow take this matter to be treason, lett him be indyted and tried by the order of the common lawe. No, not so, quoth Montague, yt shalbe better don by the parliament. For yf he be condempned by order of the commen lawe, the falte might hearafter, the king comming to his age, be imputed to vs. Yf it be don by parliament we be discharged.[21]

Sherington confesseth this faulte, and hath his pardon of lief, landes and goodes. The admirall is atteyneted and executed at the Towre Hill.[22] Howe yt was saied he hadd writen with cyfre of an oriege in paper, and sowed hytt in his shooe, and being on scaffold willed his man to remember what he saied, whoe dysclosed yt ~~who saied~~. Some saied it was only invented by the duches of Somersett and counterfayted by J. Godsalue.[23] Loocke what Mr Latimer preched after of him, and howe by that sermon he had grete hatred of many. Enquire for the end at the admiralle's deathe.[24]

---

[21] Thomas Gooderick or Goodrich (d. 1554), Bishop of Ely since 1534, later Lord Chancellor from January 1552 (*DNB*); John Gosnold (by 1507–1554), lawyer and administrator, solicitor of the Court of Augmentations from January 1547 (*HoP, 1509–1558*, II, pp. 237–238); Sir Edward Montagu (d. 1557), Chief Judge of Common Pleas since 1545.

[22] He was executed on 19 March 1549.

[23] Sir John Godsalve (by 1505–1556), courtier and administrator; *HoP, 1509–1558*, II, pp. 221–222.

[24] Seymour continued his plotting to the end. Hugh Latimer denounced him in his sermon: 'The man beyng in the tower wrote certayne papers whyche I saw miselfe. They were two lyttle ones, one to my Ladye Maryes grace, and an other to my Lady Elizabeths grace, tendynge to thys ende, that they shoulde conspyre agaynst my lord Protectours grace [...] [these two papers] [...] were founde a showe of hys. They were sowen betwene the solles of a veluet showe. He made his ynke so craftely and with suche workemanshyp as the lyke hath not sene [...]. He made his pen of the aglet of a poynte that he plucked from his hosse, and thus wrought these letters so seditiouslye.' Latimer also accused Seymour of religious indifference. When Queen Catherine had ordained twice daily prayers in her household, Seymour 'gets him out of the way like a mole digging in the earth'. Latimer continued by casting doubt on Seymour's subsequent fate: 'And as touching the kind of his death, whether he be saved or no, I refer that to God only. What God can do, I cannot tell. I will not deny, but that he may in the twinkling of an eye save a man, and turn his heart. What he did, I cannot tell. And when a man hath two strokes with an axe, who can tel but that between two strokes he doth repent? It is very hard to judge. Well, I wil not go so nigh to work: but this I will if they ask me, what I think of his death, that he died very dangerously, irksomely, horribly [...]. He was a man the farthest from the fear of God that I knew or heard of in England.' (*Latimer's Sermons, temp. Edward VI* (1549), sig. M ii–iii; Nichols, *Literary Remains*, I, pp. 123–124; G.E. Corrie (ed.), *Sermons and Remains of Hugh Latimer*, Parker Society, 16, 20 (1844–1845), pp. 161–165; cf. Hayward, *Edward VI*, pp. 83–84.).

The rebellion was throughe the realme, which began at Burye.[25]
The rebellion in the west etc.

The rebellion of ~~Kyth~~ Keth [corrected in margin] in Northfolcke,
and howe yt was supposed that the Lady Marie and her counsell were
pryvey to it.[26]
Howe Sir R. Sowthwell was accused by Sir Edmound Knight to
have ben one of the authors of this rebellion.[27]

[25] It is interesting that the East Anglian rebellion is seen as beginning in Bury: that
would lend support to the emphasis placed by Diarmaid MacCulloch (but dismissed by
Julian Cornwall) on the camps set up in Suffolk in June 1549: MacCulloch, 'Kett's
rebellion in context', pp. 38–41; J. Cornwall, 'Kett's rebellion in context', *Past and Present*,
93 (1981), pp. 160–164.

[26] The council warned Princess Mary on 18 July that 'certain of your servants are
reported to be chief in these commotions', a priest and chaplain of hers now at Sampford
Courtenay, in Devon, and one Pooley, late a receiver, 'a captain of the worst assembled
in Suffolk', and 'your household servant Lyonell is of like credit with the rebels in
Suffolk'. But the council added that 'we think you have no certain knowledge of these
servants' doings'; (PRO, SP10/8, no. 30: we owe this reference to Diarmaid MacCulloch;
D. MacCulloch, *Suffolk and the Tudors* (Oxford, 1986), pp. 300–301, 308–309). But it is
unlikely that Mary was involved in Kett's rebellion in Norfolk: her servants are mentioned
as active in Suffolk, and as MacCulloch suggests she may simply 'have been testing the
waters by sending agents to see what advantages the troubles held for her' (pp. 300–301).
Mary – if a letter printed by Burnet, the original of which cannot be traced, may be
relied upon – rejected such charges in on 20 July. She assured the councillors that the
commotions offended her no less than they did them; she marvelled that a priest and
chaplain of hers should be reported a doer at Sampford Courtenay, since, to her
knowledge, she had not one chaplain in those parts, where 'no indifferent person can
lay their [the rebels'] doings to my charge', and since she had neither lands nor
acquaintance there; her servant Pooley, sometime receiver, 'remayneth continually in my
house, and was neuer doer amongst the commons, nor came in their company'; another
of her servants of the same name rarely came to her house and she did not know whether
he had been taken by the commons; and Lionell lived near London, did not know
Suffolk or Norfolk, and was currently in London. And Mary pointedly denied the charge
that 'my proceedings in matters of religion should give no small courage to many of
those men to require and do as they do [...] for all the rising about these parts [she was
writing from Norfolk] is touching no point of religion': Kett's rebellion was not a religious
rising in defence of the old faith (Gilbert Burnet, *History of the Reformation*, N. Pocock (ed.),
7 vols (Oxford, 1865), III, pp. 327–328, VI, pp. 283–284). Moreover there is nothing in
the imperial ambassador's despatches to suggest Mary's involvement in rebellion (*CSPSp.*,
1547–1549, pp. 405, 423, 445). The rebels did not spare her: hedges around Mary's fields
at Kenninghall were pulled down (*CSPSp.*, *1547–1549*, p. 405). See also next note.

[27] Sir Edmond Knight or Knyvett (by 1508–1551), of Buckenham, Norfolk, a nephew
of Thomas Howard (1473–1555), third Duke of Norfolk, made a sortie from his fortified
manor house at New Buckenham to attack a rebel outpost during Kett's rebellion (S.T.
Bindoff, *Kett's Rebellion* (London, 1949), p. 17). Sir Richard Southwell (1502/3–1564), of
Wood Rising, Norfolk, councillor from March 1547, was one of the Catholics involved
in the conciliar protests against Protector Somerset in October 1549, in which he seized
the Tower of London (see below, p. 131). It is unlikely that Knight's accusation against
Southwell of stirring up the rebellion had any substance. Southwell's Catholicism and
associations with Princess Mary – he was keeper of her estates at Kenninghall – lent it
some plausibility in a climate in which Southwell was committed to the Tower in late

Howe the duke of Somersett being first taken, Cycill the secretary was commytted to warde.[28] And howe then Sothwell had the serche of his chamber at the Sauoye and conveyed away the ~~dysposicion~~ deposicion of E. Knyvett against him. And howe after none of the counsell resorted to Kethe in the Tower but only Southwell.

[fo. 351v]

Howe the duke of Somersett was first taken, and howe Warwick being at Stondon, Balthazer's sonn brought lettres thither from his wief and Sir R. Southwell.

Howe Sir M. Stanog and ——— Wolfe laied in wayet with bandes of men to kill Warwick by the way, and howe at supper Warwick woulde eate nothing, but sodenly in the myddest arose and went into the gallery, and there walked. But it seamed all this was withowte cause and of purpose devysed to bring Somersett in more hatred etc.[29]

Howe the duke was taken and carried to the Towre.

1549 and fined £500 for certain bills of sedition written with his hand (*HoP, 1509–1558*, III, p. 353; Nichols, *Literary Remains*, p. 232, n. 246). Curiously in his will, dated 1564, Southwell left £40 to a servant, Richard Ket: could that be the son of Robert Ket? Such links are intriguing (See MacCulloch, 'Kett's rebellion in context' , pp. 60–61, 74–75; and his reply to Julian Cornwall, 'Kett's rebellion in context', *Past and Present*, 93 (1981), pp. 171–172). MacCulloch has also cited an account 'of suche money as Robart Kette principall leader of thesaid rebelles had from Sir Richard Southwell than havyng charge of the kinges treasour sent doowne by him for the suppressing of the said rebelles', sums amounting to £497 15s, as 'convincing evidence of aiding the Norfolk rebels with royal funds'. But it is unlikely that Southwell, who was treasurer in the Marquess of Northampton's forces sent to deal with Kett's rebellion in July, could have sent the rebels such large sums with impunity. It is much more probable that this was money left behind when Kett put Northampton's forces to flight. Significantly, the rebels did not spend it and Warwick recovered it (PRO, E351/221 cited by D. MacCulloch, *Thomas Cranmer* (London, 1996), pp. 453–463). Knight's charges against Southwell may rather have reflected long-standing tensions between the two men: Southwell had been opposed by Knight in the Norfolk parliamentary election in 1539, a contest that ended in Star Chamber; S.E. Lehmberg, *The Later Parliaments of Henry VIII 1536–1547* (Cambridge, 1977), pp. 43–44.

[28] BL, Cotton MS Caligula B VII, fo. 410 (cited by W.K. Jordan, *Edward VI: the Young King* (London, 1968), p. 520). William Cecil (1521–1598), the later Lord Burghley, was Somerset's secretary, but survived to play a similar role under Northumberland.

[29] Sir Michael Stanhope (by 1508–1552), from a Nottinghamshire gentry family, was Somerset's brother-in-law (*CSPSp., 1547–1549*, p. 460), and chief gentleman in the King's chamber. Dismissed, and then briefly imprisoned in the Tower after Somerset's downfall, in 1552 he was convicted of felony in connection with Somerset's renewed intriguing, and executed. Mr Edward Wolf was one of the King's Privy Chamber (*CSPSp., 1547–1549*, p. 460; *Wriotheseley's Chronicle*, II, p. 218) who was arrested on Somerset's fall (PRO, SP10/9/48) and released on 25 January 1550 (*APC*, III, pp. 343, 372). See also *HoP, 1509–1558*, III, pp. 368–369.

Howe Wriethesley being sent for, was made one of the counsell.[30]
Equire for the articles wheron the duke was examined and for this confession was which was drawen by Pagett.[31]
The examinacion of Sir R. Fane. Only that he should robb King Henry when he went for the almaynes to be brought to Bulleyne.
Howe Sturmius and Brune were ambassadors in Fr. at that tyme for the peace, and howe by Brunoe's menes the army went not forward.[32]
Howe the duke was delyvered.
Howe Sir R. Fane had ben divers times before in pryson for Warwicke's sake, and howe he was ones his man.[33]
Howe Warewick was lodged with Somersett in his howse for feare of his brother the admirall.
Howe the first cause of breach betwene Somersett and War. was for yt Warr. desired to have money coyned and the duke with teares denied yt.[34]

[30] Thomas Wriothesley (d. 1550), Earl of Southampton, had rejoined the council on 17 January 1549 (Hoak, *King's Council*, pp. 50, 288, n. 72), just before the arrest of Sir Thomas Seymour, and not in autumn 1549 after the arrest of Somerset. He was recorded as present at the council on 17 March and on 6 October, and also on 27 July, the only day between those dates for which there are records of conciliar attendance (*APC*, II, p. 263; III, pp. 304, 330). In September the imperial ambassador instructed his agent to report that Southampton and the Earl of Arundel were plotting against Somerset. The ambassador had sent his secretary to call on Southampton to find out about this after Warwick had returned to London after defeating the rebels in Norfolk: Southampton had said that he was not hurrying to return to court after an indisposition on account of Somerset's ill-will. Clearly Southampton was in London, but not at court, by early September (*CSPSp., 1547–1549*, pp. 444–447). The apparent inaccuracy in the text – Southampton was readmitted to the council in January – may, however, simply be a loose way of emphasizing the heightened importance of Southampton once Somerset had been arrested. Southampton had fought a losing battle to stop Somerset becoming Protector in 1547: now he attempted to bring down both Somerset and Warwick and possibly to make Princess Mary regent (see below: cf. Hoak, *King's Council*, pp. 43–45, 231–239; M.L. Bush, *The Government Policy of Protector Somerset* (London, 1975), p. 80; A.J. Slavin, 'The fall of Lord Chancellor Wriothesley: a study in the politics of conspiracy', *Albion*, 8 (1975), pp. 265–286.

[31] Sir William Paget (by 1506–1563), created Lord Paget in December 1549, was closely associated with Protector Somerset's government 1547–1549, but probably advised Somerset to yield in October 1549 and arrested him; *HoP, 1509–1558*, III, p. 45.

[32] Hans Bruno was involved in diplomacy in December 1552 (PRO, SP10/15/63, 10/15/68). Andy Boyle has argued that disagreements over foreign policy, and especially the fate of Boulogne, were critical to the fall of Somerset, and the subsequent defection of key figures like the Earl of Arundel from the coalition which had brought the Protector down. Preparations for an expeditionary force to defend Boulogne proceeded in the closing months of 1549 at the same time as peace feelers with France were put out, but politicians like Arundel who had (at least in his own eyes) played a key role in its capture were not prepared to see it surrendered. See A. Boyle, 'Hans Eworth's portrait of the Earl of Arundel and the politics of 1549–50', *EHR*, 117 (2002), pp. 55–77.

[33] See above, n. 7 for Vane.

[34] According to a French report, Somerset's agents attempted to persuade people that

Howe after Somer. was depryved all the lordes had base money coyned in the Towre, which was a grete distruction.[35]

Howe Warwick was made duke of Northumberland. Herbertt, earle of Pembrock.[36]

Howe bandes of horsemen were devysed, and howe they were ~~discribed~~ distributed, and what was their wages. How they continved not longe, for the grete charge.[37] What exchaunges of landes Northumberland vsed with the king, and what gyftes he and others had of the king.[38]

[fo. 352]

Drury imprysoned in September 1559 for that it was suspected leste he would have slayne the Lord Robert, whome he thought to be vncomly to be so grete with the quene.[39]

In Nouember 1559 the Freinche King Fraunces by the counsell of the Guyses ~~of~~ his wief the Scottyshe quene's vncles vsurpeth the tytell and crownes of Eng. and maketh great ~~munition~~ provision of men, munytion and vitaylles to be sent into Scottland for the subduing therof, and so to have the better entry into England to gett the possession

---

debasement had been carried through against Somerset's advice; Hoak, *King's Council,* pp. 74, 294, nn. 188–190 and 192, citing Paris, BNF, Fonds Français, Fr 15888, fos 205 *seqq.*

[35] For the coinage of these monies by the lords, see C.E. Challis, 'The circulating medium and the movement of prices in Mid-Tudor England', in P. Ramsey (ed.), *The Price Revolution in Sixteenth-Century England* (London, 1971), pp. 119–120, n. 2. See BL, Harleian MS 660, fo. 67 which dates the order at 28 October 1551, after Somerset's fall, showing the 'Journall' to be correct here.

[36] John Dudley (1502–1553), Earl of Warwick, was created Duke of Northumberland on 11 October 1551 (G.E. Cokayne (ed.), *The Complete Peerage of England, Scotland, Ireland, Great Britain and the United Kingdom,* 14 vols (London, 1910–1998), IX, p. 725). William Herbert (c. 1506–1570), courtier and soldier, was created Earl of Pembroke on 11 October 1551 (*CPR, 1550–1553,* pp. 122, 128).

[37] The gendarmes were established in February 1551. They comprised trained bands of 850 cavalry divided into twelve companies, ten of which were commanded by members of the Privy Council. They were disbanded at Michaelmas 1552 as an economy measure; Hoak, *King's Council,* pp. 198–201.

[38] For the pattern of patronage under Northumberland, and his own exchanges of property with the crown, see Loades, *John Dudley, Duke of Northumberland,* pp. 220–224.

[39] Sir William Drury (1527–1579), captain at Calais 1557–1558 and Berwick from 1558. Drury's 'arrest' was widely reported; he was held for examination in late November or early December, after his return from a mission in Scotland in October, and not released until October 1560. According to an appeal for intercession he wrote to Dudley, his offence was words; see Longleat, Dudley Papers, II, fo. 204, (n.d.). He later became a committed Dudley follower.

therof.[40] Of this enterprise the Marques du Boefe[41] was chiefe, but these shippes were by gode's providence throughe tempest distressed, many of them drowned and the marques forced to returne to Deape Hanton.

Sir R. Sadeler to Barwick in August 1559 to practyse with the Scottes to withstande the Freinche there, who hadd 10,000 crownes ~~within~~ with him to distribut where he thought beste for the furtheraunce of the purpose, whoe taried there one yeare.[42] Require of Mr Sadeler what was don there and desire to have Mr Raylton's lettres and minutes which he had being there, with Sir R. Sadeler.[43]

At Chrystmas Anno D. 1559 was the duke of Northfolck sent livetenant of the north to the borders, for the deffence therof and for the preparacion of the army to be sent into Scottland for the deffence of the Scottes.[44]

The quene's navies sent into the north seas, who lay in the mouth of the Frythe, to lett that the Freinshe king should send no aied to the Freinshe men that were in Lythe whoe in shorte tyme fortefied yt very strongly.[45]

The Scottes refuse the olde amitie of Fraunce which had continued so many yeares, and make a league of amitie with Eng.[46] An army of Englishmen 6000 sent to the Borders who under the Lord Graye entred

---

[40] BL, Cotton MS Caligula B X, fos 63r–v, 64r–v; PRO, SP52/1, fos 279–280.

[41] René de Lorraine, marquis d'Elboeuf (1536–1566), brother of the Queen-regent, was commissioned lieutenant-général d'Ecosse to replace her (4 December 1559). He nearly reached Scotland in January 1560, but was blown back to Dieppe (*CSPF, 1559–1560*, pp. 159–160, 287).

[42] Sir Ralph Sadler (1507–1587) was sent to Scotland on 8 August with a 'slush fund' of £3,000 in gold 'to nourish the faction against the French'; *HoP, 1558–1603*, III, pp. 318–321; *CSPSc., 1547–1563*, pp. 241–242.

[43] Gregory Raylton (d. 1561), long Sir Ralph Sadler's 'inwarde man [...] who hath in a manar hoolie and doinge of all my thynges [...] wherein he showeth me both honestie and diligence', was clerk of the signet, treasurer to the Scottish expeditionary force, and secretary to Norfolk's war council. In December 1560 he received (jointly with Sadler) the office of prothonotary of chancery, among whose responsibilities was the paperwork behind diplomacy. Raylton handled Sadler's diplomatic correspondence in 1559–1560; Slavin, *Politics and Profit*, pp. 64–65, 137, 167, 170; *CPR, 1558–1560*, p. 208; *1560–1563*, pp. 62, 100; W.J. Jones, *The Elizabethan Court of Chancery* (Oxford, 1967), pp. 114–115; frequent references in *CSPF, 1559–1560*.

[44] Thomas Howard, fourth Duke of Norfolk (1538–1572). His instructions are in Haynes, *State Papers*, pp. 217–218. He arrived in Newcastle in early January 1560. Norfolk's commission is dated 25 December 1559; see *CSPF, 1559–1560*, pp. 233–237.

[45] The navy, under the command of Sir William Winter (c. 1528–1589), was delayed by the same storms which had scattered Elboeuf's fleet. He was off Berwick on 20 January, and entered the Firth of Forth on 23 January; *CSPF, 1559–1560*, pp. 302–303; PRO, SP52/2/24.

[46] Treaty of Berwick, 27 February 1560; T. Rymer, *Foedera*, 20 vols (London, 1704–1735), XV, pp. 569–571.

into Scottland in Marche and besyged Liethe.[47] Howe the Fr. men at their comming gaue them a very hoate skirmyshe.

Howe the towne was geven over to the Eng. the ———— day of ———— 1560 with condycions that they should departe with bagge and bagages and all their munytion, leaving 50 men in the Ile of ———— in the Freth, and 50 in the castle of Dumbar for saving of the Freinche k. honor.[48]

Howe those Freinshmen were transported by the Eng. navy and landed at Callies to the number of 3800 soldiers.[49]

Howe there were slaine and died 1000 of the Freinshe in the towne of Lethe. Almost as many were in the towne as did besiege them, wherat the Freinshmen marveled.

[fo. 352v]

Howe Liethe had ben threse taken by the Freinshmen's confession yf then it had ben followed. First at the comminge thither of the Eng. army in the skirmyshe of the Eng. horsemen hadd geven the on sett, which was ~~any~~ omytted, for that Sir G. Haward capitaine of them[50] was then sent to the dowager[51] into the castell of Endenboroughe, whoe desired she might talcke with the Eng. for peace and quietnes, and so Mr Barnaby[52] being his livetenant was commaunded to forbere the on sett, because he knew not his government.[53]

[47] The army was commanded by William, Lord Grey of Wilton (c. 1509–1562) After reinforcement with 2,000 additional levies which arrived in late March, it numbered 8,000 foot, 2,000 cavalry, and 700 pioneers. The only trained element in the force was the contingent of 1,000 from Berwick. The army crossed the border on 29 March and laid siege to Leith on 6 April; Haynes, *State Papers*, pp. 271–272, 274–275, 284–285.

[48] Negotiations with the French were concluded on 6 July; and peace announced in Leith on 7 July. Rymer, *Foedera*, XV, pp. 591–593, summarized in *CSPSc., 1547–1563*, pp. 440–442, and J. Hayward, *Annals of the First Four Years of Queen Elizabeth*, J. Bruce (ed.), Camden Society, old series, 8 (1840), pp. 69–72. The treaty provided for sixty French troops to remain in Dunbar and sixty on Inchkeith.

[49] 3,613 men, 267 women and 315 children were shipped out of Leith, Inchkeith and Dunbar on 17 and 18 July; *CSPF, 1560–1561*, p. 213.

[50] Sir George Howard (by 1519–1580) was captain-general of the demi-lances; *HoP, 1558–1603*, II, p. 346.

[51] Marie de Guise (1515–1560), Queen dowager of Scotland.

[52] The chroniclers of the campaign note the presence of Barnaby Fitzpatrick (c. 1535–1581); *Holinshed's Chronicles of England, Scotland, and Ireland*, 6 vols (London, 1807–1809), IV, p. 189.

[53] For the initial skirmish at Restalrig, one mile from Leith on 6 April, see G. Dickinson (ed.), *Two Missions of de la Brosse: An Account of the Affairs of Scotland in the Year 1543, and the Journal of the Siege of Leith 1560*, Publications of the Scottish History Society, third series, 36 (1942), pp. 98–101. The much criticized series of negotiations with Marie de Guise, in which Croft took a key role, were ordered by Grey on 5 April, and were pursued until about 12 April. They reflected Elizabeth's continued striving for a diplomatic solution;

Another tyme was, yf they had continued the battery where yt was laied first, which was removed, and laied against the ~~stronk~~ strongest parte of the towne by perswasion of the Spaniardes that fled owte of the towne to the Engl. Equire whether yt was of malice or of ignoraunce.[54]

The thirde was yf the assaulte that was prepared had ben don. A greate faulte imputed to Sir James Crofte, capitaine of Barwick, whoe was appointed to have the leding and conduyte of the assaultes, who all that night slepte and in the morning was owte of the waye when the feate should have ben don, wherby many that attempted the assalte were killed and maymed.[55]

Howe many of the nobilitie of Scottland were in the campe with the Eng. men, but fewe soldiers of the Scottes.[56]

Howe the Scottyshe men served by course, taried a fewe daies, and departed, and others newe cam, which they saie is the maner of Scottland because they ~~live~~ have no wages, but live for the tyme of their owne.[57]

Enquire of Mr Askam[58] for the copie of the artycles of griefs that the Scottes had against the Freinsh which were by him translated into

PRO, SP52/3/4; C.A. Mackwell, 'The early career of Sir James Croft, 1518–1570' (University of Oxford, B.Litt. thesis, 1970), pp. 138 ff.

[54] This may refer to the switch in English pressure from the middle of the west curtain wall to the flank of Saint Anthony's bulwark after the battery of 3 May which lasted eleven hours 'faisans lesdictes nuictz maintenant aussi clair que du jour' (*Journal of the Siege of Leith*, p. 138).

[55] Sir James Croft (1517/18–1590), governor of Berwick between 14 April 1559 and 21 August 1560, and the reluctant second-in-command of the expedition, became the 'fall guy'. But the failure of the assault on 7 May probably owed more to inadequate equipment and poor co-ordination than to Croft's actions. The breaches made by the bombardment of 6 May were inadequate, but Grey (doubtless goaded by Norfolk's complaints of the dilatory progress of the siege) insisted on going ahead with the assault. There is also some evidence that the assault began prematurely, which may help explain Croft's absence from the battlefield. Croft was recalled to Berwick, and sent on to the court, where he was the subject of a Privy Council investigation on about 19 August 1560, the result of which was his imprisonment in the Fleet Prison until January 1561. For Croft, see *HoP, 1558–1603*, I, pp. 672–675, and for his role in the Scottish campaign, see Mackwell, 'Sir James Croft'. The key accounts of the events of 6–7 May are PRO, SP52/3/181–182, 185, 187–188, 189; SP59/3/20–22; Haynes, *State Papers*, pp. 345–348.

[56] Valentine Browne stated on 25 May that there were only 713 Scotsmen of a total force of 12,446 after the surrender of Leith; Haynes, *State Papers*, pp. 348–349.

[57] This was known in advance by Cecil, see his 'A short discourse of the weighty matter of Scotland' (31? August 1559), printed in A. Clifford (ed.), *The State Papers and Letters of Sir Ralph Sadler*, 2 vols (Edinburgh, 1809), I, p. 381.

[58] Roger Ascham (1515–1568), Latin secretary from 1554. John Hales had worked with him during his embassy in Germany in 1551. See L.V. Ryan, *Roger Ascham* (Stanford CA, 1963), pp. 144–145.

laten and sent to King Philipp,[59] and they were declared in midsomer terme 1560 by the secretary openly in the Sterre Chamber. But in neyther was mencion of the cause of relligion, which was the chiefest cause that moved the Scottes to rebell, yf yt may be called rebellion to withstand that the prince will have don contrary to the lawes and his othe.

A booke or protestation made by the Eng. declaring the causes of the warres, in laten and freinshe printed by R Wolfey mense Junij A° 1560 which is emongest my bookes.[60]

Remember how Mr Askam being at Tuttenham in sommer 1560 I began an oration of this matter.[61]

Howe the duke of ~~Host~~ Holste was heare that same sommer, and was retayned in service with the quene, made of the garter; howe his cheefe arraunt was to sue to the quene for mariage, but hee departed (re infecta) and afterwarde ~~renuing~~ reuiuing yt by letttres, and yt was vtterly denied.[62]

---

[59] The Act of Deprivation of Mary of Guise (21 October 1559) best fits this description; it is printed in W. Croft Dickinson (ed.), *The History of the Reformation of Religion in Scotland*, 2 vols (London, 1949), I, pp. 251–255. These 'articles' are not however found in Ascham's 1558–1568 letterbook (Bodl., MS Clarendon 35). Viscount Montague and Sir Thomas Chamberlain took a 'breviat of the Scotch matter' with them on their embassy to Philip II in January 1560 (*CSPF, 1559–1560*, p. 321). For the 'Spanish' dimension to the British policy, see S. Alford, *The Early Elizabethan Polity: William Cecil and the British Succession Crisis, 1558–1569* (Cambridge, 1998), pp. 72–73.

[60] *Protestatio Christianissimi Regis Gallorum, Habita et Exhibita Praestantissimae Reginae Anglie, per Ordinarium Christianissimi Regis, ad Angliae Reginam Legatum. Excusum Londini: Apud Reginaldum Wolfium, Regiae Maiest. in Latinis Typographum.* (*STC* 11309.5, 1560), with reply from the French: *Responsum ad Protestationem, Quam Orator Regis Gallorum, Nomine sui Principis, Serenissimae Angliae Reginae Obtulit xx. die Aprilis, Anno Domini M.D.LX. Londini: Apud Reginaldum Vuolsium, Regiae Maiest. in Latinis Typographum.* (*STC* 9183, 1560). The printer whose name has been garbled is Reyner Wolfe (d. 1573) (*DNB*). The French edition prints both the protest and the response in series. *Protestation Faicte de La Part du Roy Treschrestien, Par son Ambassadeur, Resident Pres la Royne d'Angleterre, a sa Maiesté, & aux Seigneurs de son Conseil. XX. April. Anno Domini M.D. LX. A Londres.* (*STC* 11309.7, 1560). It contains 'Responce a la proteystation, faicte par l'Ambassadeur du roy Tres chrestien de la part dudict Roy son Maistre, a la Royne d'Angleterre, le vintiesme jour d'apuril. Anno. 1.5.60'. A number of drafts of the protestation and its translation into French are extant; *CSPF, 1559–1560*, pp. 564–569. In March 1560 a proclamation on the Scottish intervention was printed by Jugge and Cawood, the Queen's printers, and translated into French and Italian. Copies of this were sent to Philip II; see *TRP*, II, pp. 141–144, and *CSPF, 1560–1561*, p. 556.

[61] For the residence of John Hales and his brother Stephen at Tottenham, see the discussion in the introduction.

[62] Adolf, Duke of Schlesvig-Holstein-Gottorp (1526–1586), uncle to King Frederick II of Denmark (1534–1588, r. 1559–1588) arrived in London on 28 March and stayed until late June 1560. He was nominated Knight of the Garter on 10 June 1560 and installed by proxy on 15 December 1561; *Leicester Accounts*, pp. 140, 156, 167, 168; *Machyn's Diary*, pp. 229, 247.

[fo. 353]

Howe the Lorde Roberte's wief brake her necke at Foster's howse in Oxfordshere in die natiuitatis Marie A° 1560, her gentellwomen being gon forth to a fier. Howebeyt yt was thought she was slayne, for Sir ———— Varnye was there that daie and whyleste the deade was ~~doying~~ doing was goinge over the fier and tarried there for his man, who at leingthe cam, and he saied, thowe knave, whye tarieste thowe? He answered, shoulde I com before I had don? Haste thowe don? quoth Verney. Yea, quoth the man, I have made hytt sure. So Verney cam to the courte.[63] This woman was viewed by the coroner's queste, wherof one Smyth was foreman whoe was the quene's man being Lady Eliz. and was putt owte of the howse for his lewed behavior.[64] It was found by this enqueste that she was cause of her owne death, falling downe a paier of stayers, which by reporte was but eight steppes. But the people saye she was killed by reason he forsocke her company withowte cause and lefte her firste at Hyde's howse in Hertford shere, where she saied she was poysoned, and for that cause he desired, she might no longer tarry in his howse. From thence she was removed to Varney's howse in Warrwickshere, and so at leingth to Foster's howse. Many times before yt was bruted by the L. Rob. his men that she was ded. And P. vsed to saie that when the Lorde Rob. went to his wief he wentt all in blacke, and howe he was commaunded to saye that he did nothing with her, when he cam to her, as seldome he did. This Varney and divers others his servauntes vsed before her death, to wyshe her death, which made the people to suspecte the worse. And her deathe he mourneth, leaveth the courte, lieth at C. whither the lordes resorted to him to comforte him. Himself all his frindes, many of the lordes and gentllmen, and his famylie be all in black, and weape doloruslie, greate hypocrysie vsed.[65]

---

[63] This is one of the most interesting passages in the 'Journall'. The account of Sir Richard Verney's putative role in the murder of Amy Robsart predates the widely-known one in *Leicester's Commonwealth* by twenty years. See Dwight C. Peck (ed.), *Leicester's Commonwealth: The Copy of a Letter written by a Master of Art of Cambridge (1584)*, (Athens OH, 1985), pp. 81, 90. It is very doubtful that the 'Journall' was the source employed by the compilers of *Leicester's Commonwealth*, but it is evidence of the rumours in circulation.

[64] This may be a reference to Richard Smythe, Mayor of Abingdon in 1564–1565, who was a gentleman usher to Elizabeth as princess and Queen. See Agnes C. Baker, *Historic Abingdon: Fifty-Three Articles* (Abingdon, 1963), p. 24, and, for a reference to Smythe in 1554, BL, Additional MS 34563 [Diary of Sir Henry Bedingfield, 1554–1558], fo. 33v.

[65] For the identification of William Hyde (d. 1580) of Throcking, Herts., and clarification of Amy Robsart's movements in 1559–1560, see the full discussion in *Leicester Accounts*, appendix 1. Note, however, that Dudley never saw his wife after the summer of 1559. The identity of P is unknown, C is Kew. *Leicester Accounts*, p. 143; L. Paris (ed.), *Négotiations, Lettres et Pièces Diverses [...] Tirées du Portefeuille de [...]. Eveque de Limoges* (Paris, 1841), p. 542.

The Tuesdaie after Michelmas Daye[66] he repayreth to the courte, at Hampton Courte. And Mr Danett and I mett him, and yt was reported to the quene, that we in dyspyett would not do him reverence, but we putt of our cappes. And for my self I knewe him not, for I never sawe him before, ne ku knewe not yt was he tyll he was paste.[67]

Enquire for the conclusions of peace betwexte Eng. and Fr. for the matters of Scottland. I thinck Mr Raylton had them. Enquire for the league betwene Engl. and Scottland.[68]

The L. R. continueth his blackes till Easter following.

[fo. 353v]

The quene gaue him a licence for wolles which was worth 10000 markes, which the marchauntes much grudged at, they being restrayned from shipping, because their liberties were taken to be dissolved by the loss of Callies.[69]

The Lord Rob. in greate hoope to marry the quene, for she maketh suche apparaunce of good will to him. He geveth her many goodly presentes. His men brute hyt for trueth. The L. followe him muche. All the resorte is to him.

In winter A° 1560 before the peace betwene Eng. and Scottl Fraunce the Fre. secretly attempte to recover and put away the shame they received, by being put expelled owte of Scotland and make marvelous great preparacions. But the king dieth ———— die ———— 1560 and the authoritie was taken from the Guyses and commytted to Vandosme

---

For another discussion of Robsart's death, see G.W. Bernard, 'Amy Robsart', in his *Power and Politics*, pp. 161–174.

[66] 1 October.

[67] The implications of this passage for John Hales's authorship are discussed in the Introduction. In this context, the identity of Mr Dannet is of some importance, for a Mr Dannet had entertained Dudley to dinner in May 1559 (*Leicester Accounts*, p. 66), although Hales does not suggest that his Mr Dannet also did not know Dudley. Moreover, there are three possible candidates: Thomas Dannet the elder (d. 1569), his son Thomas the younger (1543?–1601), or his brother Leonard (c. 1530–1591). On balance the elder Thomas Dannet seems the most probable. See also Introduction, n. 55.

[68] References to Treaties of Berwick (February 1560) and Edinburgh (July 1560).

[69] *CPR, 1560–1563*, p. 321. Licence to Lord Robert Dudley, 12 April 1560 to buy 1,000 sarplers of wool notwithstanding statute of 4 Ed IV c. 2. Over the course of the next twelve months, Dudley received £5,833 6s 8d from the staplers in respect of this licence. It played a critical role in his finances; *Leicester Accounts*, pp. 116, 157. For the position of the staplers after the fall of Calais now dependent on sucessive licences from the crown before securing their new charter in 1561, see E.E. Rich, *The Ordinance Book of the Merchants of the Staple* (Cambridge, 1937), pp. 22–32.

and the constable who caused the provision of vitayle to be sold.[70] At the tyme of the kinge's death a great nomber of Frenishmen were comming downe to Callies to be transported into Scotland. Phillipp was made protector of Fraunce before the kinge's death. Also the Spaniardes in the Lowe Countrey were gathered together to Seland to be imbarked. It was supposed that Phillipp mente to have sent them into Scotland for ayed. Enquire more of the matter of Mr Gresham for yt is a greate thing etc.[71]

Phillipp in sommer 1560 suffereth greate losse in gallies and men by the Turck at Lerby.[72]

In November 1560 Earles Norton and Glincarne and the L. Ladington cam ambassadors owte of Scotland to gave thankes to the quene for their delyvery, and to be suetors for mariage with the Earle Aren. Looke over Ludington's oracion.[73]

A proclamation aboutes yt that tyme for apparell and against grete hoose but nothing observed.[74]

Mr Asteley for dyspleasure of my L. Rob. was commytted to his chamber and after putt owte of the courte Janu. 1561, but after 6 weekes restored.[75]

[70] François II, King of France died on 5 December 1560. Antoine de Bourbon, duc de Vendôme (1537–1562), and King of Navarre (1555–1562), and Anne de Montmorency (1493–1567), Grand Master and Constable of France, were the newly influential figures.

[71] Throckmorton, anxious about French failure to ratify the treaty of Edinburgh, issued repeated warnings about French troop movements in October and November 1560. Sir Thomas Gresham (c. 1519–1579), the Queen's agent in the Low Countries, had since April been monitoring the 4,800 troops that Philip II was maintaining there. There were exaggerated fears of a Spanish landfall in the Isle of Wight in late October. Whether the French would have been in the position to retaliate for the evacuation of Scotland had the death of François II not intervened is a moot point. The assumption of Franco-Spanish co-operation is exaggerated. *CSPF, 1560–1561*, pp. 28–29, 89, 136, 145–146, 298–303, 345–346, 371–372, 391–396, 408–409; P.M.D. Forbes (ed.), *A Full View of the Public Transactions in the Reign of Q. Elizabeth [...]*, 2 vols (London, 1740–1741), I, pp. 228–235, 249, 292–296, 317.

[72] The naval defeat of a Spanish expeditionary force headed for Tripoli under the command of the Duke of Medinaceli, Viceroy of Sicily and Admiral Gian Doria, off Djerba (Tunisia) took place on 10 May, and was followed by the surrender of the garrison on 31 July. The losses suffered forced Philip to recall Spanish troops from the Netherlands.

[73] James Douglas, fourth Earl of Morton (d. 1581), Alexander Cunningham, fifth Earl of Glencairn (d. 1574), and William Maitland, laird of Lethington (c. 1528–1573). The Scottish Parliament had agreed to promote the proposal of marriage to James Hamilton, third Earl of Arran (1530–1609). Elizabeth gave a negative response on 8 December and they left about a week later; *Leicester Accounts*, pp. 146–147. Lethington's oration was probably that calendared in *CSPSc., 1547–1563*, p. 495; other copies have survived, e.g., Yale University, Beinecke Library, Osborn Shelves, fa 17, art. 3.

[74] There is no proclamation extant, nor any records of action over apparel in civic records in winter 1560–1561. The main campaign against great hose was in 1562, and should have been fresh in the author's mind as the account was dictated.

[75] John Ashley (or Astley) (1507–1596), Master of the Jewel House and husband of the first gentlewoman of the bedchamber, Katherine Ashley. An undated and somewhat hysterical

The earle of Bedford in ———— 1560 is sent into Fran. to condole the late kinge's death and congratulatt the present state, who ernestly persuaded the receaving and maintenaunce of chryste's relligion, and howe yt only was the mene to make and mayntayne amytie betwene princes and contreies.[76]

The L. James passeth throughe Eng. into Fraun. to the quene of Scottes in March 1561. He was lodged at his goying over at the secretary's howse in Canon Rowe, well vsed of the quene, and in the end of May retorneth owte of Fraunce.[77]

[fo. 354]

Before the Frenishe kinge's death the duke of Namures was commyng owte of Fraunce to be a suetor to the quene for mariage,[78] but stayed at Callies. Som saied yt was by reason of the fall of Eng. base money, which was cried downe at Michellmas 1560.

The crying downe of the money made grete dearth and in many places, the people would not sell for money but vppon truste because they knew not the certenty of the fall, and in many places the price of thinges was double increased.[79]

Immediatly after gold was abated in value by proclamation, nothing is the better cheape eyther comming from beyond the sea or at home but rather encreased in pryce.[80]

The emperor was a sutor to the quene for his sonn Charles by ———— and ————, his ambassador who was a very handsome gentellman, and a good curtier. He was in grete hope, but after he was reuoked and ———— succeded who tarried not longe. The quene saied yf any successe cam of this ambassadge the prayse was.[81]

letter from her to Dudley survives (Longleat, Dudley Papers, I, fo. 201), which is obviously related to this incident but does not make clear what her husband's offence was except that Elizabeth had said 'that sche cowld never forgeve my husbond nor never love hym'.

[76] Francis, second Earl of Bedford (1527–1585) left London on 25 January 1561 and returned on 9 March 1561. He failed to convince Navarre and Catherine de Medici that France should not send representatives to Trent. *CSPF, 1560–1561*, pp. 525, 565–578: *Machyn's Diary*, pp. 248, 252.

[77] Mary's half-brother, Lord James Stewart (c. 1532–1570), made Earl of Moray on 30 January 1562.

[78] Jacques de Savoie, duc de Nemours (1531–1585). *CSPF, 1560–1561*, pp. 346, 399.

[79] *TRP*, II, pp. 150–154 (27 September 1560).

[80] *Ibid.*, pp. 155–158 (9 October 1560).

[81] Charles (1540–1590), Archduke of Austria from 1564, was the youngest son of Ferdinand I (1503–1564, Holy Roman Emperor, 1558–1564). George, Count Helffenstein (1518–1571), governor of Upper Austria, arrived in England on 20 February 1559; Caspar Brüner, Baron von Rabenstein, chamberlain to the prince arrived in late May. *CSPF, 1558–1559*, pp. 100, 242, 248, 344; *CSPF, 1559–1560*, p. 53; V. von Klarwill, *Queen Elizabeth and Some Foreigners* (London, 1928), pp. 16–18, 31–32, 80; *Leicester Accounts*, pp. 22, 135, 155, 164–165.

Phillipp pretended to be a furtherer of this mariage in wordes but secretly he wrought the contrary, by the bushoppe of Aquila his ambassador.[82] Duke John of Fineland at Michelmas 1559 cam into the realme to be a suetor to the quene for his brother the prince of Sweeden elected king who lay at Winchester Place in Southewarcke and departed at Easter 1560.[83] He kepte a very grete howse, grete fare; his owne messe was dayly hoolie geven to the poore, and freshe mete prepared for his waitors. He was wery liberall to the poore. In Southwarcke he gaue before his departure to all poore howsholdes, som 6, som 8, som 12, some 20 dollars, which made him well spoken of. He spent here for the tyme aboue 20000 dallars. He brought much bolion with him which was coyned at the Towre and parte he gave to the lordes. The earle of Hertford[84] was very familier with him, and they vsed much play at tenyce. He was a very proper man, well lerned, well nourtured and had the commendacion of all men. He had his precher.[85]

There was noe love betwene him and Holste[86] as yt seamed.

The emperor nor Phillipp's ambassador could not abyed this ~~duck~~ duke. He brought with him ——— shippes well armed and furneshed. They were balanced with coper as yt was reported. They would sufffer none to enter them.

[fo. 354v]

The Pope Pius 1560 sommoneth a counsell to be holden at Trent at in the Anunciacion of Our Ladie 1561.[87] He sendeth his nuncio abowte for that purpose called Martinengo abbat of C. and a Venetian. He commeth to the princes of Germany assembled at Venetia, a towne of Duke Johannes Fridericus where he was wery well vsed. And in the end receved this answere, that yf he were not well vsed, hit was because

---

[82] Alvaro La Quadra, Bishop of Aquila (d. 1563), Spanish ambassador from May 1559. See M. Fernandez Alvarez, *Tres Embajadores de Felipe II en Inglaterra* (Madrid, 1955), pp. 55–56. On 13 July 1559 Philip informed Ferdinand of his support for Charles's proposal (AGS, E. 811, fo. 66). There is no evidence from Spanish sources that La Quadra had secret instructions to the contrary.

[83] Johan (1537–1592), second son of Gustavus Vasa, later Johan III (r. 1568–1592) arrived in London on 5 October 1559 and left on 11 April 1560, residing at Winchester Place in Southwark. He was promoting the suit of his brother, Eric XIV (1533–1577, r. 1560–1568); *Machyn's Diary*, pp. 214, 230; *Leicester Accounts*, pp. 100, 133, 164.

[84] Edward Seymour, Earl of Hertford (1539–1621).

[85] Probably his tutor, Dionysius Beurreus (c. 1507–1567).

[86] See above, n. 62.

[87] Pius IV (1499–1565, r. 1559–1565) issued orders for the reconvening of the council, suspended since April 1552, on 29 November 1560. The council met again on 18 January 1562.

yt yt he ~~was~~ cam from the pope, but for the Venetians' sake, he was welcom, but to come to the counsell they vtterly refuced.[88]

Enquire for the copie of these ~~matters~~ newes which cam from Chrystopher Mounte.[89]

At Easter 1561 commyssioners were appointed to enquire for masse mongers and coniurers, whervpon the L. of Lugborowe, Sir Edwarde Wolgraue, Sir Thomas Whorton were apprehended whoe confessed their massing, and divers others were condempned for yt at Burnwode.[90] The heire of Geffrey Poole[91] was imprysoned, and suspicion of some confederacy was by reason of the ~~per~~ procurement of the L. of Lugborowe. This Poole should have maried the earle of Northumberland his syster, for whose mariage newe costly apparell was prepared then was thought convenient for suche personages, and many

---

[88] Girolamo Martinengo, Abbot of Leno, near Brescia in the Venetian territories, was appointed nuncio to England in January 1561. The reference to his meeting with the German princes (in fact assembled at Naumburg to reconfirm the Augsburg Confession and to frame a response to the invitation to the council) is obscure. The pope's envoys to Naumburg were Commendone and Delfino. See C.G. Bayne, *Anglo-Roman Relations, 1558–65* (Oxford, 1913).

[89] Christpher Mount/Mundt (d. 1572), Elizabeth's agent in Germany, sent to Naumburg to dissuade the protestant princes from sending representatives to Trent. The princes' meeting began on 21 January 1561; the papal envoys arrived on 28 January; and Mundt on 6 February. *CSPF, 1560–1561*, pp. 465–466; *CSPF, 1561–1562*, pp. 3–5. Cf. Hirofumi Horie 'The Lutheran influence on the Elizabethan settlement, 1558–1563,' *HJ*, 34 (1991), pp. 519–537.

[90] Lord Edward Hastings of Loughborough (by 1519–1572), Sir Edward Waldegrave (1516/17–1561), and Sir Thomas Wharton (1520–1572) were all leading Marian councillors, all in *HoP, 1558–1603*, II, pp. 35–17; III, pp. 534–535, 599–601. The indictments were taken at Essex assizes at Brentwood. Waldegrave was committed to the Tower on 22 April, Hastings to the charge of the Earl of Pembroke on the following day; *Machyn's Diary*, p. 256. On the Waldegraves and their circle, see B.C. Foley, 'The breaking of the storm', *The Essex Recusant*, 3 (1961), pp. 1–21.

[91] Arthur Pole (1531–?1570), eldest son of Sir Geoffrey Pole (?1502–1558), and nephew to Cardinal Reginald Pole. It is not clear how long his imprisonment lasted, but he continued to dabble in irresponsible plotting on his release. In September 1562, La Quadra reported that he was about to leave the country on the pretext of religion, but 'the truth is he is going to try his fortune and pretend the crown'. His claim was based on his descent from the Duke of Clarence, but La Quadra considered him lacking in credibility. Pole then approached de Foix, the French ambassador, amending his plan to support the claims of Mary, Queen of Scots, to whom it was proposed that his brother Edmund (1541–?1570) should be married. Mary's claims were to be enforced by a Guisard invasion of England from Wales. It is unlikely that the plans proceeded far, resting as they did on the predictions of an astrologer, Prestal, that Elizabeth would die in 1563. The Pole brothers were arrested (Arthur for the second time) as they were about to leave for France in October 1562. They were tried by a commission of oyer and terminer (dated 22 February 1563), and found guilty of treason (26 February), but the sentence was never carried out, and they languished in the Tower. PRO, KB 8/40; J. Strype, *Annals of the Reformation and Establishment of Religion*, 4 vols (Oxford, 1824), I.i, pp. 555–558; *DNB*.

were invyted to the feaste. Many papystes of the southe parte had mente to go thither.[92] The coniurers had were thought to have coniured to have knowen howe longe the quene should reign, and what should become of relligion. 9 of them were set on the pillory 7 Trinitatis 1561[93] emongest whome one Bylson a prebendary of Sarum and Gardener's chaplen[94] was, whoe to have his will of the Lady Cotton caused yonge Coxe, a prieste to say a masse to call on the dyvell, to make muche sorcery, which Coxe confessed and Bylson could not deny yt in the Sterr Chamber.[95]

This Bilson being in the Towre afterward wrote lettres to Coxe in Marshalsee, requiring him to declare by his lettres that he had wrongfully accused him, and promised him fauer, and so Coxe did, which letters came after to light by reason that the L. Seinte John[96] did, lamenting Bilson's case, shewe the same to the byshoppe of Winton.[97] Howe Bylson sett a grete bragge before the counsell in the Sterre Chamber as he had not ben guyltie, and on the pillory stoade with his boocke in his hand, withowte any abashment and so he did going throughe the stretes, his faier gowne with a large typett and square cape on his heade.

This terme also Symondes of Windsore's widowe was sett on the pillory for falsly accusing one Parrie and others of robberrie. Her husband with

---

[92] Thomas Percy, seventh Earl of Northumberland (1528–1572). *CSPSp., 1558–1567*, p. 208.

[93] A priest by the name of John Coxe, alias Devon, was apprehended by customs officials at Gravesend on 13 April 1561 carrying a rosary and breviary and letters intended for Catholic exiles. Examined before Hugh Darrell, a Kent justice of the peace, he named Wharton and Waldegrave for hearing mass. Further examinations before Bishop Grindal followed on 17 April, when accusations of a plot to ensure a Catholic succession based on sorcery surfaced. The conjurers were arraigned on 20 June, and pilloried in Westminster on 22 June and in Cheapside on 25 June. Those pilloried included Leonard Bylson, John Coxe, Dr Fryer (a physician, see below, n. 102), and Francis Coxe (in trouble the previous year for an attempt to kill by sorcery Lady Elizabeth St Loe and Sir William St Loe, captain of the guard). PRO, SP12/16/49; *Machyn's Diary*, p. 261; F. Coxe, *The Vnfained Retraction of Fraunces Coxe, Which He Vttered at the Pillery in Chepesyde and Els Where. 1561.* (STC 5951, 1561); *idem, A Short Treatise Declaringe the Detestable Wickednesse, of Magicall Sciences, as Necromancie, Coniurations of Spirites, Curiouse Astrologie and Such Lyke (STC 5950, 1561).* The whole episode is discussed at length by N. Jones, 'Defining superstitions: treasonous Catholics and the act against witchcraft of 1563', in C. Carlton, R.L. Woods, M.L. Robertson, and J.S. Block (eds), *State, Sovereigns and Society in Early Modern England* (Stroud, 1998), pp. 187–203.

[94] For Leonard Bylson, see A.B. Emden, *A Biographical Register of the University of Oxford, A.D. 1500 to 1540* (Oxford, 1974), p. 93; J. Le Neve, *Fasti Ecclesiae Anglicanae, 1541–1857, vi: Salisbury Diocese* (London, 1986), pp. 77, 95.

[95] Lady Cotton was the widow (née Jane Onley) of Sir Richard Cotton (by 1497–1556). *HoP, 1509–1558*, I, pp. 711–712; PRO, SP12/16, fo. 20.

[96] Oliver St John, Lord St John of Bletso (by 1522–1582). *HoP, 1509–1558*, III, p. 258.

[97] Robert Horne (c. 1519–1580).

Doctor London wore in King Henry tyme papers at Windsore for falsely accusing the gentlemen of the pryvy ~~chan~~ chamber.[98]

[fo. 355]

Enquire fullie for this conspiracy for yt was a grete matter invented by Wrothesley[99] and practised by Capon, byshoppe of Sarum[100] and Doctor Eggeworth his chaunceller;[101] yt was don at Sarum.

At this time yt was bruted that relligion should not longe continue. This was also spoken by the bushoppes that were prysoners in the Towre whoe had knowledge therof by Doctor Fryer the phisitian,[102] whoe being examyned confessed that he herd yt of the bushopp of Aquila, K. P. ambassador, who was promysed it by Sir Henry Shedney, and restitucion of the b. of Rome yf he could procure that P. should be a suetor to the quene that the L. R. might marye the quene which he undertooke, and therfore he and Pagett were ernest suetors to the quene, and the b. was so grete in the courte that it was thought he should have had a chamber in the curte at Grenewyche. Hervppon this b. laboured the comming in of the abbott, the pope's nuncio who

[98] For William Symondes (c. 1480–1547 or later), see *HoP, 1509–1558*, III, pp. 415–417. Henry Parry (d. ?1572) was chancellor of the diocese of Salisbury from 1547 to 1553, and was reinstated in 1559; W.H.R. Jones (ed.), *Fasti Ecclesiae Sarisberiensis* (Salisbury, 1879), p. 340. For Dr John London, Dean of Oxford and canon and prebendary of St George's Chapel, Windsor, see Emden, *Biographical Register*, pp. 359–360. For the conspiracies of 1543, in which London targeted Philip Hoby and Sir Thomas Carden of the Privy Chamber, see J. Foxe, *Acts and Monuments*, S.R. Cattley (ed.), 8 vols (London, 1841–1849), V, pp. 470–481; MacCulloch, *Thomas Cranmer*, pp. 300–307. Symondes and London were sentenced to the pillory at Windsor, Reading, and Newbury.

[99] Sir Thomas Wriothesley (1505–1550), at this time principal secretary.

[100] John Salcot, alias Capon, Bishop of Salisbury (d. 1557).

[101] Roger Edgeworth (d. 1560) was canon of Salisbury and chancellor of Wells; Emden, *Biographical Register*, pp. 84–85; Le Neve, *Salisbury*, p. 71; *DNB*.

[102] The Fryers were a dynasty of London physicians. This is probably John Fryer senior (c. 1499–1563). He had been an early convert to evangelical ideas under the influence of Thomas Garrett at Cardinal College, but studying medicine at Padua in 1535–1536, joined the circle of scholars around Pole, and became a 'strong papist'. Returning to England, he became physician to key establishment figures, and was president of the College of Physicians in 1549–1550. Under Mary, he returned to Pole's circle, but fell into rapid disfavour under Elizabeth, and was imprisoned in the Tower from 1561. *HoP, 1509–1558*, II, pp. 174–175; *DNB*; S. Brigden, 'Henry Howard, Earl of Surrey, and the "Conjured League"', *HJ*, 37 (1994), pp. 535–536. We are also grateful to Dr Maggie Pelling for information on the Fryers.

came downe purposely into Flaunders.[103] But the counsell noblely and stoutly resisted yt as appereth by their consultation and answere made in Maye 1561. When it appered to the examiners that the L. R. was touched, and howe also the bush. had reported the quene had promised him no lesse, that examinacion was staied, and then was the matter of coniuring and massing the more ernestly prosecuted, to showe they had not sitten in vayne.[104] But hereby the Lord R. and Seydne's ambytion appered, yt to be king he would procure the banishment of the gospell. A grete argument to prove his consent to the murdering of his wief, to have the quene, that would betray his countrey to be king. Qui maius et minus.

Paule's church borned the 4 Junij 1561. Looke the booke therof made. No hurtes besides don, a grete marvayle. The divers brutes of the causes and significations therof.[105]

The king of Swedon his chauncellor commeth to be ambassador in stede of ———— the Freinshman whoe behaved him self nobly.[106]

Howe in Maye 1561 Dymocke was commytted to warde, som say for speaking and taking vpon him whilest he was with the king of Swedon more than he had in commyssion, some saied for wrytting lettres to the quene of the reportes abroade of her and the L. Rob which were very evill favored.[107]

---

[103] Sir Henry Sidney (1529–1586), brother-in-law to Robert Dudley and president of the Council of the Marches in Wales, approached La Quadra on 22 January 1561, and Dudley followed up on 13 February. All that is known about the approaches to La Quadra by Sidney and Dudley come from la Quadra's reports to Philip II; see *CSPSp., 1558–1567*, pp. 178ff., but the 'Journall' adds details, showing how the story leaked. One of the interesting features of this account is the importance it assigns to the malign influence of William, Lord Paget of Baudesert (by 1506–1563) in these years, both here and elsewhere. Paget's exclusion from Elizabeth's Privy Council is one of the mysteries of the accession; see Rodriguez-Salgado and Adams, 'The Count of Feria's dispatch to Philip II of 14 November 1558', p. 315. The activities reported here cannot be confirmed, but Dudley later wrote of Paget with great fondness; see Adams, 'Dudley clientele', p. 248. See also nn. 111, 178, 186, 192 for Paget.

[104] The council took the decision to refuse admission to Martinengo on 1 May 1561. *CSPF, 1561–1562*, pp. 93–95, 103–105.

[105] *The True Report of the Burnyng of the Steple and Churche of Poules in London* (*STC* 19930, 1561), and see below, nn. 117, 127–132.

[106] Nils Gyllenstierna (1526–1601), Swedish chancellor, was dispatched by Eric XIV in the spring, and was in London by 4 April 1561, replacing Burreus. He stayed for twelve months. *CSPF, 1560–1561*, pp. 443, 556–557; *CSPF, 1561–1562*, pp. 27, 49, 73, 159, 208, 307, 444; below, n. 177.

[107] John Dymock, a London merchant acted as a semi-official intermediary between Elizabeth and the Swedish court in the course of 1561; Doran, *Monarchy and Matrimony*, pp. 34–35.

Sir N. Frogmorton went over ambassador into Fraunce who wysely foresawe the successe of the warres of Scottland and therfore labored muche that the quene should take vpon her the deffence of them,[108] wherunto she was very lothe at the first, being diswaded by the secrett worcking of Pagett, whoe practised with Parry the thresaurer by daye and night for that purpose, but at leingth yt proceded.[109] Howe the quene was fearefull whylest the army was in Scottland, and threatened the secretary being in Scotland with Doctor Wotton, yf the matter succeded not well, yt should lye on his sholders.[110]

The L. Montague and Sir Th. Chamberleyne ambassadors into Spayne.[111]

Anno 1561 there had ben a grete dearth of corne in Engl. had not the merchauntes of London brought grete of quantytie of corne owt of Eastland which offended farmors and husbandmen that saied they muste leve the ploughe, yf they might not sell their corne at indifferent pryces. 160 hulckes laden with corne drowned in Norwaye. A grete argumment of plenty of corne in those parties, when by this losse the pryce of corne encresed not.[112]

---

[108] Sir Nicholas Throckmorton, (1515–1571), was ambassador in France from 3 May 1559 to about 4 February 1563. He was in England from mid-November 1559 to January 1560, a critical period in the arguments over intervention in Scotland.

[109] For Sir Thomas Parry (c. 1510–1560), treasurer of the household, see *HoP, 1558–1603*, III, pp. 178–180; Haynes, *State Papers*, pp. 295–296, but note that Alford, *Early Elizabethan Polity*, pp. 66–67, 78 identifies him as originally a supporter of the war. He may have been among the sceptics of Cecil's confessional interpretation of the conflict, as Feria regarded him as a moderate on religious matters and noted tensions between him and the secretary. Lord John Grey of Pirgo, Hales's ally over the succession in 1563–1564, complained to Cecil of Parry's influence in April 1560; see PRO, SP 12/12/1, and *HMCS*, I, p. 212.

[110] Sir William Cecil (1520/1–1598) and Sir Nicholas Wootton (c. 1497–1567) were the ambassadors sent to negotiate the Treaty of Edinburgh between 27 May 1560 and 28 July 1560.

[111] Sir Anthony Browne, first Viscount Montagu (1528–1592) and Sir Thomas Chamberlain (c. 1504–1580) were sent on joint embassy to Spain on 12 January 1560. Montagu was recalled in May 1560 and Chamberlain remained as resident until mid-April 1562. Interestingly, Paget was originally appointed to the embassy to Philip II, but escaped owing to ill health. Plas Newydd, Paget Papers II, fo. 63, Throckmorton to Sir Henry Paget, 6 February 1560.

[112] The wheat harvest of 1560–1561 was poor, that of 1561–1562 good. Prices of all grains in 1560–1561 were about 22 per cent higher than in the previous three years when the harvests had been reasonably good; D.M. Palliser, *The Age of Elizabeth: England Under the Later Tudors, 1547–1603* (London, 1983), p. 386. Thomas Bates, one of the London bridgemasters, was sent to Flanders to co-ordinate grain purchases for the capital. The city's wheat was being sold at 23s per quarter in late 1560, at 24s per quarter between March and July 1561, and 22s per quarter in November 1561. CLRO, Rep(ertory of the Court of Aldermen) 14, fos 420v, 444, 457, 461, 475, 504v, 519v; Rep. 15 fo. 8.

Howe divers Engl. men were bornt in Spayne for relligion, and the ambassador Chamberleyne his men in grete daunger for that cause, and he himself forced to sue to the counsell for redresse.[113] Marchaundice forbydden to be carried owte of Spayne in straunge bottoms.[114] Our merchauntes muche troubled by the Inquysition in Spayne, putt to their fynes vpon every lyght suspicion.[115]

In ———— 1561 a proclamation was for the condemnation of all kindes of base money, which was called the victorie or conquest of the hedyous monster. Seke the proclamation.[116]

Their xv[es] in London and comen gatheringes for the reedyfynge of Paule's.[117] More charitie shewed therin then on the poore men of Callies, whoe for lack of relief storved in the streetes. The quene commeth to the Towre 10 July A 1561 and so passeth by Houndyche and Clerkenwell to Charterhowse, the lordes before her and the L.R. on horseback behind her in his whytt hose and dublet embrodered and his men in grene coates pulled owte with yollowe sarcenett.[118] It is reported that the pope, the emp. and K. Phill. send hyther with ambassadors to sommon the quene to the councell. It seameth the emp. seketh revenge fo refusall of his sonn. Manet alta mente repostum Judiciu paridis ei sprerae inuiria formae.

---

[113] *CSPF, 1561–1562*, pp. 53, 123–124, 213, 337, 370. Chamberlain reported the persecutions on 7 April 1561, but the burnings seem to have occurred a few months earlier. A London merchant named Nicholas Burton and a mariner from Southampton had been burned at Seville on 22 December 1560. Strype has a lengthy account of the harassment and imprisonment of John Frampton of Bristol at the hands of the Inquisition at about the same time. H.C. Lea, *A History of the Inquisition of the Middle Ages*, 3 vols (New York, 1887), III, pp. 445–457; Strype, *Annals*, I.i, pp. 355–367.

[114] PRO, SP70/26/155, 176, cited by P. Croft, *The Spanish Company*, London Record Society, 9 (1973), p. ix.

[115] Cf. *A Discouery and Playne Declaration of Sundry Subtill Practises of the Holy Inquisition of Spayne. Certaine speciall examples set aparte by them selues [...] wherein a man may see the forsaid practises of the Inquisition, as they be practised and exercised, very liuely described. Set forth in Latine, by Reginaldus Gonsaluius Montanus, and newly translated. (STC* 103228, 1569).

[116] *TRP*, II, pp. 169–170 (12 June 1561): 'Her majesty having now as it were achieved to the victory and conquest of this hideous monster of the base money'.

[117] On 10 June 1561, the common council of the city of London granted three-fifteenths (3,000 marks) to be levied at six-monthly intervals; CLRO, Journal of Common Council 17, fos 317, 328v. Work began on the repair of the cathedral on 1 July under the supervision of Richard Grafton, grocer and James Harrison, goldsmith; see also below, nn. 129, 132.

[118] *Machyn's Diary*, pp. 262–263; Strype, *Annals*, I.i, pp. 403–404. The Queen visited the Tower mint and was hosted for three days at the Charterhouse by Lord North. On 13 July, she began the progress into East Anglia, see also n. 137. As he had done in 1559, Dudley gave his men new liveries for the progress. The 1559 liveries were also green; see *Leicester Accounts*, pp. 21, 419.

[fo. 356]

Newes that the Turcke was prouoked to warre by another prince very mightie who pretended tytell to Turkye and howe his army was of jues, very vnlike but by liklywod invented by the papistes, for a more terror to vs: as thoughe Phillipp being nowe at libertie and fre from the Turcke, not being able to mainteyne his purpose and enterpryse in Africa and Hispania, should sett vppon the protestauntes.[119]

Newes that the Scottyshe quene goeth in August nexte into Scottland with tow gallies and foure shippes.

Grete drynes in Spaine, occasion of morren vppon their cattell and scarcytie of corne.[120]

The cytie of Excester was the vi[th] and the laste tyme besieged in the thirde yeare of King Edw. the 6 1549 by the commons of Devon and Cornewall for they not susteyning the causes of relligion then receved by lawes of the realme, clustered them selfes together in companies, to infringe the same, wherfore they cam to this cytie and vpon the 2 day of July layed siege thervnto, encamping them selfes rounde aboute the walles in grete nombers, every Hick and Tom making him self a capitan, and there continued xxxv daies, during which tyme many assaultes and soundry skirmyshes were made, the gates sett a fier, the

---

[119] Machyn's version was even more extraordinary: 12 August 'tydynges that ther was a ix trybes that have bene in a contrey ever synes they wher dryven owt of Egype, and they be rede to set on the Grett Turke with grett armes of men' (*Machyn's Diary*, p. 265). Both were clearly influenced by the translation of a 'letter' by Andrea Buonaccorsi: 'Newes Come Latle fro[m] Pera, of two most mighti armies as we of foteme[n] as of horseme[n], tra[n]slated out of Italien, to Fre[n]che and so into Engleshe. And first of the great Duke of Moscuia [and] of the Soffy, and y[e] othere of an Hebrewe people neuer spoken of before, fou[n]de not lo[n]g ago coming from y[e] mountaines called Caspii, with a newe inuencio[n] of weapons, with y[e] number of y[e] squadrons, and with the names of two earles [and] capitayns. And the cause whi y[e] great Turk hath forbydde[n] wyne, with mani other newes neuer hard of' (*STC* 4102.3, 1561). This pseudo-newsletter mixed the plausible (Muscovite pressure on the Ottomans' Tartar allies, discontent among their North African satellites, and a renewed Persian offensive) with the fantastic (the discovery and arming of the lost tribes of Israel beyond the Caspian by the Spanish, who had stumbled upon them via their new world discoveries!) The 'news' may owe something to the continuing dynastic quarrel within the Ottoman Empire. Suleyman's son Bayezid had taken refuge with the Safavid Shah Tahmasp in late 1559, having been defeated in a civil war in Anatolia by his brother Selim II. He was handed over by Tahmasp in the summer of 1561 (possibly early 1562) after long diplomatic haggling. It would appear that Tahmasp, having recently made peace with the Ottomans, wanted to extract maximum diplomatic advantage from his prize, but that he was reluctant to risk war. Charrière reports that Philip II was believed to be in touch with Bayezid. We are very grateful to Richard Repp for advice on the Ottoman succession struggle. See also D. Vaughan, *Europe and the Turk: A Pattern of Alliances* (Liverpool, 1954), p. 152.

[120] *CSPF, 1561–1562*, p. 404. Chamberlain reported that wheat in Spain was at £3 per quarter.

walles undermyned, the subvrbes burned and divers killed. And at length the cytizens having no breade were driven to suche extremyty as they were forced to eate brede made of brenn and worse, and the prisoners in the gayle for lacke of other meate were fedd with horsfleshe. And in processe suche scarcety grewe in the cytie that yt was gretly fered that eyther the people should have peryshed for famen or yelded to the commons. But the magistrates vsing the people with suche liberalitie and persuading them with comfortable promysses kepte them in fydelitie to the prince and Cytee and obteyned their consent rather to die trwe men, then to consent to such rebelles, assuring them of reskue within shorte tyme as followed, for Sir John Russell, L. Russell and l. pryvey seale and then livetenant into the west partes, after he had vanquished many rebelles about Honyton, cam to this cytie the vi[th] of Auguste, repelled and slewe a grete nomber of the rebelles, and sett the cytie at libertie.[121]

[121] Our author has the dates of the siege of Exeter in 1549 correct. The King's lieutenant was Sir John Russell, Lord Russell, later first Earl of Bedford (c. 1485–1555). The key engagement between Russell and the rebels took place at Clyst St Mary on 3–5 August, but there was further resistance and another engagement was fought at Sampford Courtenay on 17 August. A very similar short account of the siege of Exeter may be found in BL, Cotton MS Titus F VI, fos 78v–79. This is the last section of what is in the manuscript headed 'The discription of the Citie of Exetre made and done by John Vowell alias Hoker of the same Citie. 1559' (fos 76–79). Although very close, the version in the 'Journall' includes several points not in the Titus MS: the religious causes of the rebellion; every hick and Tom making himself a captain (on which see also below); the burning of suburbs; the eating of bran bred; and the efforts of the magistrates of the city to persuade the citizens to hold out for longer, but there is nothing significant in the Titus MS that is not included in the 'Journall'. The Titus MS is ascribed to John Hooker, an eyewitness of these events, who also wrote a much longer 'description' of Exeter, which includes a more substantial account of the siege set in the context of the south-western rebellion as a whole (most accessibly available in W.J. Harte, J.W. Schopp and H. Tapley Soper (eds), *The Description of the Citie of Excester by John Vowell alias Hooker*, Devon and Cornwall Record Society, 12 (1919), pp. 67–96, to which page references are given below). There is also a variant version of this text in Bodl., Rawlinson MS C 792. This longer version includes almost all the details given in the 'Journall' (the eating of bread made of bran, the feeding of horseflesh to prisoners in the gaol, the burning of the gates, the undermining of the walls, the efforts of the 'magistrates' – the word Hooker uses to describe the rulers of the city – to calm the commons) further confirming that the author of this manuscript must have had access to Hooker's writings in some form, most probably to some variant of the short version in the Titus MS. The immediately preceding pages of both the longer versions and the shorter version of Hooker's *Description* dealt with earlier sieges of the city, most recently that of Perkin Warbeck in 1497; the way this extract begins with 'the vith and last tyme' the city was besieged reinforces the claim that the author was dependent on Hooker. The only significant variation from the other Hooker texts is the phrase 'every hick and Tom making him self a captain', which is neither in the Devon Record Office nor the Titus nor the Rawlinson MSS. In the Devon Record Office manuscript (though not in the Rawlinson MS nor in the Titus MS) Hooker did describe how the commons appointed captains 'suche like the worst men and the refuse of all others' (pp. 66–67). We are very grateful to Mark Stoyle for references and for much assistance on Hooker.

1562

Mustermasters appointed in every shere, which did muster and had wages of the quene for the tyme.[122]

When Callies was taken they were afrayed of the Ile of Wyght, and sent thither to be ruler Sir Thomas Tresham, after L. of St Johnes with two ~thousand~ 2000 men for the deffence of the same.[123]

[fo. 356v]

1561 September

Many bankruptes, both in Flaund. as the company of Lixsaultes and Flechamer Italians and by reson that Phillipp and the F. K. would not paie the money they borrowed of them for their wares. And divers Londoners. Enquire the generall cause. Many that were worth 100000[li] were sodenly not worth a halfpeny. The plage of god vpon the vserers whose money caused all these alteracion of warres.[124]

Articles for the execution of divers penall lawes sent from the quene and counsell to all pustices of peace. Hyt was supposed to be don for that suche cheapnes of thinges followed not vpon the alteracion of coyne as was hoped.[125]

100000 quarters of corne brought from Dan. by the merchauntes of London which relyved many partes of the realme. Otherwyse yt was licke corne would have ben vnreasonable deare. The sommer before

[122] This initiative has not been previously noticed.

[123] Sir Thomas Tresham (d. 1559), Prior of the recently restored order of St John of Jerusalem, was dispatched as Lieutenant to the Isle of Wight on 30 January 1558 with instructions to levy 2,600 men for its defence. By the end of June he had been replaced by John Paulet, Lord St John (c.1510–1586); *CSPD, Mary I*, pp. 317, 321, 324–325, 347, 360; *APC*, VI, pp. 229, 230. For Prior Tresham, see M.E. Finch (ed.), *The Wealth of Five Northamptonshire Families, 1540–1640*, Northamptonshire Record Society, 19 (1956), pp. 67–72.

[124] Among the casualties of this year were the firms of Lixhalles and Gusman. *CSPF, 1561–1562*, pp. 282–283, 288–289; M. Battistini, *Lettere di Giovanni Battista Guicciardini a Cosimo e Francesco de Medici Scritte dal Belgio dal 1557 al 1577* (Brussels and Rome, 1950), pp. 156–157.

[125] The text of the council's instructions has not been found, and should not be confused with the 'abbreviate' of statutes issued this year. But their content can be inferred from the letter written by William Tyldesley, a Buckinghamshire Justice of the Peace, to Cecil on 3 September 1561. Tyldesley records efforts to enforce the laws relating to alehouses, apprentices, archery, plays and games, rebellion, regrators and forestallers, tillage, victuals and wood, wines, vagabonds, retainers, robberies, slanderous tales, highways, and the preservation of grain; *A Collection of the Substaunce of Certayne Necessarye Statutes to be by the Iustices of Peace Diligently Executed* (*STC* 9339.5, 1561); PRO, SP12/19/43; R.H. Tawney and E. Power (eds), *Tudor Economic* Documents, 3 vols (London, 1924), I, pp. 334–338; HMC, *Seventh Report, More-Molyneux*, p. 616; S.T. Bindoff, 'The making of the Statute of Artificers', in Bindoff, Hurstfield, and Williams, *Elizabethan Government and Society*, pp. 85–86.

was very moyest, and whete for the most parte was over growen with wyeld fetches.[126]

Lettres sent from the archbyshopp of Canterbury to all b. for a relief towardes the buylding of Paule's burnte this yeare in June.[127]

The boocke of the burning of P.[128]

The xv[es] graunted to the cytie of London towardes the buylding of P., besides a commen gathering of every man's devosion, which was accompted to be a grete deale more.[129] Commyssioners graunted for all provysions and worckmen to be taken at the quene's pryce.[130]

Greate mormoring of the people that they should carrie or sell their thinges in such sorte, considering yt was not the quene's owne worcke, and many saied the quene could graunt no such commyssions.

Grete shame to the b., deane and other prechers of P. that preching against oppression would by this menes seke to oppresse the people.[131] Suche force caused the lesse charytie.

Dyversyties of opinions whether P. ought to be reedyfied considering howe yt was dystroyed by the finger of god because yt was abused, and many thought yt was pietas in deum pietas in patriam to have buylded againe and the steple to be higher then ever yt was.[132]

---

[126] Cf. above, n. 112.

[127] J. Bruce and T. Thomason (eds), *Correspondence of Matthew Parker*, Parker Society, 42 (1853), pp. 142–144 (1 July 1562).

[128] *The True Report of the Burnyng of the Steple and Church of Poules in London* (STC 19930, 1561), licensed within a week of the fire; E. Arber (ed.), *A Transcript of the Registers of the Company of Stationers of London*, 5 vols (London, 1875–1877), I, p. 156. For a modern account, see P. Collinson, *Archbishop Grindal, 1519–1583: The Struggle for a Reformed Church* (London, 1979), pp. 153–161.

[129] See above, n. 117 for the fifteenths. The total cost of repairs was estimated at £17,738. By April 1562 the city's first two-fifteenths had yielded £813 8s 10d (rather than the anticipated £1,333 6s 8d), and the benevolence of the citizens had raised a further £1,045 7s 2d. According to Hayward, the city's eventual total contribution was £3,247 16s 2d. Although the income received was sufficient to re-roof the nave and choir, the bishop appears to have footed the bill for the transepts, and the enormously expensive task of rebuilding the steeple was never undertaken; PRO, SP12/19/64; 12/22/69; *Hayward's Annals*, pp. 88–89. See also C.J. Kitching, 'Re-roofing Old St Paul's Cathedral, 1561–6', *London Journal*, 12 (1986), pp. 123–133.

[130] PRO, SP12/17/34.

[131] Edmund Grindal (1519–1583) was Bishop of London between 1559 and 1570; Alexander Nowell (c. 1507–1602) was Dean of St Paul's from 1560 until his death.

[132] J. Pilkington, *The Burnynge of Paules Church in London in 1561[...]* (STC 19931, 1563) incorporating reply to (with extracts from) J. Morwen, *An Addicion with an Apologie to the Causes of the Brinnynge of Paules Church*. James Pilkington, Bishop of Durham, had preached at Paul's Cross on 8 June 1561, four days after the fire, and developed his argument in the printed tract, which responded to the criticisms of John Morwen, a chaplain to Bishop Edmund Bonner, and a former prebendary of the cathedral. While Catholics argued that God was delivering his judgment on the new Protestant services (the altar had burned), the Protestant establishment argued that it was a warning for a general amendment of life. But Pilkington was prepared to admit that 'we both do agree the

Grete desire of the k. of Sweden's comming of the merchauntes and Londoners, because they thought he would bring grete treasure with him, and because they sawe his brother spend so much here.

I Trinitie terme many coniurers sett on the pillory at W. and L. who first abiured that evill at the K. Benche, emongest whome was one ~~by~~ Bylson, a canon and prebendary of Sarum and Wynton, who caused a yong priest called Coxe to say a masse, and to consecratt an hooste, to the end

[fo. 357]

he might win the love of the Ladie Cotton.[133] Cruche of Sommersett shere, a justice of the peace sett on the pillory at W. and in his countrey for misvsinge of ———— Hales.[134]

The quene maketh her progresse into Essex, Suffolck and Hertford shere where she was costly feasted and many spent theron more then their yerly revenues which kind of entertaynment was the first yere of her raigne begon by the earle of Arundell at Noon suche, hooping he should have maried the quene. It coste him ten thowsand marckes at the least by reporte, wherefore afterward he was constrayned to sell a grete parte of his landes. For this president the earle had many curses of many.[135]

Eliz Symonndes wydowe ———— of Windsore sett on the pillory at Westm. and Sarum for sclaundering of Mr Parry chancellor of the cathedrall churche of Sarum.[136]

Lettres sent from the quene by way of administration for Sir John Mason chaunceller of Oxon, that no mynisters nor fellowes wieves should dwell in the colleges or in cathedrall churches. The ~~like~~ licke sent to the arche b. of Canterbury and so from him to all b.[137]

church of Pauls to be abused, and therefore justly plagued'. See Collinson, *Grindal*, pp. 154–157, and A. Walsham, *Providence in Early Modern England* (Oxford, 1999), pp. 232–234 for the controversy.

[133] cf. above, nn. 93–95.

[134] William Crowche (by 1503–1586). The reference is obscure. According to *HoP, 1509–1558*, I, pp. 735–736, he was a regular troublemaker, sued in 1562 by the dean and chapter of Windsor for detaining deeds relating to the parsonage of Puriton, Somerset.

[135] Henry Fitzalan, twelfth Earl of Arundel (1511–1580) had entertained Elizabeth lavishly at Nonsuch in August 1559; *Leicester Accounts*, p. 78; *Machyn's Diary*, p. 206.

[136] See above, n. 98.

[137] The Queen seems to have been scandalized by abuses (the 'nakedness of religion') revealed during her progress in East Anglia. Cecil reported that 'Her Majesty continueth very evil affected to the state of matrimony in the clergy'. The orders were issued from Ipswich on 9 August 1561. Archbishop Parker, deluged with complaints from the clergy, was deeply hurt by the 'progress-hunting injunction made upon the clergy with conference of no ecclesiastical person'. Inner Temple Library, Petyt MS 47, fos 372–373; E. Cardwell, *Documentary Annals of the Reformed Church of England*, 2 vols (Oxford, 1839), I, pp. 273–274; *Correspondence of Matthew Parker*, pp. 148–149, 151–152; *Machyn's Diary*, p. 265; W. Haugaard,

The Ladie Jane commytted to the Towre, because she was with chield by the earle of Hertford, who being beyond the sea was sent for home, and commytted also to the Towre. Some saied they were maried, som that they were not.[138] There she was delyvered of a sonne. Many justices of peace putt owte of the commyssion. The erle of Arundell had vii justices his servauntes, and other lordes had many, which was the cause that many were putt owte.[139] The patrons of benefices vse to geve their benefices to suche incombentes as gaue them grete somes of money, orels will lett theme have yt yn lease for lytell or no rente, orels before co covenant that suche incombent shall have a certeyn pension. Many coblers, taylers and suche licke made minesters which breade a grete sclaunder to the minestery. The licke in Quene Marie's tyme.[140]

The Scottyshe quene returned into Scottland. Rumors that she was bethrothed to the duke of Hof Holst. The Scottyshe quene rydeth abowtes in progresse with 4000 horses and is gretly feasted with all men.[141]

Elizabeth I and the English Reformation (Cambridge, 1968), pp. 200–205; E. Carlson, *Marriage and the English Reformation* (Oxford, 1994), pp. 61–62. Sir John Mason (1502/3–1566), Privy Councillor and Treasurer of the Chamber, was Chancellor of Oxford from 1552 to 1556, and from 1559 to 1564.

[138] Jane is a curious slip for Catherine. Lady Catherine Grey (c.1538–1568) was the second daughter of Henry Grey, Duke of Suffolk and Lady Frances Brandon, and by the terms of Henry VIII's will was next in line for the succession. She secretly married Edward Seymour, Earl of Hertford (c.1539–1621), the eldest son of the Protector, at Hertford's house in Cannon Row, Westminster in November or December 1560, thereby incurring the penalties of treason, as marriages of persons of royal blood required the Queen's consent. In August 1561 Catherine was sent to the Tower, but refused to confess. Her husband had departed for France with Thomas Cecil in June, but was recalled and joined her in the Tower on 5 September. Their son, Edward, was born in the Tower on 24 September. See below, nn. 187, 197–198, 204.

[139] The impact of the purges can be inferred by comparing PRO, SP12/2/17 (a list of justices of the peace compiled in 1558–1559, amended in 1559, and then annotated after July 1561 when Cecil proposed a reduction in the size of the commissions of the peace) with BL, Lansdowne MS 1218 (a *liber pacis* from November/December 1561 showing the state of the commissions after the recent purges). The purges have usually been seen as the fruition of Cecil's policy of streamlining the commissions in the interests of more efficient administration rather than reflecting the political motives hinted at here. The two interpretations are not of course incompatible. A. Hassell Smith, *County and Court: Government and Politics in Norfolk, 1558–1603* (Oxford, 1974), pp. 81–82. For Cecil's views on the size of commissions of the peace, see PRO, SP12/17, fos 100–101. For a recent assessment which questions the impact on Arundel's clients, see A. Boyle, 'Henry Fitzalan, twefth Earl of Arundel: politics and culture in the Tudor nobility', (unpublished D.Phil. thesis, University of Oxford, 2002), pp. 125–127.

[140] Cf. *Correspondence of Matthew Parker*, pp. 120–121; Collinson, *Grindal*, pp. 112–114.

[141] Mary left Calais on 10 August and arrived at Leith on 19 August 1561. A *Diurnal of Remarkable Occurents that have Passed within the Country of Scotland since the Death of King James the Fourth till the Year MDLXXV* (Edinburgh, 1833), p. 66; Croft Dickinson, *History of the Reformation of Religion in Scotland*, I, p. 7.

[fo. 357v]

The Scottyshe quene confirmeth suche relligion as was decreed in Scotland by the thre estates in parliament at Edeborough in August 1560 wherof there is a booke prynted called the confession of the protestauntes of Scotland, but yt is saied she hathe pryvely masse.[142] The Scotyshe quene choseth 4 counsellors: the governor, the L. James, the Erle Huntley, and the L. of Ludington, her secretary, and geveth them power to chuese other 4 etc.[143] The quene of Eng. suspecting this grete assembly of Scottes, causeth 2000 men to be mustered, at the borders, which the Scottyshe q. hearing, complayned to the L. James that lytell credytt was to be geven to the Eng., who answered that yf the Eng. not being prouoked by her firste did move any warre lett his heade be strocken of.[144]

The saied L. of Ludington commeth to the quene at Hertford Castell in September 1561 to aduertyse her of the Scottyshe q. arryvall at Scottland with desire of contynuaunce of amytie.[145] Sir Peter Mewtes is sent with the like message from the quene to the q. of Scottes.[146] Newes that the Scot. q. would marrie no prince, which was liked in Eng.

The dysputacion in Fr. for matters of relligion and howe the clergie offered to pay the kinges deptes, rekoned to be nyne myllions of crownes, yf he would stay yt.[147]

---

[142] T. Thomson and C. Innes (eds), *Acts of the Parliaments of Scotland* (Edinburgh, 1814–1875), II, p. 526; *The Confessioun of Faith Professit, and Beleuit, Be the Protestantes Within the Realme of Scotland. Publisched by Thaim in Parliament[...]* (STC 22016, Edinburgh, 1560); *The Confession of the Faythe and Doctrine [...]* (STC 22017, 1561).

[143] Mary's Privy Council was nominated on 6 September 1561, and had a Protestant preponderance. J.H. Burton and D. Masson (eds), *The Register of the Privy Council of Scotland*, 14 vols (Edinburgh, 1877–1898), I, pp. 158–161. Those named here are Archibald Campbell, Lord Lorne and fifth Earl of Argyle (1530–1573), James Stewart, later fourteenth Earl of Moray (c.1531–1570), George Gordon, fourth Earl of Huntly (1514–1562), and William Maitland, laird of Lethington (c.1528–1573).

[144] Assuming this is August–September 1561, Maitland advised Cecil on 14 August that Elizabeth should keep a power at Berwick in advance of Mary's return. Randolph reported on 8 September that Sarlabos had told Mary that Grey was coming to Berwick with 10,000 men (*CSPSc.*, *1547–1563*, pp. 544, 551), but we can find no verification of Lord James Stewart's response reported here.

[145] J.H. Pollen (ed.), *A Letter from Mary Queen of Scots to the Duke of Guise, January 1562*, Scottish History Society, 43 (1904), pp. 38–45; *CSPSp.*, *1558–1567*, p. 214; *Hayward's Annals*, 79–84. It was on this occasion that Lethington proposed his compromise between Elizabeth and Mary over the succession; see Adams, 'The release of Lord Darnley', pp. 134–135.

[146] Sir Peter Mewtas (c. 1500–1562) arrived in Edinburgh on 2 October, and was there until about 11 October 1561. He was sent to demand ratification of the Treaty of Edinburgh; *CSPSc.*, *1547–1563*, p. 553.

[147] The Colloquy of Poissy lasted from 9 September to 13 October 1561. Attempts at

The oration made by Beza for the dysputacion which after is printed in English.[148]
The king of Sweden betten backe with tempest, two of his shippes arrive in England, the one with bullion the other with horses.[149]
Sir Thomas Gresham reporteth that king Edward at the tyme of his death ought nothing in Flaunders. Grete deptes in Flaunders for money borrowed by Q. Mary. Quene Elizabeth soe indepted in Flaunders in September 1561 that the interest amounted to 30000[li] yerly. Grete scareytie of money in Eng and in L. 24[li] interest the houndered. For all the scarcytie of money nothing the better cheape.[150] Grete lacke of small money abroode in the countrey.[151]
A saying that the king of Sweden was landed in Denmark and there tarried the winde, and howe he had pledges in Sweden for his safetye.

[fo. 358]

October 1561
A commyssion for the sale of the quene's landes to the l. keper, l. thresaurer, the secre., and Gooderick, the quene's attorney.[152] The

theological compromise failed. By the Contract of Poissy the French clergy agreed to pay 1.6 million livres over a six-year period to redeem the alienated royal demesne and indirect taxes. Thereafter they were to clear the King's debts in respect of the *rentes sur l'hôtel de ville de Paris*, amounting to 7,650,000 livres.

[148] Théodore de Bèze (1519–1605), *Ane Oration Made [...] the IX Day of September 1561, in the Nonnery of Poyssy* (STC 2026, 1561); *The Second Oration [...] Made at Poyssy[...] The XXVI Day of September 1561* (STC 2028, ?1562).

[149] *CSPF, 1561–1562*, pp. 327, 331–332. He departed Sweden on 1 September but was beaten back by storms. See *Machyn's Diary*, pp. 267, 268; BL, Additional MS 35830, fo. 205; *CSPSp., 1558–1567*, p. 211; Strype, *Annals*, I.i, p. 405 for the arrival in London of the battered ships with presents on 3 and 6 October. The gifts included eighteen pied-coloured horses, which were prominently displayed at the Cross Keys Inn in Gracechurch Street.

[150] Mary had left debts of around £300,000, of which £92,000 was owed in Flanders, but Elizabeth had still greater recourse to Antwerp, owing £133,680 by July 1559, and £279,565 by April 1560. Gresham's account of 1562 showed that he had handled £700,000 since the beginning of the reign at a cost to the Exchequer of £127,000 Flemish. Meanwhile, the domestic debt fell rapidly: it stood at about £69,000 by the spring of 1560; D.M.Loades, *The Reign of Mary Tudor* (London, 1979), pp. 412–413, 418–420, 422; PRO, E351/26.

[151] There was a general problem in the availability of coins of small denominations in the sixteenth century, a product of currency depreciation and technical difficulties in their production. Elizabeth's government appears to have made an effort to address the problem identified here with the issue of the three-halfpence and the three-farthings in November 1561. Challis, *Tudor Coinage*, pp. 199–205.

[152] *CPR, 1560–1563*, pp. 112–113, 20 October 1561. Commission to Sir Nicholas Bacon (1510–1579), William Paulet, Marquess of Winchester (by 1488–1572), Sir William Cecil (1520/1–1598), Richard Goodrich (by 1508–1562), and Gilbert Gerrard (by 1523–1593).

confession of the protestauntes of Scottl. printed and made 1560. *24 Octob.* The graund priour, vncle to the quene commeth owte of Scotland, and Monshr Damvill, the constable's second sonn.[153] *28 Octob.* The candelstickes were removed from the alter in the quene's chapell, at the grete suete of the L. Rob. they saied, but the crosse remayned on the common table.[154] *Nouember 1561* A proclamation for golde.[155] Sir Thomas Chaloner sent into Spaine ambassador for Sir Thomas Chamberleyne.[156]

Decemb. 1561

The Sweden ambassador proponeth thre thinges to the q. to be answered: the first, the condycions of the mariage; 2, that his master's passporte might be enlarged; 3, that yf the k. and q. had issue she should goe with him into Sweden. Whervnto was answered: furste whatt cons condycions could be made where there was no certeyntey of mariage? The second that yf there were any thing in the passeporte that neded to be expounded yt should be don. The thryde as to the firste. But it was thoughte the ambasador sought onely meanes to brake of, and so that by som colour he might leve that was begon. The commen talcke is that the king of Sweden is solicited to marrye with the Scottyshe quene.[157]

The mercers be called before the counsell because they solde their sylckes so deare considering the coyne was so muche amended, who answered they coulde not sell better cheape vnles they might buy clothe better chepe. The consell willed them to see redresse, or els the quene should shoulde [*sic*] and would.[158] Fleshe better cheape commenly

---

[153] This was the return of Mary's escort to France. François de Lorraine (d. 1563), Grand Prior of the Langue de France of the Knights of St John of Malta was Elboeuf's brother. Henri de Montmorency, Comte de Damville (1534–1614) succeeded his elder brother, François, as Duke of Montmorency in 1579. They were warmly entertained in England (Dudley playing a large role) as a deliberate gesture of good will to Mary; see Adams, 'Release of Darnley', p. 135.

[154] This cannot be confirmed, but Dudley was also reported as having attempted to have ornaments removed from the Chapel Royal in January 1565; *CSPSp.*, *1558–1567*, p. 401. For the controversy over ornaments, see Haugaard, *Elizabeth and the English Reformation*, pp. 183–200; M. Aston, *England's Iconoclasts*, I, *Laws Against Images* (Oxford, 1988), pp. 306–308.

[155] *TRP*, II, pp. 179–181, announcing new small coins, and outlawing gold coins from overseas, 15 November 1561.

[156] Sir Thomas Chaloner (1521–1565) was resident ambassador in Spain from 30 September 1561 until mid-May 1565.

[157] A Swedish embassy did indeed visit Scotland in April 1562; *CSPSc.*, *1547–1563*, pp. 621, 622, 635, 650.

[158] Mercers' Company Records, Court Minutes, 1560–1595, fos 23v–25.The mercers appeared before the Privy Council on 13 December 1561, and used the interview to press their case for bringing all retailers of silk under their control. Cf. PRO, SP12/20/63. See also below, n. 162.

throughe England. The cause ys by reason of the plenty of maste, there was grete plenty of hogges killed. Corne at L. at xvj^s the quarter and soe in many places of the realme, but in Wilshere at viij^s.

On St. Stephen's day the L. Ambrose Dudley was created at W. by the quene first Vicount Lysle and imediatly earle of Warwick, the Sweden ambassadour being present. But besides the ordenary fees geven to an earle yt is —— to be paied owt of shrifewik and —— to a vicounte, he had but 300^{li} land which seemed very lytell for soe grete a personage and state. Grete suete was made that he might have had 1400^{li} landes but the quene would not graunt yt.[159]

[fo. 358v]

Controversie was betwene the two Temples, for the Inner Temple had three innes of chauncery that is Clyfforde's Inne, Lyon's Inne and Clemente's Inne, where the Midell Temple had only New Inne. It was thought good by the l. keper, and the chief justices which were all of the Mydell Temple, that the Inner Temple should have Clem. the rather because they had before Strand Inne which belonged to them, and was distroyed by the duke of Somersett. But by the suete of the L. Rob. to the quene the Inner Temple kept all three. Wheruppon in memoriall therof and of so grete a benefytt receved by the L. Robert they decreed in their parliament yt none of their howse should be of counsell against the L. Ro. nor his heyres, that his armes should be sett upp in the hall for a perpetuall monument.[160] And also they kepte a ~~somb~~ solempne Chrystmas, wherof Bashe was steward.[161]

---

[159] There are a few inaccuracies in the account. Ambrose Dudley (c. 1528–1590), Master of the Ordnance, was created Baron (not Viscount) Lisle on 25 December 1561, and Earl of Warwick on 26 December (St Stephen's Day), and received only £20 rent from the fee farm of Coventry. He did, however, receive a substantial grant of lands on 6 April 1562 (*CPR, 1560–1563*, pp. 291–293). For the complexities surrounding his titles, see Adams, ' "Because I am of that countrye and mynde to plante myself there": Robert Dudley, Earl of Leicester and the west midlands', *Midland History*, 20 (1995), p. 30.

[160] F.A. Inderwick (ed.), *A Calendar of Inner Temple Records* (1896–1936), I, pp. 215–220; Axton, 'Inner Temple revels', p. 365. The opponents of the Inner Temple's claims were Sir Nicholas Bacon, Lord Keeper, Sir Robert Catlin (d. 1574), Chief Justice of Queen's Bench since January 1560, and Sir James Dyer (1509/10–1582), Chief Justice of Common Pleas since January 1559. The Strand Inn had been demolished to make way for Somerset House. Dudley was not chosen at random: his father had been a member of the Inner Temple and so was one of his principal men of business, John Dudley of Stoke Newington. See S. Adams, 'The gentry of North Wales and the Earl of Leicester's expedition to the Netherlands, 1585–1586', *Welsh History Review*, 7 (1974), p. 140, n. 68, 143. The Christmas 1561 celebration is discussed above.

[161] Richard Bashe; Inderwick, *Calendar of Inner Temple Records*, I, p. 219.

Decemb. 1561

It was thought of the councell that by the alteracion of the coyne from base money to fyne silver, and abating of the value of gold that the pryce of all maner of thinges would also abate. But it followed not so, but all thinges were rather dearer, not only vytayll but chiefly all kind of marchandyce. Whervpon the merchauntes were sent for to the councell where yt was debated whye silckes should be so deare, considering the money was soe encreased in goodnes and willed them consulte emongest them selves for redresse, whervpon the merch. of every company assembled in their halles and consulted of the matter, and made answere howe they could not sell their wares batter chepe, vnles they might buy clothes better chepe, and howe sylckes could not be better chepe because in all partes of the worlde and especially in Spaine, they were more vsed then ever they were before.[162]

The yeare before Callies waf was loste Doctor Wotton was ambassadour into Fraunce, whoe understoode albeyt ther was no warr then betwene Eng. and Fr. that the Freinshe king made a grete preparacion for gonnes, for battery, scaling ladders, botes and all municion for warre, and yt also he mente to assaulte Callies, and howe he was advertised of the state of Callies howe yt was clene withowte soldiers, the garryson being for the moste parte olde, the towne vnvayled vnvyteled, the gonnes from the stockes, and all owte of order,[163] whervppon the earle of

[fo. 359]

Pembrocke was sent over with 300 men into Callies, and so that yeare nothing attempted.[164] But Tuckewill being suspected killed him self with a pistelett.[165] And a Freinsheman that taught Sir Thomas Cornewall his childerne was suspected, whoe being sent for by the councell to be sent to warde, was kepte at libertie, his master's promysing he should be forth comming, but he lepte over the walles and so by the yse

[162] See above, n. 158.

[163] Dr Nicholas Wootton (c.1497–1567) was ambassador in France from 2 April 1553 until about 26 June 1557. The warnings mentioned here were issued in October 1556 in connection with the intrigues of Sir Henry Dudley to destabilize the Calais garrison. John Highfield, the lieutenant of the ordnance of Calais, claimed in his report on the siege of 1558 that he had sixty canon mounted, but lacked gunners and pioneers to employ them effectively. *CSPF, 1553–1558*, pp. 267–273, 280, 281–285; D.M. Loades, *Two Tudor Conspiracies*, (Cambridge, 1965) pp. 168–169; A.F. Pollard (ed.), *Tudor Tracts, 1532–1588* (Westminster, 1903), p. 314.

[164] William Herbert, first Earl of Pembroke (c.1506–1570) was dispatched to Calais in late November 1556 after Wootton's warnings.

[165] Tuckwill=Touteville=Estouteville, a Frenchman who passed as an Englishman, and was involved in the plot with Denisot to blow up the Calais arsenal.

scaped into Fraunce.[166] By this Freinshman and Tuckwill yt was ~~disclosed~~ thought and like the secrettes and state of the towne was dysclosed, and by that menes yt was also knowen howe the castell was the wekest parte of the towne.

Divers loanes and benevolences in the tyme of K. Henry and howe ——— Reder alderman of L. was sent by Wrethesley to the borders for a man of warr because he would not lend and howe he was taken prisoner which was contrary to the liberties of London, which granteth them freedom from goyng to warr.[167]

Howe in K. He. terme the statutt of apparell was ment to be put in execution. And howe the king and the counsell wente in clothe, but yt lasted not longe.

Howe in Quene Marie's tyme the like was enterprysed and the licke successe.[168]

36 Henr. 8

The k. being at Portesmouth, Sir Thomas Seymer was appointed to lye at Dover for the deffence of those partes. After the Frenishe navye had ben at Portesmouth the gallies cam to Dover and pretended that they would lande there[169] where at the countrey ryse, and first cam to Dover to Sir Th. Seymer, Walter Moyle with x servauntes, and the second was the archbushopp of Caunterbury, Cranmer with a 100

---

[166] Sir Thomas Cornwallis (1518/19–1604) was treasurer of Calais from April 1554 to December 1557. The French tutor was Nicolas Denisot, a Protestant poet from Le Mans and former tutor to the Duke of Somerset's children. After his flight from Calais he went east to Ardres where he boasted of his exploits. C. Jugé, *Nicolas Denisot du Mans* (Le Mans, 1907). We are grateful to Cliff Davies for his advice on Calais.

[167] For the loans and benevolences of the 1540s, see M. Jurkowski, C. Smith, and D. Crook (eds), *Lay Taxes in England and Wales, 1188–1688* (Kew, 1998), pp. 142–147; I.W. Archer, 'The burden of taxation on sixteenth century London', *HJ*, 44 (2001), pp. 607, 612–613. Richard Rede, salter (d. 1550) had been elected alderman in March 1544. He refused to pay the benevolence of 2s in the pound due in 1545. Londoners had been granted immunity from military service out of the city by Edward II's charter of 1321, but the principle had already been breached. Rede left London for the Scottish front on 23 January, and was taken prisoner in March. *Wriothesley's Chronicle*, I, pp. 151, 153; A. Beaven, *The Aldermen of the City of London*, 2 vols (London, 1908–1913), II, p. 31; W. de G. Birch, *The Historical Charters and Constitutional Documents of the City of London* (London, 1887), p. 51.

[168] The specific enforcement drives on apparel referred to here cannot be identified, but the remarks are interesting on their perceived futility. The statute referred to is the act of 1533 (24 Henry VIII c. 13) which laid down apparel for the various ranks of society in elaborate detail. W.D. Hooper, 'Tudor sumptuary laws', *EHR*, 30 (1915), pp. 433–449.

[169] Seymour, at the time of the threatened French invasion of 1545, was Admiral, Master of the Ordnance, and (during the indisposition of Sir Thomas Cheyney) Lord Warden of the Cinque Ports. The French galleys had been beaten away from Portsmouth and Southampton, and turned towards Dover in the second week in August. *LP*, XX.i, pp. 63, 82, 136, 167.

horses, whoe was there by fyve of the clocke in the morning in his prevey coate with his dagge at his sadell bowe, his page wayting on him with his morion and longe peace, and with him he brought his horses with mete and necessaries, and besides had his beafes and mottons brought thither.[170]

The Cardinall contrary, when Callyes was loste and Sir Thomas Seymer appointed to levye the power of Kente, and being stewarde of his landes would not suffer his servantes to more [sic], but Christopher Roper his comptroller prohibyted them to stirr, whereby yt may be gathered, what was his affection to his countrey.[171]

[fo. 359v]

The collectours and authors of the boocke intyteled De vera differentia regie maiestatis ecclesiasticae prynted by Barthlett 1534 at L. and dylyvered to the king: Dr. Heth, Dr. Thurleby, Dr Alderege, Dr Haynes, Dr Goodrick, Dr Shaxton.[172]

A° 7 E 6 there was a synode holden at P. wherin the chief artyeles of Christian relligion were sett owte, which being confirmed by the king were sent into every diocese and all the clergie did subscribe and were sworen thervnto they be printed in the end of the Laten catechisme.[173]

[170] *LP*, XX.i, p. 647 for the defence of the south coast in 1545.

[171] Seymour is a mistake for Sir Thomas Cheyney (1482/87–1558) who was in charge of the measures for the defence of Kent in 1558. Christopher Roper (1508/9–1558/9) was receiver of the lands of Reginald Pole (1500–1558), Archbishop of Canterbury. Although there were complaints about shortage of men and the poor quality of their equipment, specific charges against Roper are othwerwise unknown. *HoP, 1509–1558*, III, pp. 213–214; *APC*, VI, pp. 226–227, 229, 248; *CSPD, Mary I*, pp. 313–315.

[172] *De Vera Differentia Regiae Potestatis et Ecclesiasticae et Quae Sit Ipsa Veritas ac Uirtus Utriusque. Opus Eximium* (*STC* 11219, 1534). The authors were Dr Nicholas Heath (c. 1501–1578), Dr Simon Heynes (d. 1552), Dr Thomas Goodrich (d. 1554), Dr Nicholas Shaxton (c. 1485–1556), Dr Thomas Thirlby (c.1506–1570), and Robert Aldrich (d. 1556). Thomas Berthelet (c.1490–1555) was the King's printer.

[173] The reference is to the Forty-Two articles approved in May 1553. The diocesan bishops undertook a campaign of subscription in June. *Catechismus Breuis Christianae Disciplinae Summam Continens, Omnibus Ludimagistris Authoritate Regia Commendatus. Huic Catechismo Adiuncti Sunt Articuli, De Quibus in Vltima Synodo Londoniensi, Anno Dom. 1552. Ad Tollendam Opinionum Dissensionem & Consensu Uerae Religionis Firmandum, Inter Episcopos & Alios Eruditos Atque Pios Uiros Conuenerat: Regia Similiter Authoritate Promulgati* (*STC* 4810, 1553); J. Ketley (ed.), *The Two Liturgies, AD 1549 and AD 1552 with Other Documents Set Forth by Authority in the Reign of Edward VI*, Parker Society, 19 (1844), pp. 526–537; C. Hardwick, *A History of the Articles of Religion*, third edn revised by F. Proctor (London, 1876), pp. 31–113; MacCulloch, *Cranmer*, pp. 503–504, 535–538; P.J. Ayris, 'Continuity and change in diocese and province: the role of a Tudor bishop', *HJ*, 39 (1996), pp. 308–311.

January 1561 A° 4° R. Elizab.

Ther was a tragedie played in the Inner Temple of the two brethren Porrex and Ferrex, k. of Brytayne betwene whome the father had devyded the realme; the one slewe the other and the mother slewe the manquiller. It was thus vsed firste: wilde men cam in and woulde have broken a whole fagott, but coulde not, the stickes they brake being severed. Then cam in a king to whome was geven a clere glasse, and a golden cupp of golde covered, full of poyson. The glasse he caste under his fote and brake hyt, the poyson he dranck of. After cam in mommers. The ~~shando~~ shadowes were declared by the chore: first, to signyfie vnytie; the 2, howe that men refused the certen and tooke the vncerten, wherby was ment that yt was better for the quene to marye with the L. R. knowen then with the k. of Sweden; the thryde, to declare that cyvill discention bredeth morning. Many thinges were handled of mariage, and that the matter was to be debated in parliament, because yt was much banding ~~because~~ but yt hit ought to be determined by the councell. There was also declared howe a straunge duke seyng the realme at dyvysion would have taken vpon him the crowne, but the people would none of hytt. And many thinges were saied for the succession to putt thinges in certenty. This playe was the ———— daye of January at the courte before the quene, where none ambassadors were present but the Spanyshe.[174]

John Onell the Frenshman who had don much myschief the sommer past in Ireland cometh by save condytt into England and was receved gentelly in the courte in his saffron shorte the twelveth day at night. He accuseth the erle of Sussex of great crymes, crueltie,

[fo. 360]

breache of promyse, putting to death of divers contrary to promyse and saue conduytt, pilling and polling etc.[175]

Moretes, the prince of Piemonte's ambassador returneth owte of

---

[174] T. Norton and T. Sackville, *The Tragedie of Gorboduc, Whereof Three Actes were Written by Thomas Nortone, and the Laste by Thomas Sackuyle [...]* (STC 18684, 1565), first performed at the Inner Temple Christmas revels in December 1561, and before the Queen at Whitehall on 18 January 1562. In his long despatch to Philip II of 31 January 1562, la Quadra makes no reference to seeing this play (*CSPSp, 1558–1567*, pp. 224–228). For a full discussion, see the introduction, pp. 48–50, and the references cited there.

[175] Shane O'Neill (c. 1530–1567), bizarrely described as a Frenchman here, arrived in London on 4 January 1562, was received at court on 6 January with the Earls of Kildare and Ormonde. He returned to Dublin on 26 May. His adversary was Thomas Radcliffe, third Earl of Sussex (c. 1526–1583), Governor of Ireland. His outlandish dress was widely remarked upon. *Machyn's Diary*, pp. 274–277; *CSPF, 1560–1562*, p. 628; *CSPIre., 1509–1573*, p. 184; J. Hogan, 'Shane O'Neill comes to the court of Elizabeth', in S. Pender (ed.), *Féilscribhinn Torna* (Cork, 1947); C. Brady, *Shane O'Neill* (Dublin, 1996).

Scotland, whither he went before Chrystmas and so departeth with rewarde home.[176]

The ambassador of Sweden 21 Januarij maketh a grete feaste for the councell, lordes and ladies. But the L. Roberte, his brother, the admirall, the earle of Pembroke, the lord chamberleyne, the erle of Bedforde cam not thither, but dyned with the L. Chandose of purpose, to deface the other. The mayer and aldermen of London were invyted to the ambassador's to dynner. They promysed but ~~cam~~ afterward sent worde they coulde not come. Some thought they durste not or they were otherwyse commaunded, but they excused yt, for that they had contrary presidentes.[177]

This moneth there was a grete talcke in London of the fall of money from v⁵ to x grotes the ounce, and the angell to vj⁵ viii^d[178] which troubled the merchauntes very muche so that well were he that coulde laye or lend owte his money for a yeare withowte gaine, to pay them money curraunt [marg: This brute of fall of money caused the quene's deptes and revenues to be better payed, then all process and privey seales could before do. Euery man brought in his money.] Many there were that would take hytt so for two yere and a half, and som did so lend yt. Some saied that this talcke grewe by reason of som of the councell sent for their credytors, and payed them when they loked not for yt. Some gathered yt because som of the ~~counsell~~ councell sold muche plate. The q. ought the merchauntes of L. 30000^li to be paied in March nexte, whoe were sent for to knowe whether they would take yt nowe or after ix monethes. Vppon deliberacion two daies, the yonge men required their money presently, the old men were content, to tarrie for

---

[176] Bertino Solario di Moretta, ambassador from Piedmont, had an audience with Elizabeth on 23 November 1561 en route to Scotland, where he stayed a fortnight from 3 December to 16 December, reaching London on 2 January. He was present at the submission of Shane O'Neill on 6 January, and seems to have left England soon after: Pollen, *Letter from Mary*, pp. xxxiv–xli, 53–59, 62–65.

[177] The absentees from Gyllenstierna's feast were Lord Robert Dudley; Ambrose Dudley (above, n. 159); Edward Fiennes de Clinton, ninth Lord Clinton and Saye (1512–1585), Lord High Admiral; William Howard, first Baron Howard of Effingham (c.1510–1573), Lord Chamberlain; the Earl of Bedford (above, n. 76); and their host Edmund Brydges, Baron Chandos of Sudeley (by 1522–1573). Cf. AGS, E815, fo. 199, cited by Doran, *Monarchy and Matrimony*, pp. 33–34.

[178] PRO, SP12/21/36, Cecil to Sidney on the rumours in London and elsewhere; *Machyn's Diary*, p. 276; *TRP*, II, pp. 181, 185–186 (proclamations suppressing rumours of coinage revaluation, 30 January and 13 March 1562). A draft proclamation dated 13 March announced a 33 per cent calling down. Oman considered it to be a forgery, but the matter was clearly debated in the council, with Winchester emerging as a key opponent and Paget working behind the scenes. The 'Journall' provides important fresh material on this episode. *TRP*, II, pp. 183–185; PRO, SP12/22/30; C.W.C. Oman, 'An alleged proclamation of Queen Elizabeth', *Numismatic Chronicle*, 12 (1932), pp. 1–12; Challis, *Tudor Coinage*, pp. 127–128; below, n. 192.

yt fearing fall, whervpon they satisfied the yonge men, and become credytors for the hoole.[179] The quene paieth her deptes and many other also were paied whoe loked not for any payment because they had ben so longe vnpaied. Money is sent to Barwick to pay the garyson. Many bring in cheynes into the mynte, and suche a quantytie of fyne plate was brought thither as hath not ben seen. This brute caused the pryces of all thynges to encrease. Some would sell nothing, and som would not take redy money, but requered the payment half yere after. The inneholders woulde not have redy money of carriers passing by the way, but would trust them for yt. It made much talcke and much vnquietnes for the tyme.[180]

[fo. 360v]

The Earle Lenoux was sent for and commyted to warde in his owne howse, tow of his men commytted to the keping of the master of the rolles, his wief sent for. The cause as hyt was suspected for that he and his wief should labour to marye their sone to the Scottyshe quene. His sonn flieth into Scotland, whervpon the earle was commytted to the Towre.[181]

The former fall of the base money was not so much grudged at as this, for that did touche only the poore sorte, for the grete and welthy men had chaunged all their base money into gold and kepte hyt.[182] This fall toucheth only or most of all the grete and rytche. Wherfore they do the more grudge at hytt, and invent all maner of excuses, som that money would be carried over, som that thinges would not be the better chepe to lett yt: wherby we may lerne that every man is for him self, and none is moved with the hurte or losse of his poore neighbour. And so yt was in the duke of Sumersett his tyme: the inclosures might

[179] For this debt to the Merchant Adventurers, see *CSPF, 1561–1562*, pp. 240, 288–289; J.M.B.C. Baron Kervyn de Lettenhove and L. Gilliots van Severen (eds), *Relations Politiques des Pays Bas et de l'Angleterre sous le Règne de Philippe II*, 11 vols (Brussels, 1882–1900), II, p. 618.

[180] *TRP*, II, p. 182 (proclamation of 10 March 1562 ordering victuals to local markets).

[181] Matthew Stuart, fourth Earl of Lennox (1516–1571) married to Lady Margaret Douglas (1515–1578). Lennox, who had been an exile in England since 1544, was imprisoned following the arrest of a messenger he had sent to Scotland in January 1562. Other charges were correspondence with the French and Spanish ambassadors, hearing mass, and mocking Elizabeth and Dudley. But the investigations were inconclusive. Lord Darnley's flight to Scotland was a rumour: see Adams, 'Release of Darnley', 130 and n. 61. For his move to the Tower, see below, n. 207.

[183] Referring to the calling-down of the coinage in 1551, which had undoubtedly caused much discontent among the poor. *TRP*, I, pp. 518–519, 525, 528–530; Tawney and Power, *Tudor Economic Documents*, II, pp. 182–188; Challis, *Tudor Coinage*, pp. 105–106.

not be touched because they touched the gretest.[183] All thinges vpon the brute of this fall encreased a thirde parte at the leste in the pryce.

A proclamation made at W. the laste of January commanding all men to sell their vitalles after the olde prices aleging that divers covetous men had stirred this rumor of fall of money to the end to make thinges deare. Vide proclamation.[184] Grete sticking in the councell for the fall of this money and the l. thes. by his lettres muche resysted yt, and saied they knewe not what they did.[185]

Februarij 4° R. Elizab.

The L. Pagett is very grete with the L. Rob. and putteth in his hede to sue for a lease of all the customes and to offer to the quene 20000[li] more yerely then ever she had and he would be the L. Rob. farmor and geve him yerely 10000[li] clere and 1000[li] to bestowe yerly emongest ten of his gentellmen. He laboreth also that the like imposition shalbe on all thinges as is in Flaunders.[186]

There is commyssion directed to the b. of Canterbury, L. and others, for the examination of the mariage of the Lady Katherine and the erle of Hertford.[187]

John Onell accuseth the erle of Sussex for killing of a gentellman whoe cam in by the coinrich [?] or saue conduyte of the erle and the earle of Kyldar, which gentell man was of the Onelle's contrey. Hervpon this Onell levyed his power, and Sussex his power, and contrary to the expectation of the Englishman the

[fo. 361]

Iryshemen lyghted from their horses and being well armed taried the fight in good order and slewe 100 Englishmen. Sussex afterward reviveth his force and mynding to to [*sic*] invade the Onell's contrey, Onell flieth with all his men and cattell into the woodes and so the iorney

---

[183] A theme of the commonwealth argument about enclosures. John Hales, an enclosure commissioner in 1548, waxed indignant about the undermining of the commissions by the rich. E. Lamond (ed.), *A Discourse of the Commonweal of this Realm of England* (Cambridge, 1893), pp. liii–lvii.

[184] *TRP*, II, p. 488; *Machyn's Diary*, p. 276.

[185] William Paulet, Marquess of Winchester (by 1488–1572), Lord Treasurer. See also n. 192.

[186] This cannot be confirmed, but on 22 October 1562, Dudley was granted an annuity of £1,000 from the customs of London until such time as he was given lands of equal value; *CPR, 1560–1563*, p. 361.

[187] PRO, SP12/21/39. Commission (31 January 1562) to Matthew Parker, Archbishop of Canterbury, Edmund Grindal, Bishop of London, William Petre, William Cordell, Richard Weston, Walter Haddon, Richard Goodrich, David Lewis, Robert Weston, and Thomas Huick.

loste.[188] Sussex thincking Kildare to be offended for killing his men sendeth for him twyse but he fayneth him self sicke. And the thryde tyme he sent 100 horsmen with three dagges a pece to bring him quick or deadd and so he commeth. Afterward Kildar commeth into England and informeth the counsell, of these thinges, who is sent againe to Ireland to persuade the Onell to come into England vpon save conduytt, who commeth and had 1000[li] lent him of the quene.[189]

Reporte that the Countesse L. is a bastard for the e. of Anguish was maried to her mother. He had another wyef lyving, which when the quene her mother knewe she sued a dyvorce, and that Anguish had a child by the other wief which she declared to the L. William then ambassador in Scotland, whoe advertysed King Henr. the 8 therof. And therwith sent to the king the woman's lettre directed to the earle of Anguish as her husband. This was declared to the Lord Devonn that he might understand his wief was no inherytor to the crowne, as he reported her to be.[190]

The L. Pagett was the occasion of the staye of the fall of the money

---

[188] The occasion of this conflict was the controversial execution of Morogh McMorysh. Whereas O'Neill claimed that McMorysh had a safe-conduct, Sussex, backed by Kildare, claimed that he had been lawfully attainted. When, in June 1561, Sussex proceeded against Armagh, O'Neill withdrew with his cattle to the borders of Tyrconnell. As a force led by Sir George Stanley, Marshal of the army, retreated from Monaghan, Shane attacked its rear, and was beaten off only with heavy losses (July). Sussex retreated to Newry to collect fresh supplies, and after fruitless negotiations brokered by Kildare, in September he mounted a fresh expedition, using 600–700 English troops reinforced by Scottish mercenaries, gallowglasses, and kernes. He achieved the considerable feat of marching through a hostile Ulster to reach Lough Foyle, but was halted there by the failure to rendezvous with a victualling fleet. Shane had disappeared, but immediately on Sussex's withdrawal raided Co. Meath. PRO, SP 63/3/69; *CSP.Ire.*, *1509–1573*, pp. 171–180; C. Falls, *Elizabeth's Irish Wars* (London, 1950), pp. 86–89; Brady, *Shane O'Neill*. We are grateful to Rory Rapple for help with this episode.

[189] Gerald Fitzgerald, eleventh Earl of Kildare (1525–1585). For his relationship with Sussex, see C. Brady, *The Chief Governors: The Rise and Fall of Reform Government in Ireland, 1536–1588* (Cambridge, 1994), pp. 91–94. Kildare received his instructions to negotiate with O'Neill on 27 August 1561, which Sussex saw as undermining his campaign. A parley between Kildare and O'Neill was held on 18 October, and O'Neill induced to come to court. *CSPIre.*, *1509–1573*, pp. 179, 181. Cf. above, n. 175.

[190] Lady Margaret Douglas (1515–1578) was the daughter of Margaret Tudor, dowager Queen of Scotland, by her second marriage (August 1514) to Archibald Douglas, sixth Earl of Angus (c.1489–1557), but since the 1530s it had been rumoured (on the basis of Angus's relations with Lady Janet Stewart of Traquair) that the union was bigamous. These rumours were probably started in high places as the Spanish ambassador reported that the Privy Council was gathering intellligence to prove her illegitimate. *CSPSp.*, *1559–1567*, pp. 230–231; Haynes, *State Papers*, pp. 381–382. Devonn is surely a bizzare error for Lennox. The claim that the countess was a bastard owing to Angus's bigamous marriage was made in the Hales Book and possibly in the parliament of 1563. It was also the subject of an investigation by the Privy Council in March 1563, which involved a deposition from Lord William Howard of Effingham, who was then Lord Chamberlain. See Adams, 'Release of Darnley', p. 133.

by sending lettres to the quene with dyvers persuasions. Whervpon the
que. declared parte in the counsell. Whervnto yt was answered yt was
but a folley, for them to debate thinges yf she followed others counsell,
and request was made that he might be brought thither to declare his
consideracions but yt was not graunted. After Pagett commeth to the
secratary and there talking was able to saye nothing, and all his excuse
was decay of memory and the lacke of practyse. And confessed he had
raysed his rentes and had many oxen to sell.

Afterward this talke was declared to my L. Rob. whoe was required
to send for Pagett, and Sir W. Mildemay,[191] and to here them both,
where Pagett declared he knewe nothing, for he understoode nothing
belonging eyther to money or to the exchaunge. This after being
reported to the quene she saied Pagett was a busie knave, and willed
he should send no more to her for he was no better then a knave. She
sendeth for

[fo. 361v]

his confession made in K. Edward his time openly in the Starr Chamber,
but yt would not be found. Whervpon yt was required yt should be
wrytten by som that herd hitt.[192]

Gresham taketh vp much money, 30000[li] withowte interest, som for 14,
some for 12, som 10 monethes, and the portes be stayed that none should
passe but his poste, which is a licklyhod that the money will not fall.[193]

The b. of Aquila suspected to be a worker with his master P. for the
mariage of Lenoux sonn to the Scottyshe quene, which dryveth him
owte of the q. favor.[194]

---

[191] Sir Walter Mildmay (by 1523–1589), Chancellor of the Exchequer; *HoP, 1558–1603*,
III, pp. 53–56.

[192] The 'Journall' sheds new light on Paget's role here. Christopher Challis has noted
that he would have expected Paget to have been influential, given his role in exploring
the possibilities of recoinage under Mary, for which see C.E. Challis and C.J. Harrison,
'A contemporary estimate of the production of gold and silver coinage in England, 1542–
1556', *EHR*, 88 (1973), pp. 821–835. Paget had written to Cecil and Parry on 3 February
1559 with devices for the amendment of the monies; Haynes, *State Papers*, pp. 207–208.
For the events of 1552, when Paget had confessed to financial irregularities as Chancellor
of the Duchy of Lancaster; see *Chronicle of Edward VI*, pp. 129, 131, 156; *APC*, IV, pp. 65,
72; PRO, SP10/14/ 33–34; B.L. Beer and S.M. Jack (eds), 'The letters of William, Lord
Paget of Baudesert, 1547–1563', *Camden Miscellany vol. XXV*, Camden Society, fourth series,
13 (Cambridge, 1974), pp. 103–105. Paget had on the occasion of his earlier disgrace
drawn on Cecil's services as mediator.

[193] For Gresham's accounts, see PRO, E351/26, E351/30, E351/31; SP12/21/60; *CSPF,
1561–1562*, p. 542; cf. R.B. Outhwaite, 'The trials of foreign borrowing: the English crown
and the Antwerp money market in the mid-sixteenth century', *Economic History Review*,
second series, 19 (1966), pp. 289–305.

[194] Henry Stuart, Lord Darnley (1546–1567).

Yaxley committed to the Towre for his grete resorte and advert-ysementes to P. ambassador.[195]

The money falleth, the money doth not fall whilest yt standeth. Thus in uncertenty the pryce of all thinges encrese to th a thryde parte as yt was thought the fall of the money would, and fewe would take redy money for wares or deptes. Many assure their deptes before hande, which otherwise would have been slacke.

The merchauntes curse Gresham as their cutthrote, in the ende of February he goeth into Flaunders and there taketh up money as he did in England before his departure, which maketh men beleve that the money shuld not fall. At his comming into Flaunders the exchaunge was 24^s sterl. for a pounde Eng. vpon usaunce and so he toocke vpe 40000^{li}. Afterward yt falleth to 22^s 6^d.[196]

March 1561 et 1562

The Earle of Hertford and Ladie Katherine were divers times convented before the commyssioners for that they maried secretly. It was thought that yt should have ben proved mariage, but both he and she stoode styffe that they were maried, albeit they could not tell the prieste's name. Many were examined in that matter to knowe yf they had understanding as Henr. Parry, chaunceller of the cathedrall church of Sarum, Stokes that maried her mother, Stukeley, the L. Henry his brother, Sir John Chympern[?owne], and others but nothinge could be founde.[197] It was thought by the people that sethence the mariage coulde not be dysproued that they would attempte to prove the L. Fraunces her mother a bastard and so to dysheritt her of the tytell to the crowne, because yt was saied Duke Charles had a wief lyving when he maried the Freinshe quene.[198]

---

[195] Francis Yaxley (by 1528–1565), Clerk of the Signet until 1559, was committed to the Tower on 5 February, and as a result much of his correspondence for these years is now among the state papers. He was acting as an intermediary between the Lennoxes and La Quadra. See *HoP, 1509–1558*, III, pp. 680–682; *CSPF, 1562*, pp. 13–14, 23; *CSPSp., 1558–1567*, pp. 230–232; PRO, SP12/21/44; *Leicester Accounts*, p. 80, n. 143.

[196] For the exchange rate, see T.H. Lloyd, 'Early Elizabethan investigations into exchange and the value of sterling, 1558–1568', *Economic History Review*, 53 (2000), pp. 75–78, where the fall is attributed to political fears about the deteriorating situation in France, though the 'Journall' seems to suggest that the fall in the exchange began sooner.

[197] The records of the commission are in BL, Harleian MS 6286. The witnesses named here are Henry Parry, chancellor of Salisbury diocese (above, n. 98), Adrian Stokes esquire, the husband of Lady Frances Brandon, Thomas Stukeley, Lord Henry Seymour (b. 1540, still alive in 1602), and Sir John Champernowne. Although the priest was never found, the depositions point to the existence of a marriage.

[198] Charles Brandon, later Duke of Suffolk, had contracted marriage with Anne Browne, a gentlewoman to the Queen in 1503, but abandoned her shortly after she became pregnant, and married her aunt, Lady Margaret Mortimer, twenty years his senior. The marriage to Mortimer was dissolved on the grounds of consanguinity in 1507

[fo. 362]

The comen brute is that the quene myndeth to establyshe the succession of the crowne. Som say that she will not do yt because she is persuaded that yf there were any heire apparante knowne the people would be more affectionated to him than to her, because the nature of Engl. men is variable, not contented with the state present but desirous of alteracions. And that the people in hearing never so lytell faulte in the prince woulde yf the successor were knowne, exaggerat yt.[199]

The ambassador of Sweden prepareth all thinges redy to departe albeit he knoweth his master will come.[200] Yett for as muche as he hath noe hope of successe of the mariage, and that he hath noe other answere, but that the realme is free for all men and he is welcome, he thincketh yt will be but vayne for his master to come, and so he saieth he hath alwaies advertysed him, and what grete vnlicklyhode yt is he shall ~~hot~~ not spede, seying the quene maketh soe much of the L. Rob.

Newes brought howe at the mariage of L. James of Scotland in February laste, the Scottyshe quene tooke a golden cuppe and caused hyt to be filled with wyne, and asked an Eng. man called Randall who was ther with the earle of Arren whether yf she did drincke to the quene of Eng., he would pledge her, whoe accepted yt very hombly, whervpon when he had pleged her she gave him the cupp.[201] These newes were soe gratfull in Engl. that forthwith yt is determined that the quene woulde goe this sommer to Yorcke and to desire the Scottyshe

and Brandon returned to marry Browne (as it were for the second time). Browne died in 1510, but Mortimer remained alive at the time of Brandon's marriage to Mary Tudor, dowager Queen of France in 1515. It was possible to argue that not only were the daughters by Browne illegitimate, but also those by Mary Tudor, and therefore that the whole Grey claim was illegitimate. S.J. Gunn, *Charles Brandon, Duke of Suffolk, 1484–1545* (Oxford, 1988), pp. 28–31, 35–36, 85–87; Levine, *Early Elizabethan Succession Question*, pp. 126–137. We are grateful to Dr Gunn for his advice on this point.

[199] Cf. the Queen's remarks to Maitland in the interview of September 1561. 'I am well acquainted with the nature of this people. I know how easily they dislike the present state of affairs. I know what nimble eyes they bear to the next succession. I know it to be natural that more (as the saying is) do adore the rising than the falling sun. To omit other examples, I have learned this by experience of mine own times. When my sister Mary was queen, what prayers were made by many to see me placed in her seat; with what earnest desire were they carried for my advancement'; *Hayward's Annals*, p. 83.

[200] Nils Gyllensternia, see nn. 106, 177 above. He left in April 1562, see below at fo. 363.

[201] The marriage of Lord James Stewart to Agnes Keith, daughter of the Earl Merischel, took place in St Giles's, Edinburgh on 8 February 1562. Thomas Randolph (1523–1590) was ambassador to Scotland between 1559 and 1566. On 12 February he reported to Cecil 'that upon Shrove Twesdaye at nyght, syttinge amongest the lordes at supper in the syght of this Quene, placed for that purpose, she dranke unto the Quenes Majestie, and sent me the cuppe of golde which waythe xviij or xx unces'; *HoP, 1558–1603*, III, pp. 276–277; *CSPSc., 1547–1563*, pp. 602–603.

q. to mete her there, and that this should be don with grete triumphe and with the attendaunce of all the nobylitie.[202]

All the winter paste was very grete raigne, not only in Eng., but also in Fraunce, Flaunders and in the easte partes. Such scarcety of corne imagyned at Dantzick that those merchauntes that be resident there wrytt howe there ys no hope of any corne there or to be gotten thence this yeares. Whervpon corne waxeth deare in all places. And nowe in London mele is solde at xxxvj^s the quarter, whete at xxiiij^s. The small pockes raigned very muche in the L. in the winter paste. They goe aboutes to make a newe custome howese in L. where and in no other place all wares shalbe landed, because yt is thought the q. is much distrayned in her customes.[203]

[fo. 362v]

The earle of Hertford case is examined at Lambeth at leinth. With grete suete he obtayneth councell. Many doubte what will come of hyt. Some thincke he shalbe dyvorced, some that she shalbe restored to the earle of Pembrock his sonn, some that the childe shalbe made a bastard, some that she shalbe dyshabled of the inherytance of the crowne, for that the L. Fraunces was not legitimat, others that the erle shalbe putt to a grete fyne. His councell commaunded not to gave any copies of their answeres and sayinges.[204]

The xiij[th] of Marche was there a proclamation made for declaracion that the quene minded not to alter the money, wherof some having intelligence the day before tooke upp as muche money as they could in the strete for moste men still suspected the fall and so gaue their money free for 12 monethes and more, and som gave 8 in the hundred for warantyse for a lytell tyeme. It was thought yt shoud have ben stayed, because every weecke the officers of the courte payed all thinges

---

[202] For the optimism of the spring, see Alford, *Early Elizabethan Polity*, pp. 89–93. The meeting had in fact been proposed to Mary by Elizabeth in the summer of 1561; see Adams, 'Release of Darnley', p. 135.

[203] The plans for a new customs house seem to have fallen through for the time being. B. Dietz (ed.), *The Port and Trade of Early Elizabethan London*, London Record Society, 8 (1972), pp. ix–x.

[204] The 'Journall' provides further evidence of the widespread public interest in the case. Sir John Mason had reported to Cecil on 28 January that 'there be abroad, both in the city and sundry other places in the realm, broad speeches of the case'. Levine, *Early Elizabethan Succession Question*, p. 28. Lady Catherine Grey had been betrothed to Lord Henry Herbert (c. 1534–1601) on 21 May 1553 as part of the Duke of Northumberland's consolidation of support (*CSPSp., 1553*, p. 46), but the marriage had not been consummated, and Mary had subsequently persuaded the Earl of Pembroke, the groom's father, to agree to the annulment of the contract, probably in the spring of 1554. Levine, *Early Elizabethan Succession Question*, pp. 138–146. See also above, nn. 138, 187, 197–198, 204.

due to all men. It was thought this staye cam by reason of some practyse of the Italians, who with money had made grete frindes, others that yt cam by lettres sent into owte of Walles from Sir Henry Shedney, whoe wrote the people were therwith offended, and imputed the faulte to the L.R. because in his father's tyme in one yere twyse the money was called downe And som saie that the Wendesday before xl persones at the courte, at the sermon made their supplication to the quene that som order might be taken for the pryce of vytelles, otherwyse by reason of the dearth they should sterve for hounger.[205]

The Marques of Beofe returneth owte of Scottland into Fraunce.[206]

The Earle Lenoux delyvered owte of the master of the rolles' keeping to the Towre. Before the counsell, as yt is saied, being examened, he saied his wief was the nexte heire to the crowne.[207] At Easter vytell was very deare: xvj^d a stone of byef, iij^s viij^d a quarter of mutton, iij^s and iiij^s a dosen of pigeons, and so small sucking rabettes.

It was supposed that by the alteracion of coyne, both the exchaunge would have encreased and all kindes of wares would have ben better cheape. But the exchaunge nothing als almoste encreased and cothe was better cheape, when the testerne at leingth called downe to ij^d quad [farthing] was xij^d then nowe the testerne ij^s pure silver.

[fo. 363]

Aprill 1562

An insurrection or rather sedytion in Fraunce. The king of Navar, the duke of Guyse, and the constable being of the one faction, and having the king, and the prince of Condij, the admirall, and Dandelott on the other parte. It is saied that the Guyse had stollen the king awaye.[208]

In Scotland the Duke Castelle Roye and the Erle Bodvell commytted

---

[205] The proclamation (13 March 1562) is at *TRP*, II, pp. 185–186. See above, n. 178 for a draft proclamation for the calling-down of the coinage. There had been rumours of a 'decrying' of the coinage in Wales in late January: PRO, SP12/21/36 (Cecil to Sidney). The Spanish ambassador reported that if the calling-down had been implemented there would have been riots; *CSPSp., 1558–1567*, p. 231. For the botched calling-down of 1551, which surely conditioned policy at this time, see Challis, *Tudor Coinage*, pp. 105–111.

[206] Elboeuf's departure from Edinburgh was reported by Randolph in a dispatch of 28 February 1562. *CSPSc., 1547–1563*, p. 607; *CSPSp., 1558–1567*, p. 230.

[207] Lennox was committed to the Tower on 11 March 1562. He remained there until November, when he was allowed to join his wife under house arrest at Sheen. Their release was made unconditional in February 1563.

[208] The protagonists were Antoine de Bourbon, King of Navarre (1518–1562); François de Lorraine, duc de Guise (1519–1563); Anne, duc de Montmorency (1493–1567), connétable de France since 1558; Louis I de Bourbon, prince de Condé (1530–1569); Gaspard de Coligny, sieur de Châtillon (1517–1572), amiral de France since 1552; François de Coligny, sieur d'Andelot (1521–1569), colonel-général de l'infanterie.

to warde, for a conspiracy as is reported to remove the L. James and others grete abowte the q. which was dysclosed by the erle of Arren his sonn, to whome the father opened the matter, and the sonn would not consent thervnto, whervpon his father locked him upp in a chamber, but he in the night by sheates went downe owte of a windoe and aduertysed the L. James therof.[209]

The ambassador of Sweden tooke his leave of the quene.

The 12 of this moneth at Newporte Panell was a calfe calved, having a double roffe two ynches deape, the necke to the very eares. Looke in Walker's lettres.[210]

The 14 the ambassador of Sweden departed by shipp.

The L.R. after in grete hope of the mariage; brutes that he should be made duke; he rovoketh his servantes who being in dyspaier of the thinge were departed from his service. He moveth Mr W.[211] whether coniurators were not leafull, and chieffly that kind that was by good aungells who answered him all kindes were evill.[212]

The morowe after St George his daie in the chapter howse of the knightes of the garter the duke of Northfolcke moveth the q. to mariage first generally, and at leingth of the L.R., and so did the most parte of all the knightes there present. It is saied the erle of Arundell and the marques of North. departed owte of the howse when they herde yt moved.[213]

---

[209] The conspiracy seems to have been a projection by the mentally disturbed James Hamilton, third Earl of Arran (1530–1609), whose feud with James Hepburn, Earl of Bothwell (?1536–1578) was causing such anxiety that Knox had been called in to mediate their differences. It appeared that Knox had succeeded when the two attended a sermon together, and on a subsequent occasion (26 March) dined together. But on the following day Arran reported to Knox that Bothwell had advised him to carry off Mary to Dumbarton and marry her, and to murder Lord James Stewart and Maitland. Knox was of the view that Arran's manner carried traces of insanity, and his father, James Hamilton, second Earl of Arran, Duke of Châtelherault (d. 1575), had him imprisoned at Kinnaird House. According to Randolph, Arran escaped from Kinnaird by his 'sheetes blanketes and other thynges above xxx fadome owte of a wyndowe in his hose and dubled, and so travayled from Ester eve at nyght upon his feete untyll Ester Tuesdaye in the mornynge to Gray's house'. Arran and Bothwell were both imprisoned, but the sanctions against Châtelherault were limited; *CSPSc.*, *1547–1563*, pp. 612–617; *CSPF, 1561–1562*, pp. 574–577, 585–586.

[210] Walker cannot be identified.

[211] Possibly the future Secretary of State, Sir Thomas Wilson (1523–1581), who was in Dudley's service at this point; see Adams, 'Dudley clientele', p. 245, n. 29.

[212] The response accorded with the standard rejection by theologians of the distinction between 'black' and 'white witchcraft'; J.A. Sharpe, *Instruments of Darkness: Witchcraft in England, 1550–1750* (London, 1996), p. 66.

[213] AGS, E 8340/234, fo. 158v (La Quadra to Philip II, 1 May 1562); Lettenhove, *Relations Politiques*, III, p. 11 (La Quadra to Duchess of Parma, 30 April 1562); Doran, *Monarchy and Matrimony*, p. 58. The opponents were Arundel (above, n. 135) and William Parr, Marquis of Northampton (1513–1571). Elizabeth announced that she needed to give the matter further consideration.

The prince of Condie with a grete nomber of the nobylitie of Fr. be assembled at Orliaunce with 50000 men to procure that the duke of Guyse might be ordered according to the lawe for the murder he commytted in March paste at Vassey, and also because he had gotten the king and quene in his possession.[214] Looke for the bookes therof made.[215]

Sir Henry Shydney sent over in ambassade to the Frennshe k. under pretence to see yf he could pacyfie the matter of Fr., as yt is reported, but by like to see in whatt state thinges there stoode.[216]

[fo. 363v]

Maye 1562

Cicilius, a Fr. man cometh from the prince of Condie and the protestantes of Fr. to the quene's Majestie to desire favor, but neyther men nor money. He was lodged secretly at Lambeth and quickley dyspatched.[217] This yeare many monsters borne withowte armes and

---

[214] The massacre of Vassy took place on 1 March 1562. Guise entered Paris in triumph on 16 March, and was soon joined by Montmorency, Saint André, and Navarre. Condé, having failed to gain control of the royal family, withdrew from Paris for Meaux on 23 March, and entered Orléans on 2 April 1562. He wrote to the reformed churches of France on 7 April, requesting men and arms to resist the enemies of the King and the Christian religion. His first manifesto, stressing the captivity of the royal family and the need to rescue the King's councillors from intimidation, was issued on 8 April; this was followed by a declaration sent on 25 April to the *Parlement* of Paris. His forces numbered 6,000 infantry and 2,000 cavalry. On 11 April he signed, with seventy-three nobles, a Traité d'Association 'pour maintenir l'honneur de Dieu, le repos de ce Royaume, et l'estat et liberté du Roy soubs le gouvernement de la Royne sa mère'. N. Lenglet de Fresnoy and D.F. Secousse (eds), *Mémoires de Condé*, 6 vols (La Haye, 1743), III, pp. 222–235, 319–333; Agrippa d'Aubigné, *Histoire Universelle*, A. Thierry (ed.) (Geneva, 1982), II, p. 15; François de la Noue, *Discours Politiques et Militaires*, F.E. Sutcliffe (ed.) (Geneva, 1950), p. 621; K. Neuschel, *Word of Honor: Interpreting Noble Culture in Sixteenth-Century France* (New York, 1989), p. 39.

[215] *A Declaration Made by the Prynce of Condé [...]* (STC 16849, 1562); *A Seconde Declaration of the Prince of Condé [...]* (STC 16850, 1562); *A Declaration of the Prince of Condé and his Associates to the Queene [...]* (STC 16851, 1562).

[216] Sir Henry Sidney's instructions are dated 28 April; he arrived in Paris on 3 May, and had an audience with the King, Queen Mother, King of Navarre, the Constable, and the Duke of Guise on 5 May, leaving on 18 May; *CSPF, 1561–1562*, pp. 636–638; *1562*, pp. 16–18, 55.

[217] M. de Séchelles, a gentleman of the King's chamber, was in England by 11 April; *CSPF, 1561–1562*, pp. 600, 601, 621, 622, 635; *1562*, 2 (de Séchelles to Cecil, 1 May 1562 from Lambeth). The Huguenots were initially reluctant to call on direct intervention by foreign troops; J. Shimizu, *Conflict of Loyalties: Politics and Religion in the Career of Gaspard de Coligny, Admiral of France, 1519–1572* (Geneva, 1970), pp. 87–89.

legges, tow bodies ioyned in one. A pigg with eight feete.[218]
The protestauntes of Fr. sent in like maner their amb. to the princes
of protestauntes in Germany for their favor.[219]
The price of corne falleth by reason yt is very faier wether and all
kind of corne faier on the grounde.

4 speciall monsters borne: the one at Colchester, annother a Dirham,
the thryd at Exceter, the 4 at Chichester, which was a childe with a
ruffe abowte the h[ead], necke and handes licke a todes fote which was
brought embalmed to the curte and kepte in a boxe, besides divers
other monsters in L. and other places, tokens of som grete thing to
followe.[220] 4 bookes translated into Eng. of the matters of Fraunce.

Advertysementes of the state of Fraunce, with the matters to the
same of the prince of Condie and against him.[221]

Mr Godericke died the ――――― daye of Maye and was buried at St

---

[218] The 'Journall' elaborates on the prodigies below, nn. 220, 226. See also J. Stow,
Annales (1592), p. 1102; Jones, *Birth of the Elizabethan Age*, pp. 42–44. The prodigies would
have been interpreted as presaging some disaster, probably related by our author to the
deteriorating international situation. Cf. J. Poynet, *A Short Treatise of Politike Pouuer* (*STC*
20178, 1556), sig. kii. 'There was never great miserie, destruction, plage, or visitation of
God that came on any nation, citie, or countrey, which as they be in dede, so they may
iustly be called woundes, but be sent of God for sinne, and be most sodaynly layed on
the people, but are before prophecied and declared by the prophetes and ministers of
Goddes worde, or by some revelationes, wondres, monstres in the earthe, or tokens and
signes in thelement'.

[219] For Condé's letters to the German princes, see de Fresnoy and Secousse, *Mémoires
de Condé*, III, pp. 254, 271, 309 (10, 12, and 20 April). Ludovic de Ber was dispatched to
the Palatinate and Württemberg, and Erlach to Switzerland. This was followed up by
an embassy from D'Andelot who left Orléans on 7 July, and toured Heidelberg, Hesse,
and Württemberg, lobbying the Elector Palatine, the Landgrave of Hesse, and the Duke
of Württemburg.

[220] W. Fulwood, *The Shape of II Monsters. M.D.LXII* (*STC* 11485, 1562); *The True Reporte
of the Forme and Shape of a Monstrous Childe, Borne at Muche Horkesleye, a Village Three Myles
from Colchester, in the Countye of Essex, the XXI. Daye of Apryll in This Yeare. 1562. O, Praye Ye
God and Blesse His Name His Myghtye Hand Hath Wrought the Same* (*STC* 12207, 1562); *A
Discription of a Monstrous Chylde Borne at Chychester in Sussex, the XXIIII Daye of May* (*STC*
6177, 1562), described also by Machyn as 'a strange fegur with a long strynge commyng
from the navyll'; *Machyn's Diary*, p. 284. For a monstrous birth at Ryton Woodside near
Newcastle, see *CSPD Addenda, 1547–1565*, p. 525.

[221] It is not clear which texts are meant here, but cf. above, n. 215; English interest in
events in France is clear from entries in the Stationers' Register: 'the Dystruction and
[As]salte Cruelly Commytted by the Duke of Guyse and his Companye in the Towne of
Wassye' (ent. 1561–1562); 'the Perfett Newes Out of Ffraunce' (ent. 1562–1563); 'a
Complante Agaynste the Barbarous Tyranny Executed in Ffraunce upon the Pore
Members' (ent. 1562–1563), 'a Warnynge to Englande Herein to Advaunce by the Cruell
Tyranny of the Guyse late of Ffraunce' (ent. 1562–1563). Arber, *Stationers' Register*, I, pp.
199, 203, 208. Cf. *An History Briefly Contayninge that whiche hath Happened sens the Departure of
the House of Guise, the Constable, and Other from the Court at S. Germanis Vntill this Present* (*STC*
12507, 1562).

Dunstone's in the Weste, at whose buriall the l. keper, the archbushoppe of Canterbury, L. Elye were there.[222]

June 1562
Many monsterous pigges with men's noses and others. It is thought to be reason of grete moyesture of the laste winter.
Sir Fraunces Knowel's childe called Dudley Warwick killed.[223]
The quene yt is saied will see the L. R.deptes ~~dischra~~ dyscharged, ~~whethe~~ wherfor he sueth to have a lycence that no clothes unwrought may passe being above the valewe of 4^{li} according to the statutt, whervpon the shippes that the merchauntes had laden to Flaunders were not at this tyme stayed.[224]
Ludington, the secretary of Scot. is sent ambassador to move the quene to come to Yorck where the quene of Scottes will mete her. The iestes be made to goe to Yorcke. Many perswasions used to hinder the iorney. Howe the Scottyshe quene is nowe farr better proportioned, more liberall, more amiable, more affable, more gentell. That the iorney would coste 10000 poundes.[225] A hegge farowed in Sir Jhon Wentworthe's parcke in Esex viij pigges, wherof one had on horne, another two, 3 thre, 4th 4 hornes, 5th 5 hornes, the 6th 6 hornes, and the other two right proportioned.[226]

---

[222] Richard Goodrich (by 1508–1562), the highly respected lawyer and administrator (cf. above, n. 152) was buried on 25 May. Machyn lists as mourners Bacon, Parker, Grindal, and Cox; *HoP, 1509–1558*, II, pp. 231–233; *Machyn's Diary*, p. 283. Cf. *An Epytaphe Vpon the Death of M. Rycharde Goodricke Esquier* (STC 17145.3, 1562).

[223] Sir Francis Knollys (by 1512–1596) Vice-Chamberlain of the Household; *HoP, 1558–1603*, II, pp. 409–414. The relationship between Robert Dudley and Knollys was extremely close. Dudley ultimately married Knollys's daughter Lettice in 1578, but a number of his sons were in his service before then. Nothing else is known of this child or his date of birth and it is possible that the Duke of Northumberland or his eldest son, rather than Ambrose Dudley, was his godfather.

[224] *CPR, 1560–1563*, pp. 244–245 for licences to Dudley to export 80,000 cloths, notwithstanding statutes of 1536 and 1542 prohibiting export of unfinished cloths worth more than £4 for white cloths and £3 for coloured cloths. (1–3 July 1562). The Merchant Adventurers bought out Dudley in March 1563 for 10,000 marks; Dudley Papers, Box 2, no. 10. See also nn. 233, 236 below. The state of Dudley's finances in the period 1558–1561 can be found in *Leicester Accounts*. In the absence of a landed estate substantial enough to finance his position at court (not granted until 1563, but see n. 186), he was dependent on export licences such as this and the earlier one for wool. Elizabeth's reasons for postponing the grant to him of a sufficient landed estate are unknown.

[225] Maitland left for England on 25 May 1562. A meeting was agreed on 6 July, but postponed shortly afterwards. The grandeur of Mary's proposed train is suggested by the arrangements for the exchange of £10,000 Scottish into sterling. *CSPSc.*, *1547–1563*, pp. 640–641; *CSPF, 1562*, pp. 162–163; Alford, *Early Elizabethan Polity*, pp. 89–96.

[226] Cf. *The Description of a Monstrous Pig, the Which was Farrowed at Hamsted Besyde London, the XVI. Day of October, this Present Yeare of Our Lord God MDLXII* (STC 12737, 1562), a similar case.

[fo. 364]

A calf there lickwyse with a childes face.

A horrible murder commytted in Chesshire by ———— Brewton, servaunt to the L. Rob. on one ———— gent.[227] This had a suet against Brewton and recovered 40^{li} of him, which when he paied he saied he would have his penyworthe for yt. Afterwarde with his wief being abroade with his rece? to see their growndes, Brewton having divers tymes with his servauntes layed wayet to kill him, beyng hid in bushes cam sodenly owte, and first B. man gaue him a grete stroke with his sworde over his face, then B. stroke him on the hedd, and so killed him. They being taken were condempned. The quene at the suete of the L. Rob. graunteth their pardon. The wief saieth the appele at W. B. man is condempned. B vppon sureties to appere in the kinge's bench goeth at large. Dyvers tyme he appereth accompaynied with the L. R. servauntes. Many knightes and gentellmen of Chesseshere were his servauntes. Grete suete is made to the widowe to leve her suete, promysses and offers of grete somes and living. The 13 of June the L. R. and the l. chamberleyne come from Grenewych to London to speake with her, but she would not come to them. Whervpon she was commaunded the nexte day to be at the curte, where she was both entysed with faier wordes, and rebucked with fowle wordes to leve her suete, which she woulde not, for she saied she woulde never sell her husbande's bloode. She is commaunded not to departe from Grenewych withowte lycence, because she should not prosecutt the appele. This caused the people to speake very evyll of the quene and of the councell that iustice should be thus staied.

There was an Italian, a jueller called ————, who had maried the doughter of ————, one of the quene's musytians. This ———— hired an Eng. man, a barbur to kill Alberto, an Italian, a brother to the saied ————. The barbur having undertaken the matter, the jueller goeth over the sea. The barbur not daring to doe yt, treateth with a serving man to do the acte, promyseth him money, and telleth him that a boate should be prepared to carie him away, when he had don the feate. The serving man having the money and the barbur dagger to doe yt with all, discloseth the matter to Alberto and willeth him to loke well to him self, and to take heade of the barbour. Whervppon the barbour is taken and adiudged by the councell to have both his eares cutt of because there was no lawe of death for yt, and yett by the old lawe

---

[227] This is an obscure episode. There is a Mr Browton in Leicester's 1567 livery list (*Leicester Accounts*, p. 426), who may be the Francis Broughton in the funeral list (*ibid.*, p. 455), but nothing more is known about him. Dudley was later to have a considerable interest in Cheshire, but not in 1562.

[fo. 364v]

voluntas reputabitur pro facto.[228]

The talke of the king of Sweden comming is renued by the comming of one Kile whoe had ben in Swetia with him; yett he had his ambassadors ~~with him~~ in Scotland to sue for mariage there.[229] Many lordes, as the erles of North. and Hunting., and barons mete at Norwich with the duke of ~~Northflock~~ Northfolck to shote.[230]

A variaunce betwene towe of the b. of Aquila's Ph. ~~Int[elligencer]~~ ambassadors servauntes, his master of his horse and his secretary. The master favored the parte of the master of the horse, whervpon the secratary getting the copies of his lettres, bringeth them to the courte, discloseth all the practyses of the ambassador, emongest the which one was, howe he had advertised Phillipp yf he would send him money, he would delyver him England within shorte tyme withowte any stroke, for he had alredy compased the good will of tenn of the beste. The ambas. having knowledge herof, excuseth himself with defacing his man. The secretary is appointed to be lodged at Lambeth with the b. of Canterbury, whyther the ambassador wryteth vnto him, intesing him to vnsay that he had saied with promesing him largely. The secretarie sendeth these lettres to the councell.[231]

Philipp's sonne had a grete fall and in grete perell of his lief; som saye by seaking meanes to come to a mayed and fearing his master's coming, rane from the place, where he had procured one to brake open a doore to come to her, and so fell downe a paier of stayers. The wounde was grete and he in grete perell of his lief.[232]

The merchauntes moved vpon the licence of clothes repaier to the courte.[233]

This moneth of June from the chainge to the laste daie was full of stormes and rayne, the waies were so foule as in winter, the medowes

[228] The protaganists cannot now be identified.

[229] John Keyle. *CSPF, 1562*, pp. 189, 190–192.

[230] Henry Hastings, third Earl of Huntingdon (1535–1595) had succeeded to the earldom the previous year. He was a potential claimant to the throne in the event of Elizabeth's death. The other attendee named here was Thomas Percy, seventh Earl of Northumberland (1528–1572), but another contemporary account also lists Surrey, Scrope, and Abergavenny among those present. F. Blomefield, *An Essay Towards a Topographical History of the County of Norfolk*, 5 vols (London, 1806), III, pp. 279–280; cf. N. Williams, *A Tudor Tragedy: Thomas Howard, Fourth Duke of Norfolk* (London, 1964), p. 83.

[231] The defector was Borghese Venturini who had mortally wounded his rival Carlos del Gesso in a fight. For Venturini's charges and La Quadra's replies, see *CSPF, 1561–1562*, pp. 641–643; *1562*, pp. 67–69; *CSPSp., 1558–1567*, pp. 247–249. For La Quadra's attempts to rebuild his relations with Venturini, see *CSPF, 1562*, p. 71.

[232] Challoner reported the accident of 19 April in his dispatch of 11 May; *CSPF, 1562*, pp. 27, 28–29.

[233] See above, n. 224.

in all places overflowen, much haye distroyed, corne grewe full of weades, and yt bread a sodayne dearth of corne vj^d in a bushell. The winde 30 daies together sowthweste.

The duke of Guyse was hurte, the cardinall of Loreyne and the prior his bretherene taken. Damvyll taken. Marshall St Andrewe h[urt] slayne, and a grete nomber besides slayne and taken by Monnshieur on the prynce of Condie's behalf.[234]

The k. of Portugall his ambassador cam to the quene to require that the Eng. merchauntes might no longer resorte to Ginea and into the Ilandes. The quene answered by lettres that she would not have her subiectes prohibited from any countrey, belonging to any prince being in amytie with her, no more then she prohibyteth other princes to resorte unto her dominions. Enquire for the copye of the answere of Mr Askam.

[fo. 365]

It was thought he tooke not the quene's lettres in good parte because she did not geve the k. his master all his tytells vpon the superscription of the lettre.[235]

It was saied that the Turcke was landed in Hyspanie and toke many prysoners, whose feare is thought to make K. Phillipp kepe home.

July 1562
The L. Ro. obteyneth, as yt is saied, a licence for 80000 clothes, yt none shall passe beyond the sea above the valewe of appointed by the statutt but by his licence, which licence groweth by this meanes, that where he was indepted in grete somes to divers marchauntes of L., they not knowing howe they should be paied, invente this licence not caring what hurte cam to the whole, so them selves gayned.[236]

---

[234] This account is misinformed; there was no major engagement in June 1562 (the implied chronology); the effect is to exaggerate the scale of early Protestant successes. The figures identified are François de Lorraine, duc de Guise (1519–1563); François de Guise, Grand Prior (d. 1563); Henri de Montmorency, sieur de Damville (1534–1614); Jacques d'Albon de Saint André, marquis de Fronsac, and maréchal de France (1505–1562). The inclusion of Charles de Lorraine de Guise, Archbishop of Rheims (1524–1574) is mysterious because he is not known to have taken any part in the fighting and left for Trent in September 1562. As for the reported casualties, the Duke of Guise received minor injury at Rouen on 15 October, Saint André was killed at the battle of Dreux (19 December 1562), where the Grand Prior also received minor injury. We are grateful to Joan Davies for assistance with this note.

[235] For the embassy of Juan Pereira d'Antas, see *CSPF, 1561–1562*, pp. 631–632; *1562*, pp. 31, 41–42, 53–54, 54–55, 75–79; *CSPSp., 1558–1567*, p. 240. For Ascham's involvement, see Ryan, *Ascham*, pp. 361–362.

[236] See above, n. 224.

The L. Hunsdon sueth for a licence that no hoppes should be brought into the realme but by his licence.[237]

The rayne continued till half Julye.

Ludington, the secretarie of Scotland returneth with newes that the quene's Majestie will mete in Septemb. with the quene of Scotes at Nottingam and hath plate worthe 100[li] in rewarde. Purveyers be sent into the north for preparacion, for the receaving of the quene of Scotes.[238]

After that the quene had ofte talked with the prince of Condie and his confederates and promysed many thynges as the prince required, understanding that Rokenborghe was entred Fraunce with 1200 pistolettes, and the Ringrave with 2 regimentes, and the papistes cantons had sent ayed, she declared that she would consent to none of ~~her~~ their requestes but would make warr on them, wherevpon the admirall saied she spake against her conscience and so departed.[239] The prince seyng him self not equall for Guyse in the filde ~~deved~~ devyded his army into divers partes and himself with the admirall kepeth the fielde. Orleaunce having 3000 fotemen and 1000 horsmen. There were at one tyme in Fr. 30 campes.[240]

The Duke Dumall besiegeth Rone but was repulsed with losse.[241]

---

[237] Henry Carey, first Lord Hunsdon (c. 1524–1596).

[238] Maitland left in high hopes of a meeting on 11 July, but the Council changed its mind on 15 July.

[239] Elizabeth received news of recruiting by the Guises in Germany and Switzerland by letters from d'Andelot (17 July) and Throckmorton (23 July); CSPF, 1562, pp. 165, 177. Christof von Roggendorf, a Frisian by birth, acted as recruiting agent for the Guises in Germany. On 8 April the King of Navarre, in the name of Charles IX, signed a convention with him engaging the services of 1,200 mounted pistoleers, and four cornets of footmen (of 300 each). His forces entered France late in July and reached Blois on 7 August. Jean-Philippe de Salm, the Rhinegrave (d. 1569) arrived in the King's camp on 1 August. The Guises had also approached the Catholic Swiss cantons which offered 6,000 troops at a diet on 21 May. Commanded by the Swiss mercenary captain, Wilhelm Fröhlich (1504/5–1562), they left on 8 July and reached Blois on 7 August. D'Aubigné, Histoire Universelle, II, p. 33, n.6, p. 76, n.3, p. 148; E. Rott, Histoire de la réprésentation diplomatique de la France auprès des cantons suisses, de leurs alliés et de leurs confédérés, 10 vols (Berne and Paris, 1902–1935), II, pp. 44–45; B.F.A.J.D. Zurlauben, Histoire militaire des suisses au service de la France 8 vols (Paris, 1751–1753), IV, pp. 278–327; H.L-V. de la Popelinière, L'Histoire de France enrichie de plus notables occurrences [...] depuis l'an 1550 jusques à ces temps, 2 vols (La Rochelle, 1581), I, p. 327; D. Potter, 'Les allemands et les armées françaises au XVIe siècle. Jean-Philippe Rhingrave, chef de lansquenets: étude suivie de sa correspondance en France, 1548–1566', Francia, 20 (2000), pp. 1–20.

[240] As the Catholic forces moved down the Loire valley, Condé detached La Rochefoucauld to deal with the threat, but Saint André's capture of Poitiers and Angoulême threatened to cut lines of communications with Orléans.

[241] Aumale arrived before Rouen on 28 May. His forces were only 3,000 strong, and he lacked siege artillery; he retreated after a few days when the garrison was reinforced by Louis de Lannoy, seigneur de Morvilliers; S. Carroll, Noble Power During the French Wars of Religion: the Guise Affinity and the Catholic Cause in Normandy (Cambridge, 1998), p. 119.

Baron des Adreses kepeth Lions and Piedemont.[242] The q. of Navar in fielde against the papistes in Gascon.[243] The warres in Fraunce began so hotte, the prince sendeth to the quene's Majestie for ayed, not of men or shippes, but of money. Dyvers com and emongest the reste the vydam of Amians, whoe offereth the q. that yf she would ioyne with the prince, they would delyver unto her Havre des Grace and that her men should have the custodie of till Calies were restored.[244]

[fo. 365v]

Vpon these newes in F. the metinges of the quenes at N. is dyspatched and Sir H. Shedney sent in post into Scotland to declare the lett of the present meting, and howe in the spring nexte it should be.[245] Some saied this meting was the more desired of the Scot. q. by the Guyse that the q. Majesties should the rather not be partaker of the doynges in Fraunce with the prince. Others saie that yt was devysed by Throgmorten the amb. who had received grete rewarde of the Scott. q. in grete silver pottes and other plate, and promysed he would doe what he coulde to bring to passe that the q. of Eng. should make and declare the Scott. q. heire apparant to the crowne of Eng. Against this meting cam Fraunces Carewe from beyonde sea, who had ben there

[242] François de Beaumont, baron des Adrets (1513–1587) held Dauphiné and the Rhône valley in the Protestant interest, and occupied Lyons.

[243] Jeanne d'Albret, Queen of Navarre (1528–1572). Her adversary was Blaise de Monluc (1501–1577), maréchal de France and lieutenant-gouverneur de Guyenne. Armand de Gontaut, sieur d'Audaux, was active in recruiting on her behalf and in clearing a path for her between Périgord and Béarn: N.L. Roelker, *Queen of Navarre: Jeanne d'Albret 1528–1572* (Cambridge MA, 1968), pp. 193–195.

[244] Francois d'Ailly, vidame d'Amiens, was one of the French hostages and had been in England since April 1560. The embassy was in fact headed by Jean II de Ferrières, sieur de Maligny, vidame de Chartres (c. 1521–1586), conseiller of the parlement of Paris, maître des requêtes, chef du conseil of the prince de Condé, and governor of Le Havre, who arrived in England on 31 July. Le Havre, the port at the mouth of the Seine constructed by François I, had been seized by Ferrières in the Protestant interest on 14 May. Elizabeth's request for the port was initially refused, and he returned to France to seek plenipotentiary powers. He was at Greenwich again on 15 August; terms were agreed on 25 August; and the Treaty of Hampton Court was signed on 20 September. See also below, n. 286. *Leicester Accounts*, p. 123; *CSPF, 1559–1560*, p. 518; W. MacCaffrey, 'The Newhaven expedition, 1562–1563', *HJ*, 40 (1997), pp. 6–12; D.J.B. Trim, 'The "foundation stone of the British army"?: the Normandy campaign of 1562', *Journal of the Society for Army Historical Research*, 77 (1999), pp. 71–77.

[245] The projected meeting at Nottingham was indeed deferred because of the deteriorating situation in France. See above, n. 225, and *CSPF, 1562*, pp. 162–163, 164. Sir Henry Sidney left London on 16 July, arrived in Edinburgh on 21 July, and had an audience with Mary on 23 July. He was instructed to tell Mary that the meeting had been postponed because of the 'duke of Guise's party's cruel procedings'. *HMCS*, I, p. 267; *CSPF, 1562*, p. 182; *CSPSc., 1547–1563*, p. 641.

longe with his brother in lawe. Thrognorton being emongest certen gentellmen spake that yf he had knowen this meting should not have taken place, he would not have come over, and besides vttered that yt were good and necessary the succession were establyshed, and that there were none so mete to be in the first place of succession as the q. of Scotes, and howe she might be maried to some Eng. gentellman and seamed to be very ernest therin, whervnto yong Mr Darcie his nephewe saied, he spake not well to say so, and he knewe howe yt cam by the grete silver pottes. And the Lady Throgmorton declared howe her husband had receved these pottes from the F. quene.[246]

One Randall being a gente in Scot. wrought the licke mater and muche solycyted the meting, and yt may by this and by the first motion therof at the L. James mariage be gathered that it was a dryfte of Throgmorton and him. Grete and ofte sending have ben betwene Throg. and Randall for the purpose.[247]

The northern iorney being stayed, the l. keeper, Pembrocke, Clinton, the secretary much advysed the quene to ~~cons~~ consider the state of Fraunce and howe yf the Guyses should have the overhand, he wold renue the olde tytell that he ~~had~~ pretented to the crowne in the right of the Scottyshe quene, and that so the realme should be in grete troble and daunger. With much a doe the quene doth here yt, whervppon the shippes be prepared to be sent owte, and men gathered in dyvers sheres to be in redines who were not mustered after the commen maner, but

[fo. 366]

taken vpp by appointement and every shire did apparell and arme their soldiers at their owne charges. It was in Hertfordshere appoyneted 600[li] for the charges of 200 men.[248]

The ambassador of Spaine being informed herof before this was

---

[246] Throckmorton's brother-in-law, Sir Francis Carew (c.1530–1611) had joined him in France in 1561, but, interestingly, Throckmorton noted his 'lack of skill in negotiation of matters'. Throckmorton was married to Francis's sister, Anne; another sister, Mary, was mother to Sir Edward Darcy (1543–1612); *HoP, 1558–1603*, II, pp. 16–17. The story of bribery cannot be verified but the whiff of suspicion was doubtless raised by the silverware the Throckmortons had received prior to Mary's departure from France; see A. Fraser, *Mary, Queen of Scots* (London, 1969), p. 128.

[247] For the co-operation of Throckmorton and Randolph at this time, see BL, Additional MS 35831, fo. 17r–v. The meeting had in fact been mooted the previous summer.

[248] For the levies authorized on 23 July, see *APC*, VIII, pp. 119, 120, 122. The estimates of the costs are not unrealistic. A recent estimate of the costs of the levy of 600 troops in London is £2,110. In the capital the troops were pressed on 26 July and kept in readiness until 19 August, only to be mobilized once again on 16 September and delivered to the captains on 19 September: I.W. Archer, 'Gazeteer of military levies from the City of London, 1509–1603', http://senior.keble.ox.ac.uk/fellows/extrapages/iarcher/levies.htm, no. 032.

resolved in the councell commeth to the courte and desireth audience,
and required the cause whie they mustered men when in deade yt was
not don, nor resolued to be don, which made the councell much
muse.[249] This ambassador muche procureth the mariage of the L. Ro.
and seaketh all meanes. And yt was he that moved by meanes that the
king of Sweden should sue for mariage to the Scottyshe quene.[250]

By certen his lettres yt is dyscovered that he practyseth this mariage
to this ende to make dyvision in the realme for yt he sawe the people
did not favor yt, and by this meanes his master Phillipp should have
the better entry into England.[251] The Elector Landsgrave[252] and other
confederattes confesionis Augustanae, make proclamation that yf any
Dutch man serve against the Prince, he should confyscatt all his goodes
and be banyshed his countrey whervpon many departed from the
Rhengrave and Rakinborogh.[253]

Those of Berna and Geneva do ayede the barron of Adresses with
13 ensignes of fote men and 4000 horses.[254]

August 1562

Colborne and Kele be commytted to the Towre, for that they wrote to
the k. of Sweden, to come into Engl. and that he should spede of his
mariage, for dyvers lordes and ladies did favor yt. Mrs Asteley is
commaunded to kepe her chamber because she was suspected to be a
doer therin, for Colborne was her man, and Mrs Dereth of the privey
chamber is commytted to the custody of the secretary. One Aleyn was
sent for and commaunded to attend at the courte. It is suspected that
he vttered all. The lettres were taken by one sent over to require that

---

[249] La Quadra followed the military preparations closely; *CSPSp., 1558–1567*, pp. 254,
255–256. He wrote to the Duchess of Parma on 25 July 1562 (Brussels, Archives Générales
du Royaume, Papiers d'Etat et de L'Audience 360, fos 177–180 [not in *CSPSp*]), enclosing
a copy and translation of the order for the levies. 'Among other things, they have
published the order that I send herewith to the governors of the provinces of this coast
to arm 12,000 men and hold them ready to muster at the five ports named. This is being
done to avoid dissension and scandal among the people should they understand that the
queen intends to send an army on this enterprise as they know that it does not please
everyone.' The unusual manner of raising troops was done to disguise the fact that they
were intended to go to France under cover of being raised for protection against invasion.

[250] His position was compromised by the revelations of his servant; *CSPSp., 1558–1567*,
p. 253.

[251] La Quadra's courier was kidnapped probably by agents of Cecil two miles from
Gravesend. *CSPSp., 1558–1567*, pp. 236, 237, 241.

[252] Philipp of Hesse (r. 1509–1567).

[253] De Fresnoy and Secousse, *Mémoires de Condé*, III, pp. 500–501.

[254] Geneva's policy was in fact one of neutrality, but Berne was more forthcoming with
military support; R.M. Kingdon, *Geneva and the Coming of the Wars of Religion in France, 1555–*
1563 (Geneva, 1956), pp. 116–117; Zurlauben, *Histoire militaire des suisses*, IV, pp. 279–281.

suche money as was due by the king here in Eng. might be paied, wherfore John Dimock stode bounde.[255] Monnshieur Vieillvill, capiten of Metz commeth owte of Fraunce ambassador from the k. to require the quene not to medell in this dyscention.[256] Henry Knowells apointed to goe to the electours to require them to ioyne in aiede of the prince of Condie with the q. and went.[257] It is saied that Dandelett commeth owte of Dutchlande with 10000 men. 8 shippes sent to the sea. 1000 archebusses cased, dyvers grete ordinances also shipped bysides the ordenary

[fo. 366v]

and necessarie of the sheppes.[258] Howe the duke of Wytenberg answered the ambassadors that came from the prince of Condie, howe they should have sett owte a ~~conffession~~ confession of their faieth before they moved the warres, but they Zwinglians withowte iust cause rebelled and moved warr against their prince, which was saied by the advyse

---

[255] The affair burst on 4 August. John Dymock (see above, n. 107) had exploited his connections with Katherine Ashley, chief gentlewoman of the Privy Chamber, and concluded that Elizabeth was well-minded towards Eric XIV. Both Francis Golborne and John Keyle had written in late July 1562 to their friends in Sweden to the same effect; Ashley and Dorothy Bradbelt (or Broadbent), also of the Privy Chamber, were incriminated by letters that they had sent to Sweden encouraging the match. It was rumoured that this was part of a wider anti-Dudley conspiracy, but no evidence was found to support it, and Ashley and Bradbelt were restored to their positions in the Privy Chamber in September. Doran, *Monarchy and Matrimony*, pp. 34–35; *APC*, VII, p. 123; PRO, SP70/39, fos 118, 119, 175–176 (for incriminating letters, 22–27 July), 62–88 (interrogations of Keyle and Goldborne, 6 August 1562); Lettenhove, *Relations Politiques*, III, p. 97.

[256] François de Scépeaux, sieur de Vieilleville (1509–1571), maréchal de France, had three audiences with the Queen, the first on 7 August; *CSPF, 1562*, pp. 249, 251–252, 253.

[257] Knollys joined Mundt. He was at Antwerp on 15 August, Heidelberg on 30 August (audiences with Friedrich III, Elector Palatine, r. 1559–1576), Worms on 3 September, Marburg on 24 September (audiences with Philipp of Hesse), Leipzig on 24 September (failed to make contact with Augustus, Elector of Saxony, r. 1553–1586), Coburg around 29 September (meeting with Johann Friedrich II of Saxony), Marburg on 8 October (meetings with Philipp of Hesse and Augustus of Saxony), Darmstadt on 17 October (meeting with Christof, Duke of Württemberg), and Frankfurt on 23 October (assembly of princes for election of King of the Romans). *CSPF, 1562*, pp. 214–215, 245, 280–281, 356–357, 360, 387–390, 466–470.

[258] D'Andelot did not in fact cross the Rhine until 22 September; C. Haton, *Mémoires contenant le récit des événements accomplis de 1553 à 1587*, F. Bourquelot (ed.), 2 vols (Paris, 1857), I, p. 267; De Fresnoy and Secousse, *Mémoires de Condé*, III, p. 267.

of Brentius,[259] who is a Lutheran and doth not allowe Calvine's doctryne of the Sacrement, who before had taken of the cardinall of Loreyne a gyfte of a guylte cuppe and 100 crownes. This unloked for answere of the ambassadors were astonied and departed, and imediatly after their departure, fell in the land of Witenberg so grete haile that yt destroyed the grapes and the vinestokes, bestes in the field, and brake downe glasse windoes.

Capita xii reformationis proposita consideranda patribus die xi° Martii Anno Domini 1562.[260]

1. Considerent patres qua ratio num ri possit, vt patriarchae, archiepiscopi, episcopi et ceteri omnes, animarum curam habentes in suis

[259] Duke Cristof of Württemberg (1515–1568, r. 1550–1568) had met François de Guise at Saverne in the territories of the Bishop of Strasbourg on 15–18 February 1562. The cardinals of Lorraine and of Guise, the duc D'Aumale and the prince de Joinville were present, along with Johannes Brenz (1499–1570), and Jakob Andreae (1528–1590), leading Lutheran theologians and advisers to the duke. This had possibly been a last-ditch attempt at theological compromise, more probably an effort to secure the neutrality of the Lutheran princes. A. Jouanna, J. Boucher, D. Biloghi, G. Le Thiec (eds), *Histoire et Dictionnaire des Guerres de Religion* (Paris, 1998), pp. 108–109.

[260] Although the later sections of the MS offer a basically chronological account of the events of 1562, this document is placed inexplicably out of sequence, and its date (11 March 1563) places it later than any other matter discussed. The document comprises headings for reform proposals presented to the convocation which met from 13 January to 14 April 1563. Its concerns with clerical residence, simony, impoverished livings, and the abuses of clandestine marriage appear in other of the various reform packages placed before convocation, but its headings do not match the contents of any other specific paper. The present text therefore provides an additional and hitherto unnoticed source for the convocation. The surviving documents have most recently been discussed by D. Crankshaw, 'Preparations for the Canterbury provincial convocation of 1562–3: a question of attribution', in S. Wabuda and C. Litzenberger (eds), *Belief and Practice in Reformation England: A Tribute to Patrick Collinson from his Students* (Aldershot, 1998), pp. 60–93. Crankshaw revises the interpretation established by Haugaard, *Elizabeth I and the English Reformation*. He establishes that, contrary to earlier views which saw key reform proposals as emanating from the 'precisians' in the lower house of convocation, they came from Archbishop Parker's circle. The obstacle to reform was not the bishops but the Supreme Governor. The key manuscripts have been printed, albeit with numerous inaccuracies by Strype, *Annals*, I.i, pp. 470–529, I.ii, pp. 562–568; idem, *The Life and Acts of Matthew Parker, The First Archbishop of Canterbury in the Reign of Queen Elizabeth* (London, 1711), II, pp. 119–123; E. Gibson, *Synodus Anglicana: Or, The Constitution and Proceedings of an English Convocation, Shown from the Acts and Registers thereof, to be Agreeable to the Principles of an Episcopal Church* (London, 1702); E. Cardwell (ed.), *Synodalia: A Collection of Articles of Religion, Canons, and Proceedings of Convocations in the Province of Canterbury from the Year 1547 to the Year 1717*, 2 vols (Oxford, 1842), II, pp. 495–527; G. Bray (ed.), *The Anglican Canons, 1529–1947*, Church of England Record Society, 6 (Woodbridge, 1998), pp. 724–765. We are extremely grateful to Professor Malcolm Parkes for his assistance with the transcription of this portion of the manuscript.

ecclesiis resideant et ab eis non nisi iustis, honestis necesariis, et ecclesiae catholicae vtilibus de causis absint.

2. Item ~~non~~ an expediat vt nemo ordinetur ad sacrae ordines nisi ad certum aliquem beneficii titulum. Compertum est enim multas ~~committert~~ committeri fallacias ex eo quibus plerique ad titulum patrimonii ordinantur.

3. Et quod ordinantes nihil omnino recipiant pro collatione quorumcumque ordinum neque etiam eorum ~~ministrii~~ ministri aut notarii.

4. An eisdem consedendum sit, vt de prebendis non servientium possint distributiones quotidianas constituere in illis ecclesiis in quibus nullae sunt distributiones, aut ita tenues, vt negligantur.

5. An parochiae omnes quae ob suam amplitudinem plures requirant sacerdotes plures etiam debeant habere titulos ab ordinario instituendos.

6. Beneficia quoque curata q idonea prouisione uictus sacerdotalis carent an sint reformanda, ita, vt a pluribus titulis, vnus tantum ab ordinario constituatur.

7. Cum rectores parochialium multi siue parum idonei, qui vel ob imperitiam, aut vitae turpitudinem destruant potius qvam edificent subiectum sibi gregem, et deteriores aliquando habeant vicarios videndum est quomodo huic malo medendum est foret, num expediat eis dari coadiutur siue vicarius idoneus cum assignationem fructuum arbitrio ordinarii.

8. Ordinariis an sit concendendum vt beneficia et capellas vetustate collapsas quae ob paupertatem restaurari nequeant in matrices ecclesias transferri possint.

9. An decernendum sit, beneficia commendata esse regularia, visitari ab ordinariis et corrigi.

10. Matrimonia clandestina an in futurum debeant declarari irrita esse et nulla.

11. Quae conditiones sint declarandae ad hoc vt matrimonium non dicatur clandestinum sed in facie ecclesie contractum.

12. Denique magnopere considerandum esset, quid constituendum sit circa quaestorum non paucos abusiis.

17 August 1562

The duke of Guyse and his partie entend to departe from Bloyes towarde Orleaunce to laye siege thervnto. The hoole power of him is 11000 fotemen and 6000 horsemen. The prince of Condie hath 6000 fotemen and 3000 horsemen in the towne.[261]

---

[261] The source for this and the subsequent data on the strengths of the various forces is PRO, SP70/40/366; *CSPF, 1562*, pp. 252–253.

The baron des Adresses is come to Schalon in Burgundie with 10000 fotemen and a thowsand horsmen for the aiede of the Prince.[262] The prince of Perceine is also comming owte of Champaigne with 2000 fotemen and 1200 horsmen for the prince.[263] Monnshieur Dandelot is entred owte of Germ. into Fraunce with 9000 fotemen and 3000 horsemen which are paied before hand for 6 monethes, all which power is thought will ioyne together to doe som other feate then to rayse the siege at Orleaunce because yt is thought the prince to be soe stronge in Orleaunce, that the towne canote be besieged, with doble the nomber the Guyse hath.

The baron des Addresses hathe lately geven an overthrowe to Monnshieur de Guset[264] and taken all his artillary. Monnshieur de Mauvanes[265] of Province and Monnshieur de Cardie,[266] sonn in lawe to the countie of Tende[267] have overthrowen Monnshieur Somariva[268] and Carses,[269] lyvetenant to the graund priour, and slane 3000 of his men and so all Provinse is at the prince his devotion.

The quene of Navar is entred into Burdeox with a grete power, and kepeth the towne and countrey in such sorte as no force of straungers should come owte of Spayne.[270]

---

[262] For des Adrets's exploits, see D'Aubigné, *Histoire universelle*, II, pp. 58–67.

[263] Antoine de Croy, baron de Seninghen and prince de Porcien (1541–1567) had been sent by Condé to raise troops in Champaigne.

[264] François de la Baume de Suze, comte de Suze et de Rochefort (1526–1587). For his defeat at the hands of des Adrets, see D'Aubigné, *Histoire universelle*, II, pp. 58–61.

[265] Paul de Richien, sieur de Mouvans or Mauvans (d. 1568), Huguenot commander in Provence.

[266] Jacques de Salusses-de-Miolans, sieur de Cardé (d. 1568), son-in-law to the comte de Tende; De Fresnoy and Secousse, *Mémoires de Condé*, II, p. 184.

[267] Claude de Savoie, comte de Tende (1507–1566), amiral de France and gouverneur de Provence.

[268] Honoré de Savoie, comte de Sommerive (1538–1572) eldest son of the comte de Tende, clashed with his father who was thought to favour a son by a second marriage. He was named lieutenant du roi in Provence by the Queen Mother, and found himself fighting on the opposite side to his father. G. Lambert, *Histoire des Guerres de Religion en Provence, 1530–1598* (2 vols, repr., 1972), I, pp. 139–141.

[269] Jean de Pontevès, comte de Carcès (1512–1582). The account is wildly misleading, as the Huguenots were hard pressed in Provence. Carcès seized Aix, driving out the Huguenots, and with Sommerive, went on to take Orange (6 June) and Sisteron (5 September). Lambert, *Guerres de religion en Provence*, I, pp. 116–186. But as Joan Davies has pointed out to us, there is a puzzle here, since Carcès is described as 'lyuetenant to the Grand Priour'. Carcès may have functioned informally as lieutenant to Sommerive in 1562 but he did not become lieutenant-governor of Provence until 1569. And it was not until 1579 that Henri de Valois, chevalier d'Angoulême (d. 1586, bastard son of Henri II), Grand Prior of the Langue de France, was appointed governor of Provence with Carcès as his lieutenant.

[270] Jeanne's arrest had been ordered by the crown and she did not stay long in Bordeaux, moving on to Béarn, and arriving in Pau in mid-August; Roelker, *Queen of Navarre*, pp. 193–197.

[fo. 367v]

The Persians are nowe in suche feare of Dandelot his comming with his power to the same towne, as they have sent to the k. desiring him to returne to Paris for their succure.[271]

The plage in so grete in Paris as by the regesters computation there die dayly above 1000 persones.[272]

By observation of accomptes of dyvers in Fra. it is certenly estemed that sethence the begynning of these troubles there there have ben murdered, drowned and killed to the nomber of 100000 persones.

It is fullie persuaded that the quene should not go northward. etc.

September 1562

All this sommer by the space of 3 monethes was grete raynes wherby till the middest of this moneth, harvest was not touched. And soe corne began to encrese in pryce – 40d the bushell of whete.

Preparation to send men over. The erle of Warwick made livetenant; all the capitaines resorte to him and to his brother, for all was don by the meanes of his brother. And so they make a grete shewe in the courte.[273]

K. Ph. suspected that the quene woulde take vpp the money in Flaunders but Gresham prevented yt.[274]

Ph. ambassador complayneth to the quene that his master coulde gett noe money in Flaunders and woulde have her release the money taken. The q. answered, if you lack money for a good purpose, I will not lett to lend him som. Then the ambassador desired the q. that her merchauntes in Flaunders might be suertie for the K. P. for 400000 crownes. Naie, saied the quene, we kepe our owne merchauntes for our owne neade and necessytye.

The Guysans labor for money in Fraunce, but they could gett none. After they send the Fre. k. iuelles to borowe money over them, but no man durste lend upon that gage.[275]

Mr Clarentius, priest taken saying masse in Fewter Lane at Sir

[271] For the state of opinion in Paris at this time, see B. Diefendorf, *Beneath the Cross: Catholics and Huguenots in Sixteenth-Century Paris* (Cambridge, 1991), pp. 65–67.

[272] Haton estimated total mortality in Paris in this year as over 25,000. Recent estimates of the city's total population put it at between 250,000 and 300,000 at this date. L. Bourquin (ed.), *Mémoires de Claude Haton, t. 1, 1553–1565* (Paris, 2001), p. 406; Diefendorf, *Beneath the Cross*, p. 9.

[273] For the role of the Newhaven venture in the revival of Dudley military patronage, see Adams, 'Dudley clientele', pp. 246–247.

[274] The Queen ordered Gresham to raise money on 19 September; *CSPF, 1562*, p. 307.

[275] For the financial difficulties of the royal forces, see J.B. Wood, *The King's Army: Warfare, Soldiers, and Society During the Wars of Religion in France, 1562–1576* (Cambridge, 1996), pp. 275–280.

Wymond Carowe's widowe's howse, and he was brought to London in his copes, and she followed him, wherat was grete gasing.[276] The q. after altered her mynde for sending men over, wherfore the secretary departed the Courte in a malencholie.[277] Fraunces the post bringeth newes owte of Fraunce.[278] Byturiges is yeldid to the k. after this maner.[279] The k. and Q. Mother were sent to the gates and required to speke with the capitayne, whoe lett them in; within two dayes the won him on these condycions that he and his should vse their relligion free; the soldiers were sworne not to be against the king or his, but against the Dutch and Eng.

[fo. 368]

Yett by and by viij ensignes of the fotemen went to the prince of to Orleaunce whoe receaved them but not their capiten, but bid him goe where he woulde, for he should in tyme answere to his othe. 4 ensignes remayne with the king. Monnshieurr Divoye capiten was promysed the order of the allowaunce of 50 grete horses, and he is but a yonge man.[280]

Whylest this parle was at Orliaunce, the yonge duke of Loreyne with Monnshieur de Traye master of the ordinaunces, went from Paris with a grete force of horsemen and fotemen to carry to Guyse's campe 8 cannons and dyvers other grete shot and a grete proportion of powder. Sir Nicholas Throgmorton for savetye went in ther company to take

[276] These events took place on 8 September 1562. Stow records that the priest in question was one Havard and gives many details about other participants. Sir Wymond Carew (1498–1549) had links with Protestants, but his widow Martha was firmly Catholic. On this occasion she was examined by the Bishops of London and Ely, but refused to give testimony under oath and was imprisoned for six months. She was in trouble again in 1568 for being present at a private mass in the parish of St Sepulchre. See *Machyn's Diary*, pp. 291–292; 'John Stow's historical memoranda', in J. Gairdner (ed.), *Three Fifteenth Century Chronicles, with Historical Memoranda by John Stowe*, Camden Society, new series, 28 (1880), pp. 121–122; P. Carter, 'Financial administration, patronage and profit in mid-Tudor England: the career of Sir Wymond Carew (1498–1549)', *Southern History*, 20–21 (1998–1999), p. 37.

[277] The troops were stood down on 19 August; see above, n. 248.

[278] Francisco Tomaso, the Queen's courier, left France under a safe-conduct on 9 September, carrying a letter from Throckmorton; *CSPSp.*, *1558–1567*, p. 254; *CSPF, 1562*, pp. 289, 290.

[279] The account seems to derive from PRO, SP70/41, fo. 113

[280] The siege of Bourges began on 19 August and the town surrendered on favourable terms on 31 August. The commander, Jean de Hangest, sieur d'Yvoy (d. 1572) was accused of betraying Condé and left for the King's service. D'Aubigné, *Histoire universelle*, II, p. 85; *Histoire ecclésiastique*, II, p. 85; De Thou, III, p. 199; De Fresnoy and Secousse, *Mémoires de Condé*, III, pp. 634–636; M.L. de Raynal, *Histoire du Berry*, 4 vols (Bourges, 1881), IV, pp. 61–63.

his leve of the King. Chastilion the admirall having intelligence mete with them, and overthrewe them, and killed a grete nomber of horsemen and fotemen, toke all the cariage, broke the ordynaunces, burnte all the powder and car carried Throg. with him into Orliaunce, but he was spoyled of all, and in grete daunger.[281]

Aboute that tyme was a grete conflicte in Bigor and Bren bordering to Hyspanie betwene Monluk of Charde, a Guysan and the capiten of the q. of Navar. Monluk was slayne, all his men and 1200 Spaniardes, and on the other parte a grete nomber slaine also.[282]

Sir Peter Mewtes died at Rhene.[283]

Mrs Astley and Mrs Doreth restored to the chamber.

The prince of Condie with the rest of that side send to the q. the vydam of Schartreis a man of good yeares and experience who had the keping of Newehaven for the prince, and Monshieur Le Haye whoe was master. eup libell. to the k.[284] These two brought from the prince in blank a parchment signed with the prince's hand, and 12 other grete personages for a league to be made betwene them and the q. which was don. The condycions be: the q. will ayed them, first in sending to the prince from Argentine[285] 140000 crownes. Item in sending 6000 soldiers for the deffence of Newehaven, Deape and Rhone yf they may be caried thither safly. Newehaven to be delyvered to the Eng., and noe Fre. soldiers to remayne therin but by lycence; all the artillary munition powder, harnesse etc. there shalbe delyvered to the q. livetenant. The q. to enioye it till the prince and his procure either by

---

[281] Throckmorton was en route from Paris to Bourges, taking a wide sweep to the west of Orléans, when Châtillon's troops attacked the Catholics (400 cavalry and 800 infantry with siege artillery intended for Bourges) under Elboeuf at La Ferté-Villeneuil, four miles from Châteaudun on 1 September. Coligny's forces killed 300. Throckmorton was escorted by his new hosts to Orléans. Forbes, *Full View*, II, pp. 36–38, D'Aubigné, *Histoire universelle*, II, p. 85; La Popelinière, *Histoire de la France*, I, p. 338.

[282] For Monluc, see above n. 243. Throckmorton reported an engagement on 1 September in which Monluc was routed, but the 'Journall' is misinformed as to his demise, and Protestant fortunes in the south-west were far less successful than is here suggested. They suffered a series of defeats culminating in the battle of Vergt (9 October), which prevented any possibility of a junction between their forces under Duras and those of Condé. Bren is a presumably garbled version of Béarn; Bigorre is the province to the east of Béarn. Forbes, *Full View*, II, p. 3; P. Courteault (ed.), *Commentaires de Blaise de Monluc*, 3 vols (Paris, 1911–1923), II, pp. 560–563.

[283] He died at Dieppe. *CSPF, 1562*, p. 291.

[284] See also above, n. 244. The vidame de Chartres was accompanied by Robert, sieur de la Haye, Condé's secretary and a *maître des requetes* (presumably the post referred to here) on his second embassy in August. La Haye remained in England as agent until the summer of 1563. A file of his correspondence survives in Geneva, Bibliothèque Publique et Universitaire, Archives Tronchin, MS 146, the most important item of which is his *seureté* of 12 May 1563 (fo. 155–v *bis*) which describes the circumstances under which the blank was employed in the making of the Treaty of Hampton Court.

[285] Strasbourg.

them selfes or at the Fr. kinge's handes the restitucion of Callies. 3000 are appointed to kepe Newehaven. The other 3000 for Deape and Rhone. The q. also sendeth grete preparation of artillary. A condytion that the q. shall not delyver Newhaven to the F. king

[fo. 368v]

nor receave Calies at his handes withowte the consent of the prince and his, the agrement at Cambraye for 8 yeares neverthelesse being saved to the q. At the delyverie of Newhaven the Eng. pledges shalbe delyvered into Deape which shall tarie there vntill the wryting signed with the quene's hand and sealed with the grete seale be delyvered to the p. of Condie, assigned by the handes of Palsgraue at Heidelberg to whome yt was sent, who shall not delyver yt till he be advertysed that Newehaven is in the q. handes.[286]

The Guysians minde to bring the Fr. k. to besiege Rhone.

Newes broughte owte of Fraunce into England 4° Septemb. 1562.

25 August, after the Guysianes had made a breche, one hundered fote wyde, at Byturiges in Berry, they gave the assault and were repulsed with the losse of 4000 men by estimacion, emongest which nomber, there was slaine Monnshieur de Randan, newe cornell of the fotemen, La Rocheposi, and Monnshieur de Nansey, apiten Charleboyes, and his brother Capteine Richleu [?], Monnshieur Valentian, the bastard of Auguin with soundry others.[287] This assaulte being geven, the Guysians wanted powder and shott and men to attempte a newe.

The governor of Burges under the prince called Monnshieur Dyvoy, brother to Monnshieur Janlies hath 3000 good soldiers within the towne sent the prince of Condie worde since the assaulte, that with godes

---

[286] The Treaty of Hampton Court, 20 September 1562; Forbes, *Full View*, II, pp. 48–51, printing BL, Cotton MS Caligula E V; *CSPF, 1562*, pp. 275–276. By the terms of the Treaty of Cateau-Cambrésis (April 1559) Calais had been ceded to France, but with a promise that 500,000 crowns would be paid at the end of eight years if it were not restored.

[287] The account seems confused. René Roch Chasteigner, sieur de la Roche-Posay (1527–1562), chambellan to Charles IX and captain of a company of *chevau-légers* was killed at Bourges. But Charles de la Rochefoucauld, sieur de Randan (1525–1562), captain of a company of *chevau-légers*, colonel-general of the infantry and captain of the gendarmerie died on 4 November 1562 from wounds received at the siege of Rouen (not Bourges) 'qui fût mal soignée'. (D'Aubigné, *Histoire universelle*, II, p. 97). Gaspard de la Châtre, sieur de Nançay, Bésigny, and Sigouneau (1539–1576), Antoine du Plessis, seigneur de Richelieu, M. de Valency, bastard son of Jean de Bourbon, comte de Soissons and d'Enghien, and Corbeyran de Cardillac de Sarlabous (probable identity of Charleboyer), formerly captain at Dunbar, all lived to fight another day. F de Cardaillac, *Deux capitaines gascons du XVIe siècle, les frères Sarlabous* (Paris-Tarbes, 1908).

grace he will warant the towne for these 6 weeckes.[288]

The power of the Gusians be in nomber as followeth. Of F. men on fote v^m wherof the best parte hurte and slaine before Burges.[289] Of almaynes under the Conte Ringrave 4000, the most parte protestantes and such as the Gusians do scarse truste, 3000 Sweses unarmed and unable men nowe lying at B. besides Bloys where they die of the plage extremely.[290] 3000 horsmen Fr. and vii^c pistoliers.

The force of the prince of Condie.

Besides those of Burges, the prince hath within Orliaunce 5000 fotemen good soldiers, and 1000 horsemen with vj^c gentell men that cam to him sence the siege of Burges.

The duke of Swaybroke alias Bypontine[291] marcheth toward them with 2000 horsmen and 3000 fotemen, and is paste Strasburgh. Monnshieur Dandelot with 6000 fotmen and 3000 horsmen by reporte, the bravest bandes that have ben seen of longe tyme, are appointed to be at Orliance with the prince the xth of this present.

[fo. 369]

The baron des Addresses and his frindes wil be at Orleans the viiith of this present with 5000 Swisses vij^m Fre. and 2000 ~~horsmen~~ horsemen, besides tow hundered pistoliers sent of late by the towne of Geneva.

The Conte Rochefocault, and Monnshieur Duras of Gasconie together with the q. of Navarre's men to the nomber of 8000 fotemen and 2000 horsemen wil be at Orlians the xijth of this moneth.[292]

The conte of Seingham, alias the prince of Porcien[293] is in Champaine besides Ch[alons?] with 3000 footemen and 500 horse against the Guysians.

Rhone, Depe, and the townes in ~~Germany~~ Normandy do nothing feare the power of Monnshieur Damvile.

The prince and all his do continue in their obedience to the k., and offer all their force to him or his bretherne or to the princes of the bloode,

---

[288] For d'Yvoy, see above, n. 280. His brother was François de Hangest, sieur de Genlis (d. 1569).

[289] Compare 'news from France', 2 September 1562, *CSPF, 1562*, pp. 278–279. For estimates of the size of royal forces in the campaign, see Wood, *King's Army*, pp. 62–65, 315–316.

[290] The Swiss were at Beaugency.

[291] Wolfgang-Wilhelm, Duke of Zweibrucken (Deux-Ponts) (1532–1569).

[292] François III, prince de Marcillac, comte de la Rochefoucauld (d. 1572) was the (Protestant) elder brother of the (Catholic) Charles, sieur de Randan, whose alleged death is mentioned above, n. 287; Symphorien de Durfort, sieur de Duras (c. 1523–1563) was the Protestant leader in Guyenne. This account is over-optimistic as Duras was pinned down by Monluc in Guyenne.

[293] For the prince de Porcien, see above, n. 263.

so as the Gusians, the constable, the Marshall St. Andrewe will retire them selfes who having broken the ordinances of Parliament and have sworne the death of the prince and all the nobilitie of Fr. assysting him. A declaration printed to the declare the causes why the q. sendeth over into Fraunce.[294] A dyalog in Laten betwene ————[295] Men prepared and gathered to send over. The charges of every man coste the countrey 4^{li} at the ~~leas~~ least, ~~as~~ as I sawe in ~~sretfordshire~~ Stretfordshere at the beginning of October.[296]

October 1562
Oure men well receved in Fr. and Newhaven delyvered to them quietly.[297] They finde there grete store of artillarie and 300 sayle in the haven, with grete plenty of fyshe, salte, wode, and brasill.

The erle of Warwick goeth over to be livetenant and Sir Mories Denys thresaurer.[298] Sir Adrian Poininges deputie in the meane tyme, and after marshall.[299]

The quene daungeruslie sicke at Hampton Courte of the small poxe; grete lamentacion made; no man knoweth the certenty for the succession; every man asketh what parte shall we take. She recovereth.[300]

It is saied a parliament shalbe called for two causes, the one for money, the other for the succession.[301]

Dyvers assaultes made to Rhone by the Guysians.

The king of Navar slaine there.[302]

---

[294] *A Declaration of the Quenes Maiestie Elizabeth [...]. Conteyning the Causes which Have Constrayned her to Arme Certaine of her Subiectes, for Defence of Both of Her Owne Estate, and of the Most Christian Kyng Charles the Nynth, Her Good Brother, and his Subiectes* (*STC* 9187.3, 1562); *Harleian Miscellany*, 9 vols (London, 1744–1746), III, pp. 177–181. A Latin version is at *STC* 9187. For French version, see De Fresnoy and Secousse, *Mémoires de Condé*, III, pp. 693–701. Copies and drafts are to be found at PRO, SP70/40/667–674; *CSPF, 1562*, pp. 311–314.

[295] *Dialogus Contra Papistarum Tyrannidem. Interloctuores. Aulus Cecinna. Cneus Heluidus. 10. Augusti. 1562* (*STC* 19175, 1562); *A Dialogue Agaynst the Tyrannye of the Papistes. Translated out of Latin into Englysse, by E.C.* (*STC* 19176, 1562).

[296] Archer, 'Gazeteer'. Compare above, nn. 248, 277. The troops in London were put in readiness again on 16 September and handed over to their captains on 19 September.

[297] The advance guard of the expeditionary force under Poynings landed at Newhaven on 4 October.

[298] Sir Maurice Denys (c. 1516–1563); *HoP, 1509–1558*, II, pp. 31–33.

[299] Sir Adrian Poynings (c. 1515–1571) arrived before Warwick and was acting commander at the outset of the campaign. *CSPF, 1562*, pp. 326–327, 342; *HoP, 1558–1603*, III, pp. 241–242.

[300] The crisis of Elizabeth's attack of smallpox occurred between 10 and 20 October.

[301] For the priority of the succession issue, see Alford, *Early Elizabethan Polity*, pp. 104–109.

[302] See below, n. 307.

[fo. 369v]

200 Engl. men and 300 Scottes in Rhone stoutly deffended the grete breache. Leighten captein.[303]

Monngomery captein there declareth him self a stout man and sendeth for his wief and childerne thither to declare that he mente to bestowe his and their lives there.[304]

The Q. Mother maketh grete meanes to ———— and offered him a blanck to make his owne condycions. He refuseth all and will do nothing withowte the prince of Condie.

The Londoners muche troubled with the commyssion for keping of horses, because they would not finde cassockes to be gownes. In the ende they finde yt soe.[305]

Rhone taken the ———— daie of this moneth. Dyvers put to execution besides the comen slaughter and emongest the Marlecorne [?] the towne sacked, neither papist nor protestant spared.[306] The king of Navar was hurte dedly at the siege of Rhone, wherof at leingth he dieth, but before he spake with the Quenes Mother lamenting muche that for the desire of a wordly kingdome, he wente aboute to lose the kingdom of heaven, and exhorteth her to take heade of her self and her children.[307]

[303] Elizabeth had forbidden English troops to assist at Rouen, but Cuthbert Vaughan persuaded Poynings to send the token force of 200, which arrived on 9 October. For Thomas Leighton (1535–1611), see *HoP, 1558–1603*, II, pp. 458–460. The English bore the brunt of the defence of the breach made in the final assault on 26 October. PRO, SP70/43, fo. 731; D'Aubigné, *Histoire universelle*, II, p. 88. The fullest account of the English participation in the defence of Rouen can be found in Amos C. Miller, *Sir Henry Killigrew: Elizabethan Soldier and Diplomat* (Leicester, 1963), pp. 84–88, but for a recent reassessment of English involvement in Normandy, see Trim, ' "Foundation of the British army?" '. We are grateful to David Trim for his advice on the campaign.

[304] Gabriel de Lorges, sieur de Montgomery (c.1530–1574), who had mortally wounded Henri II at the fatal tournament of 1559, was commander of the Rouen garrison. Despite Vaughan's indignation ('a man of that coraige and putacon to steale awaye leavinge his wyef and children behind', BL, Additional MS 35381, fo. 85), the Earl of Warwick wrote to the Queen that Montgomery had 'escaped narrowly with his life at Rouen [and] is in great repuation here amongst them'; *CSPF, 1562*, p. 409). So Montgomery's reputation among the French, at any rate, survived his escape from Rouen. His family were released and after Montgomery's death had protection and help from Burghley and Essex. We are grateful to David Trim for his help with this note.

[305] Curiously there is no record of the activities of this commission in the London records.

[306] Rouen fell on 26 October. Joan Davies has suggested to us that 'Marlecorne' may be a garbled version of the name of Antoine Marlorat, the Huguenot pastor who was executed after the fall of the city. For the siege and the fate of the city's inhabitants, see A. Heron (ed.), 'Discours abbregé et memoires d'aulcunes choses advenues tant en Normandye que en France depuis le commencement de l'an 1559, et principalement en la ville de Rouen', in *Deux chroniques de Rouen* (Rouen, 1900); P. Benedict, *Rouen During the Wars of Religion* (Cambridge, 1981), pp. 99–102, 113 (for Marlorat).

[307] Navarre was fatally wounded on 16 October, and died on 17 November at Les Andelys; De Fresnoy and Secousse, *Mémoires de Condé*, IV, pp. 116–119.

Novembr 1562

Newes of the distruction of ~~the~~ 26 gallies that cam owte of Spaine towardes Ger. as appereth by the bill.

A grete miracle ~~th~~ of god that hindereth the papistes purposes. 25 shippes at that time burnte in the river of Civill by neglygence of fier in the colking of one.[308]

The parliament somoned to be the xi[th] of January at Westm.[309]

The Erle Huntley in Scott. conspired against the L. James and others, mynding to have taken the q. owte of his handes, and to have subverted relligion. But in the field he was taken, and in the iorney toward the court ~~of~~ he fell from his horse and brake his neck. Both his sonnes put to death.[310] A newe dissease in L. and els where of the cough wherof many died.[311]

The prince of Condie with his power commeth towardes Paris. The duke in haste departeth from thence.[312]

Decemb. 1562

Lettres sent for the lending of houndred poundes throughe owte the realme.[313]

---

[308] The fleet under Juan de Mendoza had been prepared for action against Moorish pirates in Sardinia. The ships were wrecked off Velez Malaga in July; *CSPF, 1562*, p. 394.

[309] The writs for the parliament were issued on 10 November.

[310] George, Earl of Huntly had become disaffected by his displacement from the earldom of Moray by Lord James Stewart. When Mary went on progress in the north in August 1562 she found Inverness initially barred to her by his captain, who refused to allow her to enter without permission from Huntly or his son Lord Gordon. Huntly was declared an outlaw and died, probably of apoplexy, on the battlefield at Corrichie near Aberdeen on 28 October. Two of his sons were captured, but only one, Sir John, was killed; J. Wormald, *Mary Queen of Scots: A Study in Failure* (London, 1988), p. 123.

[311] Cf. Royal College of Physicians, *Annals*, I, fo. 22, where it is reported that outbreaks of catarrh accompanied by fever and pleurisy broke out in November and December 1562. We are grateful to Deborah Harkness for this reference.

[312] Condé took Etampes, thirty miles to the south of Paris, on 13 November, but was held off at the strongly defended Corbeil, giving the Parisians time to organize their resistance. The 'Journall' is misleading about Guise's movements, for he entered Paris on 13 November, with Montmorency, boosting the citizens' morale. The royalist forces, reinforced by troops from Spain and Gascony, pursued Condé, catching up with him at Dreux on 19 December. Diefendorf, *Beneath the Cross*, pp. 67–68; R.J. Knecht, *The French Civil Wars* (Harlow, 2000), pp. 99–105.

[313] The privy seal loan raised £43,886 13s 4d. It was repaid out of the proceeds of parliamentary taxation. PRO, E351/1964; BL, Lansdowne MS 102/24.

CERTAYNE BRIFE NOTES OF THE CONTROVERSY BETWENE THE DUKES OF SOMERSET AND DUKE OF NOR[T]HUMBERLAND

British Library, Additional MS 48126, fos 6–16

[fo. 6]

Certayne brife notes of the controversy betwene the dukes of Somerset and duke of Norhumberland who being fellowes togither with the cardinall and after was made knightes togither in Fraunce in a jorne vnder the leading of Charles, duke of Suffolke.[1]

After the deathe of King Henry the eight it appered that the duke of North feared muche the amitie betwene the twoo britherine, the duke of Somerset, Sir Thomas Semer, than lord admirall of Englande, seking with all diligence to vnderstande their humors; and so by lytell and a lytell to compasse them bothe; as he did; and brothe the matter so to passe that the one was condemed by acte of parliament indicta causa; and the other condemned to deathe for suspition of felony, which some butchers hathe escaped, being well proved to haue gonne abowte to murder his ennemy;[2] and so his aspiring head brought them bothe to confusion without land and reason; who after dyed himself by the ordre of lawe without reason; wherein the scriptur was fullfilled: locke what measure yow measure to others, the same shalbe measured to yow agayne.[3]

The duke of North was familiar with them bothe and loved of them bothe and trusted of them bothe and loved of them bothe and trusted of them bothe. And after the consultation of making the duke of Somerset lord protector of the realme and of the kinge's person and therevpon secretely agred and not pronunced; and that the duke of Somerset had well disgested it to be convenient and mete to haue bothe

---

[1] For the invasion of France led by Charles Brandon (d. 1545), Duke of Suffolk, see S.J. Gunn, 'The Duke of Suffolk's march on Paris', *EHR*, 101 (1986), pp. 596–634.

[2] This probably refers to the case of John Abram, butcher in St Nicholas Shambles, who was merely set in the pillory in March 1549 despite having been convicted of hiring one of the King's guard to murder the husband of his beloved: 'by fauor and sute to the Kinges counsell and rewardes geuen punishment was differred till now' (*Wriothesley's Chronicle*, II, p. 8).

[3] For discussion of the rivalry between Somerset and Seymour see Bernard, 'The downfall of Sir Thomas Seymour'. See above pp. 53–54 for some support for Dudley's alleged incitement of Seymour.

and not to be devydid for divers consideracions; and inconveniences that might fawle in partes taking if there shold fawle any inconvenience betwene them, in government as the lyke fell betwene Duke Vmphray and the Cardinall of Winchestre being vncke and great vnkell to the kingh.[4]

[fo. 6v]

The duke of North came to Sir Thomas Semour and tolde him not what was concludid, but what he ment; that the duke of Somerset sholde be the lord protector of the realme; and he sholde haue his voyse to be the governor of the kinge's person, and he sholde haue all the furtheraunce he colde make; Sir Thomas Semour did give the duke great thankes and prayed him that he wolde move it at the counselle's boord; the duke aunswered that he thought not beste to do nor any other elles but only himself king [sic: knowing?] right well if he shode demande himself it was so reasonable a request that he knewe no man wolde denye it him. Whearevpon the nexte day the borde being full, Sir Thomas came in and made his demande and showed his reason; which being ended was never aunswered but straughte the counsell roose vp and departed the counselle's chamber; and the duke of North perceving right well that the duke of Somerset was sore disconted with his brother's demand when vnto him; and tolde him, my lorde, did not I tell yow ever that he wolde withstande all yor intentes and purposes and he only wolde envye yor state and calling to this rome; his harte being so bidge that he will never rest till he do owerthrowe you agayne if yow give him never so smale accountenaunce [?] From which time the duke of Somerset

[fo. 7]

never colde broughke his brother till his deathe and the duke of Northe forsake all his familiartie with Sir Thomas Semer; and ioyned with the duke of Somerset till his heed was of his sholders; and than he begayne

[4] Somerset was referring to the quarrels in the minority of Henry VI between John, Duke of Bedford, one of Henry VI's uncles, who became regent of France, and another uncle, Humphrey, Duke of Gloucester, who was appointed 'protector and defender of the realm and church in England and principal councillor of the king' for the duration of Bedford's absence overseas by the lords in Parliament on 5 December 1422. Gloucester also wanted to be regent or have the governance of the realm, and he repeatedly tried to secure an enhancement of his constitutional position, though in vain (Bernard, 'Downfall of Sir Thomas Seymour', *The Tudor Nobility*, pp. 217–218, 236–237, n. 49, p. 232; *idem, Power and Politics*, pp. 138–139, 155–156, n. 50, 151).

to forsake the duke and to encontre with him whan he had him alone
his brother being gonne; who was very stronge and valiant, for
immediatly after his deathe he did pike quarrelles with him which he
moost diligently he followed to his deathe as being than in the duke of
Somerset howse I might well perceve and see; for as longe as Sir
Thomas Semour lyved, the duke of North never lay out of the duke of
Somersete's howse but was allwayes was at hande and after his deathe
he never lay in his howse but at the busshopp of Elye's howse in
Holburne.[5]

[The following section follows, with a few amendments, the transcription
and notes in A.J.A. Malkiewicz, 'An eye-witness's account of the coup
d'etat of October 1549', *English Historical Review*, 70 (1955), pp. 600–
609.]

In the rebellions' time the duke of North did aske licence he might
goo to Dudley Castell and to see his frendes there, and by that
time he was there, newes came that the lord marques of Northampton
was repulsed at Norwich by the rebelles there;[6] whearevpon the
duke of Somerset than protector sent to the duke of Northumberland,
than earle of Warwicke, to prepare himself to be generall against the
rebelles at Norwhiche, and he sholde haue such plentie of necessaryes
as he

[fo. 7v]

colde wishe for, and that he mynded to come to him, himself; whearevpon Holmes[7] the duke's secretary was soliciter at the courte for the
same; but the duke of Somerset came not, but was strayte in sending
of necessaryes to that proportion as the duke of North required by his
daily lettres; and this was the first grouge that did appeare vttrewardly.[8]
And after the battayle, the duke of North write to the duke of Somerset

---

[5] Thomas Gooderick[e] or Gooderich (d. 1554), Bishop of Ely.

[6] William Parr (1513–1571), brother of Henry VIII's queen, Catherine Parr, created
Marquess of Northampton in February 1547.

[7] John Holmes (by 1529–1583): *HoP, 1509–1558*, II, p. 381.

[8] Warwick's hostility to Somerset dated back, in the eyes of the writer of this text,
to the very beginning of Somerset's protectorate; during Kett's rebellion, Warwick
voiced it openly for the first time, and stirred up hostility to Somerset among his
forces.

to haue in reversion ii offices after Sir Andrew Flammocke[9] for my
Lord Ambrose his son; ~~now e~~[10] in consideration of his seruice who was
one with the first that entred the gate vpon the rebelles; the which
offices were giuen to Thomas Fisher,[11] one of the duke of Sormerset
chambre being mortall ennemy to the duke of North who take it very
euell, both to goo without his request and to haue it bestowed as it
were in spyte upon his ennemye; whearevpon the duke of North
beganne to move the hole nobilitie and gentil men, that was with him
in that iorney against the duke of Somers[et], calling him secretely to
suche of his acquaint[ance] as he might trust, a coward, a breaker of
promes, a nigard, covitous and ambitious, and suche a one as never
none of service colde hope to haue any good bye; excepte thei wolde
flatter, ley, and play the knav[e] as Fisher did; by which meanes the
duke of Somerset was dedly hated amongst the hole campe;

---

[9] Sir Andrew Flammock, a Warwickshire knight, soldier, sailor and courtier,
rewarded with monastic lands and episcopal leases for his service to the crown. He
was a neighbour of John Dudley, from whom he bought the site of Kenilworth
Abbey (*CPR, Edward VI, 1549–1551*, p. 58). On 6 September 1549 Flammock, who
had accompanied Warwick against Kett, made a will (PCC 45 Populwell), appointing
the earl its overseer and bequeathing him his best horse. The offices in question
were probably those under the Duchy of Lancaster, viz. those of constable of
Kenilworth and bailiff of the duchy liberty in Warwickshire. As early as 1540, when
Flammock and his son both fell sick and the son died while on a visit to Dudley at
Dudley, the latter wrote to Cromwell asking for 'the office of Kenilworth' after
Flammock's expected death. Dudley added that he was sorry to write it since, if
Flammock were to die, the king 'shall lose a tall man of him' (*LP*, XV, p. 386;
XII.i, p. 389 for office). Flammock died soon after Somerset's fall: both offices were
then promptly granted to Ambrose Dudley (R. Somerville, *History of the Duchy of
Lancaster*, 2 vols (London, 1953), I, pp. 561, 563).
[10] Mr Malkiewicz points out that 'several deletions, which cannot be the result of
carelessness, but only of deliberate changes in wording, indicate that we have to deal
with an original, or less probably, with the work of a copyist of initiative'; 'it must have
been his intention to call Lord Ambrose Dudley "now earl of Warwick", indicating that
this text could not have been written before that creation, namely 1561' (Malkiewicz, 'An
eye-witness's account', p. 600).
[11] Thomas Fisher (1516/7–1577), son of a Warwick fishmonger, served John Dudley as
steward of Kibworth Beauchamp, but by late 1543 was in the service of Edward Seymour,
Earl of Hertford, and had become his secretary by 1547. He served at Pinkie that year,
again in campaign with Francis Talbot (1500–1560), fifth Earl of Shrewsbury in 1548, and
once more on the Scottish borders in summer 1549 (*APC*, II, pp. 225, 323). It is not clear
why Dudley should have regarded Fisher as his 'mortall ennemy': possibly he was
concerned by Fisher's acquisition of church lands in Warwickshire (*CPR, Edward VI, 1548–
1549*, pp. 189–191, 342–345, 403; *1559–1551*, p. 19), and now at Fisher's acquisition of the
reversion of offices in Warwickshire he had long sought. And see below, nn. 13, 15; *HoP,
1509–1558*, II, pp. 136–138.

[fo.8]

making his owne case every man's; and so at their departure whom, every gentilman there fell in a great lyking of the duke of North and in a great praysing of him, in the dispysing, despraysing, and hatred of the duke of Somerset,[12] in so muche as Thomas Fisher, being sent northwarde to see the campe upon the borders, hard such rounde speches generall against his master and that in the fauor of the duke of Northumberland,[13] that he did feare great inconveniences wolde followe if the matter were not taken vp betwene them and the duke of North wonne and quieted; whearevpon he write a lettre to the master of the requestes than being Master Walpoole,[14] that in any wyse the duke of Somerset sholde see him ful[ly] recompensed for this his service donne; and that he sholde not sticke to give him iij or iiij mannors of his owne to wynne him, for he shawe elles great incoveniences lyke to ensve;[15] the which perswasion came to none effecte, but his counsell neglected, a rather a greater gruge on the duke of Somersete's parte towardes him, for there was no request that he made after his returne but he had a repulse and wente without it; in so much the duke of North was quite in despayre for ever having any lawfull fauor at the duke of Somersete's handes; so beganne to vnder mynde him; and to bringe his purpose the better to passe he went to laye at the kinge's

[12] Warwick is here clearly seen as plotting vigorously against Somerset soon after he had crushed Kett's rebellion at the end of August. There is, however, no supporting evidence, as D.M. Loades points out (Loades, *John Dudley, Duke of Northumberland*, p. 129).

[13] Fisher was indeed sent to the northern borders and on 17 September wrote, 'in such misery and shortness of life as I never was before', about the great difficulties that the English military campaign was then facing (*CSPSc., 1547–1563*, pp. 178–179). It is intriguing that Warwick should be seen as so popular and Somerset so hated by soldiers on the borders, if the author of our text is to be believed, but in the circumstances it would not have been at all surprising for the soldiers to rail at whomever was responsible for their plight.

[14] John Walpole (by 1522–1557), lawyer and Norfolk landowner, who died in 1557 as a serjeant-at-law (PRO, C142/114/2; *HoP, 1509–1558*, III, pp. 537–538), and who in these years was evidently close to Fisher and to Cecil (whom he succeeded in Somerset's household court of requests) before Somerset's fall. D.M. Loades points out that no such letter survives (Loades, *John Dudley, Duke of Northumberland*, p. 129).

[15] Thomas Fisher's attempts at conciliation failed; he was held in prison after Somerset's fall until February 1550, fined £1,000 (*APC*, III, pp. 393, 398) and though he was pardoned and the fine cancelled in March 1551 (*CPR, Edward VI, 1550–1553*, p. 8; *1553*, p. 408)), imprisoned again between October 1551 and May 1552 (*HoP, 1509–1558*, II, p. 137). He was clearly on good terms with William Cecil (PRO, SP10/4 no. 36; 10/10 no. 23). It has been suggested (by S.M. Thorpe/Jack, *HoP, 1509–1558*, II, p. 137) that this account of the overthrow of Somerset 'may be thought, both in respect of its viewpoint and by reason of the prominence which it gives to Fisher, to have been of his own composing': and that 'he could have been encouraged to write it to Cecil, with whom he was to remain on close terms throughout his life'.

howse at Grinwich[16] wheare he had rome to consulte and coonferre
with his frendes without any suspition; and the king went from
Westminster to Hampton Courte; and the duke of Somerset and the
duches were in Hampshier of hunting and sporting,[17] whyle the duke
of Northe was thoroly occupyed with conferring with all the duke's
ennemyes as well those that was for religion as other wayes; and so
broughte by his pollicy the hole faction vpon his negke vpon a pretence
that Quene Mary sholde be requent[18] and the duke to be pulled downe
from his protectorshipp.

The duke of Somerset left my lady and came on Twisday to the
courte; on Wednisday came thither my lord treasorer,[19] on of the duke
of North counsellors, and told the duke of Somerset that there was
many poore men did daly grye out to him for mony that the king
oughte them requiring his grace to syne his warrant for the payment
or

[fo. 9]

elles he must nides sende them to his grace; for he colde not elles be
ridde of them. Whearevpon the duke did syne his bill for the payment
of a very geat some,[20] which mony was in ded for the furtheraunce of
the duke of North interprise agaynist the duke of Somerset for the
nexte day after the duke did repent him of it uery much vpon hearing

---

[16] HMC, *Twelfth Report, Appendix. Part iv. MSS of the Duke of Rutland*, I, p. 44.

[17] *HMCS*, I, no. 317; *CSPSp.*, *1547–1549*, pp. 456–459. Mr Malkiewicz points out that
Somerset must have been totally unaware of the conspiracy.

[18] Although Somerset would endorse such a rumour (see below fo. 10), van der Delft,
the imperial ambassador, writing on 8 October, doubted it, since he had heard nothing
from the council to that effect: *CSPSp.*, *1547–1549*, p. 459. In September van der Delft,
aware of rivalries among councillors and increasing plotting against Somerset, was
concerned lest Mary, whom some of these councillors were sounding out, should be
trapped into an unwise commitment (*CSPSp.*, *1547–1549*, pp. 445–457, 449; J.S. Berkman,
'A reappraisal of the attack on Protector Somerset', *Bulletin of the Institute of Historical
Research*, 53 (1980), pp. 247–252). The writer of this text clearly saw any overtures that
Warwick made to councillors and noblemen with Catholic sympathies as merely tactical:
van der Delft, the imperial ambassador, noted on 8 October how 'as all the foremost
councillors are catholics, it may be that the earl of Warwick intends to range himself on
their side, for he has forbidden his household to eat meat on Fridays' (*CSPSp.*, *1547–1549*,
p. 458).

[19] William Paulet (c. 1483–1572), created Lord St John in 1539, from 19 January 1550
Earl of Wiltshire, and from 11 October 1551 Marquis of Winchester, Lord Great Master,
and from 2 February 1550, Treasurer. He was one of several signatories to a letter written
by Somerset to Lord Cobham on Friday 4 October, so the text is incorrect (BL, Harleian
MS 284, fo. 46: P.F. Tytler, *England in the Reigns of Edward VI and Mary*, 2 vols (London,
1839), I, pp. 211–212).

[20] On 3 October 1549 warrants were issued for large sums of money for military and
naval purposes: *APC*, III, pp. 328–329.

somme inkeling of their confederacy; for on Fryday nexte there was a
common talke at the courte that the duke of North was a traytor, on
Satterday the earle of Arundell was also taken and reputed for one;
whearevpon lettres were writen in the kinge's name immediatly that all
the counsell solde he at the courte ~~on Sonday in the~~ on Sonday[21] vpon
their allegiance; so that the same evening there was great cariage came
to the courte with all the lordes' stuffe against the nexte day; the duches
was sent for in all the haste, who came to the courte on Saterday at
nighte after the son set; and towardes bed time every man begayne to
prepayre himself to watche and not to

[fo. 9v]

defende himself from his ennemyes; abowte iiij of the clocke there came
a post from London that at his coming from the[re], there was suche
a sorte of horse men in the stretes that he colde not nomber them; he
thoughte there was abowte ij [ml] at the leaste; whearevpon the duke of
Somerset and the hole courte did ryse and every man to his weapon,
the which being knowen to the adversary, the horsemen was stayed at
London, and came not out; for all the duke's men did watche all the
nighte, and the hole courte was redy or euer the horse men colde
com[e]; for the did mynde to haue taken the duke of Somerset in his
bed; and that being discoured thei stayed; but the duk[e] of Somerset
went forward for his defence, being himself well armed and all the
courte in so much as all the bla[cke] garde stode in the great courte,
every one with a spite in his hande; and the stones in the courte was
digged up and carryed vp unto the leades ower the g[ate]; great logges
rampierrd vp at the bac[ke] gate that thei solde not enter no way but
at the courte gate and that was in ha[n]d to be trenched by the duke's
one appointement;[22] and he himself made an oratio[n]

[fo. 10]

on this manner ~~the~~ to this effecte in the great courte. By cause youe
sholde not marwell at thies sturres and vprores, you shall vnderstand
that my lord of Warwicke and certayne other lordes be assembled at

<hr>

[21] Somerset sent out letters on Saturday, 5 October to all subjects to repair armed and
with all haste to Hampton Court to defend the king and the Protector, against whom a
most dangerous conspiracy has been attempted (PRO, SP10/9/1–2; cf. Hoak, *King's
Council*, p. 327, n. 63).

[22] The fortifying of the gates at Hampton Court, as well as the arming of the King's
and of Somerset's servants, is mentioned in Edward VI's journal: Nichols, *Literary Remains*,
II, pp. 235–236.

London, and is mynded to make the Lady Mary regent and pulle downe me from the protectorshipp; but if you call unto mynd the story of King Richard, what devyses he had to make me self king: first to be protector and to haue the gouernement, and after murdered his two nephies, King Edward the v[th] and his brother; you may well perceve thei do not seeke me but the king; for if he were in their ha[n]des and shode miscary, thei had that thei seeke; but being in my custody, I do kepe him as the apple of my eye; whose helth is my comforthe and prefarment, and whose dethe is my fawle and ruyne; and so by all reason I sholde be as carefull of the good preseruation of his person as of my owne body and sowle. And therefore as I haue bine chosen by the good advise of his highnes' counsell, and by consent of all the piers of the realme, to be protector of his Majestie's realme, dominion, and person; so I will defende my cauling, till it shall please his Majestie

[fo. 10v]

by the advise of his consell and his said piers, to discharge me of the same; and that you shall well perceve that it is gode's quarrell and the kinge's, I myself will be one of the first that will dye in the gate, if thei come in by any forcible manner into the courte. Whearevpon all thei that stode by, with a lowde uoice thei all wolde dye and leve in the quarrell, whear[e]vpon postes was sente out in to all the partes of the realme; ~~that at~~ with lettres vnder the kinge's ha[n]d, the L Protector's hande and the rest of his previe counsell there, as Tomas Cranmer, archebusshopp of Caunterbury (who came in accorde to the kinge's lettre[s] sent the day before, accompanyed with lx horse), Sir William Paget, the comptrolor, Sir Thomas Smithe, secretary,[23] and vnder the kinge's signet; and or ever it was xij. of the clocke, there was great resorte of piople dwelling in the townes by with such weapons as thei had and armour; so that there was capitayne appointed to chose the moost hable for their purpose and to returne the reste for scarnesse of uitall.[24] The king sent to the lordes lying at London Sir William Petre,

---

[23] Sir Thomas Smith (1513–1577), scholar, close servant of Protector Somerset, serving as his secretary, author of the *Discourse of a Commonweal*, fell with his master in October 1549.

[24] Van der Delft, imperial ambassador, reported on 8 October how in response to Somerset's appeals over 4,000 peasants immediately assembled, and how Somerset then 'had the peasants divided into squadrons and assigned them quarters as if he expected to fight': Somerset, the councillors in London would allege, had 'called in the peasants to oppress the nobility and make himself master and tyrant of all' (*CSPSp.*, *1547–1549*, pp. 457–458). For consideration of the wider implications, see R.W. Hoyle, 'Petitioning as popular politics in early sixteenth-century England', *Historical Research*, 190 (2002), pp. 365–389; G.W. Bernard, 'New perspectives and old complexities', *EHR*, 115 (2000), p. 119.

one of his secretaryes, and thei did retayne him with them, wheare-
at the king did not a lytell marwell of their boldnes. The king sent
Wulfe

[fo. 11]

one of his previe chamber, secretely to take the Tower of London, and
to prepare for the king;[25] and or euer he came, it was taken by the
lordes, for lighting at Batell Brige he might see Sir William Pawlet,
earle of ~~Winchester~~ Willsher,[26] Sir Richard Sothewell and others take
the Tower for the lordes; whearevpon he returned with all speed, and
met the king on horsebacke, tur[n]ing towardes London at Hampton
Courte, going to Kingeston;[27] and so went to Wyndesor without any
warni[n]g or any manner of provision, and came thither abowte
midnighte, and after in the nighte came the cariage from Hampton
Courte and was there by iij of the clocke after midnighte; and but iiij.
tune of wynne and no great quantetie of beare for suche a company;
and fonde lytell provition of any thing at their arryval at Windesore,
by the soden coming;[28] there was great sending a brode by the authoritie
abowesaid, by the king, and the L Protector and the rest of his counsell
with him for all thinges necessary, vnder their ha[n]des and the kinge's
privie seale; and my Lord Riche, than lord chauncellor, sent in every
quarter (being

[25] See 'Journall', n. 29 for Wolf. Somerset had 'gyven order that the Tower shuld be
kept in sorte as none of his Majestes Counsail nor none other might enter into the same;
the councillors in London opposed to Somerset send for the Lieutenant of the Tower,
Sir Edmund Peckham, and ordered him to allow certain others to enter' (*APC*, III, p.
332).

[26] See above, n. 19.

[27] Mr Malkiewicz points out that if the king was on horseback 'going to kingeston',
he must have been on his way from Hampton Court to London; no doubt it was the
news of Wolf's failure that led Somerset to fall back on Windsor (Malkiewicz, 'An eye-
witness's account', p. 606, n. 2).

[28] The lords in London, on learning that Somerset had taken the king to Windsor
Castle, 'where was no maner of provision', were 'most sorrowful for the same', and
'moved with an inestimable care [...] of the good preservacion of hys majestie', ordered
on 7 October that all necessary provisions should be sent to Windsor (*APC*, III, p. 333).
Somerset, the lords in London noted on 9 October, 'had openly said in a great presence
of sundry gentlemen and others at Wyndsour that if the lordes intended his death, that
the kinges majestie should dye before him, and if they intended to famisshe him they
shuld also famishe his majestie' (*APC*, III, pp. 341–342).

[fo. 11v]

on the lordes' syde against the king) vnder the broode seale of England
to discharge their commission; so that the kinge's provison that he made
an assured accompte of, both for men an[d] uitall, was disappointed by
his trustie chaunecellor, having more attoritie by the greate scale than
the king and the protector had with the reste of his counsell, whose
Majestie being destitute of all manner of necessaryes, was compelled
to sende vnto the lordes eftsones to know the cause of their grife; and
Sir Philipp Hoby than being the kinge's ambassator resident with
Charles the vth Emperor, came ower vpon certayne speciall affayres,[29]
and came to the courte lying at Hampton Courte on Sonday in the
morning, of whom the king and the protector had a very good opinion,
of the rather for that thei toke him to be faythefull and trustie and no
partie; and therefore committed him in speciall trust to goo to the
lordes ~~both~~, with instructions, both in wordes and writing with the
kinge's [lettre?] verbatim as followeth

[Fos 12–13 are king's letter to the lords, dated 8 October 1549, printed
from PRO, SP10/9/24 by Tytler, *England in the Reigns of Edward VI and
Mary*, I, pp. 220–223.]

[fo. 13]

Who [i.e. Hoby] the nexte day after was returned from the lordes lying
at London towardes the king lying at Windesore; with divers lettres
and instructions against the lord protector; and for the better accom-
plishing of the matter

[fo. 13v]

he fayned that he had loste the lordes' lettres to the king by the
negligence of his man, and wolde not truste any body, but returned
himself to seeke the lettres, and if he colde not fynde them to optayne
newe of the lordes;[30] and sente for his excuse one of his trustie servantes

---

[29] Sir Philip Hoby (1504/5–1558), diplomat from the late 1530s (*HoP, 1509–1558*, II, pp.
366–368), was with Emperor Charles V from May 1548 to August 1550. One of the
causes of his brief return to England in October 1549, according to the imperial
ambassador, was that he was offended that Somerset had given certain offices which
Hoby coveted and which had become vacant on the death of Sir Anthony Denny on 10
September 1549, to others. Consequently, van der Delft wrote, Hoby had not tried to do
anything for Somerset in the present business (*CSPSp., 1547–1549*, p. 460).

[30] Cf. BL, Harleian MS, 363 fo. 77, quoted in Tytler, *England in the Reigns of Edward VI
and Mary*, I, p. 231.

to the courte to declare what misfortune his master had, and the cause of his longe tarying, with this generall wordes from his master that all was wel[l] and the kinge's pleasure was fulfilled in all pointes; which made the hungery and thrustie soules glad at the courte, and made the best sorte negligente, presuming of a reasonable aunswere; by which smoth messenger there was sent divers lettres of instructions to my Lord William Haward, the lord marshall of the kinge's oste;[31] and to divers others, both of the privie chamber and of the household, and to as many as was thoughte not to fauor the lord protector; with proclamations of xxix articles of high treason in printe against the lord protector,[32] the which was advisedly distributed to all the good fellowes of credite of every office, who keping in corners as the multitude went to the horses of office in the morninge, turned in a

[fo. 14]

moment all the courte, saing to every of their acquaintance tell nothing to any man in payne of deathe; so that before all such or for the moost parte that an hower before wold haue dyed and lyved with the lord protector, were in mynd to dye against him, with a generall uoices of hatred against him and all his; so that by ix of the clocke the nexte morninge[33] all the courte were conformable to Sir Philipp Hoby to do what he wolde haue them do with a becke; and as sowne as he arryuell at the castell gate, all the waye he tolde them all was well, and thereupon my Lord William Haward caused the trompet to be blowen and gave licence to all the soldiers to departe, and thei were so glad that well was he that cold get first out of the castell gate as by that time Sir Philipp Hoby was in the great chamber all were gonne in to the towne, but the kinge's howseholde seruauntes only; than was a new proclamation that no man shode weare weapon but the kinge's seruantes only within the courte; and the gates to be shotte, and no man to come in but only the kinge's seruauntes;[34] and ha to tracte the time

---

[31] William Howard (c.1510–1573), in 1554 created Lord Howard of Effingham.
[32] See J. Stow, *Annals* (1631 edn), p. 600.
[33] 10 October: cf. BL, Cotton MS Caligula B VII, fo. 410, printed in G, Burnet, *History of the Reformation of the Church of England*, N. Pocock (ed.), 7 vols (Oxford, 1865), V, p. 282.
[34] Cf. Northamptonshire Record Office, Fitzwilliam Correspondence, no. 21, fo. 20a.

[fo. 14v]

to serue the purpose, he tolde the king and the lord protector that he had lettres to eche of them, but he colde not deliver them but by the ~~counselles~~ lordes' order in the presence of them both in the chambre of presence, before all the kinge's howsholde and the gardre, that the sholde beare witnes of their true meaning towardes the king and aunswere for the causes of thies tumultes; and at the conclusion of all his talkes all is well, and the king hathe his desire; and so solemly the king came in to the chambre of the presence with the lord protector, and all the reste of his counsellors and privie chamber being full of the kinge's howsholde and of the garde; the lettres of this gratefull newes was red, fur other wayes than thei beleved; for in one lettre was to the king, what a great traytor the lord protector was, and in how many cases of high treason he had offended in; and therefore he was committed to xij of the yemen of the garde in custody till further of their pleasures, and so was the rest of the counsell there, ~~sauing~~ as Sir Thomas Smyth, Sir Mihell Stanhope, and others; and the king was committed into the tuition of Sir Thomas Rogers, knight.[35]

[fo. 15]

The next day after came to the courte from the lordes Sir Anthony Wingefild, capitayne of the garde and feechamberlade,[36] accompanyed with v^c horse, and toke the duke out of his chamber and broughte him to Beauchampe's Tower; on Saterday came the lordes to the courte; who after thei had ordered all thinges as thei thoughte best sent the lord protector with a stronge gard of horsemen to the Tower of London, with all the rest that was taken prisoners at Wyndesore, and elleswheare in gathering any power.[37] In this the protector's troble the Lord Wriotheley was very busye to followe him to deathe, by cause he being lord chauncellor of England at the deathe of King Henry the viiith was sore against him to be made protector, wheareupon he was put from

---

[35] Sir Edward Rogers (1498/1502–1568), courtier and Somerset landowner, whom the Lords appointed on 15 October as one of the four principal gentlemen of the Privy Chamber. He was a committed Protestant (*APC*, III, p. 345). For Stanhope, see 'Journall', n. 29.

[36] Sir Anthony Wingfield (by 1488–1552), served in several of Henry VIII's military campaigns (*HoP, 1509–1558*, III, pp. 638–640). Cf. *APC*, III, p. 342 for the lords of the council sending him to Windsor on 10 October; PRO, SP10/9 no. 42 for Wingfield's report from Windsor on 11 October.

[37] Mr Malkiewicz's transcript ends here.

his office and was fyne to submitte himself for the safetie of the reste.[38] Who for his wit and earnestnes was put in trust to be in commission with the earle of Arundell[39] and the earle of Wilshire[40] to examen the protector in the Tower of sertayne articles concerning his treasons in his governement; who aunswered them all directly that thei were done from article to article by the advise, consent, and counsell of

[fo. 15v]

the earle of Warwicke; and after the examination don, my Lord Wriotheslay, being hote to be rewengid of them bothe for older groges paste whan he loste his office, said to my lordes in commission, I thoughte ever we sholde fynde them traytors bothe; and bothe is worthie to dye for by my advyse; my Lord of Arundell in lyk maner gave his consente that thei were bothe worthie to dye; and concludid there that the day of execution of the lord protector, the earl of Warwicke shode be sent to the towarde and haue as he had deserved; the earle of Wilshire, howsoever he did temper his langewage there, the same night he went to my lord of Warwicke lying in Holburne and tolde him of all was donne; and bad him beware howe he did prosecute the lord protector's deathe; for he shode suffer himself for the same; who giving good care to his persuasion bente himselfe all he colde to save the protector's lyfe; and procured by the meanes of the archebusshoppe of Canterbury[41] great frendes abowt the king to preserve the lord protector and ioyned togither in the same all he colde for his lyfe; and by cause there was divers catholickes called in to counsell at that instante for the Lady Marye's sake, she hoping to haue bine regent, thei founde the frends that the Lord Marques Dorset[42] and Goodrick, busshopp of

---

[38] Thomas Wriothesley (d. 1550), Earl of Southampton had fought a losing battle to stop Somerset becoming Protector in 1547: see Hoak, *King's Council*, ch. 7; Bush, *Government Policy of Protector Somerset*, p. 80. Southampton failed: on 6 March 1547 he was dismissed, allegedly because of a complaint against him by some common lawyers, but the real reason was his opposition to the establishment of the protectorate. Hoak argues that Southampton was forced out 'not because the earl had remained a Henrician Catholic or because the common lawyers may have opposed his practices, but because [he] had from the very beginning opposed [Hertford]'s creation as Protector'. (Hoak suggests that Southampton may have refused to affix the great seal to letters confirming Somerset's elevation.) Hoak, *King's Council*, pp. 43–45, 231–239; Slavin, 'Fall of Wriothesley', pp. 276–286.

[39] Henry Fitzalan (1512–1580), Earl of Arundel.

[40] See above, n. 19

[41] Thomas Cranmer, Archbishop of Canterbury (1489–1556).

[42] Henry Grey, Marquess of Dorset, later Duke of Suffolk (d. 1554).

[fo. 16]

of Eley[43] to be of the privie counsell to encountre the other syde in nombre being protestantes; and all the hole counsell comming to Holburne Place wheare the earle of Warwicke laye sicke for the nonce; my Lord Wriothesley beganne to declare how worthie the lord protector was to dye and for how many high treasons; the earle of Warwicke hearing his owne condemnation to approche; with a warlyke wisage and a long fachell by his syde laye his hand thereof and said; my lord, yow seeke his bloud and he that seeketh his bloud wolde haue myne also; vpon his great earnestnes and sound speches being so well assisted, put all the rest to silence; and there presently ordre was taken for the duke's libertie; and the earle of Arundell and the Lord Wriothesley were commanded to kepe their howses, and so my Lord Wriothesley seing all his harte was opened against him that once before he had submitted himself to and thought now this acte colde never be forgotten and that his ambissious mynde cold take no place; he killed himself with sorrowe in so muche as he said he wold not live in suche misery if he might.[44]

---

[43] Thomas Gooderick[e] or Goodrich, Bishop of Ely. Warwick had earlier lodged at his house in Holborn (see above).

[44] In mid-January 1550 Warwick confronted Arundel and Southampton, who were dismissed from the council, Southampton subsequently dying of grief: cf. Bodl., Ashmole MS 861, fo. 340; S. Brigden (ed.), 'The letters of Richard Scudamore to Sir Philip Hoby, September 1549–March 1555', *Camden Society*, fourth series, 29 (Cambridge, 1990), pp. 107–111; H. James, 'The aftermath of the 1549 coup and the Earl of Warwick's intentions', *Bulletin of the Institute of Historical Research*, 62 (1989), p. 94. J. Poynet, *A Short Treatise of Politike Power* (1556) (*STC*, 20178) offers a comparable account of Southampton's failure : on Somerset's downfall, 'every man repaireth to Wriothesley, honoureth Wriothesley, sueth unto Wriothesley (as the Assirians dod to Ammon) and all things to be done by his advise: and who but Wriothesley?', but the Earl of Warwick 'so handleth the matier, that Wriothesley is fayne in the night to get him out of the court to his own house: wher upon narowe examination, fearing least he should come to some open shamefull ende, he either poisoned himself, or pyned away for thought'. (We owe this reference to Diarmaid MacCulloch).

MEMOIRES ET PROCEDURES DE MA NEGOCIATION EN ANGLETERRE (8 OCTOBER 1582–8 OCTOBER 1583) BY JEAN MALLIET, COUNCILLOR OF GENEVA

Edited by Simon Adams and Mark Greengrass

ACKNOWLEDGEMENTS

We should like to thank Mme. l'Archiviste d'Etat de Genève, Dr. Catherine Santschi, for her kind permission to publish this document. Simon Adams also wishes to record his gratitude to the British Academy, who financed his research in Geneva, and Mrs Gaynor Wilkin, who very kindly prepared a typescript of the text some years ago when editing and publication were first contemplated.

EDITORIAL PRACTICE

Malliet's *Mémoires* is written in a paper book, unbound and unfoliated, in two columns in small neat secretarial hand. It appears to be a fair copy from a missing original.[1] There are the occasional scribal mannerisms, including the writing of two similar consonants as double consonants (these have been corrected silently). Apart from some minor restructuring of the format (including adding foliation) and the extension of the abbreviations, the text has been reproduced in its original form. Paragraphing, accents and the spelling of English names have not been altered.

Dates

Malliet's mission coincided with the progressive adoption of the Gregorian calendar by the Catholic world. Since both England and Geneva retained the Julian calendar, none of Malliet's own dates are affected. However, both Mendoza and Mauvissière followed their home government's adoption of the new calendar (Spain in October and France in December 1582), and references to their despatches and related material in 1583 use the double form.

---

[1] The omission of the name of the minister on p. 189 would appear to be a copyist's error.

Exchange rates

Apart for the occasional use of the *livre tournois* (e.g. on p. 166), Malliet employed almost exclusively the French *écu* [*]. The exchange rate for the *écu* hovered at around 6s or slightly over three to the £1 sterling. On p. 188 below, Malliet supplies one conversion himself: 71d sterling (5s 11d). Note also his conversion of the £100 Walsingham provided for his expenses to 333 *écus* (p. 185). For ease of equation, the rate will be assumed here to be three to one.

INTRODUCTION

The collection raised in England for the financial assistance of Geneva in 1583 has interested historians of the Elizabethan Church from John Strype to Patrick Collinson.[2] A substantial amount of correspondence and other material relating to the collection survives in this country, but the single most important record it has left is the *mémoire* (or report) by Jean Malliet, the agent Geneva sent to England. Together with several files of Malliet's correspondence and accounts, the *mémoire* is now deposited in the Archives d'Etat.[3] In 1911, the Genevan historian, Lucien Cramer, published a number of extracts from it in an article on Malliet's mission.[4] While exploring the Genevan archives for another purpose in 1980, Simon Adams came across the *mémoire*, and shortly afterwards brought it to Patrick Collinson's attention. Collinson encouraged Adams to publish it, but the editing has been delayed by other demands.[5] The long delay has actually proved beneficial for the relevant volumes of the correspondence of Theodore Beza and Henry III of France have only appeared in the winter of 2000–2001.[6] Moreover, Adams has also been able bring to bring his own recent research on English foreign policy in the early 1580s to bear on the editing and Mark Greengrass has kindly volunteered his expertise in Huguenot politics and financing.[7]

The report, *mémoire* or *procès-verbal* presented to the home government at the end of a negotiation was an established feature of French and Netherlandish diplomatic practice in the sixteenth century, though not

---

[2] John Strype, *The History of the Life and Acts of [...] Edmund Grindal* (London, 1710), pp. 278–283, and *Annals of the Reformation and Establishment of Religion [...] during Queen Elizabeth's Happy Reign*, 3 vols (Oxford, 1824), III, pt 1, pp. 127–130. Collinson discusses the collection variously in Patrick Collinson, *Archbishop Grindal 1519–1583: The Struggle for a Reformed Church* (London, 1979), p. 270, *idem*, *The Religion of Protestants: The Church in English Society 1559–1625* (Oxford, 1982), pp. 126–127, and *idem*, 'England and international Calvinism, 1558–1640', in Menna Prestwich (ed.), *International Calvinism 1541–1715* (Oxford, 1985), pp. 205–207.

[3] The report itself is PH 2066. The other files are cited below. There are several variant spellings of his surname: Malliet, Mailliet, and Maillet. In keeping with the usage in the modern literature, Malliet is employed here.

[4] Cramer, 'Malliet'.

[5] Collinson employed Malliet's memoir in 'England and international Calvinism'. Adams has made reference to it in 'Eliza enthroned? The court and its politics', in Christopher Haigh (ed.), *The Reign of Elizabeth I* (Basingstoke, 1985), pp. 75–76.

[6] *Beza*, XXIII (1582) and *Henri*, V (1581–1582). References to both of these series are by consecutive item number.

[7] Provisionally entitled: *The Road to Nonsuch: The Netherlands in English Policy 1575–1585*.

of English or Spanish.[8] The reports frequently repeat information already transmitted by letter, but nonetheless they still contain a wealth of detail about day-to-day negotiations not available in other form. The Genevan collection may not have been an episode of major diplomatic consequence, but Malliet's report provides a snapshot of Protestant England and international Calvinism at work that is without rival. Its importance is heightened when it is recalled that during the reign of Elizabeth I there was only one permanent resident embassy in London, that of the French crown.[9] Better known, owing to the more extensive publication of their correspondence, are the ambassadors of Philip II, but the Spanish embassy was suspended between 1572 and 1578 and terminated in 1584.[10] These were ambassadors from Catholic powers, who negotiated with Elizabeth and her government under a greater or lesser degree of mutual suspicion. Protestant embassies were more sporadic and have left far less record – there are few Protestant reports as detailed as Malliet's.[11]

Background: La guerre de Raconis

Malliet endorsed his *mémoire* as covering the year 8 October 1582 to 8 October 1583, but it actually begins with his arrival in Paris on 21 October 1582 and ends with his arrival in Rouen on 18 September 1583 on his return from England. His mission was a consequence of the Genevan crisis of 1582 – *la guerre de Raconis* – the first of the numerous attempts by Charles-Emanuel, Duke of Savoy (1562–1630), to seize the city by force.[12] On one level, the appeal to England was a comparatively straightforward exercise in Calvinist charity, but the

[8] Relevant Dutch examples are the reports on the treaty of Plessis-lès-Tours with the Duke of Anjou in September 1580, and the various negotiations with France and England in 1584 and 1585. A good French example is the *discours au roi* by the commissioners sent to negotiate the marriage treaty with Elizabeth in April 1581.

[9] The ambassador between 1575 and 1585 was Michel de Castelnau, sieur de Mauvissière. Major historiographical problems have been caused by the erratic survival and even more erratic printing of his diplomatic correspondence. Malliet's mission unfortunately coincides with one of the larger lacunae; nothing survives from Mauvissière between September 1582 and May 1583. However, there are two copies of the *registre* of royal letters to him for the period 1580–1584: BNF, ms. français 3308 and Cinq Cents de Colbert 473 [hereafter VCC 473]. Catherine's letters are printed in Hector de La Ferrière and Gustave Baguenault de Puchesse (eds), *Lettres de Catherine de Médicis*, 10 vols (Paris, 1880–1909), [hereafter *Lettres Catherine*], Henry's to January 1583 in *Henri*, V.

[10] The ambassador between 1578 and 1584 was Don Bernardino de Mendoza, whose surviving correspondence is most accessible in *CSPSp., 1568–1579* and *1580–1586*.

[11] A permanent Dutch embassy began in the summer of 1583, but it is not relevant here.

[12] Named after the Savoyard commander, Bernardin de Savoie, Comte de Raconis, widely believed to have been the instigator of the affair.

crisis had been resolved in August 1582 and thus the necessity for the appeal was open to question. Moreover, Malliet's mission caught the English government and church at an awkward moment. The origins and resolution of the crisis lie in the complex relationship between Geneva, Savoy, the Swiss Confederation, and France, while Malliet's period in England was overshadowed by the tensions between England and France during the winter of 1582–1583. To avoid extensive commentary in the notes to the text on the numerous allusions in his *mémoire*, a brief introductory account is necessary.[13]

Even before the Reformation, the Swiss Confederation was a constitutional nightmare comprising thirteen cantons and a complex web of allies and associates. By the 1580s, religion had added a further layer of complexity. Four of the cantons (Bern, Zurich, Basel and Schaffhausen) were Reformed, two (Glarus and Appenzell) were of mixed religion, while the other seven – the four original 'Forest Cantons' or *Waldstätten* (Uri, Schwyz, Unterwalden, and Zug), together with Lucerne, Freiburg, and Soleure (or Solothurn) – remained staunchly Catholic. Geneva was notoriously not a member of the Confederation, but an ally of Bern under the 'perpetual treaty' of 7 August 1536. This treaty supplemented an earlier alliance of *combourgeoisie*, first made in 1477 and renewed in 1525–1526, 1536 and 1558. Bern's primary motive for protecting Geneva was hostility to the Duke of Savoy and this anti-Savoyard policy inspired both the perpetual treaty and Bern's military intervention in 1536. The subsequent Bernese occupation of the Savoyard territory that lay between it and Geneva (the *pays de Vaud* and the *pays de Gex*) effectively secured Geneva's independence.[14] Bern's enmity to Savoy was shared by the two neighbouring Catholic cantons, Freiburg – which also occupied Savoyard territory (the county of Romont) – and Soleure, but religion made co-operation between them increasingly difficult. Freiburg had joined Bern in the *combourgeoisie* with Geneva of 1526, but resigned from it on religious grounds in 1535.

The interests of the French crown were defined by two distinct but increasingly intertwined concerns. One was its alliance with the Confederation, the '*paix perpétuelle*' created by the Treaty of Freiburg of

---

[13] The following account is derived primarily from J.-A. Gautier, *Histoire de Genève des origines à l'année 1691*, 7 vols (Geneva, 1896–1914), esp. V, pp. 250–298; Edouard Rott, *Histoire de la représentation diplomatique de la France auprès des Cantons Suisses*, 10 vols (Bern and Paris, 1900–1935), esp. II, pp. 239–254; and Cramer, *Seigneurie. Beza*, XXIII supplies considerable further detail and corrects earlier errors.

[14] Only a few directly relevant aspects of Geneva's relationship to Savoy need be summarized here. The Bishop of Geneva was technically sovereign, under the Holy Roman Emperor, and the Duke of Savoy held only the vidamnate within the city. However, since the middle of the fifteenth century the majority of the bishops had been members of the House of Savoy, which had encouraged the dukes to make greater claims.

16 November 1516 and the subsequent military convention, the Treaty of Lucerne of 5 May 1521. The military convention was renewed by Henry II in 1549, by Charles IX in the Treaty of Freiburg of 7 December 1564, and was due for renewal by Henry III by 7 December 1582.[15] The *paix perpétuelle* gave the successive kings of France a vested interest in maintaining the status quo within the Confederation, despite the religious division. Their other concern was Savoy. Thanks to Francis I's occupation of the duchy in 1536, France and Bern became allies against the exiled duke, and this alliance included Geneva. The refusal of the Catholic cantons to admit Geneva to membership of the Confederation, and the failure of Calvin's efforts to negotiate a more formal connection with France left Geneva's survival dependent upon this informal *'paix bienfaisante'*.[16]

The restoration of the duchy of Savoy to Emanuel Philibert (1528–1580) under the Treaty of Cateau-Cambrésis reshaped the diplomatic context. After 1559 the French evacuated the duchy with the exception of five fortresses. These were eventually returned to the duke in 1574, but the continued French occupation of the marquisate of Saluces remained a source of tension. Cateau-Cambrésis did not specifically mention the future of Geneva and the Swiss-occupied territories, but it was understood that the restoration of Emanuel Philibert was to be a complete one. Coincidentally, it was at this point that Geneva's growing prominence in the Reformed world began to attract the universal hostility of the Catholic. Emanuel Philibert now initiated a dual campaign against Geneva, seeking restoration of his rights in the city and the occupied territories by negotiation on the one hand, while simultaneously appealing to the Catholic world for assistance in reducing the seat of heresy by force on the other. He scored an immediate and key diplomatic success in a treaty with six of the Catholic cantons (the four *Waldstätten*, Lucerne, and Soleure) on 11 November 1560, under which they agreed to support his campaign for restoration. The effective isolation of Bern and Freiburg intimidated them into agreeing to a compromise (the treaty of Lausanne) in May 1564. Under this treaty the three *bailliages* immediately surrounding Geneva (Gex, Thonon, and Terrier) were to be restored to Emanuel Philibert, while Bern retained most of the *pays de Vaud* and Freiburg the county of Romont. Once the duke regained possession of the three *bailliages* in the autumn of 1567, Geneva was effectively surrounded by Savoyard territory and, moreover, dependent on Savoy for food. Although the *combourgeoisie* with Berne

---

[15] The convention regulated the terms under which the Confederation supplied a military contingent on demand in exchange for an annual pension for each canton. Zurich had abstained from the 1521 convention and did not join until 1613. Bern abstained from the renewals in 1549 and 1564 on religious grounds.

[16] The phrase is Cramer's, *Seigneurie*, I, p. 38.

was preserved and the ducal rights within the city were still to be decided, future defence against Savoy was now far more difficult. Emanuel Philibert's more ambitious plans to regain Geneva by force proved less successful. Despite some encouragement from the Papacy and the enthusiastic support of Cardinal Borromeo in Milan, he encountered the opposition of successive kings of France and Philip II. For all its expressed abhorrence of the sewer (*sentine*) of heresy, the French crown regarded Geneva as the key to maintaining the *paix perpétuelle* with the Confederation and the civil peace within France.[17] It was taken for granted that both the Protestant cantons and the Huguenots would rally to Geneva's assistance should it be threatened. Philip II had his own reasons for not wishing to alienate Bern and Zurich, for they guaranteed the neutrality of the Franche Comté under a treaty made with the Emperor Maximilian I in 1511. Thus, for all the alarm created in Geneva by the Duke of Alba's march to the Netherlands in 1567, Alba was in fact under strict instructions not to be diverted by Savoy. By 1569 Emanuel Philibert had come to appreciate that effective Catholic support would not be forthcoming and that there was little likelihood that he would regain his rights in the city by arbitration.[18] He therefore agreed to a *modus vivendi* (*mode de vivre*) with Geneva proposed by Bern. In a pair of treaties signed on 5 May 1570 he granted Geneva freedom of trade with his domains for twenty-three years in exchange for Geneva's abstention from any foreign alliance without his approval.

As a further solution to this impasse, Bern revived the earlier efforts to have Geneva admitted into the Confederation. Although the proposal was supported, albeit with mixed feelings, by Freiburg and Soleure, it was firmly rebuffed by the *Waldstätten*. More surprisingly, perhaps, the French crown also emerged as a strong supporter of admission. The motive for this benevolence was the continued strategic interest in preventing future Savoyard expansion. During the 1570s the French became increasingly suspicious of Emanuel Philibert and the threat any increase of his influence within the Confederation could pose to the *paix perpétuelle*. The relationship was further embittered by Emanuel Philibert's charges that French policy was motivated by support for the rival claims on Geneva of his cousin, the Duke of Nemours.

---

[17] The phrase was used by the Cardinal of Lorraine when proposing a Franco-Spanish attack on Geneva on the eve of the death of Henry II; AGS, Estado K 1492, fo. 43a, Duke of Alba to Philip II, 26 June 1559.

[18] In 1568 the six Catholic cantons proposed a compromise over Geneva under which the duke renounced his claim to sovereignty, but retained his right to the vidamnate, though it was to be relinquished to the city in exchange for financial compensation. Emanuel Philibert refused to accept the reduction of his claims, while Geneva refused the financial compensation. See Cramer, *Seigneurie*, I, pp. 183–184.

French influence was seriously weakened by the crisis surrounding the accession of Henry III in 1574. It has recently been argued that the fifth War of Religion (1574–1576) was the decisive shaper of Henry's policies during the following decade, and his Swiss policy was no exception.[19] As they had done in the previous French civil wars, the Catholic cantons provided an important contingent of the royal army. Since St Bartholomew's, Geneva and the Protestant cantons had sheltered a shifting population of Huguenot refugees and exiles, and, while Geneva provided financial assistance to the exiles, Bern supplied troops to the army John-Casimir of the Palatinate led into France in early 1576.[20] The weak financial position of the crown forced Henry into what he considered to be the humiliating surrender of the peace of Monsieur (6 May 1576) and the notoriously enormous compensation awarded to John Casimir and his army. In the event, Henry effectively reneged on paying the compensation, which made John Casimir a bitter enemy during the following years.[21] But at the same time the financial commitments created by the peace of Monsieur effectively prevented Henry from honouring the claims of the allied Swiss, to whom substantial arrears of pension were also due.

Emanuel Philibert now saw his chance to capitalize on Catholic disenchantment with France by offering an alternative military alliance of his own. The Treaty of Lucerne with the four *Waldstätten*, Lucerne, and (eventually) Freiburg was agreed on 8 May 1577 and concluded in August 1578.[22] This more or less open out-bidding exercise was accompanied by increased tension with France over Saluzzo. In an equally obvious counter to Savoy – or perhaps more accurately act of revenge for the treaty of Lucerne – in July 1578 Henry proposed to Bern and Soleure that Geneva now be included in the alliance between France and the Confederation. Soleure was unwilling to recognize the Genevan regime so formally and, after considerable negotiation over the winter of 1578–1579, a more complex agreement was reached in the treaty of Soleure, agreed on 8 May 1579 and ratified by Henry on 29 August. Although Geneva itself was not one of the contracting parties, Henry agreed to subsidize whatever measures Bern and Soleure found necessary to protect the city from any future threat. Moreover, Huguenot assistance was also permitted: 'si aucuns des subjects de Sadicte

---

[19] This theme is developed in Pierre Chevallier, *Henri III roi shakespearien* (Paris, 1985), p. 324 *et seq.*

[20] Pfalzgraf or duke (1543–1592), younger son of the Elector Palatine Frederick III, an enthusiastic if impulsive supporter of Protestant crusades. *Briefe Johann Casimir* is an excellent edition of his correspondence.

[21] However, the death of his father and the succession of his Lutheran brother, Louis VI, in October 1576 crippled him financially and militarily.

[22] To win over Freiburg, Emanuel Philibert ceded the county of Romont.

Majesté les veulent venir ayder et secourir [Geneva], il ne leur sera aucunement deffendu ny empesché par Sadicte Majesté, ny par ses ministres et officiers'.[23] The Treaty of Soleure was one of the many diplomatic manoeuvres by the French crown in defence of its perceived interests that ran counter to the prevailing religious tensions of the period. Not only did it shock the wider Catholic world, but it was also no less controversial within France. Most of Henry's council opposed it, as did Catherine de Medici, who was then away from court on her famous voyage in Languedoc.[24]

Henry appears to have hoped that Charles Emanuel (who succeeded on 30 August 1580) would prove less ambitious than his father. Here he miscalculated, for in 1581 Charles Emanuel began preparations for a full-scale attack on Geneva and approached the papacy for a subsidy. His request was rejected as too exorbitant, and this rebuff may have caused him deliberately to keep Philip II in the dark, possibly in the hope of forcing his hand by a *fait accompli*. As a result his enterprise was a distinctly amateurish one, which hinged on a conspiracy of disaffected Genevans to provide an entry into the city. The plot (the *conspiration de Desplans*) was discovered on 11 April 1582, by which point Charles Emanuel had only managed to assemble 1,200 to 1,500 miscellaneous French, Italian, and Swiss troops under the command of Raconis. The premature exposure of the conspiracy left him with no alternative but to occupy the regained *bailliages* with this 'army' (which had no artillery) and blockade the city in the hope that something would turn up.

Much depended on assistance Charles Emanuel would now get from the Catholic world, an issue confused by the claims of widespread support that he broadcast in the succeeding weeks. Both Gregory XIII and Philip II responded to the news of the enterprise by advising him to abandon it, despite Gregory's expressed desire, as the French ambassador in Rome reported, for an end to 'le vent pestilent qui a soufflé depuis quarante ans du costé de ce Lac'.[25] Only Cardinal Borromeo and the *Waldstätten* backed him openly. During the first week of May the *Waldstätten* (who may have known something of his plans

---

[23] The text of the treaty is printed in H. Fazy, 'Genève, le parti huguenot et le traité de Soleure (1571 à 1579). Etude historique', *Mémoires de l'Institut National Genevois*, 15 (1883), pp. 190–201. The treaty was the work of Jean de Bellièvre, sieur de Hautefort (1524–1584), president of the parlement of Grenoble and ambassador with the Swiss in 1573–1579. He was the brother of Pomponne de Bellièvre, *surintendant des finances* 1574–1588, now the subject of a full biography: Olivier Poncet, *Pomponne de Bellièvre (1529–1607): Un homme d'état au temps des Guerres de Religion*, Mémoires et Documents de l'École des Chartes, l (Paris, 1998).

[24] The response to the treaty in France is discussed in Cramer, *Seigneurie*, I, pp. 272–274. Precedents can be found in the German policy of Henry II and in Catherine de Medici's dealings with the Protestant world after St Bartholomew's Day.

[25] Quoted in *Lettres Catherine*, VIII, p. 32, n. 1.

in advance) agreed to send him a further five companies of infantry (1,500 men), but they took some time to muster and did not arrive in Turin until the end of June. The Spanish authorities in Milan had been worried that Charles Emanuel might use his army to seize the marquisate of Montferrat instead, so they discreetly supported his Genevan enterprise with a company of 500 Spanish arquebusiers, which reached him on 19 June.

Bolstered by the support of the *Waldstätten*, a majority of the Savoyard council decided on 22 May to continue the blockade even at the risk of open hostilities. A further factor in the equation was a new development in the Netherlands. The *Joyeuse Entrée* of the Duke of Anjou in February had enabled the Prince of Parma, Philip's governor-general, to persuade the provinces of the Union of Arras to agree to the return of the 'foreign' troops, which had been withdrawn under the Treaty of Mont St Eloi of May 1579. During the spring some 10,000 Spaniards and Italians were mustered in Milan and there is evidence that Charles Emanuel hoped until the last minute that Philip would allow him to use this substantial force for his enterprise. However, in early July they passed by Geneva on their way north under strict instructions (as in 1567) not to be diverted by Savoy, even collecting en route the company sent to him several weeks earlier.

Once the conspiracy was discovered there were those in Geneva (Theodore Beza among them) who wished to exploit Charles Emanuel's military weakness by taking the offensive and driving the Savoyards out of the three *bailliages*. However, for this they needed the co-operation of Bern, and despite some sympathy the Bernese decided to try diplomacy first. At the end of April the Genevans also turned to the King of Navarre, the Huguenot churches and John Casimir. If more distant, they proved more obliging.[26] In May John Casimir informed Geneva that he was ready to come to their assistance with 2,000 horse whenever they were needed. At the same time Navarre sent them a military engineer and made clear his willingness to help further. Navarre was supported by the delegates at the Huguenot assembly held at St Jean d'Angély in May who urged that, in the event of a prolonged blockade, 'ou les assiegez ne s'en voudroient despartir trouuer bons qu'elle [Geneva] soit secourue par lesdites eglizes comme estant de l'alliance et confederation de sadite maiesté'.[27]

The most enthusiastic response came from Henry, Prince of Condé (1552–1588), and the son of the Admiral Coligny, François de Coligny,

[26] This was not the first occasion. During the crisis over Alba's march in 1567, Geneva had recruited three companies of Huguenots at the expense of the churches of France; see *Beza*, XXIII, 21.

[27] Paris, Bibliothèque Mazarine, MS 2604, fo. 126v. For Navarre's offer, see *Beza*, XXIII, 1516; for John Casimir's, Cramer, *Seigneurie*, III, pp. 23–24.

comte de Châtillon (1557–1591), both of whom had taken refuge in Geneva (most recently in 1581) and retained close contacts with the city. On 19 June, Châtillon responded to the appeal from the Genevan magistrates with an open offer of assistance: 'Je pense que vous trouverez un chacun disposé à s'employer pour vous: mais particulièrement je me sens obligé à vous par la promesse que je vous ay faicte, oultre ce que naturellement je vous doy.' He promised Beza at the same time that: 'Le danger et la difficulté ne m'empêcheront jamais de me jeter dans les feux et les piques de voz ennemys pour m'ouvrir un chemin au travers d'eulx, avec l'assistance de Dieu qui me guide au lieu où je puisse rendre tesmoignage de ma résolution et fidélité à vostre service, tout ensemble.' These letters together with a verbal offer of 4,000 to 5,000 arquebusiers reached Geneva at the end of the month. Châtillon's offer revived the issue of an offensive war against Savoy, but the debate in the Genevan council concluded with a decision to consult Bern first, not least because Geneva itself could not afford to finance so large an army.[28]

Geneva's defiance was not in doubt. On 10 July the city informed the Huguenot leader in Dauphiné, François de Bonne, seigneur de Lesdiguières, that its citizens were 'tous résolus de nous défendre et maintenir [...] jusques à la dernière goutte de nostre sang'.[29] Thanks to the Treaty of Soleure, however, Henry III played the key role in the affair. Coincidentally, he was about to renew the military convention with the Confederation, which was due to expire later in the year. An embassy for this purpose had been prepared in September 1581, but it was then postponed, presumably to raise money for the payment of the arrears of the Swiss pensions, which was considered essential for renewal of the treaty.[30] The embassy was revived early in April 1582 and then formally commissioned on the 22nd. Six hundred thousand écus were provided towards the arrears and more generous terms offered for the future pensions, but under the condition that the Confederation now publicly recognize the alliance with France as 'préférée' – an almost explicit warning to Savoy. It was at this point that news of the Genevan crisis reached Paris, where it was immediately appreciated that an open war over Geneva could jeopardize the treaty.

On 13 May Henry sent his ambassadors an additional set of instructions.

[28] *Beza*, XXIII, 1524 (Châtillon to Beza), annexe 8 (to Geneva); see also the note on pp. 249–250, which corrects important errors in Jules Delaborde, *François de Chastillon, comte de Coligny* (Paris, 1886).

[29] Cited in E. Choisy, *L'Etat chrétien calviniste à Genève au temps de Théodore de Bèze, thèse présentée à la Faculté de théologie de l'Université de Genève* (Geneva, 1892), p. 214.

[30] See *Henri*, V, 4326, 4337, 4505–4506, 4520–4524. The embassy consisted of Hautefort, François de Mandelot, sieur de Pacy (the governor of Lyons), and Henri Clausse, sieur de Fleury-St-Martin (d. 1613), who replaced the resident ambassador and served until 1586. Fleury was the brother of Anjou's agent in England, Pierre Clausse, sieur de Marchaumont.

He would, he admitted, prefer to see Geneva reduced to cinders, 'neantmoins, estant assise en telle assiette qu'elle est, elle ne pourroit estre reducte en l'obeissance de quelque prince que ce soyt de mes voisins'.[31] The embassy was to attempt a peaceful solution of the crisis, and specifically to prevent the Catholic cantons aiding Charles Emanuel. Henry was aware that Charles Emanuel was seeking to recruit in France and claiming publicly that he enjoyed his secret support. Therefore Savoyard recruiting (though not Genevan) was to be banned and he made it clear in Turin that while he would support Charles Emanuel's legitimate rights in Geneva, he was equally determined to uphold the treaty of Soleure.

The French embassy coincided with the opening of the diet of Confederation at Baden on 20 May. The diet then went into recess until 24 June while a delegation from the Confederation went to see Charles Emanuel. The French were unable to prevent the *Waldstätten* from sending their five companies, but they had more success in dissuading Bern from an offensive war and preventing the other Protestant cantons from sending to troops either to Bern or to Geneva. For their part, the Genevans regarded the French embassy with suspicion, especially Mandelot, whom Beza persisted in describing as the butcher of Lyons.[32] They were also distinctly worried by rumours that Henry intended to implement the Treaty of Soleure by providing a garrison for the city that might include Swiss Catholics.

The tension was broken in mid-July when Charles Emanuel suddenly announced that he was standing down his troops, although he still intended to see his rights over Geneva maintained and held Henry III to his promise in that regard. Precisely why Charles Emanuel decided to give up is unclear. It may have been Henry's public declaration that he would uphold the Treaty of Soleure. It has also been suggested that he was frightened by the Huguenot mustering, particularly the threat of an invasion of Savoy by Lesdiguières from Dauphiné. A further influence may have been the departure of the Spanish troops for the Netherlands, conclusive evidence that Philip II would not assist him, and that he was on his own.[33]

The news of the Savoyard retreat reached the diet of the Confederation shortly after it resumed at Soleure to negotiate the French treaty on 21 July. At this point Bern demanded further guarantees from Savoy before agreeing to a permanent secession of hostilities. It was not until early August that a settlement was reached in which Charles Emanuel's rights in Geneva were to be put to arbitration in a new diet,

---

[31] *Ibid.*, 4543.
[32] 'Lugdunensis carnifex'; for his role in St Bartholomew's, see *Beza*, XXIII, 1513.
[33] See the discussion in Cramer, *Seigneurie*, III, pp. 33–34.

which was to meet at Baden on 30 September. The news of the settlement reached Henry III by 13 August and was accepted by Geneva on 16 August. The Genevans wrote immediately to call off the Huguenot recruiting – the cause of some embarrassment for Châtillon was already en route and one Huguenot contingent actually reached the city on 18 August. The Genevans were not enthusiastic about the settlement, but did not feel strong enough to carry on alone. The revival of the issue of the ducal rights was a particular worry, and they were determined to resist any involvement by the *Waldstätten* in the arbitration. But for all the Genevan anxiety, in the event Bernese obstructionism prevented the diet from agreeing a formula of arbitration in October, and the issue was held over to a further diet in January 1583.

By this stage the Genevan settlement had been overshadowed by the renewal of the military convention with France. The terms were actually agreed by the majority of the cantons at Soleure on 22 July, for Savoy's failure undercut any resistance by the *Waldstätten*, who were afraid of loosing their pension arrears. The French also hoped to gain the adhesion of all the Protestant cantons, but, while Bern finally agreed discreetly on 20 November, Zurich continued in its abstention. At the beginning of November a large Swiss delegation went to Paris for the solemn celebration of the treaty, which was held in Notre Dame on 22 December. The delegates from the *Waldstätten* used the occasion to make a public appeal to Henry to abandon Geneva, but he made it equally clear that he would not reconsider his decision.

The appeal to England

On the surface the resolution of the crisis of 1582 had been a triumph for the Treaty of Soleure. Yet the mood in Geneva was anything but confident. It was clear that the *modus vivendi* of 1570 was at an end and that Charles Emanuel was now an open enemy. Moreover, it was difficult to believe that he had undertaken the enterprise without the support of the greater Catholic powers, although as Edouard Rott has observed, it was early days yet and Charles Emanuel's 'esprit remuant n'avait point encore, il est vrai, donné sa mesure'.[34] Nor were Henry III's actions entirely comprehensible. In a long letter to Beza on 6 September John Casimir's councillor Pierre Beutterich (by no means an impartial judge) expressed his conviction that Henry had manipulated the whole episode for his own devious ends.[35] Lastly there was a strong feeling of having been abandoned

---

[34] *Histoire de la représentation*, II, p. 246.

[35] *Beza*, XXIII, 1546. Beutterich (1545–1587) a Burgundian lawyer, served both Frederick III and John Casimir. He was the most active – and most controversial – of John Casimir's agents.

by the Confederation and a particular resentment at Bern's failure to act decisively in April. Huguenot assistance had proved more reliable, but the potential financial implications were discouraging.

It was in this climate that the decision was taken at the end of September to appeal to England for financial assistance. The immediate background is something of a mystery. The relevant entries in the registers of both the city council and the Company of Pastors for 28 September state specifically that the idea came from Beza. The council register reads 'suyvant ce que M. de Bèze a faict cy devant avoir heu advis du costé d'Angleterre et de Paris, qu'escrivant Messeigneurs à la royne d'Angleterre, au mayre [etc.] on pourroit obtenir quelque chose en don pour ayder à supporter les frais passés et debtes créés'. The company of pastors' register states more simply that Beza 'rapporte quil a appris qu'on pourrait obtenir des dons et des secours d'Angleterre grace à la reine [etc.]'.[36] Beza's surviving correspondence supplies no evidence as to the source of this information. Beza's relations with England were not particularly close, for Elizabeth had always held Calvin personally responsible for allowing the printing of Knox's *First Blast of the Trumpet* in Geneva in 1558. In December 1581 Beza had sent via Lord Burghley a polyglot Pentateuch and the manuscript now known as the *Codex Bezae* as gifts to Cambridge University Library, and he was distinctly annoyed at having received no acknowledgement, which he assumed was a deliberate snub.[37]

On the other hand, as will be discussed below, Beza was well informed about events in Britain and the English were no less aware of the course of the blockade. Yet no Englishmen visited Geneva during the summer and if there was at least one English student at Geneva at the beginning of the year, he left during the blockade.[38] The obvious candidates for Beza's informants are the ministers of the French Church in London, Robert le Maçon, sieur de La Fontaine and his colleague, the recently-appointed Genevan, Jean Castol, both of whom were regular correspondents of his.[39] Yet nothing survives from them in 1582, and La Fontaine's almost frosty reception of Malliet eliminates him. One possibility, though there is no direct evidence, is that the advice

[36] The council register is quoted in Cramer, 'Malliet', p. 391. See also Olivier Labarthe and Bernard Lescaze (eds), *Registres de la Companie des Pasteurs de Genève: IV (1575–1582)* (Geneva, 1974), p. 214.

[37] *Beza*, XXIII, 1549–1551 (to the Sr de La Fontaine, Burghley and Walter Travers, 10 October 1582). In fact Cambridge had written on 18 May (*ibid.*, annexe 7), but delivery had been prevented by the blockade. Beza's letter to Burghley also reveals his continued worry about the effects of *The First Blast*.

[38] Emanuel Barnes, son of the Bishop of Durham.

[39] On La Fontaine (1535?–1611), see Charles Littleton, 'The French Church of London in European Protestantism: the role of Robert le Maçon, dit de La Fontaine, Minister, 1574–1611', *Proceedings of the Huguenot Society of London*, 26 (1994), pp. 45–57. Castol became second minister of the church in 1582 and served until 1601.

came from Pierre Beutterich, who had his own contacts with England. However, the reference to Paris suggests a further alternative, the Huguenot minister François de Laubéran, sieur de Montigny. As both Malliet's dealings with him in Paris in October and his own correspondence with Beutterich in the summer of 1582 reveal, Montigny was very well connected and informed.[40] Yet, whatever the source, no less striking are Beza's worry about the reception the appeal would meet in England and his instruction to Malliet to rely on La Fontaine's advice. If La Fontaine considered it unwise to proceed, he and Malliet were to burn all the letters of credence.[41]

The choice of Jean Malliet (1550–1625) as the city's agent, which was also agreed on 28 September, was far more straightforward. Malliet came from an established magisterial family and was to have a stormy political career.[42] In 1570, together with his friend Paul Chevallier, the future Genevan *secrétaire d'état*, he had taken a Protestant grand tour, first to Heidelberg, then Paris, and finally London. In May 1572 he reported that he had agreed to act as tutor to Charles Stewart, Earl of Lennox, at the request of certain 'principaux personnages du royaume'. How long his London residence lasted is not clear, for he was elected to the council of the 200 at the end of the year. Nevertheless, in 1582 the council considered him 'bien cogneu' in England, with a full command of the language, something few other Genevans would have had.[43]

Malliet took with him to England two sets of letters of credence and introduction, one from the city and one from Beza. Beza's were sent unsealed, those from the syndics under an open seal ('cachet volant'), so that La Fontaine could help Malliet address them.[44] A number of copies of both survive.[45] However, two very important documents have disappeared: such written instructions as were issued to him and the

[40] See *Briefe Johann Casimir*, I, pp. 478, 503. Montigny was, or would be, seigneur at Ablon, later authorized as the place of worship for Paris Protestants under the terms of the Edict of Nantes. He also became chaplain to Catherine de Bourbon and co-moderator of the Synode national of Montpellier in 1598, see 'Les deux temples de l'église réformée de Paris sous l'édit de Nantes', and 'Les pasteurs de l'Eglise de "Madame"', *Bulletin de la société de l'histoire du protestantisme français*, 2 (1854), p. 246; 57 (1908), p. 313.

[41] *Beza*, XXIII, 1549, Beza to La Fontaine, 10 October 1582.

[42] See Cramer, 'Malliet', for a full biography

[43] Beza referred to Malliet's 'cognoissance du pays, de la langue et des personnes' in his letter to La Fontaine.

[44] *Beza*, XXIII, 183 (to La Fontaine, 10 October).

[45] *Beza*, XXIII prints four from Beza (arts. 1549–1552, to La Fontaine, Burghley, Walsingham, and Walter Travers). To these should be added one to the Earl of Bedford, calendared in Albert Peel (ed.), *The Seconde Parte of a Register*, 2 vols (Cambridge, 1915), I, p. 155. Although they are all dated 10 October, they are quite individual in content. Those from the city (dated 6 and 7 October) survive in Geneva in minute form (Cramer, 'Malliet', pp. 391–392) while some originals (to Elizabeth, Walsingham and Sir Henry Cobham) are in the State Papers; see *CSPF, 1583*, addenda, pp. 638–639.

factum justifying the city's stand against the pretensions of the Duke of Savoy, which, as can be seen from the *mémoire*, he distributed widely in Paris and London.[46] In the absence of his instructions, precisely what he was to ask for and how he was to proceed are unknown. All we can say is that on 28 September the council intended him to ask for a gift, but at a subsequent meeting on 2 October it was decided to request an interest-free loan of 30,000 *écus* instead.[47]

The problem of the *factum* is complicated by contemporary references to several documents that might fit the description.[48] On 8 August Beza had presented to the council on behalf of the Company of Pastors a written justification of the city's resort to arms. At a later date a document described as a *factum* was drafted to defend the city's independence and repudiate the ducal rights that Charles Emanuel claimed, intended in the first instance for the arbitration proceedings at the diet of the Confederation. However, the one clear reference to this document is found in the council register for 25 October: Beza was to be commissioned to draft a *factum*, which was to be published in various languages. However, not only has no text of this document survived, but it was also commissioned too late either to be supplied to Malliet on his departure or to be presented to the diet that met at Baden on 30 September. There also exists a further *mémoire* defending the city's position, drafted by Michel Roset and dated 19 September, which was to be sent in the first instance to Beutterich for circulation among the Protestant cantons.[49] In the absence of any text of the *factum* distributed by Malliet, the question remains an open one.

Malliet's Paris interlude

Malliet's *mémoire* begins with his arrival in Paris on 13 October and, without any introduction, launches into a detailed narrative of the many items of business that he conducted over the following fortnight. In the absence of his instructions, it must be assumed that these were matters he was commissioned to undertake en route to England, but what they were can only be reconstructed from the references in his report. In the main they were issues arising from tangled financial relationship between Geneva and the Huguenot churches.

The first among them was the debt due to the city from its co-religionists in France. Huguenot financing is a complex and little

---

[46] No copies of the *factum* have yet been discovered in either Britain or Switzerland.
[47] Cramer, 'Malliet', p. 91. For the exchange rate for the *écu* see p. 139.
[48] See the discussion in *Beza*, XXIII, xiii, xv.
[49] *Ibid.*, annexe 9.

researched subject.[50] Although Geneva had played no part in the complex arrangements that financed the army John Casimir had raised in 1575–1576, the city had lent 1,151 *écus* to Condé during his exile after St Bartholomew's. Then he had set up court in Basel and Strasbourg and acted as the nominal head or 'chef, gouverneur général et protecteur' of the Huguenot movement, the position accorded him at the assembly of Millau in July 1574.[51] The Genevan loan was underwritten by his family jewel collection, which had also been pawned to various German and Swiss banking houses in return for loans. In the peace of Bergerac (September 1577), Henry III had agreed to underwrite the repayment of the debts incurred by the Huguenots to John Casimir.[52] But some of the debts were to be repaid directly by the Huguenots themselves. The King gave permission for them to raise 224,656²/₃ *écus* through the mechanism of their political assemblies, part of which would include the reimbursement of the loan secured by Condé himself for his own expenses. These assemblies (or 'estates' as Malliet terms them) are to be distinguished from its national and provincial synods. By 1577 they had evolved to the extent that they were now essential to the political accountability and credit-worthiness of the Huguenot movement.[53] As far as possible, the assemblies included delegates representing the fifteen 'provinces' into which the various colloquies of French churches (over fifty of them) were divided.

The levying of this large amount of money from the churches was extensively discussed and arranged at the next assembly, that at Montauban in July 1579.[54] It was repartitioned in accordance with the financial districts by which taxes were accounted in the French kingdom (*généralités* – the divisions of the offices of the *trésoriers-généraux*) rather than by the provinces and colloquies of the church, a distinction that was no doubt not without its problems when it came to collecting the sums involved. Nicolas Payot was appointed *receveur*.[55] Part of the amount, 22,000 *écus* in total, was agreed with Condé as a contribution to the repayment of the 'plusieurs grandes et notables sommes de

---

[50] For a preliminary enquiry, see M. Greengrass, 'Financing the cause: Protestant mobilisation and accountability in France (1562–1589)', in Philip Benedict *et al.* (eds), *Reformation, Revolt and Civil War in France and the Netherlands* (Amsterdam, 1999), pp. 233–254.

[51] 'Articles arrestez en l'assemblee de ceux de la Religion pretendue refformee a Millau', Paris, Bibliothèque Mazarine, MS 2604, fos 64–72v.

[52] Article 12 of the secret articles appended to the treaty, see *Articles secrets du XVII septembre MDLXVII* (Paris, 1671).

[53] See L. Anquez, *Histoire des assemblées politiques des réformés de France (1573–1622)* (Paris, 1859).

[54] Paris, Bibliothèque Protestante, MS 97, pièce 8 [procès-verbal].

[55] Or Pajot, *trésorier* of the king of Navarre in the period 1578–1582; see *Beza*, XXIII, 21, 23.

deniers, par luy empruntées, pendant qu'il estoit hors de royaume, et emploiées au profit et pour la deffence desdictes églises aux guerres passées'.[56] The city of Geneva in turn agreed to advance him this money so that he had could satisfy the various creditors that were assailing his estates on the understanding that Geneva would be repaid in due course by the French churches. As it turned out, little (if any) of it was collected by the time of the following assembly, again at Montauban, in May 1581. Pierre Beutterich appeared before the assembly in person to ask for its assistance in persuading Henry to honour his obligations to John Casimir under the treaty of Monsieur of 1576. Condé followed him with a petition that he be 'promptement payee suiuant le despartement quy en a cy deuant en ladite assemble esté faict dont ledit sieur prince n'a aucune chose receu affin de le descharger des grandz interestz quil en a porté sur ses terres et reuenu ordinaire, et qu'il puisse retirer ses bagues engagees en alemaigne et suisse'.[57] The interest on the debt was also mounting up and he had been forced to borrow money from La Rochelle and elsewhere to meet it.[58] The delegates agreed to a new repartition of the amount, now totalling 27,333$^{1}/_{3}$ écus, around the provinces of the kingdom and undertook to see that the levy was completed by Christmas 1581.[59]

Such an optimistic promise was to ignore, however, the real resentments felt by individuals in the French Protestant churches at being asked to fund the debts of a notably adventurist aristocrat at the same time as they were beset by demands to fund the needs of churches, pastors' salaries, student bursaries, and charitable bequests of all sorts. A letter to the King of Navarre from the north of France from this period revealed tellingly the resentments that had built up towards this levy. Gentlemen were reported as staying away from churches so that they could not be touched for such payments.[60] At the assembly of St-Jean d'Angély in May 1582, the deputy for the Ile de France, Pierre de La Tour, rose to argue that Condé's debts had been misapportioned and that this, too, was causing discontent. As La Tour told Malliet later

---

[56] Fazy, 'Soleure', *pièce justificative* 35, deputies of the churches of France to Geneva, 25 July 1579.

[57] Bib. Mazarine, MS 2604, fo. 113v.

[58] These sums were raised through the late sieur de Vigean, governor of Lusignan, and the sieur Dumont.

[59] Bib. Mazarine, MS 2604, fo. 114 –v. The repartition provides an interesting picture of the provincial distribution of resources of the Huguenot movement at this date: (by generality, sums in *écus*) Paris: 1,468; Orléans: 1,468; Rouen and Caen: 2,947; Champagne: 700; Picardie: 700; Bourgogne: 700; Metz: 368$^{1}/_{3}$; Tours: 1,200; Limoges: 360; Bretagne: 3,193; Bourges: 1,000; Montpellier and Toulouse: 4,100; Bordeaux: 2,320; Limoges: 1,620; Poitiers: 1,600; Dauphiné: 1,906; Provence: 800; Roan: 396

[60] Simon Goulard to the Company of Pastors, 14/24 January 1583, printed in L.C. Jones, *Simon Goulart, sa vie et son oeuvre, 1543–1628* (Geneva and Paris, 1917), pp. 361–362.

in the year, Condé's demands 'refroidit la charité de plusieurs'.[61] But, with the deputies at St-Jean d'Angély aware of Geneva's plight, it was a good moment to press the case for individual churches to honour the promises made on their behalf and (no matter how they had originated) pay up in what was confessionally a good cause.

So one of Malliet's tasks in Paris in October 1582 consisted in obtaining reimbursement in liquid money wherever it was to be found. Small amounts had trickled in from Normandy and Picardy. The churches in Metz and Paris were prepared to advance substantial portions at current rates of interest (*denier* 15, or 6.6 per cent and *denier* 12 or 8.3 per cent respectively). The churches in and around Paris offered to find the interest payments that were mounting up at 1,000 *écus* per annum. For the rest, although other churches had received letters on the subject, they had not replied. It remained, therefore, for Malliet to pursue the *assignation* of the debt. *Assignations* were the predecessors of promissory notes, issued generally by the French *conseil des finances*, which assigned a particular pension or sum to be paid to an identifiable receipt. The arrangement allowed the French monarchy to avoid the costs of moving money around the kingdom and also to advance upon its receipts. In times of financial malaise there were lots of *assignations* chasing the same receipt and the *assignations* were even handed over, or rescripted, to other parties who might be better placed to secure their payment. In this instance, Malliet seems to have entertained the possibility of the rescript of an assignation on the receipts of the amounts being levied in Burgundy and Provence in favour of nearby Geneva. Whether the arrangement ever worked is not known, but the proposed *assignation* without a named party on it (such as Payot proposed) would have been likely to meet with a refusal from French treasurers if it had been presented. And, in any case, it would not be long before Payot himself found himself imprisoned and his accounts and papers seized, the King having countermanded any permission to the Protestants to raise money in this way.[62]

Malliet's other important task in Paris involved the settlement of two matters arising from Châtillon's recruiting in the summer. The first was Châtillon's demand for financial compensation, the second the issuing by the Parlement of Toulouse of an *arrêt* condemning his levying of

---

[61] See below, p. 168. La Tour was minister at Rouen and deputy to the previous assembly in 1581 (Bib. Mazarine, MS 2604, fos 89, 123, fo. 132). A Pierre de La Tour *de Rouen*, probably the same individual, appears on the rectors' register at Geneva on 16 December 1570, although his name was subsequently crossed out (S. Stelling-Michaud and S. Stelling-Michaud, *Le livre du Recteur de l'Académie de Genève, 1559–1878*, 6 vols (Geneva, 1956–1980), IV, p. 275).

[62] BNF, ms français 15905, fo. 674 (undated copy of the ordinance for his arrest).

troops within Languedoc as illegal.[63] Châtillon's defence was that his recruiting was legitimate under the Treaty of Soleure. On 28 September Châtillon and Condé had sent the sieur de La Vacqueresse to Geneva from Montpellier with a carefully worded letter of reproach: 'Vous me permettrés aussi, s'il vous plaist de vous dire que vous m'avez mis en une extrȩme peine [...] Nous nous sommes tous mis en de très-grandes dépenses, pour vous monstrer l'envie que nous avions de vous bien servir [...] et tout soudain, tant que nous pensions vous faire sentir le fruit de nostre peine et les effects de notre bonne volonté, sans pourvoir, ni à nostre seureté, ni à mon honneur que j'avoir engagé pour le contentement de ceux qui m'ont fait cest honneur de m'accompagner pour vostre service'.[64] From Geneva, Vacqueresse set off for Paris, possibly accompanying Malliet on this part of his journey. The Genevan magistracy doubtless hoped to extricate Châtillon (and themselves) from the embarrassing situation by (at least) saving him from the charge of levying troops without the king's permission. In his audience with Henri III, Vacqueresse did not hesitate to refer to the Toulouse decision, with the clear implication that, once again (so far as the Protestants were concerned) this ultra-conservative court was trying to make the law suit its own agenda. The King, intelligently aware of the subtleties of the moment, contented himself with an ambiguous reply to the effect that he graciously embraced Geneva in his protective care. He quietly rescinded the order of the Toulouse court in early November, and Châtillon and Condé were left to contemplate their bruised fortunes in Montpellier, which is where the latter wrote on 18 October to Geneva to request on the former's behalf that he receive 'son remboursement très raisonnable des grands frais et dépenses nécessaires auxquelles ladite levée l'a réduit'.[65]

Malliet in England

By the time he arrived in London on 13 November, Malliet's mission was overshadowed by greater matters. Even before Geneva decided to send him to England, Beza was aware of two of the three recent events that threw Anglo-French relations into turmoil and dominated the attention of the English government during the winter of 1582–1583.[66]

---

[63] *Arrêt* of 23 August 1582 forbidding any raising of troops without the specific permission of the king and the provincial governors and lieutenants; A[rchives] D[épartementales] Haute-Garonne B 86, fo. 464. There was also a specific court order against Châtillon and those who had levied for him that has not been found, perhaps because it was rescinded a few months later.

[64] 'Fazy, Soleure', *pièce justificative* 51, Condé to Geneva, 28 September 1582.

[65] *Ibid.*, 52. On the rescinding of the *arrêt*, see also Delaborde, *Chastillon*, pp. 217–218.

[66] He knew of both the Ruthven Raid and the defeat of Fillipo Strozzi by 22 September; see *Beza*, XXIII, 1547.

The Duke of Anjou's *Joyeuse Entrée* had initiated the final phase of the complex negotiations surrounding his proposal of marriage to Elizabeth. In December 1581, Elizabeth had offered to supply £60,000 towards his military costs, and by the autumn of 1582 he had drawn £40,000 of this. However, Elizabeth would make no further commitment without an equal one from Henry III; but the King's financial support for his brother, phrased in deliberately vague terms, would only become operative after the celebration of the marriage. Elizabeth in turn refused to proceed with the marriage until Henry's commitment was made more explicit. The extent to which either side was acting in good faith has been queried, but what is relevant here is that by September Elizabeth had refused to supply Anjou with any further money until a suitable answer was received from Henry.[67]

On 22–23 August, the Protestant councillors of the adolescent James VI of Scotland were able to separate him from Esmé Stuart, Duke of Lennox, in the episode now known as the Ruthven Raid. This was welcome news in England, but tempered by the fact that Lennox was still at liberty in Scotland. It was important that Henry III be persuaded to accept the new status quo in Scotland and refuse any assistance to Lennox. During September the new Scottish regime also supplied London with some major intelligence. Firstly, it was discovered that Castelnau de Mauvissière had been sending information to Lennox during the earlier part of the year, supposedly about English-backed plots to unseat him. Secondly, confirmation was provided of the negotiations in Paris in the autumn of 1581 over 'The Association' between Mary, Queen of Scots, and her son. This was Mary's plan under which she would recognize James as King of Scots if he revoked her abdication of 1567 and governed with her advice. Since these discussions apparently had Henry and Catherine's approval, it could be argued that the French crown still harboured hostile intentions, for all the proposals of Anglo-French co-operation in support of Anjou.[68]

The French response to the Scottish crisis was tempered by a third event. On 11 August Henry left Paris for Lyons and then the baths at Bourbon-Lancy and did not return until 8 October. In his absence the Queen Mother was given charge of affairs. On 11 September final confirmation reached Paris of the defeat in July of the fleet sent to the Azores to aid the Portuguese pretender, Dom António, and the death

---

[67] PRO, 31 [Deposited Transcripts], 3/28/378–379, Mauvissière to Henry, 13 September. In the meantime Henry had responded with letters patent exempting Elizabeth from any financial commitment to Anjou (8 September, *CSPF, 1582*, p. 311). The debate over this assurance lasted for the remainder of the year.

[68] This intelligence came from the confession of George Douglas (dated 14 September), *CSPSc.*, *1581–1583*, pp. 166–167. For Elizabeth's response, see *CSPF, 1582*, pp. 353–355, Walsingham to Cobham, 26 September.

of its commander, Catherine's favourite, Fillipo Strozzi. Rumours that Strozzi had been deliberately executed shocked Catherine, and Henry was no less moved when the 'piteuse nouvelle' reached him.[69] Catherine's response was to throw her energies into the mustering of a large reinforcement for Anjou, as well as organizing a new fleet to be sent to the Azores in 1583. It thus appeared to many that the French crown was on the verge of war with Spain in last months of 1582. On the other hand, news of the Ruthven Raid had been followed by appeals for a strong stand in Scotland from the Queen of Scots, who claimed that her son was being returned to the captivity he had escaped after the fall of the Regent Morton in 1581. But this was not the moment to quarrel with Elizabeth. The upshot was the appointment in late October of the former ambassador to England, Bertrand de Salignac, sieur de La Mothe-Fénelon, on a special embassy to London and then Edinburgh to see if a compromise could be brokered that would enable Lennox to remain in Scotland.[70]

Malliet makes a number of allusions to this complex situation at the beginning of the English section of his report, but thereafter he makes little reference to wider events, with the main exception of Mauvissière's hostility to the Geneva collection in April 1583.[71] Unfortunately, the only comment on the collection in Mauvissière's surviving despatches dates from 16/26 May 1583, over a month later.[72] In the absence of his other reports from this period, what lay behind it can only be deduced from what the King wrote to him. The primary cause was an event Malliet does not mention, but which overshadowed the whole of 1583, Anjou's use of the reinforcements sent to him in an attempted coup at Antwerp, the 'French fury' of 7/17 January. To many Protestants the Antwerp fury appeared to be a new St Bartholomew's Day that revealed yet again a deep-seated Catholic design within the French royal family, and justified those (both in England and elsewhere) who had been suspicious of Anjou and France all along. It both corresponded with and stimulated a new restlessness in the Protestant world. Just before the Antwerp fury, Gebhard Truchsess, the Elector of Cologne, had

[69] *Lettres Catherine*, VIII, pp. 405–406, Villeroy to Henry, 12 September; *Henri*, V, 4638, Henri to Villeroy, (n.d.). Nicolas de Neufville, sieur d'Alaincourt, Magny and Villeroy (1543–1617) was the most influential of the three *secrétaires d'état*.

[70] (1523–1599), ambassador 1568–1575. He was chosen precisely because he was believed to be well regarded in England. His letters of credence were dated 25 October (see *Henri*, V, 4688–4689) but he did not leave France until mid-November. It is revealing of the difficulties of French policy that he was expected to combine negotiating a compromise over Scotland with persuading Elizabeth to accept Henry's letters patent for Anjou, and to permit Catherine to hire English ships for the new Portugal expedition.

[71] See below, p. 184.

[72] For the treatment of dates subsequent to the adoption of the Gregorian calendar, see above, p. 138.

published his conversion to Protestantism, which initiated the 'War for Cologne'. In April 1583, Philippe du Plessis-Mornay informed Walsingham that the Huguenots would not surrender the six *places de sûreté* that they were obliged to do in the autumn of 1583, even at the risk of a new civil war.[73] A further manifestation of this new Huguenot attitude was the embassy of Jacques de Ségur from the King of Navarre to all the Protestant princes to propose the formation of a grand confessional alliance. Ségur arrived in England in September 1583 just before Malliet's departure.

Henry III, on the other hand, was haunted by the spectre of a conspiracy within France involving a disgruntled Anjou, Henry, Duke of Montmorency, and the Huguenots.[74] Anjou's putative motive was the belief that his Netherlands expedition had been sabotaged financially by his brother. Immediately after the Antwerp Fury, Mauvissière reported strong expressions of hostility to France in England, only mitigated by Elizabeth herself, and his concern that the English might now stir up the Huguenots. Henry ordered him in turn to 'pénétrer leurs deliberations'.[75] These instructions may have caused Mauvissière to turn his attention to the collection. On 7/17 May Henry answered letters from Mauvissière from late April and early May reporting that the English had received news that a new religious civil war was about to break out in the south of France. This Henry was at pains to dismiss, but nonetheless he wished Mauvissière to discover the source.[76] In his letter of 16/26 May Mauvissière reported that the 'ceulx de Geneve' had raised 'plus de cent mil écus' (nearly £30,000, five times the actual sum) from the churches of England, because everyone had contributed.[77] In the following month Mauvissière sent a now-missing *discours* on the 'menées, ligues et considerations de ceaulx de la religion et autres protestans'. Henry did not think 'quils puissent accumuler de si grandes sommes' – but Mauvissière was to continue his efforts to find out what was going on.[78]

In the absence of further comment in his diplomatic reports, is it difficult to tell whether Mauvissière was being completely honest when

---

[73] *CSPF, 1583*, pp. 233–236 (the dating of this memoir to March is an error). Under the treaty of Bergerac of 1577 they were to hold them only for six years.

[74] For an early expression of his concern, see Henry's long letter to Villeroy in September 1582; *Henri*, V, 4678.

[75] BNF, VCC 473, 380–381, 18/28 February (misdated to January), and 375, 28 February/8 March. (This volume is paginated rather than foliated.)

[76] *Ibid.*, pp. 410–411. Note the reference to the churches of Languedoc in the text, pp. 166, 190.

[77] Printed in A. Chéruel, *Marie Stuart et Catherine de Médicis* (Paris, 1858), p. 243. This particular collection of his reports contains most of those that survive from the summer of 1583. Unfortunately, it was made for the benefit of a future French ambassador in Scotland and only those relevant to Scottish affairs were included.

[78] BNF, VCC 473, 429–430 (18/28 June).

he later assured Malliet that he was now satisfied that the collection was free of ulterior political purpose. What had undoubtedly attracted his suspicions was the secrecy under which it was carried out, for he appears to have had a very exaggerated idea of its success. It is also interesting that Mendoza's one reference to the collection is equally exaggerated and that he too claimed that it had a secret political purpose, which was to aid Truchsess, an issue of greater immediate relevance to Spain.[79]

Malliet also encountered some of the major tensions within the English church and government at this juncture. As has been noted above, there is no evidence of any direct communication between Geneva and England during the summer of 1582. However, Elizabeth's government had been kept informed of the blockade by Sir Henry Cobham from Paris, while Walsingham had consulted a former resident of Geneva about the city's ability to stand a siege, and the Earl of Leicester had been sent full accounts by John Casimir and Beutterich.[80]

On one level, Beza's apprehensions about Malliet's possible reception were unjustified, as the friendly and generous treatment he encountered first in Paris from Cobham and then generally on his arrival in England soon revealed. But on the financial level, they were, for Elizabeth was certainly 'not in the giving mood today'. Yet Elizabeth's response was shared by La Fontaine, and for not dissimilar reasons. Although it has been nearly axiomatic for English historians to emphasise the financial weakness of Elizabethan England, this was not the view of continental contemporaries. England's escape from religious civil war and Elizabeth's international reputation for parsimony had created an image of a queen presiding over swelling coffers. Both Elizabeth – and the foreign refugee churches (who had their own financial problems) – had been the recipients of regular appeals for monetary assistance, and the earlier history of Huguenot borrowing was not conducive to further generosity.[81]

The various financial demands on Elizabeth and her recent expenditure to which Malliet refers can be summarized briefly. Apart from the £40,000 supplied to Anjou in 1582 mentioned above, Elizabeth had given him £30,000 in October 1581, making a total of £70,000.

[79] See below, *Mémoires*, n. 96.

[80] Sir Henry Cobham (1538–1592) was ambassador in Paris from 1579 to 1583. His reports on Geneva (beginning in May) can be found in *CSPF, 1582*. See pp. 63–67 for the memoir for Walsingham (4 June). The anonymous author considered that Charles Emanuel had little chance of besieging Geneva successfully and that the whole scheme was a cover to enable a Catholic army to assemble for an invasion of England. For Leicester's correspondence, see below, *Mémoires*, n. 30. There were also more informal accounts from English travellers in France, e.g. BL, Lansdowne MS 36, arts 69, 79.

[81] See below, p. 170.

There were also long-standing debts (a total of £98,374) owed by the States General of the Netherlands, some going back to 1576, for which she was making regular demands for repayment.[82] Precisely what she had spent on Dom António to date is unclear, but £11,000 had been spent towards a possible military intervention in Scotland to save the Earl of Morton in the spring of 1581.[83] The greatest burden, however, was the £200,000 to £250,000 that the repression of the Desmond Rebellion in Ireland had cost between 1579 and 1582.[84] Elizabeth, who always read the fine print, knew from Cobham of the renewal of the Franco-Swiss military convention. So far as she was concerned the crisis over Geneva was over. If a 'good cause', Geneva was far down the list of *grandes affaires* at this moment.

No less important was the peculiar political context. Walsingham's denial of access to Protestant embassies because he did not think the climate was right was not unique to Malliet.[85] But Elizabeth's delegation of the Geneva collection to the Privy Council and Walsingham's assertions to Malliet that she did not know precisely what they were up to are very interesting. Equally striking, given the supposed factionalism of the Council, is the high degree of co-operation among them. There may an answer to this in the terminal illness of the most discordant member in recent years, the Earl of Sussex.[86] On the other hand, the tension between the Council and at least some of the bishops is almost palpable. One problem was the Archbishop of Canterbury, Edmund Grindal, 'sequestered' since 1577. Now in poor health, nearly blind, and arranging his resignation on grounds of ill health, the Geneva collection was one of the last two major acts of his life – the other was blocking at the last minute plans to adopt the Gregorian calendar.[87] However, if Grindal (who was still used by the council as the formal means of communicating with the church) was the safe pair of hands in which to leave the collection, this was less true of his colleagues. Walsingham's dismissive comments about the bishops and the Bishop of Lincoln's efforts to keep the collection from the clergy out of lay hands reveal a striking degree of hostility. No less interesting is the

---

[82] See the statement conveniently compiled by Burghley in August 1582; BL, Cotton MS Caligula E VII, fo. 224.

[83] See *CSPSc., 1581–1583*, pp. 184–185, note of expenditure relating to Scotland compiled in September 1582.

[84] F.C. Dietz, *English Public Finance, 1558–1641* (New York, 1932), p. 431, gives £262,775 for expenditure in Ireland 1579–1584.

[85] He had done the same to a proposed embassy from the Netherlands in January 1579.

[86] Sussex, who died on 9 June 1583, had been reported as gravely ill by Mauvissière on 14 September 1582; PRO 31, 3/28/415.

[87] See Collinson, *Grindal*, esp. p. 270. His resignation was to take effect in the autumn of 1583.

meeting between Malliet and what appear to have been the central figures in the Puritan classical movement. Although, given the episcopal involvement, they were prepared to stay their hands, their involvement in the collection is in itself revealing of their growing importance at this juncture.

The final issue is the emphasis on discretion and secrecy, and the limiting of the collection to the committed. The council does not appear to have shared the cheerful cynicism of Alderman Martin, and they placed no direct pressure on Catholics to contribute. In Protestant circles the emotional appeal to repay Geneva for its charity in Mary's reign was an effective one – though it may have been intended to counter any debate about Knox and *The First Blast*. Certainly most of those who supported the collection enthusiastically were former exiles, even if they had not taken refuge in Geneva itself. Yet if there appear to be genuinely voluntary contributions, the surviving evidence suggests that the majority were rated primarily by rank. Unfortunately, the evidence for the collection on the ground is (so far) limited, though more may be uncovered by a search in ecclesiastical archives.

Mémoires et procédures de ma negociation en Angleterre des mon depart du 8ᵉ d'Octobre 1582 jusques au 8ᵉ d'Octobre de l'an 1583, par le commandement de Messeigneurs Par moy J. Malliet[1]

[fo. 1]

Octobre

Arrivé a Paris le 21 d'Octobre 1582,[2] m'enquis le lendemain de Monsieur de Montigny[3] touchant l'action intentee par M. Groullier pour le faict des Perrolliers, lequel me dict avoir sceu de la part de Monsieur de Belieure,[4] que l'affaire n'avoit esté produit en conseil, et qu'il n'y avoit aucun octroy de lettres de marque.

Que lon sçaura ce qui aura esté intenté par le dict Groullier par le moyen de la requeste qu'a entre main [*sic*] Monsr de la Protiere procureur de Messeigneurs en ce dict procez.

Que M. Groullier est à Paris avec Messieurs de Mantelot et de Hautefort.[5]

Que Monsr de Montigny est d'advis, que lon aye les parcelles du procez de Perolliers,[6] que le factum ne sert que pour informer, et non pour estre produit.

M. de Montigny me toucha aussi des 12000* que prestent les Eglises de Metz, offertz au denier 12. Que les Eglises de Paris payeront le surplus de la cense, qui pourroit monter plus hault qu'au denier 15.

Monsieur de Chassincour[7] me dict au contraire, que Monsieur de

---

[1] Endorsement.

[2] The text actually reads 1572, with a later note by an archivist, 'au lieu de 1572 lisez 1582'.

[3] See above, p. 153.

[4] Pomponne de Bellièvre, see above, Introduction, n. 23. Like his brother, he had considerable diplomatic experience in Switzerland, and was one of the few councillors involved in the making of the treaty of Soleure (Cramer, *Seigneurie*, I, p. 272, n. 4).

[5] They returned from their embassy in Switzerland in mid-September.

[6] Lawsuit, probably before the Parlement of Paris, involving the Peyroliers, a merchant family from Lyons, and presumably involving trade with Geneva. No further details of it are currently known.

[7] Imbert de Biotière, sieur de Chassincourt, councillor of the King of Navarre and his agent at the court from 1578. He was also appointed representative of the churches at court by the assembly of St Jean d'Angély; see Bib. Mazarine, MS 2604, fos 104v, 125, 129 v.

Clerevant[8] estoit allé a Metz, et respondroit pour la dicte somme en faisant sa debte, et que les Eglises de Paris et la aupres payeroyent tout l'interest, scavoir est mille escus par an: et qu'estant sur le lieu on sçauroit pour quel terme on s'en pourroit servir.

Les Eglises de Picardie ont faict 200* lesquelz avec 600* faictz en Normandie ilz envoyeront ensemblement.

Qu'ilz n'ont receu response des autres Eglises ausquelles ilz avoyent escrit à mesme fin.

Touché a Monsieur de Chassincour de la partie de 20000£ deues par les Eglises et des 2600 et tant d'escus assignez sur le departement de Bourgogne et en apres sur la Provence par les Estats tenus à Montauban,[9] lequel pour n'en estre bien informé, m'a renvoyé a Monsieur Paiot recepveur du Roy de Navarre,[10] lequel dict estre de besoing qu'on en escrive à M. de Chassincour pour le faire sçavoir au Roy afin qu'il en face sa debte, et par ainsi que Mess. de Geneve soyent remboursez de la somme entiere. Ou bien qu'il trouvait encores meilleur, qu'au lieu des 8000 livres assignees sur la Provence Messieurs tirassent les 13000 et à quoy elle est cotisee, le faisant scavoir au Roy de Navarre, et le priant d'envoyer mandement au dict Monsr Paiot d'assigner les dictz 13000 livres sur la Provence pour Messieurs de Geneve, et que lon procederoit à la levee des dictz deniers sans nommer aucun.

Que le somme qui restoit des 20000 livres s'assigneroit à la prochaine assemblee des Estats, laquelle se pourra tenir en brieff.[11]

Et que quant à eux pour estre officiers de sa Maiesté, qu'il ne leur est seant d'en faire ouverture.

Touchant la revocation de l'arrest de la Cour de Parlement de Toulouze, donnée à l'encontre de ceux que se sont mis en debvoir de secourir la ville, Monsieur de Chassincour m'a dict en avoir escrit au

---

[8] Claude-Antoine de Vienne, seigneur de Clervant (or Clervaut) (d. 1588), councillor of the King of Navarre. He had come to court at the beginning of August and then departed in October (having been delayed by Henry III's absence) on a mission first to John Casimir and then to Charles Emanuel. This mission concerned Navarre's proposed attack on Spanish Navarre and his response to Charles Emanuel's proposal of marriage earlier the summer to his sister Catherine. The latter may have been an attempt to distract Navarre from aiding Geneva, but it collapsed over Charles Emanuel's insistence that she change her religion; see J. Berger de Xivrey (ed.), *Recueil des Lettres Missives de Henri IV*, 7 vols (Paris, 1843–1860), I, pp. 467–469, 472–473. Beutterich makes some very some interesting sceptical comments on both Clervant and the attack on Spain in his letter to Beza of 6 September (*Beza*, XXIII, 1546). Clervant finally saw Beutterich in November, see *CSPF, 1582*, pp. 417, 424, and *Briefe Johann Casimir*, II, p. 23.

[9] For the assembly at Montauban in 1579, see above, p. 155. Note that the sums involved here are in *livres tournois*.

[10] Nicolas Pajot, see above, Introduction, n. 55.

[11] The next Huguenot assembly was not in fact held until 1584, despite a certain notion that there should be one every three years.

Roy de Navarre, et qu'il trouvoit bon en attendant response d'en parler à Messieurs de Mandelot et de Hautefort et à Monsieur de Belieure, de peur que ne leur estant la chose communiquee, et passant sans leur sceu, ilz ne fussent peust estre enaigris par ce moyen.

Qu'il ne failloit parler que simplement de rescinder l'arrest, sans avancer tant de choses à coup, et qu lon se serviroit de ceste revocation pour tous les aultres.

Que Monsieur de La Vaqueresse[12] presenta lettres au Roy de la part de Monsieur de Chastillon son maistre, et aultres papiers pour informer le Roy de sa droicte intention en levant les armes, que estoit non pour troubler la France mais seulement pour secourir Geneve comme le traicte du Roy avec eux le portoit expres: donnant permission à tous ses subiectz tant capitaines chefs souldatz qu'a tous aultres d'y aller avec armes pour la defense d'icelle, come il le pouvoit monstrer par la copie qu'il en avoit.

Que le Roy fist response que de vray tel estoit son vouloir et s'il ne l'avoit faict à aultre respect qu'il luy seroit Roy bon et gracieux, et le recevroit en sa protection.

[fo. IV]

Monsieur de Villeroy Secretaire d'Estat[13] receut les dictz papiers pour les veoir, et en faire rapport.

Le 24 d'octobre Monsieur de Belieure promist qu'il s'employeroit en ce faict en ce qu'il pourroit, si le Roy luy en parloit, parce, me dict il, qu'il n'en avoit la principale charge. Et me conseilla d'en parler à Monsieur de Mandelot et Monsieur d'Hautefort deputez à cest affaire avec Monsr Brulart.[14]

Que n'ay eu moyen d'acoster Monsr de Mandelot: toutefois que Monsr d'Hautefort promit luy en parler et à Messieurs de Villeroy et Brulart et qu'il se trouveroit quand la depesche de M. de la Vaqueresse seroit presentee au Roy.

A promis le dict Seigneur de moyenner la dicte revocation avec l'adveu general tant de Monsieur de Chastillon, que des aultres Seigneurs at gentilzhommes qui s'estoyent mis en debvoir pour la defense de la dicte ville.

---

[12] For the mission of La Vacqueresse, see above, p. 158.
[13] See above, Introduction, n. 69.
[14] Pierre Brulart, sieur de Crosnes and Genlis (1535–1608), *secrétaire d'état*. The Swiss were in his *département*; see N. Sutherland, *The French Secretaries of State in the Age of Catherine de Medici* (London, 1962), p. 37.

Quant à l'interiner[15] à la Cour de Parlement de Paris, il faudra poursuivre cela par apres.

Ay tiré promesse de Monsieur de Chassincour d'advertir Messeigneurs des aussitost que la dicte depesche seroit faict, et que la Cour de Parlement y auroit passé dessus.

Rendu les lettres de Messieurs à Monsieur Cobham Ambassadeur pour la Royne d'Angleterre en France, auxquelles il faict response. Et a escrit lettres en Angleterre en faveur de Messieurs à Mess. de Lestre, Walsyngham et Hatton, lesquelles il m'a faict veoir avant les sceller.[16]

Livré au dict Seigneur Ambassadeur un factum des Pretensions de Mosr. de Savoye et de noz defences au contraire.[17]

Monsieur de Montigny escrit en Angleterre à Monsieur Walsyngham et Monsr de La Fontaine en faveur de la cause.[18]

A Rouen Monsieur de la Tour[19] me dict avoir presque perdu l'esperance qu'il avoit eüe du present de 15000*, que les Eglises de Normandie vouloyent faire par ensemble: leur estant survenue une assignation de 27000*, que Monsieur le Prince de Conde demande presentement estre fournie: laquelle chose refroidict la charité de plusieurs, et ne veoict moyen d'en tirer somme, si Messeigneurs ne trouvent la dessus quelque expedient.

Qu'il ne laissoit de solliciter les Eglises et les rechauffer en la continuation de la bonne affection qu'ilz avoyent au soulagement de la dict ville comme il faict de mesmes en Angleterre.

En Angleterre

Novembre

Arrivé le 13 Novembre à Londres, et ayant rendu mes lettres à Monsieur de La Fontaine, il ne trouvoit estre temps idoine et propre a mouvoir cest affaire, le siège estant leve, les troubles à demy assopis, l'occasion passee lors que la ville estoit en destresse, et aultres discomoditez survenuës depuis six semaines en ça: comme entre aultres la comission par deça de la part du Roy de Navarre a mesme fin, le mescontentement de la Royne envers les François, qui en leur nécessité l'ont sceu implorer

---

[15] i.e. *enregistrer* – the process by which a legal document was given the full sanction of the authority of the Parlement of Paris.

[16] Cobham's letter to Walsyngham for Malliet, 25 October, is found in *CSPF, 1582*, pp. 409–410. For the credence, see Introduction, n. 45.

[17] The *factum* is discussed above, p. 154.

[18] For La Fontaine, see above, p. 152.

[19] See above, pp. 156–157.

et hors de peine n'ont tenu conte d'elle, jusques à ne daigner la remercier.²⁰

Que les Rochellois ayans eu en prest £40,000 de la maison de ville de Londres pendant leur siege, se soucioyent peu de rembourser les dictz deniers, requerans qu'on leur en fist present.²¹

Le 15 de Novembre presentay à Wynsor²² celles de Messeigneurs à Monsieur Walsyngham Secretaire d'estat de sa Majesté: auquel ayant declaré ma charge, et descouvert les Practiques du Duc sur l'estat de la ville de Geneve, les fraix soustenus par les troubles de longue duree, et la request que faisoyent Messeigneurs à sa Majesté: me fist response que cela ne luy estoit du tout incogneu,²³ et qu'il estoit si affectioné et à la Religion et au dict bien public, que quand il verroit l'opportunité, il se mettroit en debvoir, de sonder la volonté et intention de la Royne envers la dicte ville, et quelle resolution elle prendroit.

[fo. 2]

Quant à son advis pour parler franchement et sans palliation, qu'il n'avoit grande esperance du costé de sa Majesté, et qu'il y voyoit de grands empeschements: comme entre aultres la mauvaise opinion conceue d'eux de longue main a cause d'un livre imprime pendant le Reigne de la Royne Marie, impugnant la succession des femmes aux Royaumes. A quoy neantmoins Monsieur de Beze principal ministre du dict lieu, auroit suffisamment respondu en un livre qu'il a faict, monstrant assez qu'il n'y avoit ny consentement ny mandement du

---

²⁰ Anglo-French relations at this point are discussed above, pp. 158–162. In July Navarre informed Cobham and Burghley that he was sending one of his chamberlains, the Baron de Senégas, to see Anjou and then Elizabeth over his proposed attack on Spain, as Clervant (above, n. 8) was doing elsewhere. Senégas accompanied Clervant to Paris in August, and on 4 October Clervant sent Walsingham a letter of introduction for him; see *CSPF, 1582,* pp. 234, 250–251, 370–371, and BL, Lansd. MS 35, art. 58. Nothing, however, survives from this period in England. Mauvissière mentions an exchange of missions between Elizabeth and Navarre in his despatch of 25 June 1582 (Chéruel, 227), but the reference to Navarre is an error for the King of Denmark.

²¹ This is probably not a reference to the famous siege of 1572–1573, but to the complex agreement for the supply of money and munitions to La Rochelle in the autumn of 1568, outlined by Cecil in September 1568; PRO, SP 12/47/194–195. A later undated minute of a letter from Elizabeth to La Rochelle, assigned to 1573, regrets her inability to modify the repayment terms, *CSPF, 1572–1574,* p. 452.

²² The court had removed to Windsor at the end of September, concluding a 'little progress' in Oatlands and Nonsuch, and remained there until 12 January 1583, when it removed to Richmond. This was unusually late in the year for Elizabeth to stay at Windsor and was probably an attempt to avoid the plague in London, to which reference is made below.

²³ See above, p. 162.

Magistrat, et partant que les faultes d'un particulier n'estoyent valables pour prejudicier à tout un public.[24]

Oultre que sa Majesté avoit depuis nagueres faict grands fraix en Irlande, Escosse et Flandres, estant par ce moyen espuisee d'une grandissime somme de deniers.[25]

Que pour bien acheminer le tout, il failloit attendre la venue à la Cour de Monsieur le Comte de Lestre que s'estoit retiré a Northhal a cause d'un laquay qui luy estoit mort de peste:[26] et de Monsieur Burghley grand Tresorier qui estoit avec Monsieur Myldmay à Erford, ou le Terme se tenoit a cause de la contagion qui estoit grande dans la ville de Londres.[27]

Le dict Seigneur me dict aussi, que je pourroye bien m'absenter de Cour pour quelque temps, et n'y saluer aucun que Monsieur Marchemond agent pour Monsieur en Angleterre: de peur que venant à ses oreilles par quelque aultre moyen, il ne chanssast à sa Majesté quelque sinistre opinion de nostre faict.[28]

Qui fut cause que le dict iour ayant salué le dict Seigneur, luy fys un breff recit de ma commission: a quoy estant attentif, ne trouvoit bon le delay au retour des susdictz Seigneurs en Cour; et fut d'advis, cas advenant que Monsieur le Secretaire le trouvast bon; que me transportasse par devers Mess. de Burghley et de Lestre et leur fisse ouverture du faict afin d'apprendre d'eux, comment je m'y debvrois gouverner. Et que cela serviroit mesmes pour advancer les affaires de son maistre.[29] Ce que Monsieur Walsyngham approuva.

Le 18e je livray celles de Messieurs à Mylord de Lestre en sa maison à Northal et iceluy ayant entendu les menees et practiques de noz adversaires, dict que ny la Royne d'Angleterre, ny le Roy de France

---

[24] *The First Blast*, see above, p. 152, and the comments in *Beza*, XXIII, p. 192, n. 7.

[25] See above, pp. 162–163.

[26] A servant fell ill of the plague at his house at Wanstead on the 9th, and Leicester dispersed his household and retired to Northaw – his brother, the Earl of Warwick's, house – with 'a fresh company'; see BL, Lansd. MS 36, art. 10, to Burghley (13 November) 1582.

[27] The Westminster law courts were sitting in Hertford Castle. Burghley, together with Sir Walter Mildmay, Chancellor of the Exchequer, and the barons, was presiding over the exchequer court.

[28] Pierre Clausse, Sieur de Marchaumont, the brother of Fleury, the French resident in Switzerland (see above, Introduction, n. 30). Initially one of the commissioners for the marriage treaty between Anjou and Elizabeth in the spring of 1581, he had remained in England as Anjou's agent. He was then at Windsor; see his letter to Leicester of 28 November, P.J. Blok (ed.), *Correspondance inédite de Robert Dudley, comte de Leycester, et de François et Jean Hotman* (Haarlem, 1911), pp. 118–119.

[29] This may be a reference to Anjou's extensive recruiting in Switzerland during 1582 for his Netherlands army, from which Henry was careful to distance himself; see *Henri*, V, 4563.

ne debuoyent permettre que le Roy d'Hespagne passast au pays Bas sans empeschement, qu'il estoit par [*sic*] trop grand.

Que je fisse a sçavoir à Messeigneurs le désir qu'il a de s'employer pour eux et l'affection qu'il porte au bien de ceste Republique.

S'enquist si Monsieur Casimire estoit fort esloigné de nous, parce qu'estant serviteur de sa Majesté, la Royne le prieroit et luy aussi par lettres à ce qu'il ne permist que l'Estat de la dicte ville fut aucunement alteré ou innové.[30]

Que le plaisir de sa Majesté estoit, qu'elle fut garantie et protegee a l'encontre de tous, estant come une lampe que a servi pour esclairer toutes presque les Eglises de l'Europe.

Que le perte d'une telle ville ne seroit moins deplorable, qu'elle toucheroit de pres leur Estat, en souffrant que l'ennemy empietast si avant.

Que Monsieur mesmes, lequel la Royne favorisoit, y avoit de l'interest.

Mais que touchant la requeste que faisoyent Messieurs de Geneve, il seroit malaysé de pouvoir tirer somme de sa Majesté, ayant icelle depuis quelques mois en ça debourse £300,000 st. Que toutefois dans 8 jours il seroit en Cour, et ne faudroit d'en faire ouverture à sa Majesté.

Le dict Seigneur me donna advis d'arrester à Londres quelque temps, et que cependant il en escriroit à Monsieur Walsyngham.

Le 19ᵉ je presentay celles qui s'adressoye à Mylord Burghley grand Tresorier,[31] lequel pour les grandes negoces qu'il avoit au Terme ne me peust faire response sur le champ, promettant que sçaurois son advis de la bouche de Monsieur le Secretaire auquel ce jour là ou le lendemain il escriroit.[32]

Decembre

A Wynsor le 2 de Decembre Monsieur Walsyngham me dict qu'il se doutoit que je n'avancerois rien avec sa Majesté qu'elle n'impartiroit aucuns deniers.

---

[30] Leicester was far better informed than this answer would imply. Both John Casimir (6 September, *Briefe Johann Casimir*, I, pp. 537–538) and Beutterich (7 September, Blok, *Correspondance de Robert Dudley*, pp. 112–114) had written to him about the settlement of the Genevan crisis, and he had answered on 8 October (*Briefe Johann Casimir*, I, pp. 553–554). Casimir was about to take up the cause of the Elector of Cologne, about which he wrote to Elizabeth and Leicester on 5 December (*ibid.*, II, pp. 29–30).

[31] The letters are now BL, Lansd. MS 35, arts 64–65, printed in Strype, *Annals*, III, pt 2, pp. 198–202. See *Beza*, XXIII, 1550, for a more accurate version of the letter from Beza.

[32] On 21 November Burghley informed Walsingham that he and Mildmay would be finished in a week and asked if the Queen wished them to return to court then, but did not mention Malliet. Walsingham answered on 26 November that she wished him to come as soon as possible in order to reach a decision on the mission of La Mothe-Fénelon (see above, p. 161), PRO, SP 12/155/184, 190. As Malliet notes below, Burghley and Leicester returned to court on 3 December.

[fo. 2v]

Me dict en oultre que Mylord Burghley ny Mylord de Lestre n'avoit pas escrit, et demanda quelle response i'avoye euë d'eux.

Le dict iour fys tenir à Yorck la lettre de Messeigneurs à Monsr. le Comte de Huntingdon avec un factum par le moyen de Monsieur le Secretaire.[33]

Le 3 jour les Seigneurs de retour en Cour, Monsieur le Secretaire s'enquist de moy, quelle somme on demanderoit bien: je fy response que petiteurs ne doivent faire choix.

Urgé derechef de dire à mon advis quelle somme les pourroit accomoder pour le present, je respondy qu'en faict de prest, 30000* sans aucune interest et pour 5 ou 6 annees leur fairoit grand service. Il repliqua que c'estoit une bien grosse somme.[34]

Demandé derechef quelle some pour une fois les pourroit gratifier, je fy response de dix à douze mille escus de la liberalite de sa Majesté.[35]

Il repliqua qu'il seroit expedient que je parlasse aux Seigneurs de Lestre et de Burghley, et leur ramenteusse la promesse qu'ilz m'avoyent faicte. Qu'il sçavoit ce que lon debvroit faire, mais non ce que lon fairoit.

Que quant aux Evesques ilz sont paovres et assez refroidis: que les particuliers fairoyent plus qu'eux, combien qu'a la contribution de Mompellier lon ne fist jamais plus en Cour que £200 st.[36]

Que si Monsieur le Tresorier n'advance l'affaire rien ne se faira.

Le 4 Decembre presentay à M. le Secretaire les lettres qui s'adressoyent à sa Majesté: lequel me demanda le nom de tous ceux auxquelz Messieurs escrivoyent.

Adjousta le dict seigneur qu'il avoit bonne envie de s'employer, mais qu'il ne pourroit y vaquer que Monsieur de la Motte Fenelon Ambassadeur pour le Roy et qui s'acheminoit en Escosse, n'eust eu ses depesches: que j'eusse un peu de patience.[37]

---

[33] Henry Hastings, third Earl of Huntingdon, Lord President of the Council in the North.

[34] This was the sum he had been instructed to request, see above, p. 154.

[35] i.e. £3,500–£4,000, some £2,000 less than they actually obtained.

[36] Little is known about the collection for Montpellier. The town had appealed to England in the spring of 1580 for financial help following an earthquake. An undated draft circular letter from Elizabeth to the leading laymen in each shire survives, which requests them to raise money discreetly out of Christian charity; (PRO, SP 12/138/65, assigned to May 1580). The French Church in London also contributed; see Fernand de Schickler, *Les Églises de Refuge en Angleterre*, 3 vols (Paris, 1892), I, p. 242.

[37] Fénelon arrived in London in late November and left for Scotland about 10 December, escorted by William Davison. The English tried by various means to obstruct or delay his journey to Edinburgh until Lennox had left Scotland.

Le 5ᵉ parlay à Mylord de Lestre, lequel me dict qu'il ne m'avoit oublié: qu'il en parleroit le lendemain à sa Majesté.

Le 6 livray les lettres pour M. Sidney à M. Philippe Sydney son filz,[38] et pour Mons Pawlet à Monsieur son frere avec des mien[s] que je luy adressois.[39]

Le mesme jour Monsieur le grand Tresorier promist derechef d'en parler à la Royne. Que Geneve estoit un des principaulx pilliers [de] l'Eglise, qu'il ne seroit des derniers à faire debvoir.

Le mesme jour livray celles qui s'adressoyent à Monsieur Walter Myldmay, qui m'asseura d'en parler à M. le grand Tresorier, et à M. Walsyngham, et que de sa part il y contribueroit volontairement. Et s'enquerant de l'Estat de la ville luy presentay un factum des pretensions.

Le 7 presentay celles de Messieurs à Monsieur Warwick[40] qui dict qu'il auroit l'affaire pour recommandé.

Le 8 acostay M. le grand Tresorier au parc lequel me dict avoir comuniqué noz affaires à M. le Comte de Lestre, et qu'ilz y avoyent donné ordre: qu'il failloit avoir un peu de patience. Que Monsr le Secretaire en fairoit ouverture à sa Majesté, et qu'il estoit requis de le laisser faire, qu'il espieroit l'opportunité.

Le 9 je rendy les lettres de Messieurs à Monsr Hatton,[41] lequel envoya un de ses gentilzhomes M. Flour[42] par devers M. le Secretaire afin que pour l'amour de luy il eust nostre faict pour recommandé.

L'11 Monsr le Comte de Lestre me dict qu'il n'avoit conceu trop bonne esperance du costé de sa Majesté pour les grands fraix soustenus par elle en Irlande, Flandres, Escosse et Portugal toutefois que l'amitié de M. le Duc Casimire y serviroit beaucoup si lon tiroit lettres de luy. Mais que, puis que M. de la Motte estoit party entre cy et Dimanche il en parleroit à la Royne. Monsieur Walsyngham n'est d'advis que je presente lettres à Mylord Maire de Londres, ny aux Archevesques et Evesques que sa Majesté n'en eust esté premier informee.

Le 15 Monsr le Secretaire me dict qu'a cause des grand affaires survenus les uns sur les aultres, il n'avoit trouvé bon de presenter les lettres à sa Majesté d'autant qu'elle ny prendoit goust: mais qu'au pis aller on rembourseroit les fraix faictz venant de si loin.

---

[38] Sir Henry, Lord President of the Council in the Marches, was then presumably at Ludlow and Philip either at court or in London.

[39] Sir Amyas Paulet, ambassador in Paris 1576–1579. He had two brothers. The reference to 'my letters' suggests that Malliet had some previous acquaintance with him.

[40] Ambrose Dudley, Earl of Warwick, Leicester's brother.

[41] Sir Christopher Hatton, then Vice-Chamberlain of the Household.

[42] Hatton's friend and follower, Francis Flower (d. 1596).

[fo. 3]

Qu'il trouvoit bon que je les presentasse moy mesme, et qu'il en parleroit le lendemai au conseil, et m'en rendroit response à la chambre du conseil, m'ensoignant de m'y trouver. Que M. de Lestre et Burghley en avoyent conferé ensemble, et ne voyoyent point qu'il y eust apparence d'obtenir chose que ce fut de la Royne.

Quant aux Evesques come il m'avoit ia auparavant dict, qu'ilz estoyent paovres et n'avoyent moyen de faire somme notable: mesmes que Daniel Rogers estoit entre les mains des Espagnols detenu pour l'appetit de £3000 de rançon, et n'avoyent peu fournir à la susdicte somme.[43]

Que toute la sepmaine ilz seroyent occupez à Grennwich pour les affaires du Duc de Moscovie: que le temps ne permettoit point d'avancer rien.[44]

S'estant enquis qu'il auroit a declarer de bouche à sa Majesté, et l'ayant instruict me pria ne faillir me trouver le lendemain a 9 heures à la chambre du Conseil.

Le 16 le dict seigneur me fist response à la dicte chambre, avoit presenté les lettres de Messeigneurs à sa Majesté, et combien qu'il eust esté quasi de besoing des lettres de M. le Duc Casimire, toutefois le temps ne le pouvant porter, qu'il auroit declaré a sa Majesté la necessité a laquelle estoit reduicte la ville de Geneve, et discouru tous les troubles, et l'estat d'icelle.

A quoy sa Majesté auroit respondu, que Messieurs de Geneve n'avoyent à craindre nouvelle guerre: et que le Duc de Savoye sçait combien cela luy vaut: qu'il aura cogneu a cause de leurs amis et alliez, la partie estre trop forte: qu'ilz auroyent les Souisses pour eux. Que le Roy de France mesmes luy auroit faict entendre avoir moyenné la paix et s'estre proposé les assister si la necessité l'eust requis. Qu'elle a plus faute d'argent que ceux de Geneve, estant à present menacee de

---

[43] Daniel Rogers (1538–1591) had been seized on a mission to the Empire in the autumn of 1580 and then held by the Prince of Parma on the grounds that he was instigating rebellion in Philip's domains thanks to papers he was carrying about Dom António. Getting Rogers released proved difficult. Leicester and Walsingham wanted to imprison Mendoza in retaliation, but Elizabeth would not agree; neither would she pay a ransom. A compromise was reached in early 1582 to raise the money by a charitable levy on the clergy, but with little immediate success and Rogers was not freed until early 1584. See J.A. van Dorsten, *Poets, Patron and Professors* (Leiden, 1962), pp. 68–73.

[44] The embassy of Theodor Andreevitch Pissemsky, sent by Tsar Ivan IV to negotiate an alliance and an English bride. Pissemsky arrived in September 1582 and left on 22 June 1583. See T.S. Willan, *The Early History of the Russia Company* (Manchester, 1956), pp. 162–163.

plusieurs costez, et entre aultres du costé d'Escosse, d'ou il y avoit grandement à craindre.

Que le Roy de France, les Souisses et Seigneurs d'Allemagne ne permettroyent qu'ilz fussent reduictz à grande necessité: leur estant le dict affaire de telle consequence.

Monsieur le Secretaire dict avoir remonstré la dessus à sa Majeste les grands frais par eux soustenus, et la despense du personage qu'ilz avoyent depesché par devers elle ne pouvoir estre petite, la priant humblement d'y avoir esgard. A quoy sa Majeste auroit respondu que Messieurs de son conseil eussent à y adviser, et donner quelque ordre.

Le dict Seigneur m'ayant laissé le communiquer a Mylord de Lestre, qui pour toute response dict qu'il en failloit parler à Monsieur le Grand Tresorier et y adviser.

Mais parce que les seigneurs avoyent ja prins leur places en Conseil, il falloit sortir. Et quoy que l'on fut, fut arresté des procedures à ce requises.

Le 17 Mess. de Burghley, de Lestre, Hatton et Walsyngham partirent de cour pour ouir les Ambassadeurs Moscovites à Grennwich. Le dict Sieur Secretaire dict à son homme M. Tomson[45] qu'il me fist sçavoir que je me pouvois retirer à Londres pour 5 ou 6 jours, et que j'eusse quelque peu de patience, qu'il luy avoit comandé de despescher lettres à Messieurs les Archevesques et Evesques de la part de Messieurs du Conseil en faveur de Messeigneurs prestes à sceller à leur retour.[46]

Le 24 M. Walsyngham me dict que M. le Grand Tresorier et luy avoyent conferé ensemble, et qu'il estoit de cest advis avec Mylord de Lestre qu'au nom des Seigneurs du Conseil lon escrivist aux deux Archeveques et à un chacun des Evesques particulierement, que les lettres estoyent dressees, mais qu'a cause que le dict Sieur Burghley s'en alloit à sa maison et que l'Aumosnier de sa Majesté M. Piers Evesque de Salisbury[47] qui devoyent l'un soussigner et l'aultre m'accompagner avec les susdictes lettres chez M. l'Archevesque de Canterbury,[48] seroyent empeschez toutes les festes de Noël: me seroit force d'attendre 10 ou 12 jours pour plus entiere expedition.

Le 26 j'envoyay les lettres de Mylord de Bedford à Mylord Rossel son filz pour les luy faire tenir au pays. Au dict Sieur Rossel livray un

---

[45] Laurence Tomson (1539–1608), Walsingham's personal secretary.
[46] The council register for the period June 1582 to February 1586 has disappeared. In its absence the process can only be reconstructed from the surviving correspondence. These letters (signed but not dated or addressed) were those taken by Malliet and the Bishop of Salisbury to Grindal on 5 January; see below, pp. 176–177.
[47] John Piers, Bishop of Salisbury 1577–1589, Queen's Almoner from 1576.
[48] Edmund Grindal, see above, p. 163.

factum des pretensions des Ducs de Savoye, et allegations au contraire par ceux de Geneve.[49]

[fo. 3v]

Janvier

Le 2 Janvier M. Philippe Sydné dict avoir receu lettres de Monsr. son pere, par lesquelles il luy mandoit qu'il envoyeroit mandement de tous costez en son gouvernement de Galles pour faire levee de deniers. Ce qu'il obtint tost apres.

Le 3 de Janvier je baillay les lettres de M. de Beze a M. l'Evesque de Sarisbury, lequel de sa part promist toute faveur ayde et assistance, non seulement par son travail, mais ainsi de ses propres deniers. Le lendemain me dict avoir mandement des Seigneurs du Conseil de m'accompagner avec le Doyen de Wynsor[50] chez M. l'Archevesque de Cantorbury et que lon assisteroyent l'Evesque de Londres,[51] et le Doyen de Pauls[52] pour adviser à quelque bon ordre: et qu'il ne foudroit le 7 du mois de se trouver à Lambeth sur les 2 heures apres midy avec les deputez.

Le Doyen de Wynsor me dict avoir receu le mesme mandement.

Monsieur Walsyngham me fit recit que Messieurs du Conseil avoyent deliberé d'essayer premier ceste voye susdicte, et en apres selon les occurences adviseroyent à quelque aultre expedient.

Le 5 jour Monsieur Beal[53] me livra les lettres des Seigneurs du Conseil à M. l'Archevesque,[54] les aultres particulieres des Evesques estans livrees à M. de Sarisbury.[55]

---

[49] Francis Russell, second Earl of Bedford, and his son, Lord John Russell. Beza's letter to Bedford is referred to above, Introduction, n. 45.

[50] William Day, Dean of Windsor 1572–1595, Bishop of Winchester 1595, d. 1596.

[51] John Aylmer, Bishop of London 1577–1594.

[52] Alexander Nowell, Dean of St Paul's 1560–1602.

[53] Robert Beale (1541–1601), clerk of the Privy Council.

[54] The council's letter to Grindal (5 January) was entered in his register and is printed in William Nicholson (ed.), *Remains of Edmund Grindal* (Parker Society, 1843), pp. 432–433. It recommends the bearer, who will explain his purpose, saving them having to do so. With him and the Bishop of Salisbury they are sending their letters to the bishops, which Grindal is to send to 'such of your lordship's brethren as to your lordship shall be thought meet' and they hope that he will accompany them with his own. They leave the further order and direction to Grindal, but they want the collection made secretly and discreetly. They recommend he consult Piers and Day as well as Aylmer and Nowell.

[55] These were the council's letters to the bishops (see previous note), from the appearance of the copy entered into Grindal's register (printed in both Strype, *Grindal*, pp. 281–282, and Nicholson, *Remains*, pp. 434–435); it was left to Grindal to address and date them, for they are dated only January 1582[3]. They briefly describe the needs of Geneva, state that owing to the demands on the Queen's resources (especially Ireland) she is unable to give as she would like to, and propose that money be raised from the

Le dict Sieur Beal me dict que M. l'Evesque de Sarisbury se retiroit de la Cour et que je fairois bien de le prier de donner charge à son Viceaumosnier[56] de faire collecte en Cour, et gagner temps à son absence. Ce que le dict Seigneur Evesque me promist.

Je receu aussi les copies des lettres escrites à Messieurs les Archeveques et Evesques, et de celles que lon avoit minutees pour envoyer par devers le Maire de Londres,[57] lesquelles il receut tost apres.[58]

Le 6 M. le Secretaire me donna advis de comuniquer à M. l'Archevesque et les deputez, que j'avois lettres qui s'adressoyent à M. l'Archevesque d'Yorck[59] et l'Evesque de Durham,[60] et d'aultres à le Maire de Londres de la part de Messieurs de Geneve: et que j'eusse a suyvre l'advis qu'ilz me donneroyent.[61]

Le 7 consultation fut faicte à Lambeth domicile de M. l'Archevesque de Cantorbury ou je presentay les susdictes lettres, tant de la part des Seigneurs du Conseil de la Royne, que de Messeigneurs, et des ministres de la ville de Geneve. Leur consultation couchee par escrit fut renvoyee à Messieurs du Conseil par le Doyen de Wynsor me prians par mesme moyen de m'y trouver le Jeudy matin: luy pour declarer sa charge et moy afin de prier Messieurs du Conseil de me favorir de leurs lettres à M. le Maire, à l'Archevesque d'Yorck et aux aultres Evesques de son ressort.

Le 10 parlay à Wynsor à M. le Secretaire lequel sur la commission que j'avois de la part des Seigneurs deputez dict que Mess. du Conseil escriroyent pareillement à M. l'Archevesque d'Yorck, aux Evesques de son Evesche et a Monsr. le Maire de Londres. Le mesmes me fut confirmé par Monsieur le grand tresorier.

Le 15 M. Paulé Secretaire de M. le Comte Huntingdon[62] dict que son maistre avoit receu les lettres de Messieurs, et qu'il advanceroit la dicte contribution autant qu'a luy seroit possible.

wealthier and best affected persons of their dioceses. The contribution was to repay the courtesy shown in the late persecution in Queen Mary's time.

[56] William Absolon (d. 1586), sub-almoner to the Queen and Clerk of the Closet by 1574, Master of the Savoy 1576; see John Bickerseth and Robert W. Dunning, *Clerks of the Closet in the Royal Household* (Stroud, 1991), p. 15.

[57] The Lord Mayor in 1582–1583 was Thomas Blanke.

[58] Malliet's copies and translations of the council's letters to Bedford, the Lord Mayor of London, the two archbishops, and the bishops can be found in PH 2045, all of which are dated 20 January 1582/3, possibly by him.

[59] Edwin Sandys, Archbishop of York 1577–1588.

[60] Richard Barnes, Bishop of Durham 1577–1587, whose son was a student at Geneva; see above, Introduction, n. 38.

[61] The letter from Geneva to the Lord Mayor of London (7 October) is calendared in Peel, *The Second Parte of a Register* (I, p. 155).

[62] Identity not clear. Henry Cheke (c. 1546–1586) was secretary to the Council in the North from 1581. Claire Cross, *The Puritan Earl: The Life of Henry Hastings, Third Earl of Huntingdon 1536–1595* (London, 1966) does not mention a private secretary.

Demandant lettres aux Provinces de M. le Secretaire, il me fist response que la chose requeroit du temps, et que lon pourroit faire tenir lettres à quelques Provinces les plus affectionees, comme en Gales, West [*sic*], Kent et lieux circumvoisins, et qu'en apres lon adviseroit au reste.

Le 17 Monsieur Noël Doyen de Pauls me dict que les deputes avoyent ja depeschez les lettres des Seigneurs du Conseil à leurs freres avec la copie des lettres de M. Beze tant particulieres que generales jointes au leurs particulieres de recommandation.

Que l'Archevesque de Cantorbie avoit promis pour sa part 100 marcs, les Evesques de Londres et de Salisbury un chacun 50 marcs, le Doyen de Wynsor 20 marcs et luy tout autant.

Que lon donnoit ordre que le tout fut icy à Pasques.[63]

Le 18. M. Randol[64] et M. Kilgray[65] m'asseurerent qu'ilz recommanderoyent l'affaire aux Eglises.

[fo. 4]

Le 20 baillay une copie du factum à M. Randol.

Le 21 je conferay à Londres avec 8 ministres des Eglises du pays ou M. Travers[66] presida portant la parolle et secondé de M. Crook,[67] Charck[68] et Kreck,[69] en la presence de Monsr. de la Fontaine: ou fut consulté, s'il estoit necessaire que lon fist collecte particuliere de leur authorité propre ou non, oultre la generale ordonnee par le conseil: out fut conclu, que de peur qu'ilz ne s'emblassent soubsminer les dictz Seigneurs, qu'ilz attendroyent que la collect fut faicte par les Evesques,

---

[63] This basically summarizes Grindal's letter. Grindal's contribution of 100 marks (£66 13s 4d) appears to have been the largest single individual gift, followed by Bedford at £40, Leicester at £30, and Burghley at 40 marks (£26 13s 4d). It was, however, still unpaid at his death in July; see below, pp. 192, 194.

[64] Probably Thomas Randolph (1523–1590), Master of the Posts from 1567.

[65] Probably Henry Killigrew (c. 1528–1603), like Randolph actively employed in Protestant diplomacy.

[66] Walter Travers (1548?–1635), then lecturer at the Temple.

[67] Thomas Crooke, rector of Great Waldingfield (Suffolk) and preacher to Gray's Inn.

[68] William Charke, preacher to Lincoln's Inn 1581–1593, expelled from Cambridge for supporting Thomas Cartwright in 1572.

[69] Richard Crick, central figure in the Dedham *classis*. Malliet's final account (PH 2082) records a contribution of £9 14s. from the towns of 'Diddam, Barfold, and Buckstead' [Dedham, Barfold, and Boxted], where the *classis* met. Unfortunately the minute book of the *classis* [which held its first meeting at Barfold on 3 December 1582] contains no reference to the Geneva collection, although the meeting held on 8 April 'where the time was spent in extraordinary prayer wth fasting' may have been suitable; Roland G. Ussher (ed.), *The Presbyterian Movement in the Reign of Queen Elizabeth as illustrated by the Minute Book of the Dedham Classis 1582–1589*, Camden Society, 3rd series, 8, (1905), p. 29. However, it is also possible that as elsewhere the collection was made at Easter.

et y procederoit ou lors si la necessité le requeroit, ou bien par apres sur quelque nouveau accident.[70] Le 22 je fus en Cour à Richemond,[71] ou M. le Secretaire me dict avoit lettres de Mess. du Conseil à M. le Maire de Londres de mesme teneur que les aultres et que je les presenteroye.[72] Et quand ce fut à les demander de son Secretaire Milles,[73] luy dict les avoir ia livrees à un poursuivant: qui fut cause qu'il me requist aller en diligence au dict Sieur Maire, et luy dire que j'estois le personage mentioné dans les lettres, et que j'eusse à luy rendre par mesme moyen les lettres de Messeigneurs, et luy declarer les troubles et Estat de la ville, prenant pour m'acompagner et m'authoriser de leur part Monsieur Bodeley marchant de la ville de Londres.[74]

Le 23 M. Bodely et moy parlasmes à Mylord Maire, luy presentay mes lettres, luy declarant ce qui m'estoit enioinct: lequel m'asseura de sa bonne volonté, et qu'il esperoit trouver Mess. les Aldermans ses compagnons prompts et volontaires.

Le 24 je fus à la maison de Monsieur Beal Secretaire du Conseil privé pour m'enquirer touchant la charge que Monsr. l'Evesque de Sarisbury disoit luy avoit laissee pour la contribution de la Cour: que me fist response, qu'il ne luy en avoit communiqué que fort legerement, toutefois qu'il tacheroit d'en parler à son beau frere M. Walsyngham,[75] afin que pendant le sejour des Seigneurs en Cour on y pourvent.

Que Mylord de Lestre, Mylord de Bedford, Mylord Gray,[76] M. Walsyngham et quelques aultres faisoyent assez larges offres.

Il me monstra aussi la liste qu'il avoit faicte des gentilzhomez nomez

---

[70] A highly significant gathering of some of the key figures in the classical movement, it is a pity the other four are not identified. It is also a pity that Malliet does not record how he came into contact with them. Beza had asked Travers to use his influence with eminent persons on Geneva's behalf, but not to organize a collection (*Beza*, XXIII, 1551). La Fontaine had his own contacts with the classes (see his undated letter to Oliver Pigge and the brethren of Buckinghamshire asking for financial help for the French church in London; Peel, *Second Parte of a Register*, I, p. 156).

[71] As noted above, the court had removed from Windsor to Richmond about 12 January. It remained at Richmond until mid-April.

[72] For these letters, dated 20 January, see above, n. 59. They are also calendared in Peel, *Second Parte of a Register*, I, p. 155. The collection was to be made 'in secret manner, and as nere as can be, of the wealthier sorte, that therof ther maye growe neither common speche nor grief to the poorer'.

[73] Francis Mylles (d. 1618), in Walsyngham's service from c. 1566.

[74] The former Exeter merchant, John Bodley, had been an exile in both Wesel and Geneva. From 1571 onwards he was an active elder of the French church in London; see Charles G. Littleton, 'Geneva on Threadneedle Street: the French church of London and its congregation, 1560–1625', (unpublished Ph.D. thesis, University of Michigan, 1996, pp. 208–209). It is interesting that, despite these impeccable Genevan credentials, his involvement in the collection was initially through Walsingham's nomination.

[75] Beale's wife and Walsingham's wife were sisters.

[76] Arthur, fourteenth Lord Grey de Wilton, Lord Deputy of Ireland 1580–1582.

par toutes les Provinces du Royaume et des Insercourtz.[77] Ce qui depuis ne fut entierement suyvi.[78]

Le 25 M. Mylles secretaire de M. Walsyngham me dict à Westminster à la chambre de l'Estoille,[79] que Mylord de Bedford avoit impetré lettres pour les quartiers de son ressort.

Le dict jour Mylord de Bedford me dict que l'uniformité des volontez et de la religion, et la charité exercee envers les Anglois pendant les troubles de la Royne Marie en Angleterre, ne nous nuyroyent point: qu'il estoit raisonable de rendre bien pour bien. Et luy et M. le Secretaire promisent qu'on seroit ramentu en Cour.

Je livray les lettres qui s'adressoyent à M. l'Archevesque d'Yorck et à l'Evesque de Durham, entre les mains de Monsr. Wilcks[80] Secretaire aussi du conseil privé, pour les enfermer avec celles qui leur estoyent depeschees à mesme effect.

Le 30 Monsr. le Comte Huntington m'asseura de sa bonne voloné envers Messeigneurs, et que pour son regard il s'y employeroit, si on luy en bailloit charge.

Le dict jour je fus trois grosses heures avec Monsieur le Comte de Bedford, lequel m'ayant faict grand accueil, et apres s'estre enquis de toutes choses particulierement, tant touchant l'Estat qu'aultres particularitez, me protesta tenir la dicte ville aussi chere que son pays propre, et que moy venant de la part de telle Republique, luy estois à son endroit aussi bien venu que l'Ambassadeur du plus grand Duc, Roy ou Monarque qui fut sous le ciel: que si l'avois faulte d'hommes, serviteurs, chevaux ou argent cependant, que je m'adressasse à luy familierement, hardiment et sans bruit. Qu'il ne le disoit selon la façon coustumiere de Cour, que le coeur parloit aussi bien que la bouche. Il me fist lire les lettres du Conseil qui luy avoyent esté adressees pour

---

[77] Inns of Court.

[78] The explanation for this comment may lie in the very interesting letter Thomas Cooper, Bishop of Lincoln, wrote to his senior clergy on 5 February (Peel, *Second Parte of a Register*, I, p. 155), explaining how an assessment of 6d in the £ was to be made of parsons and vicars, with curates and poor vicars exempted. He then went on to claim the credit for having prevented the council from implementing a scheme whereby the clergy would be rated 'not by my L. of Canterbury and the ordinaryes, but by certaine noblemen and gentlemen in eche county by authoritye of the councell. Into which bondage yf we shall once fall by our slacknes, we shall never rydd ourselves out of it, but in such cases for vjd. shall paye xxtie tymes sixpence. What affection they bere towards the mynisterye in eche counterye, I know by to[o] good experience. Upon this occasion some of the Councell have sent me worde that all the Clergie of England are beholding to me. This danger I praye you imparte to the mynisters when they appeare.' See Collinson, *Religion of Protestants*, pp. 126–127, for the method of rating employed by the archdeaconry of St Albans.

[79] Star Chamber.

[80] Thomas Wilkes (d. 1598), clerk of the Privy Council from 1576.

nostre faict. M'asseura que les [*fo. 4v*] Conseillers estoyent tous pour nous, et desireux d'advancer ceste charité.

Que M. le Tresorier, et M. de Lestre s'estoyent declarez fort noz amys, et que M. le Secretaire Walsyngham et M. Myldmaye usoyent de grande diligence à nostre advantage.

Febvrier

Le 5ᵉ de Febvrier j'obtins de M. de la Fontaine que lon communiquast aux trois Eglises estrangeres Françoise, Flamende et Italiene la necessité à la quelle estoit reduicte nostre ville afin que lon y pourvent selon qu'ilz trouveroyent leur estre commode sans les interesser aucunement: toutefois il estoit d'advis que de la à un mois seroit assez tost, et que les dictz deniers fussent rapportez à l'usage des paovres estrangers: mais luy ayant declare le soing que lon avoit des paovres par devers noz quartiers, il acquiessa.

Le 6 M. Walsyngham me dict qu'il prendroit luy mesme la charge de la collecte en Cour: que j'allasse cependant en son nom à M. le Maire, le priant qu'il eust a diligenter l'affaire et haster les commis.

Le dict jour Mylord Maire me dict qu'ilz s'estoyent assemblez.

L'11 les Aldermans Osburn[81] et Weabe[82] me firent recit de l'ordre estably pour la ville de Londres: qu'ilz avoyent choisix 5 des Aldermans, et 4 des Communes ou Tribu: entre lesquelz estoyent Alderman Martin,[83] Hart,[84] Bon,[85] Digsay[86] et Audley:[87] et M. Fish[88] du nombre des communiers avec M. Jong.[89]

Le 12 M. l'Archeveque me dict avoir depesché 21 lettres aux Evesques, et qu'il les avoit prié de se haster, et rapporter leurs sommes à Pasques.[90]

---

[81] Edward Osborne, Lord Mayor 1583–1584.

[82] William Webbe, Lord Mayor 1591–1592.

[83] Richard Martin, Lord Mayor 1594 and Master of the Mint.

[84] John Harte, Lord Mayor 1589–1590.

[85] George Bonde, Lord Mayor 1587–1588.

[86] Wolstan Dixie, Lord Mayor 1585–1586.

[87] Probably Thomas Audley, skinner.

[88] Probably Walter Fisshe, merchant taylor.

[89] Probably Richard Young, grocer; 'communier' is presumably common councillor.

[90] This letter is copied in Grindal's register (printed in both Strype, *Grindal*, pp. 281–282, and *Remains*, pp. 429–432) but dated only January 1582[3]. In it Grindal states that while he is forwarding the Council's letter, he also feels it his duty to aid the collection. The collection is to be undertaken with all secrecy and detailed advice is given on how to approach the clergy. With regard to the laity, the bishops are to consult two or four of the gentlemen of the shires in their dioceses, take their advice and appoint them collectors. Full returns of all contributors are to be made both to him and to the Council before Easter. To set an example Grindal rated himself at 100 marks, the two bishops at 50 marks and and the two deans at 20 marks (identified above, p. 176). Peel, *The Second Parte of Register*, I, pp. 154–155, calendars the Council's letter to the Bishop of Lincoln as dated 29 January and Grindal's 30 January According to what Grindal told Malliet, he wrote to all the bishops, not just the selection the Council had advised.

Le 17 Monsieur Bodely me vint dire que les Aldermans s'assembloyent le lendemain et que ilz me prioyent de leur bailler la copie des lettres de Messieurs à Monsr. le Maire parce qu'elles estoyent esgarees et ne se trouvoyent point: et parce que je n'en avois aucune copie come je luy fy response, ilz desirerent pour le moins d'en avoir le sens. Ce que je fy pour le lendemain. Toutefois dela a 6 ou 7 jours on les retrouva.

Le 18 M. Molins Archidiacre de Londres m'asseura avoir convoqué tous les ministres et curez des Paroisses de Londres, afin d'entendre leur habilité et affection.[91]

Le 19 M. Travers ministre me dict qu'il ne vid [sic] jamais, que les Sieurs du Conseil embrassassent un tel affaire avec plus grand soing, comme ilz faisoyent cestuy cy: qu'on s'en esmerveilloit fort.

Alderman Bon disoit que Messieurs de la Rochelle nous faisoyent grand tort, par ce qu'ilz estoyent cause que lon se monstroit plus froid qu'on n'eust este, pour ne s'estre monstre soigneux de restituer ce qu'ilz avoyent receu en prest.[92]

Le 25. M. Walsyngham dict n'avoir rien encores encommencé en Cour, par ce qu'il s'estoit apperceu que les dictz Seigneurs se refroidissoyent, contens de nous ayder de leur nom, authorité, faveur et creditz mais qu'ilz n'ont oreilles à mettre la main à la bourse.

Le dict jour M. l'Alderman Bonn me demanda un factum des pretensions que je luy livray.

Mylord Rossel en receut aussi un aultre.

Mars

Le 5e de Mars proposay devant les ministres des susdictes trois Eglises estrangeres, afin qu'ilz dressassent un ordre pour la levee de quelques deniers en leurs Eglises.[93]

A quoi le ministre Flamand[94] portant la parolle pour tous respondist, qu'ilz le communiqueroyent à leurs Consistoires, et qu'en breff en auroyent resolution.

M. Fisch l'un des 12 Tribu[95] me dict qu'apres qu'ilz auroyent achevé

---

[91] John Mullins, Archdeacon of London 1560–1591. There is a nice irony here, for Archdeacon Mullins had been a member of the Frankfurt congregation during Mary's reign, and his sermon on the 'Frankfurt troubles' in October 1573 had (according to the preface) inspired the publication of the famous *A Brieffe Discourse of the Troubles Begonne at Frankford* in 1575.

[92] See above, n. 21.

[93] This has not survived, but the reponse from the Dutch church in Norwich of 14 April 1583 is printed in J.H. Hessels (ed.), *Ecclesiae Londino-Batavae Archivum*, 3 vols (Cambridge, 1889–1897), II, p. 708. Owing to poor commercial conditions, they had collected only £14 10s.

[94] Godfrey van Winghen was minister of the Dutch church in London from 1563 until his death on 30 December 1599.

[95] Livery companies.

en leurs 12 Tribu qu'ilz tiroyent quelques aultres sommes des petites compagnies au nombre de 21: ce qui fut faict executé tost apres.[96]
Le 13 Mess. de la Fontaine et Castol[97] ministres de l'Eglise Françoise me redirent response, que lon m'avoit accordé ma demande et que lon avoit arresté que le Dimanche avant Pasques on le fairoit sçavoir aux assemblees, et que le jour de Pasques lon contribueroit; hommes estans à ce deputez, tant à Londres, que par toutes les Eglises foraines esparses en ce Royaume.

[fo. 5]

Le dict jour M. Estiene le Sieur[98] natif de Geneve et serviteur à M. Philippe Sidné, dict avoir ouy, que la femme de Daniel Rogers[99] s'estoit presentee à la Royne, et que sa Majeste luy auroit dict que lon auroit dans deux mois argent pour la rançon de son mary, que lon avoit depesché lettres aux Evesques à cest effect: et partant disoit il, qu'il se doutoit que cela fut cause que lon rongnast quelque partie de la benevolence: come de vray il y a eu depuis quelque apparence.[100]
Le 20 M. Fromton Secretaire de M. l'Archevesque. de Cantorbie[101] receut lettres des Evesques de Winchester[102] et Lyncoln [103] qui l'avoyent prié, qu'a cause de leurs assemblees qui se font en Apuril, on n'eust à les presser par trop, que M. son maistre estoit certainement informé du debvoir que faisoyent ses freres. Et que iaçoit que M. l'Archevesque se disposast de ceder à la charge qu'il a, que neantmoins il donneroit ordre que le tout fut rapporté entre les mains de M. Walsyngham, ou de ceux auxquelz il donnera ceste charge.
Le 24 fut presché par M. Castol touchant la charité pour subvenir à l'affliction des saincts, et fut appliqué à la necessite presente de Geneve, les exhortant que le jour de Pasques, ilz se dispossassent à s'eslargir

---

[96] On 7/17 March Don Bernardino de Mendoza reported that the amount being collected was being kept very secret, but that there were rumours it was actually intended for the Elector of Cologne; *CSPSp., 1580–1586*, p. 454. This, as noted above, was his sole reference to the collection.
[97] For Castol see above, p. 152.
[98] Stephen Lesieur (c. 1550 – by 1638), then Sidney's secretary.
[99] Her identity is a mystery, for in 1588 Rogers wrote to a friend that he had married Susanna, daughter of the French Secretary, Nicasius Yetsweirt, the year before (Van Dorsten, *Poets, Patrons*, 11). No earlier wife is known.
[100] i.e. to employ (literally 'trim') some of the collection to contribute to Rogers's ransom, on which see above, n. 43. On 15 March Malliet reported to Geneva on the methods of collection and on Bedford's diligence 'au pays de son gouvernement' (PH 2066).
[101] Richard Frampton, see Collinson, *Grindal*, p. 297.
[102] John Watson, Bishop of Winchester 1580–1584.
[103] Thomas Cooper, see above, n. 78.

envers la dicte ville, chacun selon l'opulence et benediction que Dieu leur aura donnee.

Le 30 fut faict cueillette aux 3 susdictes Eglises par 4 des Anciens et 4 des Diacres deputez à chacune d'icelles.[104]

Apuril

Le 1 jour d'Apuril Monsieur de la Fontaine, M. Castol et M. de l'Aulne[105] me raconterent, avoir ouy parler du grand mescontentement qu'avoit Monsieur de Mauvissieres Ambassadeur du Roy touchant la levee des deniers qui se faisoit en Angleterre, ayant conceu une jalousie grande avec soupçon que cela se practiquast par les Eglises du Languedoc au nom de Messieurs de Geneve, et que pour l'asseurer, il seroit bon que je parlasse à luy: adioustant que Geneve n'estoit en si grande disette, et que si Messieurs de la ville eussent envoyé aucun, ilz ne l'eussent celé, veu que le Roy leur est allié.[106]

Le 4 du dict mois Mylord Maire me dict que lon avoit faict assez bonne somme: et que iaçoit que leur ville fut chargee d'impostz, que le peuple estoit si affectioné envers Geneve, que de leur bon gré ilz s'offroyent et presentoyent largement.

Que je m'en allasse à Alderman Martin et luy disse de sa part, qu'il eust à haster les commis.

Le 5e Monsieur Bodley estant en Cour, fut authorisé pour recevoir toutes les sommes levees de toutes parts pour la dicte contribution.

Le 7 Monsieur le Chevalier Jerome Bowes[107] m'asseura, que s'il plaisoit à sa Majesté luy bailler £10000 st et 500 souldatz, il vendroit tout le sien, et se rendroit dans nostre ville pour la garder et defendre.

Le 8 je parlay à M. l'Ambassadeur de ce qu'il se formalisoit que d'aucuns soubs couleur d'une raccolte pour la ville de Geneve, faisoyent amas de deniers pour le prince de Condé, qui tendoit à nouveaux desseins et remuements: en quoy l'ayant satisfaict et asseuré de la verité, et m'estre excusé de ne luy avoir faict la reverence, m'a dict, qu'il n'y nuiroit aucunement: et que de son particulier, si la chose luy eust esté communiquee, qu'il y eust contribué, iaçoit qu'il ne fut des plus riches, aussi avant que ceux qui ont plus de moyens, puis que c'estoit la volonté de son maistre que lon advançast les affaires de ceux qui luy sont alliez. Me demandant si j'estois natif de pere et de mere de

[104] Easter Sunday 1583 (according to the Julian calendar) was 31 March. It may have been used as the collection day elsewhere, despite Grindal's instruction that the collection be made before Easter.

[105] [*Sic*], possibly Jean Baptist Aurele, who signed the letter from the London churches to Geneva in September; see below, n. 159.

[106] See above, pp. 161–162.

[107] Sir Jerome Bowes. On 22 July he accompanied the Russian ambassador on his return to Moscow and remained there as Elizabeth's ambassador until the summer of 1584; see Willan, *Early History of the Russia Company*, pp. 163–165 for further references.

Geneve, et des quand j'estois icy, je luy fy response que n'estois venu luy baiser les mains à mon abbord, parce que Messeigneurs desirans que cela se tinct secret, n'avoyent tiré response de sa Majeste que deux mois apres mon arrivee: se tenant pour satisfaict ceste fois la.[108]

[fo. 5v]

Le 9ᵉ Monsieur Beal secretaire du Conseil dict que luy et M. l'Evesque de Sarisbury avoyent conferé ensemble, et arresté qu'a la S. George[109] la cueillette se fist en Cour, et que j'en resouvinse Monsieur Walsyngham.

Le 12 Monsieur le Secretaire auquel delivray celles de Messieurs à la Royne qu'ilz luy envoyoyent pour la remercier dict que sa Majesté n'avoit sceu particulierement comment le tout s'estoit passé et comment on y avoit procedé, et partant qu'il retiendroit encores les dictes lettres par devers soy, a cette fin que s'il advenoit que M. l'Ambassadeur se plaignist envers elle, les dictes servissent pour tesmoigner la volonté et bonne affection de Messieurs de Geneve envers sa Majesté. Que j'avois bien faict d'avoir parlé au dict Sieur Ambassadeur, et de luy l'avoir satisfaict.

Qu'il garderoit les dictes lettres a tant qu'il en seroit besoing luy monstrant la copie d'icelles.[110]

Le 16 lettres furent depeschees du conseil à M. l'Archevesque de Cantorbie, afin qu'il livrast l'argent receu des Evesques entre les mains de M. Bodely.

Le dict jour M. Bodely receut lettres de M. Walsyngham pour me delivrer £100 st.[111]

Le 18 par la lettre de l'Evesque de Carleil,[112] estoit faicte mention que le dict Evesque donoit £10£ st., Mylord Scrop[113] £10 st., et Mylord Warton[114] oultres £20 st. Alderman Martin a doné £20 st.

Le dict jour Mylord de Bedford estant de retour du pays, dict avoir amassé une bonne somme de deniers, voire plus grande qu'il n'avoit

---

[108] Malliet reported this conversation with Mauvissière and his reassurance that he was not collecting for Condé to the syndics on 9 April (PH 2066).

[109] St George's Day.

[110] Malliet reported this conversation with Walsingham to Geneva on 20 April (PH 2066). Walsingham had also told him that Elizabeth 'n'avoit sceu comment on y avoit procede, ny quel ordre on y avoit donne jusques a present', that he expected £5,000 would be raised from the court, and to beware of Mauvissière, who was jealous of Geneva's relations with England.

[111] In his account of his expenses (PH 2082) Malliet records receiving 333 *écus* from Walsingham towards his expenses in England.

[112] John May, Bishop of Carlisle 1577–1598.

[113] Henry, ninth Lord Scroop of Bolton (1534–1592), Lord Warden of the West March from 1563.

[114] Philip, third Lord Wharton.

estime. Que d'aucuns des bonnes gens du pays, voire la pluspart d'eux, donnoyent £2, 3 et 4 par teste, et ça librement et sans contrainte: qu'il ne cogneut jamais le peuple mieux disposé. Que quant à la contribution de la St George qu'il en parleroit, et qu'il employeroit et credit et moyens, et femme [*sic*] et tout s'il estoit requis.

Le 19 M. le Capitaine Yorck[115] s'est offert de venir et 4 ou 5 gentilzhomes de commandement si besoing, et y attireroit d'aultres si on se vouloit servir d'eux.

Le 21 en Cour à Grennvich[116] Monsieur l'Evesque de Sarisbury apres l'avoir prié de se resouvenir de Messieurs le dict jour de la St George, fit un presche devant la Royne et le Sieurs de la Cour, ayant choisy texte expres, leur recomandant ceste charitable contibution, et insistant la dessus un fort long temps.

M. le Chevalier Amies Paulet a doné £10 st.

Le 22 je saluay M. le President de Gales Henry Sydney, lequel dict avoir faict depesches par tout son gouvernement et que lon y marchoit de bon pied.

Monsieur l'Evesque de Sarisbury à ma requeste et le mandement qu'il eust depuis fut content d'exiger des seigneurs leur benevolence, iceux estans en Cour un fort grand nombre.

Le 24 Mylord de Bedford me declara que luy et Monsieur le Secretaire avoyent trouvez les Seigneurs de Cour bien disposez à nostre endroit, et que n'eust esté que M. l'Aumosnier estoit malade le iour precedent ont eust desja commence à y proceder.

Le dict jour le dict Sieur Evesque encommença et me monstra la liste de quelques Seigneurs qui s'estoyent soussignez sçavoir est de Mylord Burgley 40 marcs, de Mylord de Lestre £30 st., de Mylord de Bedford £40 st., de Mylord Warwick £20 st., de Mylord Huntington £20 st., de Mylord de Pembrook £20 st., de Mylord Gray £15 st., de Monsr. le Chevalier Sydney £10 st. de Monsieur le Chevalier Myldmaye £10 st., de Monsr. le Chevalier Walsyngham £10 st: les aultres n'avoyent encores soussigné.[117]

Le dict Sieur Evesque me dict avour aussi obtenu lettres de Messieurs

[115] Of the several Yorke brothers, probably the notorious Rowland (d. 1588).

[116] The court had removed to Greenwich about 18 April and remained there till the end of July.

[117] Three undated copies of a list answering this description survive (PRO, SP 12/159/136–138), naming seventeen members of the council or court (as well as these ten, the Lord Admiral, Lord Hunsdon, the Earl of Arundel (in one copy, Howard of Effingham in another), Lord St John of Bletso, Sir Francis Knollys, Sir Christopher Hatton, and Sir Ralph Sadler). SP 12/159/138 gives the rates for all except Hunsdon, Howard of Effingham, and Hatton, and notes that all those rated have accepted, but only Grey had actually paid at that point. The rates seem to reflect rank as much as any voluntary offer.

du conseil pour les gentilzhomes de son Diocese, et que luy mesmes s'y acheminoit la sepmaine prochaine.

Le 25 Monsieur Bodely et moy arrestasmes que le plus seur pour la remise des deniers estoit estoit [sic] que Messieurs tirassent de Lyon, Rouen ou Anvers pour payer icy.

[fo. 6]

Le 27 je saluay Monsieur Paulet, et le remerciay du travail et de la peine prinse en Sommersetshyre pour la Republique qui s'excusa de n'avoir si bien faict qu'il seroit requis, que neantmoins le peuple s'estoit monstré volontaire, et avoit mieux faict, qu'il n'avoit esperé d'eux.

Le 29 Monsr le D. Wilson,[118] et Monsr Frompton secretaire de Monsieur d'Archevesque m'appellerent pour livrer entrer les mains de M. Bodely la somme de £1434 st, que le dict Seigneur Archevesque avoit ja receu de quelques Evesques.[119]

Le 30 Mylord de Bedford parla à M. le Chancelier[120] pour la contribution des Insercourts, et demanda lettres aux provinces de Bouckingham et de Bedford, mais il en fut esconduit.

May

Le 2 de May je fis escrire Monsr Bodely à Monsieur le Secretaire Chevallier pour plus plaine intelligence de la remise de 10000* qu'avions ja entre mains.[121]

---

[118] Probably Grindal's chaplain Wilson; see Collinson, *Grindal*, pp. 29, 281.

[119] On 19 April Whitgift sent the council the contributions from the diocese of Worcester (a total of £289) as well as the schedule of contributors, which has not survived (PRO, SP 12/160/31). The city of Coventry received a receipt from the Bishop of Coventry and Lichfield dated 1 May for £20 collected (Coventry Record Office, A 79/69). The mayor made a contribution (possibly from city funds) of 27s 1d to bring it up to a round £20 (A.7.b, p. 88). The only surviving schedule of contributors is that for the diocese of Canterbury (PRO, SP 12/161/49ff, undated). It records a total of £470 16s 5d, of which the clergy (headed by Grindal) contributed £196 7s 4d, and the laity (headed by Sir Thomas Scott of Scot's Hall) £274 9s 3d. Collinson, *Grindal*, p. 345, n. 25 erroneously gives £470 as the total from the laity alone. From this sum, 34s 8d was deducted for the expenses of preparing the schedule. The rating also appears to be by rank. The Canterbury schedule may have been the only one retained, for a later list of papers relating to the Geneva contribution (PRO, SP 12/185/196–v, which may have been part of a larger schedule of Walsingham's papers) includes only seven items. Apart from the Canterbury list, these were the list of noblemen contributing (see above, n. 117), an estimate of the collection [missing], a possible copy of the *factum* [missing], letters from Geneva to the Queen and the councillors (probably those now calendared in the *CSPF*) and two papers on the blockade.

[120] Probably Sir Thomas Bromley, Lord Chancellor 1579–1587.

[121] This is probably Bodley's letter to Chevallier of 10 May (PH 2063) stating that he had already received a large sum, expected more in a few days, and wanted Geneva's advice on the method of remitting it.

Le mesme jour M. Aldersay,[122] M. Jong, M. Audley et M. Fish furent deputez par Mylord Maire pour rendre ce que la ville de Londres avoit faict entre les mains du dict S. Bodley.

Le 3 de May à la chambre de l'estoille[123] Monsieur Beal me dict, que parlant avec Monsieur l'Ambassadeur pour des affaires d'Estat qui concernoyent la Royne sa maistresse, qu'il luy auroit dict, avoir receu lettres le jour precedent du Roy son maistre ou entre aultres choses, qui concernent ses Estats et ceux de la Royne, il escrivoit avoir entendu de luy, que lon avoit faict levee de Deniers pour Geneve, qu'il en estoit joyeux, et seroit content de n'estre exempt de la dicte contribution pour le desir qu'il a que la dicte ville alliee à la Couronne fut conservee et gardee en son entier à l'encontre de tous.[124]

Souhaitant le dict Sieur Beal que quelcun y fut envoyé par devers sa dicte Majesté et qu'au pis aller le refus ne pouvoit estre honteux.

Le 5 de May parlay à Grenwich à M. l'Evesque de Salisbury, lequel dict que ayant faict fin aux Comtes, Barons et Seigneurs, Monsr Walsyngham assigneroit un aultre pour les gentilzhommes.[125]

Le 10 envoyay lettres à Messieurs pour tirer 1000* de Raymond de Not espissier pour les payement de Pacques.[126]

L'11e je fy tenir lettres à Messieurs pour tirer 651²/₃* de Mathieu Spont Allemand à Lyon pour les payements de Paques, sur le conte de Nicolas de Cozzi Italien.[127]

Le 17 renvoyay la copie d'icelles lettres.

Le 18 furent remis 2000* pour Rouen aux Chauvins[128] a 71d.st. par Monsieur Bodley, pour les tirer dela par marchands seurs.[129]

Mylord de Bedford dict avoir parlé ia par trois fois à Monsieur le

---

[122] Thomas Aldersey, haberdasher and common councillor.

[123] Star Chamber.

[124] No letter from Henry to Mauvissière in VCC 473 answers this description or mentions his desire to contribute to the collection.

[125] Presumably of the court. There are general references to the Geneva collection in Walsingham's leigerbook under the dates 12–13 May (the only ones in the book), but what precisely they refer to is unclear. See BL, Harleian MS 6035, fos 10–11.

[126] One letter from Malliet to the syndics on 10 May survives (PH 2066), reporting that he had obtained £2,000 from the lords of the Council and hoped to get another £2,000 from the City of London, that Henri III had commended Elizabeth's charity, and that Beale had advised him to strike while the iron was hot (presumably a reference to their conversation on 3 May). See also Bodley to Chevallier 10 May, mentioned above, n. 121.

[127] A letter from Bodley to Chevallier of 11 May to this effect survives (PH 2063), the bill of exchange was to be paid at the next Easter fair (presumably at Lyons).

[128] Jean, Nicolas and possibly Pierre Chauvin, sons of Jean Chauvin, sieur de Varangeville, a merchant family with Protestant leanings at Rouen.

[129] Bodley reported this transaction to Chevallier on 20 May (PH 2063); it was a transfer to Rouen to be forwarded on to Geneva.

Chancelier au nom de Mylord de Lestre et de M. le Secretaire, mais qu'il n'y voyoit aucune apparence.

Le 25 ce qu'avoit faict Mylord de Bedford et M. Paulet aux provinces de Cornuailles Devon et Sommerset fut rendu et rapporté.

Le 27 Monsieur l'Alderman Martin dict qu'ilz avoyent tenu cest ordre en la contribution de Londres, que ayans appellé toute une compagnie, leur declaroyent, que Messieurs du Conseil n'entendoyent que ceux qui estoyent Papistes et mal afectionez à la religion contribuassent, mais seulement ceux qui avoyent pitie de leurs freres affligez. Qui estoit cause que ceux qui estoyent tels, contribuoyent plus largement afin de n'estre suspects et de religion contraire.[130]

Le 30 M. Tomson secretaire de M. Walsyngham avoit parlé a Monsieur Ministre Anglois [sic] d'une des maisons des Insercourts, luy disant, qu'il ne seroit trouvé bon de Messieurs du Conseil si lon urgeoit aultres lettres d'eux, que si on ne le faisoit par le moyen de M. le Chancelier, rien ne se fairoit.

Juin

Le 3 de Juin parlay derechef à Monsr Walsyngham touchant les Insercourts, qui me dict qu'il ne failloit remuer davantage l'affaire: autrement qu'il y aura opposition, qu'on se contente de ce qu'il y a.

Monsieur le Doyen de Pauls me donna advis de rechercher ou faire rechercher le conte des Evesques, qu'aultrement quelques uns d'eux passeroyent sans payer soubs la collecte generale de leur provinces.

[fo. 6v]

Le 4 faisant la reverence à Monsieur l'Archevesque d'Yorck, et le remerciant de sa diligence en nostre faict, me dict que si Messieurs du Conseil luy eussent donné mandement aussi bien pour les Lays, comme pour le clergé, qu'il eust faict plus de trois fois autant.

Qu'il s'y estoit employé de bon coeur et gayement et quant à son particulier quand il n'auroit eu chose en ce monde il eust plustost engagé sa chemise en acte de si grande compassion et charité.

Le 18 Monsieur le Comte de Bedford dict qu'il s'estoit apperceu qu'on n'avanceroit rien aux Insercourts, qu'il faudroit se contenter de ce que lon a desja, combien que plusieur gentilzhommes des dictes maisons fussent fort affectionez à nostre party, et souhaitassent lettres ou mandement.

Le dict seigneur estant prest pour se retirer au pays, me pria de faire

[130] Mendoza had reported in March that the aldermen had seen everyone individually, threatening the Queen's displeasure if the sum was small, so that the collection was in effect obligatory; see above, n. 96.

ses humbles recommandations à Messieurs de la ville et à M. de Beze et qu'il prioit Dieu pour eux: que si ses moyens estoyent suffisants pour les subvenir, il vendroit tout ce qu'il a en ce monde en un besoing, pour leur faire du bien.

Le 19 je receu de M. Fromton toutes les lettres adressees à M. l'Archeveque son maistre pour ce faict pour les conferer, et coster les arrierages.

Il me dict aussi avoir escrit a M. l'Evesque de Glocester[131] afin de haster, comme de mesmes à l'Evesque de Hereford.[132]

Que lon n'eust à s'attendre de rien recevoir des Evesques de S. Davids[133] et Assaphen[134] parce qu'ilz estoyent paovres.

Le 28 parlay au Registre de l'Evesque de Rochester,[135] afin que lon receut la partie receuë au Diocese de M. son maistre, il me respondist qu'il estoit expedient, que tirer nouveau commandement de Messieurs du Conseil pour retirer les dictz deniers, montant le tout a £80 st., oultre la benevolence de Monsieur son maistre.

Le 29 S. Walsyngham m'octroya lettres aux Evesques de Rochester et Glocester pour la reddition de l'argent receu, dont ilz avoyent faict refus.

Je luy communiquay aussi que j'avois lettres de Messeigneurs à Monsieur l'Ambassadeur de France, sur le mescontentement qu'il avoit de ma negociation: afin que si cela fut venu d'ailleurs à ses oreilles, il n'eust esté pris à mauvaise part.

Quant aux lettres de faveur que requeroyent Messieurs de la Maiesté de la Royne aux Seigneurs Cantons, il m'a prié luy en bailler un memoire pour s'en resouvenir, et le proposer quand il seroit temps propre.

Le 30 je presentay lettres de Messeigneurs au dict Sieur de Mauvissieres Ambassadeur du Roy, lequel apres la lecture d'icelles me dict, que ce qu'il m'avoit dict au commencement il le me disoit encores, que puis que Messieurs de Geneve estoyent alliez à la couronne de France, que c'estoit le plaisir du Roy qu'ilz fussent conservez, et que pour ce respect, il combattroit luy mesmes pour eux et les aideroit de sa bourse propre aussi avant qu'aucun aultre. Que Messieurs de Geneve l'avoyent fort satisfaict, que je les remerciasse en son nom, et que la

---

[131] John Bullingham, Bishop of Gloucester 1581–1598.

[132] John Scory, Bishop of Hereford 1559–1585.

[133] Marmaduke Middleton, Archbishop of St. Davids 1582–1590/2. On 16 September Middleton informed Walsingham at the end of a long letter of complaint about the financial state of his diocese that 'Concerning the collection for Geneva I have dealt with some of the best of my dicocese which I finde not greately willing because it is in another countrie. And as for the clergie they all alleage povertie, beseching your honour's further resolution herein.' (PRO, SP 12/162/54, quoted in Strype, *Grindal*, p. 283).

[134] William Hughes, Bishop of St Asaph 1573–1600.

[135] John Young, Bishop of Rochester 1578–1605.

ou il auroit moyen de s'employer pour eux ou avancer leurs affaires, qu'il le fairoit de bien bon coeur. Qu'il n'a jamais esté contraire à ceux de la Religion, que feu Monsr de Chastillon[136] en eust peu tesmoigner, qu'il avoit congedié les Reistres trois fois, qu'il avoit faict la paix aux premiers troubles.[137] Que son Maistre ne cherche que la paix et union de son peuple: que ceux de la Religion ne cherchent aussi que de se maintenir, qu'ilz avoyent protesté, qu'ilz ne desirent que la paix, et de vivre comme bons subjects.

Que de ce que Messieurs de Geneve demandoyent ayde et subvention, estans molestez et assaillis, n'estoit trouvé mauvais. Que c'estoit le plaisir du Roy que pendant leurs troubles on leur fournist tous les mois tant de deniers comtens pour leur tuition et defense.

[fo. 7]

Qu'il envoyoit les lettres de Messieurs au Roy, et que par le tesmoignage qu'il avoit par icelles et de moy, il s'asseuroit de leur syncerité et rondeur. Que si je le venois veoir ayant [*sic*] luy ayant receu response de sa Majestez, il m'impartiroit ce qu'on luy en auroit escrit.

Promist lors d'escrire à Messeigneurs et peust estre à Monsr de Beze.[138]

Jueillet

Le 1 de Jueillet ayant communiqué mes lettres à Mess. de La Fontaine et Castol ministres, je dressay memoires pour la minute de deux lettres, l'une à tout le corps des ligues et l'aultre particuliere et speciale aux 4 Cantons de la Religion, dont ay baillé la copie à M. le Secretaire.

Le dict jour escrivay lettres à Monsr Fromton pour le prier de solliciter par ses lettres et au nom de Monsieur l'Archevesque, les Evesques d'Ereford, de Rochester, Glocester, et St Davids, qui n'avoyent rien rapporté encores, et qu'il sollicitast de mesmes les arrierages de Norwich,[139] de Lyncoln et de quelques autres que estoyent longs en leurs procedures.

Le 3 presentay à M. le Secretaire le roole de la contribution qu'il

[136] The Admiral Coligny.

[137] Mauvissière had been employed the settlement of the First War of Religion in 1563, and in the paying off of the Huguenot German auxiliaries in several of the later wars.

[138] Mauvissière wrote to Geneva on 2/12 August (PH 2077), thanking them for the letters presented to him by Malliet (presumably these). He claimed to have helped Malliet, contributed himself and written on their behalf to Henri III. He was now persuaded they had no desire to see a civil war in France and wished to maintain the peace.

[139] Edmund Freke, Bishop of Norwich 1575–1584.

m'avoit demandé, et le priay au nom de Messieurs d'impetrer en leur faveurs, les susdictes lettres de sa Majesté.

Le 6 mon nepveu partist et ce jour là je receu 16* de M. Bodley pour son dict voyage, mais il n'en voulut prendre qu'11 pour avoir lettres de change de M. Bodley à Rouen aux Chauvins de la somme de 40*.

Le mesme jour je receu du dict seigneur Bodley les lettres de Monsr le Comte de Bedford à Messeigneurs et à M. de Beze.

Le dict jour Monsr l'Archeveque mourut[140] et M. Fromton me dict que l'Archedoyen de Cantorbury nommé D. Redman[141] avoit encores environ £50 st payez pour une fois, et £30 st payez à une aultre.

Item que M. Bodley devoit avoir receu £107 st. de l'evesque de Norwiche oultre £15 st. payez pour une fois & £30 st. payez à une aultre.

Que M. Purefey[142] gentilhomme, servant le dict Evesque avoit tiré quitance de luy pour la dicte somme le 7 de May. Ce que le dict S. Bodley nyoit avoir receu, ne le trouvant sur ses livres, et estoit d'advis d'en escrire au dict S. Evesque.

Le dict jour receusmes lettres de Raymond de Not, faisantes mention que les 1000* avoyent esté livrez à Mathieu Spon comme procureur.

Le 8 de Jueillet je receu lettres du 5ᵉ de Juin, afin de payer 10000* à Messer. Horatio Michaeli,[143] ou à ses commis Mess. Pompeo Michaeli et Fabio Arnolphini banquiers à Lyon, et deduisant de la susdicte somme 1651²/₃* payer à Mathieu Spont.[144] Dont ce qui restoit à payer, montoit a 8348* 6s 8d. dor.[145]

Le 9 parlay à D. Redman executeur du testament du feu Archevesque et Archdoyen de Cantorbury, qui promist faire obligation de £48 12s. 4d st d'arrierages pour tout le terme de la St Michel.

Le 10 M. Bodley et moy fusmes parler à Absalom[146] pour sçavoir nouvelles des £107 mandees par l'Evesque de Norwich: qui dict les avoir eues 3 sepmaines en sa custode, et que M. Purevey les estoit venu

---

[140] Grindal died on 6 July. On 20 May Malliet had informed Chevallier of the expectation that Whitgift would succeed him, as the Archbishop of York had been compromised in the Stapleton scandal (PH 2066). Nicholas Faunt (below, n. 151) knew this as well; see Collinson, *Grindal*, p. 277.

[141] William Redman, Archdeacon of Canterbury 1576–1595.

[142] Not identified.

[143] Italian merchant resident in Geneva: see E. William Monter, *Studies in Genevan Government (1536–1605)* (Geneva, 1964), p. 43.

[144] The bills of exchange for the 651²/₃ écus and 1,000 écus referred to above, p. 188.

[145] Malliet reported this transfer to the syndics on 12 July (PH 2066), informing them again that Walsingham had told him that 'la Royne n'avoit cognoissance de l'ordre de ceste collecte, pour l'avoir du commencement remis a la discretion de ses counseillers'.

[146] The queen's sub-almoner; see above, n. 56.

querie accompagné d'un vestu de noir qui se disoit serviteur de M. Bodley.

Qui fut cause que M. Bodley escrivit lettres au dict gentilhomme M. Purefey pour descouvrir la verité.

Le 18 Monsr le Secretaire dict avoir escrit à son homme Tomson qui l'eust à dresser les lettres, pour lesquelles je faisois requeste.

Le 20 M. Bodley dict avoir ruminé de pres ses affaires, et n'avoir pourveu assez à toutes occurrences. D'un costé de ce qu'il avoit faict tenir 12000* sans commandement expres du Conseil, sa charge ne s'estendant plus oultre que la recepte. De l'aultre de ce qu'il n'avoit eu meilleure asseurance de la remise des deniers de la part de la Seigneurie, ses lettres n'estant authorisees que d'un Secretaire et non du seel de la ville.

[fo. 7v]

Qu'un jour il luy en faudroit rendre conte.

Qui fut cause que luy et moy fusmes à la Cour, et receut de M. le Secretaire lettres qui l'authorisoyent pour la dicte remise des deniers soit receus ou à recevoir pour la contribution de Geneve. Des mesmes me pria d'en escrire à Messieurs, afin qu'il eust garant plus suffisant d'eux.

Que d'autant que plusieurs pieces d'or n'estoyent de mise [?, *obscured*] seroit besoing les vendre avec perte.

Le 21 M. Frompton dict avoir envoyé lettres aux Evesques que l'avois prié fors qu'a l'Evesque de Rochester avec lequel il en parleroit aux funerailles de son Maistre.

Le 26 M. Bodley dict avoir receu response de M. Purefey gentilhomme et officier de M. l'Evesque de Norwych, et marques si suffisantes du payement des £107 st, qu'il s'estimoit satisfaict, et me monstra comme il avoit mis receu la dicte partie sur son livre, et l'avoit mise en conte.

A Grennwich Monsr le Secretaire dict qu'il estimoit valloir mieux ne parler à sa Majesté des susdictes lettres, dautant qu'icelle ne vouloit faire à l'encontre de M. de Savoye pour le respect qu'il luy sembloit deferer depuis quelque temps. A quoy faisant replique luy dy[s], qu'elles ne fairoyent directement contre luy, ne faisant aultre mention les dictes lettres que le desir qu'elle a d'entendre la pacification des dictz troubles tant pour leur propre respect que de leurs voysins. Il me respondist, que je m'asseurasse qu'il fairoit son pouvoir quand la commodité se presenteroit.

Que l'Ambassadeur[147] instoit [*sic*, insistoit?] si fort envers sa Majesté sur la collecte derniere, qu'il ne sçavoit par quel bout commencer pour acheminer cest affaire.

Le 27 eusmes advis de 10000* remis à Lyon par les deputez de M. Horatio Michaeli.

Le 30 M. Beal m'asseuroit avoir veu 100 marcs leguez par le testament de M. l'Archeveque de Cantorbie: mais depuis a cogneu son erreur, ayant pris la despense pour les legatz.[148]

Le dict Sieur Beal promist de s'employer à l'octroy des susdictes lettres de faveur et en parleroit à son beau frere.

Aoust

Le 3 d'Aoust M. Bodley receut advis que £30 st. mandees de la part de l'Evesque de Wynchester estoyent en ville, mais on n'avoit moyen de recevoir la dicte somme que les officiers du dict Evesque ne fussent venus.

Le 4 manday lettres à M. Walsyngham le priant se resouvenir des dictes lettres.

Le 5 Madame Bacon donna £20 st. [149]

Le 13 M. Bodley aprist nouvelles de £130 st. mandees par l'Evesque de Glocester mais le marchand n'estoit arrivé que les apportoit.

Le 14 M. Bodley me manda querir, et dict qu'il avoit essayé de vendre les angelotz legers rognez, cassez, sodez, bordez et de bas or, lesquelz ne se pouvoyent mettre qu'en partant 100 francs sur £158 st. Que Alderman Martin maistre de la Monnoye les prendroit sans encourir aucune perte, pourveu qu'on l'attendist jusques au 12 de Decembre. A quoy pour la grand perte qu'il y auroit j'ay condescendu, considerant qu'il y auroit lors argent prest à retourner, et que le demourant ne montoit à grand somme. Par ainsi le dict Sieur Bodley a receu du S. Alderman Martin oblige des dictz £158 st. à payer le 12 Decembre prochain.

Le 15 M. Tomson me monstra la minute qu'il avoit faict des lettres de faveur aux Cantons, la laissant à M. Fond[150] son compagnon pour la mettre au net en son absence, faisant compagnie à M. le Secretaire son maistre depesché avec commission en Escosse.[151]

Le 16 prins congé de M. Walsyngham, lequel promist recommander

---

[147] Mauvissière.

[148] Malliet reported Grindal's legacy of 100 marks (equated to 670 *livres tournois*) as well as the sending of 2000 *écus* to the Chauvins at Rouen in a letter to the syndics on 2 August (PH 2066). It is not mentioned in Collinson's survey of Grindal's legacies in *Grindal*, pp. 280–283.

[149] Lady Anne Bacon (c. 1529–1605), widow of Sir Nicholas, Lord Keeper, 1559–1579.

[150] Nicolas Faunt (1554–1608), Walsingham's secretary from c. 1578.

[151] Walsingham's famous Scottish embassy, the consequence of James VI's escape from the Ruthven regime on 27 June.

les susdictes lettres à M. Beal, et que touchant le reste de la contribution, il donneroit que le tout fut tenu seurement à Geneve.

Que presentasse ses recommendations à Messeigneurs et m'avoit dict qu'il escriroit à M. de Beze mais j'estime que ses negoces et le peu de loysir qu'il avoit ne le permiront.

[fo. 8]

Le 18 Monsr Scoré [152] filz de l'Evesque de Hereford promist escrire à son pere et que ce ne seroit la cause de mon plus long sejour.

Le 20 j'eu la reveuë des lettres escrites en faveur de Messieurs.

Le 23 M. Fand Secretaire aussi de M. Walsyngham s'en alla en Cour[153] avec les susdictes lettres, pour les faires soussigner à sa Majesté par l'adresse de M. Beal.

Le 25 receusmes advis de M. Horatio Michaeli et ses compagnons de Lyon de payer 3500* qui estoyent prests, comme aussi de l'ordre de la remise des 2000* qui estoyent à Rouen entre la main des Chauvins.

Le 28 M. Beal me livra les lettres de sa Majesté en faveur de Messieurs, ja signees, afin qu'on prinsse la copie et les communiquasse à M. de la Fontaine.

Le mesme jour luy baillay une copie du memoire des Arrierages tant du Clerge que des Lays, le priant de les solliciter par ses lettres: ce qu'il accepta et en print la charge. Promist aussi d'avancer la contribution de la Cour.

Le 29 il signa les dictes lettres et me les livra, avec un passeport pour passer sans recherche au port de Diepe.[154]

Le 30 M. Bodley me monstra le recepisse de Hypolite et Scipione Buyamonti de la somme de 3500* par l'adresse du Seigneur Horatio Michaeli: ensemblement les lettres des Chauvins, comment ilz avoyent remis la somme de 2000* par la mesme adresse du dict Horatio.

Septembre

Le 2 de Septembre je fus en Cour à Sonninghill[155] et receu lettres de Mylord de Lestre à Messeigneurs, et me dict qu'il estoit marry, que la somme n'estoit plus grande, et qu'il n'avoit tenu à luy: qu'il y avoit employé son credit pour le bien qu'il souhaite à cest Estat.[156]

Le 4 je receu Passeport de Monsr l'Ambassadeur de France.

---

[152] Sylvanus Scory (d. 1617).

[153] The court had removed to Oatlands at the end of July, and during August and September went on another 'little progress' in Surrey and Berkshire.

[154] Exemption from customs search.

[155] Sunninghill (Berkshire).

[156] Leicester's letter, dated 2 September (PH 2078) also includes his regret that the sum was not larger.

Le mesme jour je fy conte avec M. Bodley et restoyent £256 19s. 4d st: dont 158, comme dict est dessus, entre les mains de M. Alderman Martin, et le reste il a pardevers soy qui monte a £98 19s. 4d st. Ce jour là parlay à Monsr l'Archevesque de Cantobury nomme M. Whytgyfft,[157] et luy recommanday les Evesques qui sont en derriere, et les arrierages des aultres lieux, lequel promist d'en tirer notes de Monsr Frompton qui seroit à luy, de solliciter nostre faict, et d'escrire à Monsieur de Beze par la premiere commodité.

Le 5e je fy derechef conte avec le susdict Sieur Bodley: et ayant soustraict 15500* (qu'avons remis qui valent en monnoye sterlin £4662 2s 1d) et £120 12s 8d, deboursez que pour la despense de moy et de mon nepveu, que pour le change des susdicts 15500*, reste receu entre ses mains £256 19s 4d st, qu'il faira tenir avec ce qu'il pourra recepvoir cy apres.

La Totale somme de la recepte montant à £5039 14s 1d st lors que party de Londres, qu'estoit le 6 de Septembre 1585.[158]

Le dict jour sur mon depart, Monsr Bodley m'envoya dire par son homme que l'Evesque d'Hereford luy avoit escrit avoit £160 st. tout en monnoye d'escus de Flandre, prestes a les faire tenir par le premier messager.[159]

Le 18 de Septembre je receu à Rouen de Messieurs les Chauvins 50* pour mon voyage par l'adresse de M. Bodley, qui les mettra sur son conte.

---

[157] Whitgift was confirmed as Archbishop of Canterbury on 23 September.

[158] This is the total entered in Malliet's main account covering the period 16 April to 6 September (PH 2082). It includes the separate contributions from the dioceses, the foreign churches, the City of London, Devon from Bedford, Somerset from Paulet, Lady Bacon, and the Dedham *classis*. A second undated account (also PH 2082) gives a total of £5,730 7s 6d, but this included contributions that arrived after Malliet's departure. Bodley was still arranging for the transfer of outstanding payments in the first half of 1584; see his letters to Malliet of 8 February and 2 May (PH 2063).

[159] Malliet also took with him a letter from the London Strangers' Churches to the Company of Pastors (printed in Schickler, *Eglises*, III, p. 102). Signed by La Fontaine, Castol, Winghen, and Jean Baptiste Aurele and dated the 5 September, it regretted their inability to do more, but they had been burdened by numerous other requests for financial assistance, both domestic and foreign.

LETTERS FROM SIR ROBERT CECIL TO SIR CHRISTOPHER HATTON, 1590–1591

Edited by Paul E.J. Hammer

ACKNOWLEDGEMENTS

I am grateful to University College London Library, and especially the Director of Library Services and the Librarian for Manuscripts and Rare Books, for kind permission to publish this edition of Ogden MS 7/41, folios 2–35.

EDITORIAL PRACTICE

Like other contributions to this volume, Cecil's letters to Hatton have been edited in accordance with the principles laid out in R.F. Hunnisett's *Editing Records for Publication* (London, 1977).[1] As a result, punctuation and capitalization have been modernized, abbreviations have been silently expanded,[2] ellisions separated (eg. 'thissue' becoming 'the issue'), and the use of 'u' and 'v', 'i' and 'j', and 'c' and 't' have been regularized (eg. 'accion' becoming 'action'). In the case of possessives, an apostrophe has been added before or after the final 's' (as appropriate), but no new 's' has been added. Editorial interventions are signalled by square brackets, while round brackets reflect parentheses in the original manuscript. All dates are Old Style, but the year is treated as beginning on 1 January.

[1] British Records Association, Archives and the User series, no. 4, 1977.
[2] Except in a few cases where silent expansion might potentially introduce and conceal editorial error, such as 'my L[ord] A[dmiral]' (Letter 2) or 'an earle of N'. (Letter 26). Note also that abbreviations have been expanded in accordance with the practices of this particular scribe. Hence 'your lo' becomes 'your lordshipp' and 'at com' becomes 'at command' unless there is evidence of a final 't' (in which case it becomes 'at commandment').

INTRODUCTION

The manuscript

Ogden MS 7/41 is one of a collection of manuscript commonplace books, known as the 'Bacon-Tottel MSS', which were bequeathed to University College London by C.K. Ogden.[3] Ogden purchased them in the mid-1940s under the impression that they were manuscripts which had been compiled by (or for the use of) Francis Bacon. This Bacon provenance, trumpeted in the sale catalogue of 1943, ultimately proved to be erroneous. In fact, the collection was gathered together by William Drake (1606–1669), a seventeenth-century bibliophile who owned the house where the documents were discovered, Shardeloes, near Amersham in Buckinghamshire.[4] Most of the fifty-four volumes which constitute this collection were actually copied out by Drake himself or by his amanuensis. However, Ogden MS 7/41 is one of twelve items in the collection which were originally compiled by other copyists. There was a large and buoyant market for historical books and manuscripts of all kinds in seventeenth-century England.[5] Amongst this mass of historical writings, Elizabethan materials seem to have enjoyed a considerable vogue, driven partly by nostalgia for the bold action of Elizabeth's reign and disaffection towards the politics of James I and Charles I. William Drake, who was an eager participant in this world of gentleman collectors and commercial dealers, undoubtedly acquired the volume from one of his various contacts in the trade.[6]

The manuscript is a small volume measuring 95mm on the horizontal axis and 155mm on the vertical. It contains approximately 100 folios,

---

[3] For detailed discussion of the 'Bacon-Tottel MSS', see Stuart Clark, 'Wisdom literature of the seventeenth century: a guide to the contents of the "Bacon-Tottel" commonplace books', in 2 pts, *Transactions of the Cambridge Bibliographical Society*, 6 (1972–1976), pp. 291–305; 7 (1977–1980), pp. 46–73.

[4] For Drake, see K. Sharpe, *Reading Revolutions: The Politics of Reading in Early Modern England* (New Haven CT and London, 2000), esp. chs 2–3.

[5] For a general overview of scribal culture in this period, see H. Love, *Scribal Publication in Seventeenth-Century England* (Oxford, 1993). See also H.R. Woudhuysen, *Sir Philip Sidney and the Circulation of Manuscripts, 1558–1640* (Oxford, 1996); A.F. Marotti, *Manuscript, Print and the English Renaissance Lyric* (Ithaca NY and London, 1995); P. Beal, *In Praise of Scribes: Manuscripts and their Makers in Seventeenth-Century England* (Oxford, 1998); Sharpe, *Reading Revolutions*.

[6] Hence Drake's notes included reminders to 'enquire from tyme to tyme in Duck Lane', and with the 'booksellers hard by Bedlam' (Woudhuysen, *Sir Philip Sidney*, p. 50, n. 22).

of which only the first 38 are numbered. Almost all the documents contained in the volume have been copied in the same hand. This is a clear scribal hand typical of the late sixteenth century and the first two or three decades of the seventeenth century. Folios 2–35 are copies of letters by Robert Cecil (1563–1612, later created first Earl of Salisbury), while the remainder are copies of letters by Francis Bacon (1561–1626, later created Viscount St Albans). The initial folio has been lost. The Cecil letters are dated in 1590 or 1591. The Bacon letters, which are familiar from other compilations of his correspondence, consist of documents ranging from the early 1590s to 1607/8. Ogden MS 7/41 therefore cannot have been compiled any earlier than 1608 and was probably written nearer 1620, or slightly later.[7] The scribal errors which are apparent in the Cecil letters also strongly suggest that the manuscript was copied from another compilation, rather than from the original letters themselves. The documents contained in this volume are therefore only second-generation copies, or copies of copies.

In addition to the dominant scribal hand, there are also a few brief documents which have been added to the volume in the later hand of William Drake himself. These items include a reference to Robert Doleman's *A Conference About the Next Succession to the Throne of England* (Antwerp, 1594) and a letter written by Sir Thomas Wentworth (later created Earl of Strafford) as Lord Deputy of Ireland in 1635. There is also a copy of a letter written by Sir Robert Cecil to Lord Mountjoy, c.1600–1601 (folio 36r–36v). This has been added on what was formerly a blank folio separating the Cecil letters from the Bacon letters. The same hand seems to have scribbled a marginal comment on folio 34v and probably also the cross-reference ('Se[e] 18') on folio 27v. Drake therefore studied the Cecil letters with some care and it seems likely that he was also responsible for the extensive underlining of key phrases in many of these letters. This would be consistent with the intentions which he expressed in various jottings in other volumes in the collection: 'to enforme my selfe thorouly in the state of this kingdom and proceedings therof, I think fit to reade and meditate uppon the histories of this kingdom; to get all matters of publick nature whether printed or divulged by pen, preserved by the authors themselves or by others'; 'get as many choise things concerning law and concerning busines and emploiments in the generall as you may and studdy them, Mr Cotton for iournalls of parlaments and Sir

---

[7] Unfortunately, the evidence of watermarks seems to offer no assistance in advancing a more precise date for the volume. The c.1620 date is suggested by the nature of the hand and the discernible boom in copying Elizabethan manuscripts following the outbreak of the Thirty Years' War and the execution of Sir Walter Ralegh (both in 1618).

Simmonds Dewes'.[8] Reading for Drake, as for many of his contemporaries, was not merely a pastime but an active process designed to extract very practical guidance for his own future actions in public and private life: 'when a man is deliberate and governed by order, rules and principles [derived from reading], no difficulty he meets with faints or abates his courage'.[9]

In addition to informing himself 'thorouly' for the needs of his own life, Drake's close study of these letters reflects the contemporary fame, even notoriety, of Robert Cecil.[10] Cecil's remarkable political career culminated in his virtual domination of English government from the closing years of Elizabeth's reign to the middle years of James I, his elevation to the earldom of Salisbury and the entrenchment of two branches of the Cecil family among the high nobility of England.[11] However, Drake also had a more direct interest in Cecil, for he admired the statesman's rhetorical skills and consciously sought to pattern himself after him. Unfortunately, he found it difficult to acquire many of Cecil's papers, which forced him to turn elsewhere for much of his reading: 'to supply his defect of writing many things, read much Lord Bacon and Sir Robert Cotton's writings'.[12] In this light, the twenty-seven Cecil letters copied into Ogden MS 7/41 must have represented a rich haul. The letters were perhaps especially intriguing to Drake because they are all dated 1590 or 1591 and therefore documented the start of Cecil's political career.[13]

For modern scholars, these documents are also significant.[14] Although

---

[8] Clark, 'Wisdom literature', part 1, pp. 297–298.

[9] K. Sharpe, *Remapping Early Modern England: the Culture of Seventeenth-Century Politics* (Cambridge, 2000), p. 340.

[10] P. Croft, 'The reputation of Robert Cecil: libels, political opinion and popular awareness in the early seventeenth century', *Transactions of the Royal Historical Society*, 6th series, 1 (1991), pp. 43–69.

[11] For Cecil, see A. Cecil, *Robert Cecil, First Earl of Salisbury* (London, 1915); P.M. Handover, *The Second Cecil: The Rise to Power, 1563–1604, of Sir Robert Cecil, Later First Earl of Salisbury* (London, 1959); D. Cecil, *The Cecils of Hatfield House* (London, 1973), pp. 91–161; A. Haynes, *Robert Cecil, Earl of Salisbury, 1563–1612: Servant of Two Sovereigns* (London, 1989); W.D. Acres, 'The early political career of Sir Robert Cecil, c.1582–1597: some aspects of late Elizabethan secretarial administration' (unpublished Ph.D. thesis, University of Cambridge, 1992). A full-scale study of Cecil as *de facto* chief minister is currently being written by Dr Pauline Croft.

[12] Sharpe, *Remapping*, pp. 340–341; *idem*, *Reading Revolutions*, pp. 84, 86–87.

[13] Drake was also interested in, and admired, the means by which Cecil's father climbed to power: *ibid.*, pp. 98, 117.

[14] The 'Bacon-Tottel MSS' have been the subject of intermittent scholarly interest since the announcement of their discovery in 1943. Ernest Strathman, for example, searched many of the volumes in pursuit of documents relating to Sir Walter Ralegh and wrote a two-page report on his finding in 1964 ('Some notes on the Bacon-Tottel Manuscripts'). He suggested that the Cecil letters in Ogden MS 7/41 'should be checked against known sources', but did not include the volume among those 'worth closer study

they are not originals or even first-generation copies, they constitute the only versions of these letters which are known to survive. Moreover, their significance is heightened by the fact that they are all written to the same correspondent, who can be easily identified as Sir Christopher Hatton (1540–1591). Hatton was one of Elizabeth I's great royal favourites and was Lord Chancellor from May 1587 until his death in November 1591.[15] These letters therefore demonstrate the linkage between two of the most important figures of Elizabethan politics: Sir Robert Cecil in the formative period of his career and Sir Christopher Hatton in the very twilight of his career.

The letters: corroboration and dating

Folios 2–35 of Ogden MS 7/41 contain some twenty-seven letters from Cecil to Hatton, one of which is incomplete because of the missing first folio. They have been copied into the manuscript in no particular order. According to the dates which they bear, these letters cover the final year of Hatton's life, from 10 November 1590 to 16 November 1591. Unfortunately, some of these dates are clearly incorrect. Two of the letters are also incompletely dated. This means that the dates of all the letters need to corrected, or corroborated, by reference to external sources of evidence. Broadly speaking, these external sources relate to the movements of Cecil, Hatton and the royal court during the period supposedly covered by the letters. Further evidence comes from the date of events and documents which are mentioned in the letters.

During much of the period covered by these letters, Elizabeth I and her court were occupied with the fortunes of expeditionary forces which had been sent to fight in Normandy and Brittany and with a royal progress through Surrey, Sussex, and Hampshire. The war in France, and especially in Normandy,[16] generated a large amount of paperwork, as orders, reports and private advice flowed back and forth across the Channel. Many of these documents help to corroborate the contents of Cecil's letters to Hatton and confirm or correct their dating. The most important source is the archive of the royal secretariat, which was

for a possibility of "new" materials' (Strathman typescript, held by UCL Rare Books Library).

[15] For Hatton, who died on 20 November 1591, see H. Nicolas, *The Memoirs of the Life and Times of Sir Christopher Hatton* (London, 1847); E. St J. Brooks, *Sir Christopher Hatton: Queen Elizabeth's Favourite* (London, 1946); A.G. Vines, *Neither Fire nor Steel: Sir Christopher Hatton* (Chicago IL, 1978).

[16] For the expedition to Normandy, see H.A. Lloyd, *The Rouen Campaign, 1590–1592: Politics, Warfare and the Early-Modern State* (Oxford, 1973); R.B. Wernham, *After the Armada: Elizabethan England and the Struggle for Western Europe, 1588–1595* (Oxford, 1984), chs 13–16. For operations in Brittany during the time of Cecil's letters, see *ibid.*, ch. 12.

controlled at the time by Cecil's father, William Cecil, first Lord Burghley.[17] Cecil's own papers for this period are disappointingly thin, but they contain many of the surviving papers of Robert Devereux, second Earl of Essex, who commanded the army in Normandy.[18] Unfortunately, there is no corresponding body of material for Hatton, very few of whose letters for this period have survived.[19] This makes Cecil's letters to Hatton in Ogden MS 7/41 all the more important. Another valuable source for this period is the letter-book kept by Sir Henry Unton, who served as Elizabeth's ambassador to France during 1591–1592.[20] This contains copies of most of the letters which he sent and received. Unton also kept a separate private record of his activities,[21] roughly paralleling Burghley's practice of maintaining specific diaries relating to events in France.[22] Further light is cast on government business by the register of the Privy Council[23] and the declared accounts of the treasurer of the chamber.[24] Finally, there are more narrowly-focused sources such as Sir Thomas Coningsby's journal of the campaign

[17] The secretarial archive now constitutes the core of the state papers classes at the PRO. The most relevant here are SP classes 12 (domestic, Elizabeth I), 15 (domestic, additional, Edward VI–James I) and 78 (foreign, France). The domestic classes were calendared in the nineteenth century, while the state papers foreign are detailed in *L&A*. Since the division between official and private documents remained fluid in this period, these sources must be supplemented by Burghley's 'private' papers in BL, Lansdowne MSS 1–122.

[18] These are well calendared in *HMCS*, IV. A few stray holograph letters from Essex to the Queen survive in BL, Additional MS 74286. This volume is part of what was formerly called the Hulton MS (which resided for many years at the BL as Loan 23): *Elizabeth and Essex: The Hulton Letters* (Sotheby's sale catalogue for 14 December 1992). These letters are also printed (with some inaccuracies) in Devereux.

[19] Nicolas prints only four letters by Hatton which were written in 1591, the last of them written to the Earl of Essex on 5 October (490–495). The difficulties in tracking the details of Hatton's activities as Lord Chancellor are illustrated by the fact that Nicolas prints only three letters by Hatton for 1590, three for 1589, and one for 1588. By contrast, Nicolas prints seven letters by Hatton and thirty-four letters to Hatton for 1582. Even allowing for the incompleteness of Nicolas's sample, it is apparent that much of Hatton's correspondence for his last years must have been lost.

[20] This has been printed by R.J. Stevenson in *UC* from a composite of the original letter-book (Bodleian Library, Oxford, MS eMus 18), Unton's drafts (BL, Cotton MS Caligula E VIII, which has been damaged by fire) and the letters received by Burghley from Unton which survive in PRO, SP 78.

[21] BRO, TA 13/2, photostat copy of Unton's diary, which ends on Friday 1 October 1591. The original manuscript is held at the Alderman Library, University of Virginia.

[22] Burghley's holograph 'jornall of sondry matters concerning the armyes sent into Normandy', covering the period 15 June–1 October 1591, is BL, Cotton MS Titus B VI, fos 34r–35v. Burghley also drew up another diary relating to events in both Brittany and Normandy between March and 21 September 1591: PRO, SP 78/25, fo. 346r–v.

[23] Printed *in extenso* in *APC*.

[24] PRO, E 351/542.

in Normandy[25] and the later memoirs of Sir Robert Carey, which were probably written in 1626.[26]

These sources enable Cecil's letters to Hatton to be dated both by their contents and by the location of the court, from where most of the letters were written. The most difficult and important aspect of determining the physical location of the court involves reconstructing Elizabeth's progress to Portsmouth and Southampton during August and September 1591. Having undertaken a mini-progress to Theobalds in early May,[27] during which she had knighted Cecil,[28] the Queen settled at Greenwich for the early part of the summer. On 19 July she visited Burghley's house at Westminster to watch Essex parade his cavalry before leaving for France.[29] Elizabeth moved the court to Nonsuch on 31 July, breaking her journey for dinner (ie the midday meal) at Lady Blanke's house at Mitcham.[30] The progress finally began on 3 August,[31] when the Queen and her entourage travelled to Thomas Cornwallis's house at East Horsley, stopping for dinner along the way at Edmund Tilney's house at Leatherhead. Thereafter, she visited Sir Henry Weston's house at Clandon Park (dinner only: 4 August), Guildford (4 August), Sir William More's house at Loseley (5–9 August), Katherine Hall (dinner only: 9 or 10 August), the Bishop of Winchester's palace at Farnham Castle (10–13 August), Edward Marvin's house at Bramshot (14 August), Lord De La Warr's house at The Holt, Viscount Montagu's house at Cowdray (15–20 August), Richard Lewknor's house at West Dean (dinner only: 20 August), Chichester (20–23 August), Lord Lumley's house at Stanstead (23–26 August), John Carrill's house

[25] This journal (covering the period 13 August–24 December 1591) survives only in the form of two incomplete copies: BL, Harleian MS 288, fos 253–279 and Bodl., MS Eng.hist.c.61, fos 5v–9r. The former was printed in J.G. Nichols (ed.), 'Journal of the siege of Rouen, 1591, by Sir Thomas Coningsby', *Camden Miscellany*, I (1847). Omissions from this document were supplied from the Bodleian manuscript in R. Poole, 'A journal of the siege of Rouen in 1591', *EHR*, 18 (1902), pp. 527–537.

[26] F.H. Mares (ed.), *The Memoirs of Robert Carey* (Oxford, 1972).

[27] *HMCS*, IV, pp. 108, 115. The latter document seems to represent an early draft of the Queen's itinerary because it lists the stay at Theobalds as four days, instead of the ten which the court actually spent there.

[28] Robert Cecil was knighted on 20 May 1591.

[29] BL, Cotton MS Titus B VI, fo. 34r.

[30] Margaret, Lady Blanke, widow of Sir Thomas Blanke, a former lord mayor of London (d. 1588). Unless otherwise stated, details of the Queen's hosts listed below can be found in *DNB* and/or *HoP, 1558–1603*.

[31] The following reconstruction of the Queen's itinerary is based upon E.K. Chambers, *The Elizabethan Stage*, 4 vols (Oxford, 1923), IV, pp. 105–106, but supplemented and amended by additional sources and fuller use of the treasurer of the chamber's accounts. For discussion of how a progress was organized, see Z. Dovey, *An Elizabethan Progress: The Queen's Journey into East Anglia, 1578* (Stroud, 1996).

at Bedhampton[32] (dinner only: 26 August), Portsmouth (26 –28 August), John White's house at Southwick[33] (28 August to 1 September), the Earl of Southampton's house at Titchfield (2–3 September), the Earl of Sussex's house at Southampton (3–7? September), Mr Caplen's house at South Stoneham[34] (dinner only), Francis Serle's house at Fairthorne[35] (dinner only: 8? September), the Bishop of Winchester's house at Bishop's Waltham (8–9 September), William Neale's house at Warnford,[36] Sir Benjamin Tichborne's house at Tichborne (dinner only), the bishop of Winchester's house at Winchester,[37] Abbotstone (11 September), William Wallop's house at Wield (mid-journey dinner: 11 or 12 September), Sir Henry Wallop's house at Farleigh Wallop (12–13 September), the Marquess of Winchester's house at Basing (13–19 September, with a visit to Lord Sandys's house at The Vine, c. 18 September), Edward More's house at Odiham (19–20 September), the Earl of Hertford's house at Elvetham (20–23 September), Farnham Castle (23–25 September), Sir Henry Weston's house at Sutton, Woking (25 September), Bagshot (26? September), and her palace at Oatlands (27 September–4 October), before settling back into a more sedentary existence at Richmond Palace (5 October–12 November).

With this structure of dates and places established, the dating of Cecil's letters to Hatton in Ogden MS 7/41 can be reconsidered. The results of this exercise are reflected in the following table overleaf, which lists the letters in chronological order. This shows that *all* of the letters which bear a date of November 1591 have been misdated, an error which may reflect corruption in the source from which the scribe copied these documents. In most cases, the correct date simply involves replacing 'November' with 'September'. However, internal evidence indicates that this approach cannot be applied to Letters 19 and 24.

---

[32] John Carill or Caryll (c.1554–1613), whose family was seated at Warnham, Sussex. Bedhampton was owned by his father-in-law, George Cotton, Esq., who lived at Warblington; *VCH, Hampshire*, III, pp. 135–136, 143; J.L. André, 'Warnham: its church, monuments, registers and vicars', *Sussex Archaeological Collections*, 32 (1883), pp. 144, 176–177.

[33] John White, son of Edward (d. 1580). For Southwick, see below.

[34] John Caplen or Capelin, whose father, grandfather, uncle and stepfather had been mayor of Southampton. He became sheriff of Southampton in 1592–1593, but moved into royal service in 1594 as controller of customs for the port. He died c.1607–1608 (A.L. Merson *et al.*, (eds), *The Third Book of Remembrance of Southampton, 1514–1602*, III (1573–1589), Southampton Record Series, 8 (1965), p. 55, n. 1; IV (1590–1602), Southampton Record Series, 22 (1979), p. 74, n. 125; p.,90, n. 384; p. 93, n. 416).

[35] The accounts of the Treasurer of the Chamber clearly describe the Queen dining 'at Mr Shirleye's at Fayrethorne' (PRO, E 351/542, m. 153d). However, it seems that the manor of Fairthorne (itself part of the manor of Bishop's Waltham) was held by Francis Serle, whose family had been connected with the property since the 1540s (*VCH, Hampshire*, III, p. 279).

[36] William Neale, an auditor of the exchequer.

[37] T. Atkinson, *Elizabethan Winchester* (London, 1963), p. 119.

Letters from Sir Robert Cecil to Sir Christopher Hatton, 1590–1591

Letter	Date	Place	Folios
1.	10 November 1590	Cecil's house, London	3r–v
2.	19 February 1590/1	Cecil's house, London	2r–v
3.	7 April 1591	Cecil's house, London	5v–6r
4.	6 August 1591	Loseley	7r–v
5.	8 August 1591	Loseley	11r–12r
6.	22 August 1591	Chichester	9v–10r
7.	23 August 1591	Stanstead	8r
8.	26 August 1591	Portsmouth	13v–15v
9.	27 August 1591	Portsmouth	12v–13v
10.	31 August 1591	Southwick	15v–16v
11.	2–3 September (3 November) 1591	Titchfield	18r–19r
12.	3–4 [2] September 1591	[Southampton]	17r–v
13.	4 September 1591	Southampton	19r–21r
14.	6 Sepember (6 November) 1591	Southampton	27r–v
15.	7 September (7 November) 1591	Southampton	26r–v
16.	9 September (9 November) 1591	Abbotstone	25v–26r
17.	10 September (10 November) 1591	Abbotstone	29r–30r
18.	11 September (11 November) 1591	[Abbotstone]	28v–29r
19.	13 September (19 November) 1591	Farleigh Wallop	30v–32v
20.	16 September (16 November) 1591	Cecil's house, London	30v
21.	[19 September 1591]	Odiam	32v–35r
22.	24 [September] 1591	Farnham	4r–v
23.	24 September 1591	[Farnham]	5r
24.	c.28 September (20 September) 1591	[Oatlands]	21r–22v
25.	8 October 1591	[Richmond]	22v–23v
26.	21 October 1591	[Richmond]	24v–25r
27.	27 October 1591	[Richmond]	24r–v

Note: Dates within parentheses are erroneous dates assigned by the copyist. The correction of these dating errors is explained in the accompanying text. Dates and places within square brackets represent editorial interpolations based upon external evidence.

The dating of Letter 19 must instead be fixed by the stated location of the court, the date of a letter written by the privy council to Essex and his advisers in France, and reference to a council meeting which ordered the convoying of ships sailing to Bordeaux. Letter 24 cannot be dated with such precision. It was clearly written after the Queen had sent Thomas Smith and Francis Darcy as messengers to Essex, but before Robert Carey arrived at court bearing a message for the Queen from Essex. Smith left court on 26 September and Carey arrived on 1 October. Since Darcy left some time after Smith, a date of c. 28 September seems reasonable, especially if the copyist's date of '20ᵗʰ' reflects a corruption of '28ᵗʰ' written on the original letter. Letters 21 and 22 lack full dates in the manuscript, but this is easily remedied by reference to the places from which Cecil wrote these letters, the day of the week named in Letter 21 and internal evidence.

The dating of Letters 11 and 12 raises more complex problems. Although bearing the date of 2 September, the contents of Letter 12 suggest a slightly later date. In particular, its reference to Elizabeth arriving at Southampton and the disproving of an alarmist rumour that Essex had been betrayed in France indicate that it must have been written the day after Letter 11. Letter 11 has been misdated as '3 of November', but its contents and apparent place of composition demonstrate that it must have been written on 2–3 September. Accepting a date of 3 September for Letter 11 would, in turn, force a re-dating of Letter 12 to 4 September. However, this would mean that Cecil wrote both Letters 12 and 13 on the same day, even though neither letter betrays any indication that Cecil had already written another letter to Hatton that day. Letter 12 was also clearly written in the evening, which would place it after Letter 13, even though its contents tie it closely to Letter 11. In these circumstances, it seems necessary to recognize the uncertainty which the copyist's unreliable dating has introduced into the manuscript by dating Letter 11 as 2 or 3 September and Letter 12 as 3 or 4 September.

The twenty-seven letters from Cecil to Hatton contained in this manuscript fall into two basic groups. Letters 1–3 were written before Cecil was knighted (20 May) or became a member of the Privy Council (2 August). As such, they show him desperately seeking to cement his favour with the Lord Chancellor and make his way in the world of royal service. The remaining letters show Cecil interacting with Hatton as a fellow member of the council board – albeit as the most junior member corresponding with a veteran councillor who was second in order of precedence. These letters are full of council business, reporting to Hatton on the actions of the Queen and on the contents of letters newly received at court by Cecil's father, Lord Burghley. These letters therefore show Cecil acting as an intermediary between Hatton, Burghley, and the Queen. This rôle was important because Hatton spent very little time at court during the summer and autumn of 1591, which subsequently proved to be the last months of his life. By mid-September, ill health and affairs in London had kept Hatton away from the Queen for longer than at any time since his visit to Spa in 1573.[38]

Hatton's prolonged absence from court helps to explain why these letters were actually written, while his occasional presence there explains gaps in the correspondence. Hatton remained a fixture at court and in council meetings until the very eve of the Queen's summer progress. On 2 August he helped to swear Cecil as a member of the council at

---

[38] Letter 21.

Nonsuch, but he did not join the progress which began the next day.[39] Instead, he returned to London and relied upon Cecil's letters to keep in touch with the court and council business. For his part, Cecil reported on Hatton's activities in London to the Queen and Burghley. Hatton rejoined the court by the time of Elizabeth's visit to Cowdray, between 15 and 21 August.[40] This meant that he could receive copies of important letters directly from Burghley and could confer with the Queen and his conciliar colleagues in person. Cecil's letter-writing, which always represented a second-best option to face-to-face contact,[41] naturally ceased. However, Hatton again left court after the visit to Cowdray and Cecil promptly resumed his correspondence. Another brief pause occurred during Hatton's short visit to the court at Oatlands between 29 September and 4 October.[42] A much longer gap separates Letters 25 and 26 (between 8 and 21 October). Although one or more letters from Cecil for this period may have been lost, much of the hiatus seems to be explained by the court's arrival at Richmond, which was close enough to Hatton's house at Holborn for daily communication: 'I have forborne to trouble your lordshipp with my lettres these few dayes because I knew I could not sooner advertize your lordshipp of any thing then yourselfe had yt att loud'.[43]

Cecil's constant attendance at court means that his letters also constitute an invaluable new source of information about the progress itself. Although Elizabeth often made last-minute changes to her trips through the countryside, this progress involved much more confusion than usual. As the court prepared to leave Chichester and move into Hampshire, the Earl of Sussex's plans for receiving the Queen at Portsmouth were cancelled and then promptly reinstated.[44] When she arrived at Stanstead late in the evening of 23 August, Elizabeth still planned only a single night's stay at Portsmouth on 24 August, before turning north towards Basing.[45] However, hopes of a visit at Portsmouth from Henri IV of France or the Earl of Essex now caused her to change her plans.[46] The Queen delayed her departure from Stanstead

---

[39] *APC*, XXI, p. 358.

[40] *Ibid.*, pp. 386, 396.

[41] Hence, when Cecil sought permission to leave court for a quick visit to London, the Queen instructed him to meet and speak with Hatton (Letter 20).

[42] *APC*, XXI, pp. 468, 471; *UC*, p. 105. The council meeting on 30 September was the last which Hatton ever attended. This visit also helps to suggest that Letter 24 could not have been written any later than 28 September.

[43] Letter 26.

[44] Letter 6.

[45] Letter 7.

[46] This presumably explains why advance preparations for the Queen's arrival at Abbotstone in August proved to be wasted effort: 'at which tyme she came not' (PRO, E 351/542, m. 153).

for Portsmouth until 26 August, arriving there about 8pm.[47] The following day she went to view the Downs from a specially-constructed platform and was entertained in very different ways by Sir George Carey and Lord Strange. Despite a fire near her lodging that night 'which hath bredd noe small feare and trouble',[48] she apparently stretched her stay in Portsmouth for one more day before moving five miles north to John White's house at Southwick. From there, she made a completely unplanned visit to Portchester Castle on 30 August, where she finally abandoned any hope of holding a summit at Portsmouth and decided to move on to Southampton.[49] The Queen and her court therefore headed west from Southwick on 1 or 2 September, spending a day or two at Titchfield before completing the move to Southampton on the evening of 3 or 4 September.[50] Once at Southampton, Elizabeth decided that she would make a trip to the Isle of Wight on 6 September with only a small retinue.[51] This decision clearly caused deep alarm among her advisers. Much to their relief, the Queen cancelled the trip on the evening of 5 September, thanks to a forceful explanation of the practical difficulties involved by Sir George Carey. This marked the end of her stay on the south coast,[52] clearing the way for the court to begin its journey northwards a day or so later, heading homewards via Bishop's Waltham, Winchester, Basing, Odiham and Farnham.[53] Remarkably, despite all this chopping and changing, Elizabeth finally arrived at Oatlands only two days after the revised schedule which she had laid out on the eve of her departure from Stanstead for Portsmouth.[54]

The letters and their significance for late Elizabethan politics

The opening years of the 1590s were a deeply troubling time for Elizabeth I and her regime.[55] The war against Philip II of Spain, which

[47] Letter 8.
[48] Letter 9.
[49] Letter 10.
[50] Letter 12.
[51] Letter 13.
[52] Letter 14.
[53] The decision to return home via Farnham, where Elizabeth had stayed on her journey southwards in August, apparently represented another sudden change of plan. A team of royal servants had been preparing for the court's return to Oatlands when they 'were sente for backe to Farneham in all haste by the space of three dayes' (PRO, E 351/542, m. 153d).
[54] HMC, *Calendar of the Manuscripts of the Marquis of Bath, Preserved at Longleat, Wiltshire,* II (Dublin, 1907), p. 37: Cecil to Michael Hickes, Stanstead, 25 August [1591].
[55] For fuller discussion of the points made below, see P.E.J. Hammer, *The Polarisation of Elizabethan Politics: the Political Career of Robert Devereux, 2nd Earl of Essex, 1585–1597* (Cambridge, 1999), esp. chs 3–4.

had brought the *Gran Armada* to England's shores in 1588, was escalating in ominous fashion, along with its human and financial cost. On land, the fighting had expanded dangerously from the Low Countries into France, threatening the prospect of defeat for the Protestant Henri IV and the establishment of Spanish bases just across the Channel. At sea, England's hopes of delivering a knock-out blow to the enemy remained frustratingly unfulfilled, while its naval superiority in the Atlantic was being eroded as Spain built a new ocean-going fleet. Elizabeth and her Privy Council were also forced to cope with death and dislocation much closer to home. Beginning with the sudden death of Robert Dudley, Earl of Leicester, the council was convulsed by the loss of seven of its most experienced members between September 1588 and November 1590, having already weathered another series of deaths in mid-1580s. Such rapid and painful change was especially difficult for Elizabeth, who hated personal upheavals and had loved Leicester like no other man in her life. The decimation of her inner circle of advisers and courtiers inevitably also raised questions about Elizabeth's own mortality. She turned fifty-seven in September 1590 and was well aware that some of her more ambitious subjects had already been cultivating James VI of Scotland for some time, believing that she could not live much longer.

Leicester's death also broke up the triumvirate of great officers of state which Elizabeth had established in 1587: Leicester as Lord Steward, Hatton as Lord Chancellor, and Burghley as Lord Treasurer. This placed a crushing burden of administration on the shoulders of Hatton and Burghley, especially when the death of Sir Francis Walsingham forced Burghley to add the secretaryship of state to his existing portfolio of responsibilities in April 1590. As Elizabeth grew older, she found it increasingly difficult to appoint new men to key posts in her government. In part, this was perhaps because she did not want to acknowledge her own advancing years, but it also reflected her distaste for having to forge new working relationships and for fighting a fresh round of subtle little battles to ensure that her personal authority remained untrammeled. However, even if the Queen did not want to face the problem, Burghley and Hatton felt increasingly old and worn out. For the sake of their own health and to help deal with the swelling demands of the war, they knew that a younger generation must soon be brought into the council. They believed that their task was to convince the Queen of this necessity and to oversee the process, like masters of a trade supervising the final training of apprentices.

In 1590, there were two obvious candidates for advancement, Burghley's younger son, Robert Cecil, and Leicester's stepson, the Earl of Essex. Hatton, who never married, had no obvious heir for his position. Until fairly recently, it was fashionable for historians to portray Cecil and Essex as natural rivals, continuing and deepening the alleged antipathy between Leicester and Burghley. In reality, both sets of relationships were far more complex and friendly than this over-simplification suggests. Burghley had been Essex's guardian and helped to win him to achieve his aim of commanding the army sent to Normandy in 1591. Whatever misgivings he might have harboured about Essex's over-enthusiasm for war, Burghley clearly believed that the earl would be a vital ally for his son and a fixture in English politics for many years to come. Hatton apparently held a similar view. As Cecil's letters to Hatton demonstrate, the Lord Chancellor remained consistently supportive of Essex: 'the queen saith your lordship is one that hath ever cockered the earle and would not suffer her to chasten him'.[56] In mid-September, when he had himself been absent from court for several weeks, Hatton handed Cecil a jewel to give to the Queen with a request 'that to the distressed earle yt might be sent'. This served the double purpose of lessening Elizabeth's fury with Essex and reminding her of Hatton's own qualities: 'shee fell into so great prayse of your nature, your faith and constancy'.[57] For Hatton, as for Burghley, evincing such personal concern for the rising stars of English political life at once helped to demonstrate his zeal for the Queen's service and reinforce his own hold upon her affections.

Although both Burghley and Hatton gave open support to Essex during this period, their efforts on behalf of Robert Cecil were complicated by Burghley's unwillingness to be seen to advance his son in too obvious a manner. Moreover, whereas Essex's ambitions had focused on winning command of the army being sent to assist Henri IV in the siege of Rouen, the target for Cecil was no less than the vacant secretaryship of state. In the weeks immediately following Sir Francis Walsingham's death in April 1590, Essex had lobbied for William Davison, Walsingham's former assistant in the post, to be given the charge. Whether out of sympathy for Davison's continuing suspension from duty since the execution of Mary, Queen of Scots or good will towards Essex, Hatton supported this effort.[58] However, once it became apparent that Elizabeth would never rehabilitate Davison and that Burghley wanted his son to become secretary, Hatton put his

---

[56] Letter 11.

[57] Letter 21. Hatton gave the jewel to Cecil when the latter visited him in London on 17 September. Although Cecil presented the jewel to the Queen on the following day, she was still unwilling to part with it on 20 September.

[58] BL, Harleian MS 290, fo. 244r: Essex to Davison, [c. April–May 1590]. Davison was the scapegoat for the Privy Council's decision to expedite the execution of Mary, Queen of Scots in February 1587. Following his release from prison in late 1588, he continued to be paid as junior secretary of state until his death in 1608, but was never allowed to return to service: R.B. Wernham, 'The disgrace of William Davison', *EHR*, 46 (1931), pp. 632–636.

weight behind Cecil. The results of this decision can be seen throughout the letters edited below. Cecil repeatedly protests that he is Hatton's 'creature' and that Hatton is 'my only oracle' or 'patron', who has more 'interest in mee or mine' than anyone except his own father.[59] In Letters 1–3, when Cecil felt his prospects were being batted about like a tennis ball, the language of his dependence upon Hatton is particularly emotive.

Hatton's willingness to become Cecil's 'cheefest undertaker'[60] dismayed rival candidates who had believed they would enjoy the Lord Chancellor's support. It also allowed Burghley to play a more subtle (and negative) rôle in his son's advancement, undercutting the suits of other contenders for the post, such as Edward Wotton, Edward Dyer, Henry Killigrew, and Thomas Wylkes. However, Elizabeth proved strongly resistant to both Hatton's urgings and Burghley's more indirect efforts to secure Cecil's appointment. Even when Burghley hosted the Queen at Theobalds for ten days in May 1591 and staged a mock retirement to live as a 'hermytte', she refused to do more than bestow a knighthood upon Cecil.[61] In the Queen's eyes, Cecil was too young and inexperienced for such a vital office, even in tandem with a more seasoned colleague. Elizabeth was also probably simply unwilling to be seen to give way too readily to the combined efforts of her two chief councillors, especially for the sake of Burghley's own son. However enthusiastically her Lord Chancellor and Lord Treasurer might agree on the matter, she was determined to preserve her own royal authority at all costs – and to be seen to do so.[62] The full force of Hatton's suasions over the summer of 1591 could extract only the lesser, but still substantial, prize of a seat for Cecil on the Privy Council. In the days immediately following this appointment, it seems that Cecil, at least,

---

[59] Letters 2, 3, 8.

[60] *UC*, p. 16: Unton to Burghley, 28 July 1591.

[61] For Elizabeth's visit to Theobalds, see J. Nichols, *The Progresses and Public Processions of Queen Elizabeth*, 3 vols (London, 1823), II, pp. 76–78. Upon her arrival at Theobalds, the Queen was addressed by a hermit who complained that Burghley, still grieving for the deaths of his daughter (1587), his mother (1588), and his wife (1589), had abandoned living in the main house and taken over his poor cell (BL, Egerton MS 2623, fos 15r–16v). Elizabeth therefore issued a mock charter to the hermit, co-signed by Hatton, which guaranteed the hermit possession of his 'olld cave' (BL, RP 2895), forcing Burghley to return to life as a great landowner. The symbolism of this exchange was obvious, especially as Theobalds was the centrepiece of the estates which Cecil would inherit upon his father's death. See M. Airs, ' "Pomp or glory": the influence of Theobalds', in P. Croft (ed.), *Patronage, Culture and Power: The Early Cecils* (London, 2002), pp. 3–19.

[62] This was certainly how Elizabeth explained her similar refusal to appoint Francis Bacon as Solicitor General in early 1594: the open support of both Burghley and Essex for Bacon intimidated other potential candidates, encouraged men to praise Bacon with an eye to pleasing Burghley and Essex, and prevented her from exercising her royal discretion (Lambeth Palace Library, London, MS 650, fos 33r, 45r, 148r, 197r).

feared that even this success would prove a mere sop, opening the way for another man to be appointed secretary over his head. His letter to Hatton of 7 August is therefore almost gleeful in describing the rebuffs which Mr Cavendish received from the Queen.[63] Elizabeth's dashing of the hopes of Cavendish and 'his councell' probably served to advertise that the question of the secretaryship was now closed. The office was not mentioned in any of the remaining letters from Cecil to Hatton and, despite occasional flutterings over the following years, remained vacant until Cecil was finally confirmed in the position in July 1596.

The efforts of Hatton and Burghley to advance Cecil and to support Essex in 1590–1591, and their success in doing so, sheds important light on the nature of the Privy Council during these years and its relationship with Elizabeth. Recent scholarship has begun to characterize the council of the early 1590s in terms of fragmentation and incipient division. In particular, the issue of religion – or, more accurately, the means and implications of punishing puritan dissidents – caused bitter arguments between Burghley, on the one hand, and Archbishop Whitgift, supported by Hatton and Lord Buckhurst, on the other.[64] However, the more striking phenomenon is perhaps that the fierce passions which this issue raised were kept in check. As one observer noted after reporting the lack of consequences which stemmed from another 'jarre' between Burghley and Whitgift in February 1591: 'in truthe, there is little mettell in these men that now are about the queen to worke uppon by devision'.[65] Although they both disagreed with Burghley over the treatment of puritans, Hatton ensured that Buckhurst backed Cecil's suit to become secretary.[66] Burghley, Whitgift, Hatton and other councillors also shared a common concern to punish the false prophet, William Hacket, with the greatest severity and to ensure that his offences stirred public outrage.[67] Clearly, the forces which bound the

---

[63] Letter 5. This is probably Richard Cavendish (see below). It is unclear which of Cecil's rivals for the secretaryship Cavendish and his advisers were seeking to assist. If the phrase 'the oracle of his profession' was intended to suggest a leaning towards Catholicism, Cecil *may* have been hinting at Edward Wotton, who ultimately converted to Catholicism during the reign of James I.

[64] J. Guy, 'The 1590s: the second reign of Elizabeth I?', in *idem* (ed.), *The Reign of Elizabeth I: Court and Culture in the Last Decade* (Cambridge, 1995), pp. 6, 11ff.; *idem*, 'The Elizabethan establishment and the ecclesiastical polity', in *ibid.*, pp. 126–149.

[65] PRO, SP 15/32/7 (fo. 10r): notes by Thomas Phelippes for a letter from Thomas Barnes to Charles Paget, 12 March 1590 [1591].

[66] Letter 1.

[67] For Hacket, see below. In an important article, Alexandra Walsham ('"Frantick Hacket": prophecy, sorcery, insanity and the Elizabethan puritan movement', *HJ*, 41 (1998), pp. 27–66) has argued that anti-puritan polemicists sponsored by Archbishop Whitgift deliberately avoided any concession that Hacket might have been insane, in order to claim that Hacket's conspiracy reflected the treasonable extremism of puritanism (*ibid.*, pp. 51–58). Letter 4 suggests that this argument must be modified. Even if Burghley

council together were still more important than the issues which divided them. Hatton's moderating role, and the respect which Burghley accorded him, was one of the most important of these binding forces. This relationship was undoubtedly eased by Hatton's lack of a political heir and the shared experience of holding high and burdensome office. As Cecil had written to his father at the time of Hatton's appointment as lord chancellor, 'he hath left his hat and feather, and now wears a flatt velvet cap, not different from your lordship's':[68] the courtly favourite had become the same sort of administrator as Burghley. Burghley himself touched upon this sense of comradeship after Hatton's death, when he described his late colleague as 'the principall counsellor of this realme, to whose interrement I shall tomorrowe geive attendance at Pawle's, and so leade the way for myselfe, for others to doe the like, in via universae carnis'.[69] In the event, Burghley survived for another seven years, but Hatton's death unbalanced the council and prepared the way for trouble later in the decade.

In 1591, unity and consensus among the Privy Council was also still encouraged by a corporate sense of duty to the Queen and recognition of the exigencies of war. This unifying impulse was perhaps all the stronger because the realities of war sometimes seemed to conflict with the councillors' loyalty to the Queen. Cecil's letters to Hatton frequently

had been willing to dismiss Hacket as insane before the latter's trial (*ibid.*, p. 56), Cecil's letter to Hatton shows that the Lord Treasurer had changed his mind by 6 August and that it was Burghley – not Whitgift – who deemed it 'not convenient by any writeing authorized to bee spreade abroad' to suggest that Hacket was merely 'a madd distracted person'. Whitgift had apparently overseen the writing of a treatise which portrayed Hacket in precisely this light (perhaps a very hasty first draft – Hacket was only executed on 28 July – of the work by the archbishop's protégé, Richard Cosin, which was later published as *Conspiracie for Pretended Reformation* (London, 1592, *STC* 5823)), but Burghley (and perhaps also Hatton, who had sent it on to Burghley) rejected the draft and suggested that Whitgift be sent interrogation notes to help the revision process. Almost certainly, Burghley changed his position towards Hacket because of legal considerations: the crown's prosecutors had explicitly argued against insanity at Hacket's trial on 26 July to ensure that he could not escape condemnation. Burghley may well have thought that, following this very public statement of the crown's views, it would have been inconsistent (and damaging) for an officially sanctioned publication to raise any doubts about Hacket's sanity. If this is correct, then it seems likely that the anti-puritan potential of a polemic, describing Hacket as a calculating plotter against the state, was not immediately apparent to either Whitgift or Burghley and that this only emerged during the revision process itself. If so, there is a certain irony that Burghley's intervention in this matter, however well intentioned, actually helped to shape a political weapon which was later deployed to justify the sort of ecclesiastical inquisition which he was desperately trying to oppose.

[68] W. Murdin, *A Collection of State Papers Relating to Affairs in the Reign of Queen Elizabeth, From the Year 1571 to 1596 [...]* (London, 1759), p. 588: Cecil to Burghley, 30 April 1587.

[69] *UC*, p. 209: Burghley to Unton, 15 December 1591, *In [...] carnis*: 'according to the way of all flesh'. For a depiction of Hatton's funeral at St Paul's on 16 December, see Folger Shakespeare Library, MS Z.e.3.

touch upon the notion of 'the common cause', in which England propped up the Protestant Henri IV of France against his rebellious Catholic subjects and the forces of Spain. However, the term often almost seems to signify a common burden for the Privy Council: to prevent Elizabeth's growing personal dislike of Henri IV from triggering actions which might damage her public interests. Cecil's letters show the Queen constantly trying to withdraw her forces from France and lashing out at her representatives there whenever they failed to conform to her expectations, however unreasonable they might be. Her chief targets were Sir Henry Unton,[70] her ambassador in France, and Essex, the commander of her army in Normandy. Elizabeth's blistering letters to Essex have frequently been cited as evidence of the earl's incompetence as a general.[71] In fact, these letters show Elizabeth herself at her worst as a war-leader – angry that her favourite would willingly spend time away from her court, out of touch with events on the ground, unrealistic in her expectations, and utterly scathing in her criticisms. Cecil's reports to Hatton portray a queen whose behaviour combined shrewd political calculation with injured pride and a tendency to knee-jerk reactions. When Essex sought leave to stay in France if his troops were withdrawn, she fumed at 'his so small desire to see her as shee doth requite him accordingly with crossing him in his most earnest desire'.[72] On hearing of his prolonged trip to meet Henri, her immediate reaction was even to wish Essex dead: 'the queen seemeth so offended with this journey and adventure as shee, in height of passion, wisheth him to pay for yt, so that her troupes may not miscarry'.[73] When Unton and others wrote in support of Essex's actions, they shared in the blame. On one occasion, Burghley stood up for Unton ('by God, madam, I would have written as hee did'), but Elizabeth was so intent upon making him 'knowe his error' that she forced the Lord Treasurer to pen a rebuke to the ambassador, even though she had 'infinitely [...] praysed him [Unton] for the same lettre not an hower before'.[74]

With such erratic leadership – at times, princely, perceptive, affectionate, spiteful, and irresolute – it seems that the Privy Council's chief task, or at least that of its leading members, was to sustain Elizabeth's support for 'the common cause' and to delay the implementation of

---

[70] For Unton, see J.G. Nichols (ed.), *The Unton Inventories, Relating to Wadley and Faringdon, Co. Berks. in the Years 1596 and 1620*, (Berkshire Ashmolean Society, 1841), esp. pp. 1–48; R. Strong, *The Cult of Elizabeth: Elizabethan Portraiture and Pageantry* (London, 1977), pp. 84–110.

[71] A more balanced – but still critical – assessment of Essex's generalship during this campaign is given by Lloyd, *Rouen Campaign*, pp. 106–126. Cf. Hammer, *Polarisation*, pp. 103–107.

[72] Letter 22.

[73] Letter 11.

[74] Letter 24.

any impetuous decisions which were taken in the heat of the moment, in the hope that she might change her mind 'after her second bethinkinge'.[75] News which was considered likely to provoke precipitate action was also often deliberately held back from the Queen: 'therefore is yt thought good by my lord to lett yt fall out heerafter, when with yt some other pleaseing matter may bee delivered'.[76] Elizabeth herself was well aware of her councillors' efforts to 'handle' her, which made the prolonged absence of Hatton, who had a special ability to deal with the Queen, all the more critical. While Elizabeth frequently lamented the continued absence of her old favourite ('her swete lyddes') during the late summer and autumn of 1591, Burghley (and presumably the rest of the council) continued to hope for his return to court for more practical reasons: 'till your lordshipp come to joyne your helpe, his lordshipp cannot but doubt the continewance still of her Majeste's offence'.[77] Nevertheless, government business in London and ill health kept Hatton away.[78] Although Hatton wrote letters to the Queen and sent her artful tokens, such as a jewel in the shape of a bagpipe,[79] Burghley was ultimately forced to carry the chief burden of preventing Elizabeth from overturning 'the common cause' on his own.

This subtle – and often not-so-subtle – struggle between the Queen and her councillors also played itself out in Cecil's mind. Cecil's letters show him trying to project an image of himself as Hatton's perfect dutiful correspondent and protégé, conspicuously displaying 'an honest minde frawghte with so much dutie and true reverence'.[80] However, the experience of joining the Privy Council and attending upon the Queen also introduced him to the practical dilemmas of working with Elizabeth. On the one hand, Cecil shared the council's belief that 'the common cause' with Henri IV was an inescapable necessity, despite the Queen's misgivings: 'yf this occasion overpass, halfe a million next yeare will not so much helpe him'.[81] On the other hand, Cecil was profoundly impressed by the Queen's 'royal absolute estate'[82] and often seems inclined to echo her sentiments as a matter of duty. The conflict between these perspectives sometimes made it difficult for Cecil to strike the right tone in his letters. When discussing Elizabeth's frequent explosions of fury against Essex, for example, he seems increasingly

---

[75] Letter 21.
[76] Letter 25. Cf. Letters 19, 27.
[77] Letter 23.
[78] Hopes that Hatton might rejoin the court at Basing (Letters 7, 9) or Elvetham (Letters 16, 21) or Oatlands (Letter 21) were repeatedly dashed by his worsening health.
[79] Letters 9, 13.
[80] Letter 17.
[81] Letter 19.
[82] Letter 22.

drawn towards the Queen's position: 'I pray God to put his minde to make her Majestie's absolute will his perfectest reasone and to frame his actions to her Majeste's likeinge'. Nevertheless, Cecil constantly reassured Hatton that he 'wisheth him [Essex] all honorable fortune', conscious that the Lord Chancellor was not only his 'patron' but also a friend of the earl.[83] The tensions between Cecil's sense of duty to the Queen, to his father, and to Hatton are also evident in his occasional bewilderment at the Queen's behaviour and his consequent difficulty in rationalizing her actions: 'I find that att some time good is badd and, another time, worse is not so ill taken'.[84] Indeed, Elizabeth's conduct towards Unton was so mercurial that it seemed like a fable from Ovid's *Metamorphoses*.[85]

Cecil's letters also offer other insights into the workings of Elizabethan politics at the start of the 1590s. The importance of catching the Queen's ear, and the difficulty of doing so for those who lacked an office which gave them ready access to the Privy Chamber, can be seen in Mr Cavendish's 'pretence of access': 'to diswade her Majesty from goeing further, alleadging that shee was to pass through a tyckle countrey and places fraught with suspected and discontented persons'.[86] This tactic of using an audience with the Queen for one purpose in order to help further quite different aims was probably a common practice at court,[87] although Cavendish's poor reception suggests that Elizabeth could react badly to such deception if the suppliant did not play his/her hand very carefully. Cavendish's ostensible reason for speaking with the Queen is also significant. Having been profoundly doubtful, even fearful, of Catholic loyalties at the time of the Armada, the Elizabethan regime still remained uncertain about the patriotism of most English Catholics, despite their proven unwillingness to aid the Spanish. The fact that Cavendish was able to secure an audience to warn the Queen against trusting southern Catholics suggests that at least some key officials at court remained deeply suspicious. Nevertheless, whether because of geography or a conscious effort at bridge-building, many of the stops on Elizabeth's progress occurred at houses which were owned by open or suspected Catholics. This could result in some curious, almost schizophrenic, coincidences. Elizabeth stopped

---

[83] *Ibid.*
[84] Letter 25.
[85] Letter 24.
[86] Letter 5.
[87] Hence a very similar approach was suggested by Ralph Lane in March 1592, when he heard that Burghley was in ill-favour with the Queen and apparently unable to dispell 'harde constructions' against him. As a 'wellwyller' of Burghley, he offered to write a 'projecte' on a matter of war, such as fortifying the shore near Southsea Castle (of which Lane was captain), which would include praise of Burghley and 'vouchesafe my personalle speeche with her Highness aboute yt' (SP 12/241/101 (fo. 148r–50r)).

at two of Sir Henry Weston's houses (Clandon Park and Sutton), for example, only a few months after the Privy Council had ordered Sir William More (who also hosted the Queen) to search Weston's house at Sutton for 'one Morgan, sometymes of her Majestie's chappell, an obstinate and seditious papist' who had been seen nearby 'in lurcking sorte'.[88] Sir Benjamin Tichborne, who hosted Elizabeth for dinner at the house where his family had been resident since the twelfth century, had many relatives who were outright recusants, including one who had been executed for plotting to kill the Queen in 1586 and another who had died in Winchester gaol three years later.[89] Cavendish may have been correct in describing this as 'a tyckle countrey', but he underestimated both Elizabeth's determination not to be cowed by men's fears for her safety and her ability to inspire loyalty across the confessional divide.

There are also hints in Cecil's letters about the important, but often obscure, part played by women in high politics. Although the Queen herself was notoriously hostile towards women who meddled too openly in politics, female involvement in bringing together families and as go-betweens and purveyors of advice and hospitality provided much of the glue which held the Elizabethan élite together. In his missives to Hatton, Cecil refers to his wife several times,[90] using her alleged feminine simplicity and emotionalism as a foil for his own more sophisticated qualities: 'humbly, but foolishly [...] according to her plaine woomanish fashion'.[91] This rhetorical strategy depended for its success upon Hatton's own personal acquaintance with Lady Cecil and his awareness that Cecil was very far from regarding the behaviour of 'my life's companion' as merely 'idle matter'.[92] Indeed, because Hatton had known Lady Cecil before her marriage (as a daughter of his fellow councillor, Lord Cobham), Cecil deliberately played upon this bond to reinforce his own relationship with Hatton. For her part, Lady Cecil accompanied her husband during much of the summer progress,[93] magnifying his presence at court. When the question of Cecil's advancement had still hung in the balance, she also spoke directly with Hatton about his prospects, reiterating the reliance upon Hatton's patronage which Cecil expressed in his letters.[94] The furtherance of Cecil's

[88] HMC, *Seventh Report, Appendix*, p. 649. For Weston, see *HoP, 1558–1603*, III, p. 605.
[89] *Ibid.*, p. 508; *VCH, Hampshire*, III, p. 337.
[90] Letters 2, 8, 13, 17. For Cecil's wife, see below.
[91] Letter 13.
[92] *Ibid.*
[93] She was at Stanstead and Portsmouth at the end of August (Letter 8; HMC, *Manuscripts of the Marquis of Bath*, II, 37) and at Portsmouth (Letter 13) and Abbotstone in September (Letter 17).
[94] Letter 2.

career was therefore a joint project to which both husband and wife contributed, working in tandem within their own specific spheres of endeavour.

This complementarity of male and female politicking, in their different forms, also seems to have been tried, but thwarted, in the case of the Earl of Essex. As Cecil informed Hatton from Loseley, attempts by various unnamed courtiers to 'urge the matter of the gentlewoman lately gonn from courte' had backfired and made the Queen even more 'apt to take exception' to Essex's actions.[95] Reading between the lines, it seems that there was a concerted attempt to win favour for Essex's wife, whom Elizabeth had dismissed as an unsuitable bride for the earl when news of their marriage became public in late 1590. By the summer of 1591, friends of Essex and his wife presumably thought that enough time had passed since this rejection, and since the birth of a son in January, to seek the Queen's forgiveness. Significantly, this overture was also launched at precisely the time when Essex himself went abroad, suggesting that the countess was expected to help protect his interests at court in his absence. However, Elizabeth's obduracy scotched the plan and any hopes that the Countess of Essex might contribute to her husband's political career were stymied. Indeed, the Queen was so irritated by this effort – whether because of her continuing dismay at Essex's choice of bride, or because this attempt to install the countess at court was so transparently political – that she counted it as a black mark against Essex himself. In this case, as so often during her reign, Elizabeth's innate suspicion of other women worked against the interests of the man whom a woman sought to assist.

Finally, Cecil's letters are also instructive for what they do not report. Perhaps most significantly, they underline the extent to which Essex's chief rival for royal favour, Sir Walter Ralegh, was completely excluded from the beneficent machinations of Hatton and Burghley.[96] Despite his later close association with Cecil, Ralegh is mentioned only twice in these letters. On the first occasion, Ralegh is described simply as one of those courtiers who conveyed to Cecil a message from the Queen.[97] The other mention of Ralegh, however, shows him striking a blow against Essex by reporting the news which had been concealed

---

[95] Letter 4.

[96] According to one (unidentified) observer, Essex was 'mightelie backt by the greatest in opposition to Sir Walter Ralegh, who had offended manie and was maligned of most'; BL, Egerton MS 2026, fo. 32r. For Ralegh's controversial rise to royal favour and his rivalry with Essex, see P.E.J. Hammer, ' "Absolute and Sovereign Mistress of her Grace"? Queen Elizabeth and her favourites, 1581–1592', in J.H. Elliott and L.W.B. Brockliss (eds), *The World of the Favourite* (New Haven CT and London, 1999), pp. 43ff.; *idem*, *Polarisation*, pp. 64ff., 83ff.

[97] Letter 2.

from her of Essex's mass dubbing of knights outside Rouen.[98] Moreover, the fact that Ralegh deliberately waited until Hatton had left the Queen's presence suggests that the Lord Chancellor was also in his sights, at least as one who knew of Essex's action and had deliberately prevented the Queen from hearing of it. As a frequent companion of the Queen, Ralegh would presumably have known of her conviction that Hatton had always 'cockered' the earl and his intervention was perhaps therefore intended to re-ignite this suspicion, hampering Hatton's ability to defend Essex and increasing the Queen's indignation with both Essex and Hatton.

Ralegh's attack ultimately did Essex little harm, but it may perhaps have done more serious damage to Hatton because it came at precisely the time when Elizabeth launched proceedings against him to recover the huge debt which he owed her as the receiver of tenths and first fruits. It is impossible to claim that Ralegh's intervention actually provoked the Queen to demand repayment of the money, especially as the matter had apparently been raised in the past[99] and the ballooning cost of the campaign in Normandy now made it increasingly difficult for the government to overlook a debt of more than £40,000.[100] Nevertheless, it is possible that Ralegh's action helped to prevent Hatton from convincing the Queen to delay repayment during those vital few days before he was fully incapacitated by his sickness. Once it became apparent that the illness which kept Hatton from returning to the court was likely to prove fatal, Elizabeth returned to the sort of affectionate behaviour towards her old favourite which is described in Cecil's letters.[101] According to a later poetic tribute to Hatton, she spent five days tending to him at his London house, Ely Place.[102] However, the imminence of Hatton's death did little to deflect Elizabeth's determination to secure her money. Following his death on 20 November, the Lord Chancellor's estate was promptly extended, just as Leicester's had been some three years earlier for the debts which he had owed. Many of Elizabeth's chief servants had to endure a similar final

<hr/>

[98] Letter 27.

[99] Lord Campbell claims that Hatton had told the Queen that he still could not afford to repay the debt because of the continuing financial burden of his installation as Lord Chancellor four years earlier and his unwillingness to impose higher fees on litigants: J. Campbell, *Lives of the Lord Chancellors and Lord Keepers of the Great Seal of England*, fifth edn, 10 vols (London, 1868), II, pp. 287–288.

[100] Various figures are given for Hatton's debt. Nicolas cites a figure of £42,139 5s (*Memoirs of Hatton*, 495).

[101] Thomas Phelippes noted that Hatton's sickness was likely to prove terminal on 31 October (PRO, SP 12/240/53 (fo. 84r–v)), but the only firm date for Elizabeth's visits to Hatton is 11 November (St J. Brooks, *Hatton*, p. 353).

[102] John Phillips, 'A commemoration on the life and death of the Right Honourable Sir Christopher Hatton', cited in St J. Brooks, *Hatton*, pp. 353, 356–357.

reckoning. In this perspective, and above all in light of the contents
and tone of Cecil's letters, the old romantic notion that Hatton died of
a broken heart because Elizabeth had spurned him[103] – and, even more
so, the idea that this alleged rejection occurred because the Queen
shifted her affections to Essex[104] – cannot stand up to any serious
scrutiny. Like most of his peers, Hatton died in enormous debt to the
crown, but Cecil's letters show that he retained an equally enormous
political influence almost to the day he died, despite his increasingly
long absences from the royal presence.

---

[103] W. Camden, *The History of the Most Renowned and Victorious Princess, Elizabeth* (fourth
edn, London, 1688), p. 458; T. Fuller, *The History of the Worthies of England*, 3 vols (London,
1840), II, p. 508; Campbell, *Lives of the Chancellors*, II, pp. 287, 294; Nicolas, *Memoirs of
Hatton*, pp. 495–496. St J. Brooks, *Hatton*, p. 351; and Vines, *Hatton*, p. 201 are correct in
rejecting this interpretation, even though they lack strong evidence to support their
contention.
[104] Campbell, *Lives of the Chancellors*, II, p. 294.

LETTERS FROM SIR ROBERT CECIL TO SIR CHRISTOPHER HATTON, 1590–1591

Ogden MS 7/41, University College London, folios 2–35

Letter 1: Robert Cecil to Lord Chancellor Hatton, 10 November 1590
[fo. 3r–v]

My most humble dutie remembered to your lordshipp. Since my lord my father's retourne from the courte today after dynner, his lordshipp hath imparted unto mee the inward care your lordshipp, with infinite favors, hath taken to effecte that for mee which I shall never bee able to deserve. With whom, seeing I have determined to make religiouse conscience never to dissemble, I must needes to your lordshipp unfeynedlie avowe[1] that yt was so farr from my lord's owne thoughtes to hold mee worthy the nomination and so much farther from his minde ever to have pursued yt directly or indirectly, I being his sonne, as ever I did hold yt a most desperate fortune for mee to compasse, both in regarde[2] of mine owne wantes (wherof I am best able to to judge) [and] of the cross thwarts from undeserved badd frindes, wherof daylie I find sharpe fruites, and espetially of the impossibillitie in this age to finde so noble, so constant and so powerfull an intercessor as, by your lordshipp's manner from[3] the first breath delivered of the matter hitherto, I have most sensible cause to holde your lordshipp, to whom, though I cann profess noe more of love and dutie then I have alreadie vowed.[4] Yet, being not so conveniently to attend your lordshipp, by takeing this day some light phisicke, I cannot hold my penn from being the messenger of my thankfull minde nor yet, without betraying my hearte,[5] *[fo. 3v]* forbeare to profess my true and reverend affection, next my dutie to him from whom I have my beinge, most absolutely of any creature liveinge, to bee att your lordshipp's disposition, whom I humblie beseech to accept of this poore sacrifice till I may see the hower to bee so happy to doe your lordshipp service, whose dayes I wish may long and happilie bee numbred for her Majeste's saftie and our countrie's preservation. And so, craving pardon for my

---

[1] 'unfeynedlie avowe' underlined.
[2] 'a most [...] regarde' underlined.
[3] 'Thwarts [...] from' underlined.
[4] 'sensible cause [...] vowed' underlined.
[5] 'some light [...] hearte' underlined.

presumption[6] thus to trouble your lordshipp from your important affayres, I humbly take my leave. From my howse[7] this x[th] of No. 1590.[8]

Your lordshipp's most humbly to doe yow service
Ro: Cecyll

[*Marginated*] Postscript:
I doe find that your lordshipp's speeches to my lord of Buckhurste[9] hath purchased me his furtherance,[10] for which I must only thanke your lordshipp, for hee hath to some neer me so professed.

Letter 2: Robert Cecil to Lord Chancellor Hatton, 19 February 1591'
[fo. 2r–v]

[**Note:** the earlier part of this letter, written on fo. 1, is missing]

feare to buylde on future hopes nor entended to have made any cortlyer suites then gratious acceptation for reward of my endevours. I did besides excuse my absence[11] by being loath, after the quicke apprehension that the world conceived of my preferrment, though I knew they voyced yt with contrary affections, to appeare ambitious by repaire to the courte to stand for a place which I durst not betray my thoughtes to seeme to hold myselfe capeable of, but[12] through her Majeste's owne goodnesse, which only I trusted to, and to no mediation. I did heerin, I trust, not much digress from your lordshipp's speech,[13] whom ever I must honor for your substantiall favor, to whom I presume this to deliver, that your lordshipp, beinge my only oracle, may not bee unacquainted with the proceedinges of your poore follower,[14] whose heart unfoyled, I assure your lordshipp, shall ever reverence yow as my seconde father and, so your lordshipp will hold mee your creature, I care not what condition of fortune befall[15] mee. I have bynn not a little greived that your lordshipp was founde faulte withall for your direct dealeing with mee, which her Majestie, I perceave, did not like to have

---

[6] 'happilie bee [...] presumption' underlined.
[7] Cecil's house was a small mansion on the east side of Burghley (or Cecil) House, which was located between the Strand and Covent Garden.
[8] 'take my leave [...] No.' underlined.
[9] Thomas Sackville, Lord Buckhurst (1536–1608), a privy councillor since early 1586.
[10] 'purchased me his furtherance' underlined.
[11] 'any cortlyer [...] absence' underlined.
[12] 'durst not [...] capeable of' underlined.
[13] 'much digress [...] speech' underlined.
[14] 'my only oracle [...] followe' underlined.
[15] 'lordshipp will hold [...] befall' underlined.

mee feele or understande. But I trust your lordshipp shall finde, yf ever I speake with her, that her Majeste's purpose was delivered mee by diverse others, as Mr Vicechamberlain,[16] my L[ord] A[dmiral][17] and Sir W[alter] R[alegh].[18] But God forbid I should looke for good by contestation with so absolute a prince.[19] And therfore I was sorry that by others' errors your lordshipp might have any cause to bee offended with mee or reprehended by her Majeste for my unfortunate matter. *[fo. 2v]* Thus, haveing only presumed to prepare your lordshipp yf her Majeste doe take notice of the partes of my letter wherwith I heare her Majestie was very well satisfied, I doe humbly take my leave, careless of envy for enjoying your favor, because yt is ever accompanyed with their goode that are of any worth to preserve yt, which I was not a little proude by my wife[20] to understand yow did so nobly continew towardes mee, whose power cann never be able in any sorte to deserve yt, but by praying for your long life, honor and happiness, wherwith I humbly take my leave. From my poore howse this 19th of Febr. 1590 [1591].

> Your lordshipp's most humbly
> Ro: Cecyll

Letter 3: Robert Cecil to Lord Chancellor Hatton, 7 April 1591

[fos 5v–6r]

My humble dutie remembred to your lordshipp. I trust your lordshipp will pardon my boaldnes in importuning your lordshipp in the middest of your greater affaires with my private tedious cause, so tenderly touching now my poore reputation, wherin what good soever shalbee from the queene derived (of whom I have so slenderly deserved), I must and will accompt the same, not cheifely but wholely, attayned by your lordshipp's directe and honorable mediation,[21] whose power I must only trust to (in regard of my many oppositions) for the conclusion,

---

[16] Sir Thomas Heneage (c. 1532–1595), vice-chamberlain and privy councillor since 1587.

[17] Charles Howard, second Lord Howard of Effingham (1536–1624), Lord Admiral and privy councillor since 1585.

[18] Sir Walter Ralegh (?1552–1618), a royal favourite since the mid-1580s. Although he became captain of the Queen's guard after Hatton's death (not in 1587, as most modern sources claim), Ralegh never became a member of the Privy Council.

[19] 'forbid I should [...] prince' underlined.

[20] Elizabeth Cecil, née Brooke, daughter of William seventh Lord Cobham. Married to Robert Cecil on 31 August 1589, she died on 24 January 1597.

[21] 'meditation' in MS.

as I have bynn alreadie bound really and singly to your lordshipp's favor[22] for the beginning and proceeding so farr forth and so much exceedinge my meaness to requite or require it att your handes. I have long and generally honored yow for that virtue which is apparrant in your lordshipp to all the world, but such and so particuler sence have I now had of your lordshipp's undevided and irremoveable good opinion of mee as I must ever continew my honest profession of the same as a fayth I will dye in, which, though yt have altered the formallitie of others' former frindshipp, who (since they discovered your lordshipp's fast favor to have answered my constante beleife) leave now noe strategems *[fo. 6r]* unpracticed underhand (knowing that by open opposition they were like by your lordshipp's greatnes to bee overweighed). Yet I am desireous for their better understanding (yf any of them expecte thankes from my handes) to leave it under my hande that in this of mine so substantially concerneing my poore fortune,[23] only begunn and wholy continewed by your lordshipp, without possibilitie of private respecte of mee or my freindes, as those whose love your lordshipp little needed, I doe disdayne from thought or confession that I have truly bynn att all, or desire to bee, bound to any man liveing[24] but to your lordshipp (myne owne father excepted). My case hath a long tyme bynn tossed (right honorable and my singuler good lord) like a tennis ball, dandled by them att first till tyme discovered their fyness but, now that yt hath appeared that noe devise cann directe your favor from mee, I doubt not that any invention shallbee spared to strike the ball under the lyne. And therfore my humble suite is to your lordshipp, seing your presence is only the life of my crossed fortune, that, even according to your noble nature, yow wilbe pleased to free mee from the uncerteyntie I live in by driveing that to some periode (happen as yt shall) which only your lordshipp hath moulded to the[25] forme yt is already fashioned. Wherin, yf my happ bee not agreeable to your favor, the contentment *[fo. 6v]* to knowe yt in time wilbee so much that I shall as little quarrell with my destiny as any creature liveing. Yf better befall mee, even so doe I desire to prosper as I ever will shew my unfeyned dutie and devotion by all publique and particuler demonstration to lett the world know whom I have chosen for the patron of that life which in her Majeste's service (dearer to mee then my life) I shall most faythfully and lyally imploy att her sacred pleasure and comandement. It is, I know, noe newse to your lordshipp, in regard of your greatenes and quallitie, to heare many formall and greate

---

[22] 'I must only [...] your lordshipp's favor' underlined.
[23] 'better understanding [...] my poore fortune' underlined.
[24] 'Disdayne [...] any man living' underlined.
[25] Followed by 'fashion', struck through.

protestations, whose favor daylie men of other condition then[26] ever I shalbee doe, need and use. But surelie, sir (before God I speake yt), to my minde yt is not suteable to betray yt with my wordes and, therfore, leaveing all thwartes to bee remedyed by your wisdome and favorable regard, for that noe man cann bee farther interested then I am in the suspence therof, in symplicitie of heart by this messenger of my minde doe I desire to bee layde open to yourselfe and to all the world besides. And so most humbly take my leave. From my house this 7th of Aprill 1591.

Your lordshipp's most humbly to command
[no signature added]

Letter 4: Sir Robert Cecil to Lord Chancellor Hatton, 6 August 1591

[fo. 7r–v]

Since my writeing to your lordshipp this morneinge,[27] I am commanded by my lord my father to let your lordshipp understand that, in his peruseall of the booke which my lord [of] Canterbury[28] sent your lordshipp, which likewise was delivered mee by your lordshipp to shew to my lord heer, hee doth find that in this booke is not aptlie conveied what were fitt to bee published. For, wher by Arthington's[29] confession the supposed maddnes of that monster Hackett[30] was laide open and proved but only a dissembled frensy, this pamplet in the end doth noate him to bee a madd distracted person, which were not convenient by any writeing authorized to bee spread abroade and therfore, in my lord father's judgement, yt doth not meete with that which yt should doe.[31]

---

[26] Followed by 'myselfe', struck through.

[27] This letter has apparently not survived.

[28] John Whitgift (c. 1530–1604), Archbishop of Canterbury since 1583.

[29] Henry Arthington, a puritan gentleman from Yorkshire. With Edmund Copinger, he publicly proclaimed William Hacket (see below) as a messiah in London on 16 July 1591. After his arrest, Arthington disavowed Hacket and pleaded his innocence in the affair. He was still a prisoner in the Counter in February 1593 when he published his *Seduction of Arthington by Hacket* (*STC*, 799), also called *Arthington's Seduction and Repentance*.

[30] William Hacket was hanged, drawn and quartered for treason (denying the Queen's sovereignty) on 28 July 1591. He had claimed to be a messiah and 'king of Europe' and publicly challenged the authorities at Cheapside twelve days earlier: Camden, *History of Elizabeth*, pp. 451–455. The official account of Hacket's treason was presented in Cosin, *Conspiracie for Pretended Reformation*. See Walsham, ' "Frantick Hacket" ', and C.C.Breight, 'Duelling ceremonies: the strange case of William Hacket, Elizabethan messiah', *Journal of Medieval and Renissance Studies*, 19 (1989), pp. 35–67.

[31] 'aptlie conveied [...] which yt should doe' underlined.

The confession of Arthington is in Mr Doctor Awbrey's[32] handes, out of which was collected those articles which Mr Vice Treasurer[33] shewed your lordshipp att my lord mayor's, with certeine cautelous[34] answers to them made by Arthington, full of evasions and only charging those two that are deade. To the entent therfore that now better matter may bee now[35] drawen from him and some more substantiall interrogatories ministred, my lord doth send to the archbishopp of Canterbury to use his pleasure therin and hath comanded mee to write to Mr Doctor Awbrey to lett my lord of Canterbury see the whole writeinge which Arthington sent his lordshipp, out of which Mr Awbrey drew the last interrogatories which were sent to Mr Foskew,[36] [fo. 7v] to examine him of the answeres wherunto (such as they were your lordshipp saw and quickly perceived his cunninge slender devises therin).[37] Since the comminge of Sir Thomas Gorge[38] and Mr Nicholas Darcy,[39] who both brought lettres from my lord of Essex,[40] the queene is nothing satisfied with the earle, espetially because hee forgott to answere some pointes of her Majeste's last letter written with her owne hande conteyning a divine prayer and full of all princely favor.[41] Ther

[32] Dr William Aubrey (1529–1595), a civil lawyer who served the Elizabethan regime in many capacities, including as a master in chancery, master of requests, a judge of the Admiralty Court, and (by 1593) member of the Court of High Commission.

[33] Presumably Sir John Fortescue (see below), Chancellor and under-treasurer of the Exchequer.

[34] i.e. crafty.

[35] Interlined.

[36] Sir John Fortescue (?1531–1607), Chancellor of the Exchequer and Privy Councillor since 1589. Fortescue and another councillor, John Wolley, the Latin secretary, led the interrogation of Hacket at the Lord Mayor's house, beginning on the afternoon of 18 July: APC, XXI, pp. 293, 297; PRO, SP 12/239/93 (fo. 124r)); Cosin, Conspiracie for Pretended Reformation, pp. 59–60.

[37] The second parenthesis is placed after 'your lordship saw' in MS.

[38] Sir Thomas Gorges of Longford, Wiltshire (1536–1610), a groom of the Privy Chamber since 1572 and gentleman of the Garderobe of the Queen's Robes (HoP, 1558–1603, II, p. 208; BL, Lansdowne MS 59, fo. 43v; PRO, SO 3/1, fo. 581). He frequently served as high-powered messenger from the Queen.

[39] Nicholas Darcy was the seventh son of Sir Arthur Darcy of Brimham, Yorkshire: C.B. Norcliffe (ed.), The Visitation of Yorkshire in the Years 1563 and 1564, Harleian Society, 16 (London, 1881), p. 93. Like Gorges, Darcy had been with Essex at Dover, where he delivered a cipher and letters from Burghley on 28 July (PRO, SP 78/25, fo. 105r–v). Prof. R.B. Wernham understandably confused him with his younger brother Francis (tenth son of Sir Arthur Darcy: see below) in his mention of this delivery: L&A, 1591–1592, p. 328, §546).

[40] Presumably, PRO, SP 78/25, fos 105r–v, 112r, 121r, 124r: Essex to Burghley, 28 and 29 July 1591, written from Dover.

[41] This letter has apparently not survived. It may have been written in response to Essex's letter protesting that 'I must nott lett this second day passe without complayning to your Majestie of the misery of absence' (BL, Additional MS 74286, fo. 9r; Devereux, I, pp. 219–220).

are besides [some] that urge the matter of the gentlewoman lately gonn from courte,[42] which her Majestie apprehendeth the more and so is apt to take[43] exception to him and his whole actions. I am afraid to importune your lordshipp any longer and therfore humblie take my leave. From Sir William Moor's,[44] this 6th of August 1591

Your lordshipp's most humbly att commandment
[no signature added]

Letter 5: Sir Robert Cecil to Lord Chancellor Hatton, 8 August 1591

[fos 11r–12r]

May yt please your lordshipp. It is to mee noe small comforte that my poore myte is acceptable to your lordshipp, of whom unfeynedly I protest to have received more favor, continewance and helpe to my preferment then of any person that liveth on earth, uppon which I wish I may treade noe longer then while I acknowledge yt by all the meanes my fortune cann yeild mee. In the reporte of that your lordshipp delivered att Guildhall,[45] I trust your lordshipp doth assure yourselfe that I was as spareing as became mee, knowing how easily I moughte have marred the life of your sub-stantiall speech (gravely by yourselfe conceived and uttered) by my light reporte and therfore, more then to avoide her Majeste's opinion that I had not made the best observation I coulde, I did not any way dispose myselfe to any enlargement, as one that knoweth full well the approved experience that her Majeste hath of that in your lordshipp, which yieldeth her a most constant assurance that her country is indebted unto her not a little for being contented to spare from herselfe so worthie a magistrate in such and so high a place of justice.[46]

Since, my lord, I wrote to your lordshipp by Mr Ashelie's[47] handes of the French occurrences, nothing hath bynn brought worthy your lordshipp's understandinge, only out of Scotland. Yt is advertized that the Earle Bothwell now,[48] by late peremptory presumption purposeth to kill the Chancellor, hath so exasperated the king as hee proceedeth

---

[42] This seems to refer to Frances Walsingham, daughter of Sir Francis Walsingham and widow of Sir Philip Sidney (d. 1586), whom Essex had secretly married in 1590.

[43] 'take' interlined.

[44] Loseley, Surrey, house of Sir William More (1520–1600).

[45] Cecil may be referring to a speech by Hatton to the justices following the conclusion of the Trinity law term on 23 June.

[46] 'I did not any way dispose [...] place of justice' underlined.

[47] Anthony Ashley (1551–1628), a clerk of the Privy Council since March 1587 (*APC*, XIV, p. 385).

[48] 'the French occurrences [...] Earle Bothwell now by' underlined.

seriously to his apprehension. *[fo. 11v]* And yf hee doe not come in hee
will award a confiscation of all his landes and goodes, which hee
promiseth the duke of Lenox, the better to embarque him in the
prosecution of the said Bothwell.[49] I am commanded by my lord to
recomende his most loveing comendations to your lordshipp, hopeing
to meete your lordshipp att Cowdrey.[50]

Hither came yesternight lame Cavendish,[51] who had longe speech
with the queene. His pretence of accesse was to diswade her Majesty
from goeing further, alleadging that shee was to pass through a tyckle
countrey and places fraught with suspected and discontented persons,
but his errand was to speake for the oracle of his profession, that hee
might bee chosen to the place of hir Majeste's secretaries. More
comforte then in heareing him the queen gave him not, as himselfe
hath confessed to some of his councell. Neyther in his owne particuler
suite, for the like benefitt which hee had by Mr Tyrwhit's[52] recusancie
(who is now dead), did her Majesty give him any good contentation. I
doe finde (yf yt please your lordshipp) that by some your lordshipp is
judged not to bee so carefull to drawe on their fortunes as yow were
to further mee, for that yf yow had their election, being so neere, yow
might have drawen on theires then or else have suspended myne. If
therfore (my good lord) I thus doe finde that yow are noted for
particularity to mee by others in like competition, surely, *[fo. 12r]* sir, I
will pray your lordshipp to bee assured that this your extraordinary
favor to mee hath taken such deepe impression in my hearte as,[53]
whensoever by their advancement their meanes may bee encreased to
shew their good wills to doe yow service and reverence, they shall
never goe before mee in all true honor to your lordshipp, as farr as, in
this condition of mine, I may bee able to the world to publishe it or to

---

[49] See *CSPSc.*, X, (1589–1593), pp. 550–552: Robert Bowes to Burghley, Edinburgh, 31
July 1591.

[50] Cowdray, Sussex, house of Anthony Browne, first Viscount Montagu (1529–1592).
Montagu staged an elaborate series of entertainments for Elizabeth there, 15–21 August.
See J. Wilson, *Entertainments for Elizabeth* (Woodbridge, 1980), pp. 86–95; C.C. Breight,
'Caressing the great: Viscount Montague's entertainment of Elizabeth at Cowdray, 1591',
Sussex Archaeological Collections, 128 (1989), pp. 147–166. Two accounts of this visit were
soon published in London: *STC* 7582.5 and 3907.5 (which was also published in another
edition, *STC* 3907.7).

[51] Probably Richard Cavendish (d.c.1601), a former client of the Earl of Leicester who
had performed diplomatic work abroad and enjoyed some reputation as a mathematician
and man of letters (*HoP, 1558–1603*, I, p. 567).

[52] William Tyrwhit of Kettleby, Lincs (d. 1591), who had been paying £400 p.a. for
pre-1587 recusancy fines and £260 p.a. for his fines from October 1586: H. Bowler and
T.J. McCann (eds), *Recusants in the Exchequer Pipe Rolls*, Catholic Record Society, record
series, 71 (1986), p. 171. Cavendish's claim probably explains why Tyrwhit's will was not
probated until 17 June 1592.

[53] 'extraordinary favor [...] my hearte as' underlined.

your lordshipp in any parte to express yt, wherin I desire nothing more
then that your lordshipp will vouchsafe to serve yourselfe of mee, which
shall not a little glad my minde. And so, with my humble dutie,[54] I
take my leave. From the court this 8th August 1591

> Your lordshipp's most humbly att command dureing life
> R. Cecyll

Letter 6: Sir Robert Cecil to Lord Chancellor Hatton, 22 August 1591

[fos 9v–10v]

May yt please your lordshipp. I am ashamed I cann write your lordshipp
noe more matter of importance, seing your favorable acceptation of
my poore service which is such as, to my hearte's contentation, I may,
by your lordshipp's manner of usage of myselfe and my lettres, feelingly
conceive. From any forraine partes ther hath come noe dispatch since
your lordshipp's departure[55] and therfore to fill upp my paper must I
presume to inserte the newse of courte and progress. Howsoever my
lord of Sussex's[56] provisions were countermaunded (to his displeasing)
by objections against her Majeste's comeing to Portesmouth, it is now
otherwise ordered to double his trouble, for the queen will needes to
Portsmouth for a night and then make her retourn homewarde. Shee
hath bynn heere presented by the corporation with a cupp of mother
of perle and 30[li] in gold, by the bishopp[57] with a purse and 20[li] and
today, by one of the prebendes, with a noteable sermon to her Majeste's
likeing in the kathedrall church.

This her Majeste understood from the French embassador att
London: that the state of the king's army in all 17000 foote and 5000
horse [*marginated*: This is confirmed by Sir Roger Williams' letter][58] but
hee doth send downe to Roan under conducte of the Marshall Byron[59]
but 12000 foote and 2000 horse, to bee joyned with her Majeste's
troupes under my lord of Essex his charge. *[fo. 10r]* The other 5000

---

[54] 'your lordshipp in any parte [...] dutie' underlined.

[55] Hatton had been at court at Cowdray until at least 18 August (*APC*, XXI, p. 396).

[56] Henry Radcliffe, fourth Earl of Sussex (c.1532–1593), captain of Portsmouth and
joint Lord Lieutenant of Hampshire.

[57] Thomas Bickley (1518–1596), Bishop of Chichester since 1585.

[58] Sir Roger Williams (?1540–1595), veteran soldier and frequent envoy to Henri IV.
The relevant letter was written to Burghley from Dieppe on 15 August (PRO, SP 78/25,
fo. 202r–v) and carried to England by Thomas Smith. Williams commanded the advance
guard of English troops sent to Dieppe before the arrival of the main force and was
subsequently appointed marshal (second-in-command) of Essex's army (*APC*, XXI, pp.
318–319).

[59] Armand de Gontaut, baron of Biron and marshal of France.

foote and 3000 horse hee carrieth himselfe to the frontiers to receive in the reyters[60] for their more safe passage now att their entry into Champaigne. Her Majeste much misliketh my lord of Essex's goeing to meete the king[61] and seemeth to scorne the kinge's goeing away and his leaveing her generall with his marshall. But, for all this, her Majeste doth send favorably by Mr Smith,[62] my lorde's man, so as your lordshipp may perceave her Majeste's displeasure to the earle is not so permanent as sharpe in the beginning, which is the fruite of her gratious nature, best knowen to your lordshipp by your most inward conversation and continewall attendance on her royall person.

Out of Spaine yt is written that all Arragonia is upp in armes against the king of Spaine uppon an injurious committment of a greate man there into the Inquisition, which howse his freindes have broken upp and rescued his person, so as by this sacrilegious outrage yt wilbee hard to make their peace and therfore not held unfitt heer to have the fire kindled ther so neer his gates.[63] For all advertizementes doe confirme yt, that hee spares noe cost nor looseth any occasion to make his title in Brittanie past disputation by getting possession,[64] which, yf hee

[60] German mercenaries or *reiters*. These troops consisted of mounted troops armed with pistols or carbines (*reiters*) and heavy infantry (*landsknechts*).

[61] For Essex's long and dangerous ride through enemy territory to meet Henri IV, accompanied only by his small force of cavalry, see Nichols, 'Journal by Coningsby', pp. 13–22; E.M. Tenison, *Elizabethan England: Being the History of this Country 'in Relation to all Foreign Princes'*, 12 vols in 13, pr. for subscribers (Leamington Spa, 1933–1961), VIII, pp. 401–413. The glittering arrival of Essex and his entourage at Henri's camp is described in Palma Cayet's *Chronologie Novenaire*: M. Petitot (ed.), *Collection Complète des Mémoires Relatifs à l'Histoire de France*, 52 vols (Paris, 1819–1826), XL, p. 284. Essex and his horsemen left the bulk of his army on 15 August and did not link up with them again until 4 September.

[62] Thomas Smith (c.1556–1609), Essex's chief secretary and public orator of the University of Oxford: P.E.J. Hammer, 'The uses of scholarship: the secretariat of Robert Devereux, Second Earl of Essex, c.1585–1601', *EHR*, 109 (1994), pp. 27–28, 32–33, 42. Smith made two trips back to England during the period covered by these letters. On the first, he left Dieppe on 15 August and returned there on 28 August (having left the court at Chichester on 22 August). On his second trip, he left Dieppe on 13 September and arrived at court on 18 September. He was paid £10 for carrying letters on both trips by a warrant from Burghley dated at Farnham on 25 September (PRO, E 351/542, m. 158d). He set out for France on the following day (BL, Cotton MS Titus B VI, fo. 35v).

[63] The 'greate man' is Antonio Perez, former secretary to Philip II, whose imprisonment and subsequent rescue sparked revolt in Aragon: J.H. Elliott, *Imperial Spain, 1469–1716* (London, 1963), pp. 271–278; J. Lynch, *Spain 1516–1598: From Nation State to World Empire* (Oxford, 1991), pp. 472–481. Perez escaped to France and entered the service of Henri IV. He lived in England as a guest of the Earl of Essex (with Elizabeth's approval) during 1593–1595: G. Ungerer, *A Spaniard in Elizabethan England: The Correspondence of Antonio Perez's Exile*, 2 vols (London, 1974–1976).

[64] Fresh intelligence asserted that 3,000–4,000 Spanish troops at Corunna (the Groyne) were about to be shipped to Brittany: *UC*, p. 45: Burghley to Unton, 22 August 1591. For Philip II's efforts to establish a claim to the duchy of Brittany, see *L&A, 1591–1592*, p. 269, §417.

doe, your lordshipp's wisdome cann deepliest consider of the dangerous consequence, when all traffique, entercourse and almost daylie passengers shalbee so impeached as ther must ever bee a navye maynteyned to waft over all that passeth by our Channell. Your lordshipp knowes [fo. 10v] ther was a booke lost or else ill bestowed. Ther is another send over by Mr Smith, which I hope wilbee better received or remembred.[65] My love and dutie carries mee further then good manners. Your lordshipp's favor towardes mee hath not bynn formall, but essentiall. When my mind shalbee ingratefull, I wish my life att an ende. In which minde, most humbly I take my leave, wishing your lordshipp all honor, health and multyplied yeares. From the court att Chichester this 22 August 1591.

Your lordshipp's most ready to doe yow humble service
[no signature added]

[*Marginated*] Postscript:
The queene gave mee instructions, because shee could not speake with my lord,[66] to write a letter to my lord embassador[67] fraught with princely care and kindnes in his particular visitation of sicknes, as also very royall and prudent councell for his carriage of the publike affayres, comaunding him to write to the king or to his secretary[68] (being himselfe not yet presented) how jelous shee is least eyther his absence or division of his forces should weaken or discomfitt his troupes left behind him for Roan, requireing him neyther to use delay in the begininge nor rashe leadeing her men to the butchery in the course of the action. This was the substance which, being conceaved in a letter, she hath signed herselfe.[69]

Letter 7: Sir Robert Cecil to Lord Chancellor Hatton, 23 August 1591
[*fos 8r–9r*]

May yt please your lordshipp. This progresse growes wearesome, though yt will not bee confessed, and hither to Stansteed[70] her Majesty came

---

[65] The nature of the book which Smith took back to France is unclear. It may have been a copy of the military regulations issued for the Earl of Leicester's army in 1585. Essex had been directed to use these articles to enforce discipline upon his own army, but he still did not have a copy of them when he left for France (PRO, SP 78/25, fo. 105r).

[66] i.e. Burghley, who performed the role of Secretary of State while the office remained vacant.

[67] i.e. Unton. See PRO, SP 78/25, fo. 226r–v; *UC*, pp. 43–44.

[68] Followed by 'being', which is repeated within the parentheses in the MS.

[69] PRO, SP 78/25, fo. 226r–v; *UC*, pp. 43–44.

[70] Stanstead, house of John Lord Lumley (c.1533–1609).

very late on Munday[71] night by moonshine. The howse is fayre, well builte without and not meanely furnished within, but want of water is a greate inconvenience. Tomorrow her Majestie goeth to Porthmouth to bedd, next day att night hither againe and so towardes Basing,[72] wher I trust your lordshipp will meete the queene, of which her Majestie, as yt seemeth, doth make full reckoninge. But of that your lordshipp best knowes, for I only speake that which in discourse her Majestie pleaseth accidentally sometimes to utter.

From Diep her Majestie received advertizement that Dreux is rendred to the king, which is a towne of good importance.[73] It is the place wher the admirall fought the battell.[74] Ther is also written that Homflen,[75] which is a towne neer Roan, doth now begin to shew ytselfe against the Leaguers. The governor of the place hath a brother resideing in the king's camp, so as ther is greate hope that, so soone as the king shall make his approach, that towne will hold for the king, which was one of the first peices that the king ment to have summoned before his sittinge downe before Roane.

On Satturday these letters were written from Deip, but my lord of Essex was not then arrived from the king, which, yf yt could have bynn well, accompanyed [fo. 8v] with the declaration therof. Hee is looked for and I doe conceive by the lettres that hee is by this time come thyther.

The ratification of the contract which was confirmed att Tours[76] is come to Dyep and hither yt shalbee brought by[77] Monsieur de Reiux,[78] whose comeing the queene misliketh for that, the knowen occasion of his message being of noe[79] greater importance, yt doth threaten some purpose of unknowen further demaundes accidentally, which the queen

[71] i.e. 23 August 1591.

[72] The house of William Paulet, third Marquess of Winchester (c.1533–98), joint Lord Lieutenant of Hampshire. Travelling towards Basing reflected a northerly, homeward journey which was soon postponed. The Queen's intention to visit Basing not only reflected the dictates of geography and the attractions of Basing itself (built on a grand scale by the first marquess), but also a desire to balance her entertainment by Sussex. Although they shared the lord lieutenancy of the county, there was a bitter local rivalry between Winchester and Sussex which encouraged frequent and acrimonious disputes.

[73] PRO, SP 78/25, fos 222r–223r, 224r: Sir Edmund Yorke to Burghley and Otwell Smith to Burghley, both dated Saturday 21 August 1591.

[74] The Battle of Dreux, December 1562, in which a Huguenot army led by Admiral Coligny and the Prince of Condé was defeated by Catholic forces.

[75] Honfleur.

[76] This is the agreement specifying the terms under which Elizabeth agreed to send troops to Normandy. Signed and sealed at Greenwich on 25 June, it required ratification by the parlement and chambre des comptes at Tours.

[77] 'The ratification [...] brought by' underlined.

[78] Antoine de Moret, sieur de Reau.

[79] 'misliketh for that [...] noe' underlined.

now utterly distasteth, attending rather some sound effectes of her Majeste's succors and forces already yeelded to the king,[80] in whom her Majestie noteth a playne irresolution in that hee cometh not to Roan but is gonn himselfe upp higher, thinkeing yt some towch to her Majeste's generall to accost himselfe to any leiuetenant or marshall of any king in Chrystendome, but in these passages, when her Majestie hath spoken, ther following no alteration or revocation, so as yf the effect bee good all these circumstances wilbee past calmely over.[81]

The partie that brought these lettres[82] to my lord and to Mr Vicechamberlain[83] from Otwell Smith[84] did leave Sir Henry Unton (thankes be to God) uppon amendement on Satterday night last. God send him life and health to serve her Majestie, for all men find his judgment most apt and his mind not spareing of [fo. 9r] his purse for her honor, which by all men that come thence, I assure your lordshipp, is confirmed and yet not without an underhand repineing heerof, some that think noe man praysed but that they are blemished.[85]

Your lordshipp sees how tediously I trouble yow with these thinges which come to my knowledge,[86] wherin I must end with craveing pardon of yourselfe and with wishes to myselfe of some occasion to make knowen my fayth full affection to your lordshipp, whom Almighty God preserve for your countrie's[87] good and her Majeste's greatest contentment, whom all men finde not halfe well satisfied this long to spare yow, yf shee could help yt. From the court att Stansteed this 23 August 1591.

Your lordshipp's humbly att command
[no signature added]

---

[80] 'sound effectes [...] king' underlined.

[81] 'effect bee good [...] over' underlined.

[82] Edward Hills, who was paid 100 shillings for this service by a warrant from Burghley dated at Stanstead, 24 August 1591 (PRO, E 351/542, m. 158d.).

[83] Heneage and Burghley had jointly taken over much of the foreign correspondence and intelligence-gathering which had previously been controlled by the late Sir Francis Walsingham (d. 1590): Hammer, *Polarisation*, pp. 154–155; *idem*, 'An Elizabethan spy who came in from the cold: the return of Anthony Standen to England in 1593', *Historical Research*, 65 (1992), pp. 280, n. 23, 283.

[84] Otwell or Ottywell Smith was an English merchant based at Dieppe, who provided both financial and intelligence-gathering services for the English crown.

[85] 'underhand [...] blemished' underlined.

[86] 'tediously [...] knowledge' underlined.

[87] 'knowen my [...] countrie's' underlined.

Letter 8: Sir Robert Cecil to Lord Chancellor Hatton, 26 August 1591

[fos 13v–15v]

May yt please your lordshipp. As I chaunce to light uppon any convenient messenger, I am bold to continew my dutie, though to your lordshipp's trouble. When I sent your lordshipp my footman of purpose, your lordshipp's gentleman made him so sawcy and yourselfe, with a rewarde (in such a couloured coyne as hee hath not often seen in his purse), made him so rich in his owne conceipte as hee hath ever since rune heavier then hee did. If your lordshipp should followe on as yow have begonne, yow may buy your newse much cheaper in the markett. And yf your lordshipp remember, yt is asmuch as the quarteridge my lord father gave my lady Veare to play *[fo. 14r]* att kardes a fayre angell in golde.[88] But your lordshipp hath begunn with the master to bynde him as fast to your service as ever love, dutie or serious intention to become worthy of your favor and protection cann tye any man. I would I were so happy therfore as to have occasion by any comandment of yow to requite the same to the meanest person towardes your lordshipp, seeing yt were a service to imagine that the greatnes of your lordshipp's quallitie cann need or have use of oughte in my power to promise or performe to yourselfe, to whom I confess next her Majestie greatest obligation. This being often repeated must needes bee tedious, sed ex abundantia cordis[89] proceedeth the error and not of other formality or complement, for which ever this paper shall bee a recorde. Yesterday Monsieur de Rieu, long spoken of, is come from the king to Portsmouth,[90] not deceiveing the former expectation of her excellent Majestie, for yt is certeynly advertized that hee meaneth to make diverse demaundes for martiall provisions as munitions, pyoners and carriages, with proposition also for a longer continewation of the forces for a moneth longer after the second moneth shalbee expired, the first being now newly ended. And also to this doth hee meane to make addition that the king is not fully resolved whether to beseige Roan or Paris. Hee landed yesterday night heer and to Stansteed yesterday night was brought the newse of *[fo. 14v]* his arrivall to her Majestie and

---

[88] Lady Elizabeth (de) Vere (1575–1627), daughter of Edward, 17th Earl of Oxford and Burghley's granddaughter. This token allowance for 'play' (worth 10s) presumably reflects her arrival at court and the early stages of Burghley's effort to match her with a suitable husband. For her difficult early career, see P.E.J. Hammer, 'Sex and the Virgin Queen: aristocratic "concupiscence" and the court of Elizabeth I', *Sixteenth Century Journal*, 31 (2000), pp. 80, 85–88.

[89] 'sed [...] cordis': 'but from an abundance of devotion'.

[90] Noted by Burghley in his journal of matters relating to the Normandy campaign: BL, Cotton MS Titus B VI, fo. 34v; PRO, SP 78/25, fo. 346r.

withall a slender excuse that hee would not present himselfe to her royall presence ther or heer before hee had conferred with the king's legier embassador att London,[91] whither hee is gonn and hath baulked the queene, being not 8 miles from Portesmouth nor 2 miles out of his way to London. This parte of his, and his free knowledge given of his negotiation, dubles in the queen a settled purpose to refuse all his demaundes and, finding that her forces have thus longe idlely attended and that promise is not kept by some expected att Portsmouth (wherin your lordshipp knowes my meaneing), but that they are gonn farther as her Majestie is come neerer, even as lande will suffer,[92] I doe assure your lordshipp I doe thinke it is parte of the causes that her minde is somewhat unquieted, though for her bodie, health, stomach and bookes I saw yt not better these 7 yeares, praysed bee God.

This afternoone Sir Thomas Leighton is come from Gernsie[93] and, as hee saith, goeing for Deipe, was put in heere and, heareing of her Majeste's neernes, came to her dyneing howse,[94] aboute 5 miles from Portsmouth in her way as shee came from Stansteed. Newse hee bringeth none and, for ought that I find, her Majestie could have bynn content [fo. 15r] to have heard of him att Deipe as well as to have seene him heer. Hee reporteth that our men in Brittanie dye of a new sickness. The French king, haveing ben from the queen expostulated with for his negligent provision in Brittanie of new supplies, hee answereth with a faire promise that, so soone as the reyters come, hee would send thither 5000 foote and a 1000 horse.[95] But when all is donne, in my poore opinion, in that province res agitur nostra.[96] I trust your lordshipp beares with my bolde manner of scriblinge. I make noe [more] scruple to lay open my thoughtes (imperfect and vaine as they are) unto your lordshipp's grave wisdome then I doe, or would, to mine

[91] Jean de la Fin, seigneur de Beauvoir la Nocle, who served as Henri IV's resident ambassador in England from 1589 until 1595. He maintained a house at Hackney.

[92] This is an allusion to Henri IV. Henri had raised the prospect of meeting Elizabeth if she travelled to Portsmouth in a letter to her dated at Noyon on 5 [15 n.s.] August (PRO, SP 78/25, fo. 161r–v; HMCS, IV, pp. 132–133). While waiting for Henri, Elizabeth also ordered Essex to return to meet her at Portsmouth, but the letter informing the earl of her plans was lost in transit and he consequently failed to appear (PRO, SP 78/25, fo. 275r–v: Essex to Burghley, 7 September 1591).

[93] Sir Thomas Leighton (c.1535–c.1610) was governor of Guernsey and a veteran of the French wars, going back to the early 1560s. He had been ordered to serve as an 'adviser' to Essex, despite his claim of poor health (PRO, SP 15/32/19, fos 29r–30r). This task was made all the more delicate because his wife, Elizabeth Lady Leighton, née Knollys, was both a long-serving member of the Queen's Privy Chamber and an aunt of Essex. Leighton arrived at Dieppe on 31 August (PRO, SP 78/25, fo. 246r).

[94] Presumably the temporary dining house constructed for the Queen at Bedhampton: PRO, E 351/542, m. 153d.

[95] PRO, SP 78/25, fo. 194r: Prince of Dombes to Elizabeth, 22 [12] August 1591.

[96] 'res [...] nostra': 'the business being done is ours'.

owne father, next whom your lordshipp hath all interest in mee or mine [wife?], who sweares, in spite of jelowsy, that shee is and wilbe att your lordshipp's commandment yf your lordshipp please to use her service. Wherwith I humbly take my leave. From Portsmouth, wher even now the queen is arrived att 8 a clocke att night, the 26th of August 1591.

> Your lordshipp's most assured at command
> R. Cycell

[*Marginated*] Postscript:
I am so ashamed of my idle writeinge to your lordshipp as I beseech yow make my lettres no towches of my poore discretion in the ballance of your grave wisdome but only as the messengers of my affections and dutie, which, by absence, cannot otherwise bee declared. Tomorrow her Majestie turnes homeward. Shee hath [*fo. 15v*] diverse suiters for Sir Thomas Williams' office,[97] as Mr Skypwith the escuyrrie[98] and my lord of Hunsdon for Mr Robert Carye.[99] Of the honorable embassador att Deipe, I heare by Bellingham,[100] to my greife, that his bodie is visited with the black jaundice, and by everybodie else that cometh, that his chardges are exceedingly to her Majeste's honor. Pardon I beseech your lordshipp this lettre sine modo et forma.[101]

[97] Clerk of the check and muster-master for English forces in Ireland. Sir Thomas Williams was a cousin of Sir John Perrot and had been appointed by him when the latter was Lord Deputy of Ireland (PRO, SP 12/241/7.i, fo. 14r). When Perrot was charged with treason, Williams fell with him. Sir Henry Wallop (see below) and Sir Richard Bingham accused him of corruption (PRO, SP 63/154/4, 7; 156/10; 157/49) and Sir Dennis O'Roughan accused him of complicity in Perrot's alleged treason (PRO, SP 12/239/127.i, 158, fos 181r, 241r–242r); HMCS, IV, p. 117). Imprisoned in the Marshalsea Prison by late 1590, he was moved to the Tower in March 1591 (LPL, MS 3199, 258). He was dead by 6 August 1591 (PRO, SP 12/239/127.i, fo. 181r). His office was ultimately taken by Ralph Lane (PRO, SP 63/166/9).

[98] Richard Skipwith, equerry of the Queen's stables (like Ralph Lane). Perhaps in consolation for missing out on Williams's office, Skipwith was promised a grant of £60 p.a. from the temporalities of the diocese of Ely in April 1592 (HMCS, IV, p. 430). This grant was ultimately issued in August as a lease of Caldrose Manor, Cambridgeshire (PRO, C 66/1394, mm. 33–34).

[99] Henry Carey, first Lord Hunsdon (1524–1596), was a cousin to the Queen and had been Lord Chamberlain since 1585. He was appointed to the Privy Council in 1577. Robert Carey (see below) was his youngest son.

[100] Henry Bellingham, a naval officer who operated in the channel and narrow seas. He had overseen Essex's departure for Dieppe in July and later received a commendation from Essex (PRO, SP 78/25, fo. 273r: Essex to Burghley, 11 December [1591]). He had arrived at Portsmouth from Dieppe on 25 August, probably having escorted de Reau across the Channel (BL, Cotton MS Titus B VI, fo. 34v).

[101] 'sine [...] forma': 'without balance and shape'.

Letter 9: Sir Robert Cecil to Lord Chancellor Hatton, 27 August 1591

[fos 12v–13v]

My humble dutie remembered to your lordshipp. Being with her Majestie today to shewe her the lettres from her embassador,[102] shee shewed mee a jewell of your lordshipp's sending, in forme of a bagpipe, which shee weareth on her ruffe with the word uppon yt, which doth very much please her and with your token doth shee make much sporte, remembring your lordshipp by the name of her mutton, adding to her other speeches of yow this protestation, that, being in her coach uppon the toppe of all her plattforme today, where she veiwed the Downes covered with sheepe, shee had rather then x^{Mli} that yow had bynn there with her in that stately place, expressing unto mee how sorry her Majestie was of your lordshipp's newe accident that woulde stay yow. Shee is exceedingly well pleased with my lord of Sussex his entertaynement, which is very honorable indeede.[103] Sportes shee hath had both in martiall kind by Sir George Carye's souldiers of the Isle[104] and in another kind by my Lord Strange,[105] who became an hermytt and rann the course of the feilde for her Majeste's sake. The particularities of all these to my freind Mr Morgan,[106] your lordshipp's serveant, I referr.

This day att fower of the clocke arrived two French shipps with messengers from Deipe, who brought the lettres from the queen's embassador *[fo. 13r]* and withall the ratification, signed and sealed by the king and lord chancellor but not emologned by the court of parliament, but the duplicate is sent thither for that side.[107] This yt was beeleeved alwayes that Monsieur de Reau should have brought, but hee leaving yt behind him, yt confirmes the queen's jelousie that his access to her presence wilbe for more supply, whose messuages yet not

---

[102] PRO, SP 78/25, fos 228r, 232r: Unton to Burghley, 23 and 24 August 1591; *UC*, pp. 46–48.

[103] Elizabeth stayed at Sussex's house in Portsmouth.

[104] Sir George Carey (1547–1603), eldest son and heir of Lord Hunsdon. He had been governor of the Isle of Wight since 1582. Recorded expenditure for the Queen's visit includes construction of 'a standinge for her Majestie, without Portesmouth, to see the soldiours' (PRO, E 351/542, m. 153).

[105] Ferdinando Stanley (c.1559–1594), eldest son and heir of Henry, third Earl of Derby. A poet himself, he was renowned as a patron of the arts, especially of poets and players.

[106] This was probably James Morgan. Hatton rewarded his service by granting him a share of the profits from the great seal (BL, Lansdowne MS 69, fo. 195v).

[107] The document's arrival, 'but not the emologation by parlement', was noted on this date in Burghley's journal: BL, Cotton MS Titus B VI, fo. 34v. The duplicate is the copy which had already received formal ratification in England and was destined to held by the French.

delivered her Majestie prepares to receive with as constant denyall as yf shee knew[108] already his argumentes.

The embassador's lettres were of Twesday nighte the 23 and the next day.[109] My lord generall was at Deipe attended.[110] One of his greatest advertizementes is that the king hath an assured partie in Newhaven,[111] whither my lord with the Marshall Byron shall give the first attempte, yt appeareing by his lettres that the king's ministers and serveants att Deipe make of yt small doubt. Hee writes of yt to bee kept secrett because yt depends uppon a well executed stratageme.

I thanke God hee is well amended and when I delivered to her Majestie his great greife to bee visited now with any thinge that should impeache his service and withall reade his lettres, whose substance and methode deserved greate commendations of such as are worthy to censure him (wherin I am both unable and partiall), her Majestie conceived great and gratious opinion of his worth and will to serve her. Thus hath your lordshipp all I know and, yf I could express my dutie according to the measure of my heart, your lordshipp should have cause to accounte your former greate favors well bestowed, wherin now I cann appeale[112] [fo. 13v] only to the worth of your lordshipp's most noble disposition, who doth, I see, accept my minde and not my meanes to doe yow all honor and service, wherwith I humbly take my leave.

From[113] my lodgeing in Portsmouth att ix of the clocke, being newly come from the quenching of a fyer close to the queen's howse, which hath bredd noe small feare and trouble, Fryday nighte the 27 of August 1591.

Your lordshipp's humbly att command
R. Cycill

Letter 10: Sir Robert Cecil to Lord Chancellor Hatton, 31 August 1591
[fos 15v–16v]

My humble dutie remembred to your lordshipp. Since my last lettres noe newse of importance have happened and therfore am I boald to

---

[108] 'yt confirmes [...] knew' underlined.

[109] PRO, SP 78/25, fos 228r, 232r; *UC*, pp. 46–47, 47–48: Unton to Burghley, 23 and 24 August 1591.

[110] i.e. Essex's arrival was being awaited. Unton's letter of 24 August states that Essex 'will without faile be with us here [ie Dieppe] tomorrow at night'. Burghley underlined this and wrote 'on Wednesday' in the margin (*UC*, p. 47).

[111] Le Havre.

[112] 'methode deserved [...] appeale' underlined.

[113] 'For' in MS.

lett your lordshipp even know the worst in the beginninge, which is that these lynes are to as small purpose as the other, in regard of your lordshipp's troble, though they are to myselfe an ease, when I dare imagine that they doe present the disposition of my minde to doe your lordshipp agreeable service yf my power could any way stretch to yt.

Yesterday the queen, from Southwicke (within 5 miles of Portsmouth), wher shee lay, being a gentleman's howse called White,[114] did ride to dynner to Portchester, not so meaneing att her goeing forth, but, being come so farr, rather chused so to doe then to turne backe uppon the sunne att xi of the clocke. Yf your lordshipp had seen her entertaynement *[fo. 16r]* you would have also seene the difference of her likeinge of her usage when shee was to bidd herselfe welcome. The castell hath only in yt a poore man and his wife that keepes the howse and, when the queen was lighted, the fflowers[115] of the castell were so rotten as noebody durste adventure her Majestie uppon them and therfore was shee fayne to goe even to the stately bedd-chamber of the hows-keeper, wher his bedd was newly made and ther did shee dyne and was as merry as could bee. Instead of her sweete perfumes, the chamber was as full of rwe and isop[116] as ever yt could holde and yet noe fault found with any thinge, &c. Ther did shee with a settled resolution determine to goe to Southampton, and so to tarry 4 dayes uppon the coaste longer. Your lordshipp knowes what to judge of yt and by this meanes shall your lordshipp perceave that shee makes noe hast homewardes and that from Deipe we hear nothinge. This I beseech your lordshipp to accept, with the alterations of the removes for this tyme agreed on, being ashamed to have noe other matter worthy your readinge, only this: I have often heard my lord say that, when embassadors would forbeare to write because they had noe matter of moment, hee would always entreate them to send some lettres though they write nothyng else but this that att that instant they had noe matter to advertize, which sometimes was as good a hearing as greater *[fo. 16v]*. And thus, with my humblest dutie, doe I take my leave. From my lodgeing neer Southwicke this last of August 1591.

> Your lordshipp's most humbly att command
> [no signature added]

---

[114] John White, whose grandfather (a servant of the then Sir Thomas Wriothesley) had been granted the manor of Southwick in 1538 (*VCH, Hampshire*, III, pp. 162–163).

[115] i.e. floors. Although some work had been done on Portchester Castle as recently as 1583–1584, the poor state of the main buildings was explained by a survey of 1609. They were 'for the most part very ruynous, by reason the leade hath bene cutt and imbezeled, whereby the water hath had issue to the timber and rotted it'. H.M. Colvin (ed.), *The History of the King's Works*, III, 1485–1660, part I (London, 1975), p. 291.

[116] Rue and hyssop: strongly aromatic plants used for medicinal purposes. These plants seem to be being used here as herbal disinfectant.

Since the writeing of this, may yt please your lordshipp to understand that out of France yt is written, an intilligencer, that diverse of my lord of Essex his gard are combyned to betray him and some souldiers of his corrupted. Their names are sent over and lettres now written to apprehend them by the queen's commandement yesterday night.[117] The pynnace that carried over him that went with the queen's last lettres from Cowdre to Sir John Norrice found him gonn upp into the country to Rhenes[118] with the Prince d'Ombes[119] and, as yt was expected, hee was not sooner departed but the Iland of St Brieux[120] was straight wonn and diverse Englishmen killed and taken prisoners that were left behinde sicke when Sir John marched from them, so, as for ought I cann, perceave nihill inde boni.[121]

Your lordshipp may see my boaldness by my blotted scribling, which I humbly crave pardon for.

Letter 11: Sir Robert Cecil to Lord Chancellor Hatton, 2 or 3 September 1591

[fos 18r–19r]

May it please your lordshipp. I have received your favorable lettre with testimony therin of your good interpretation of my poore services, which, yf yt could make any addition to my desire to appeare in your sight a man devoted in constant dutie, I must confess (proceedinge from suche a personage),[122] yt woulde double my comforte. Even now when the queen had dispatched her lettres to the king and to the earle (of which I wrote your lordshipp the substance in my lettres yesterday)[123] by a man of Sir John Hawkins,[124] ther is come one Bostocke that was captaine of the shipp wherin Sir Thomas Leighton went lately over to Deipe. Hee ther found all our 4000 men risen and gonn from Deipe towarde Pont de Larche, not 12 leagues from thence, wher, within 4 miles, the earle of Essex with his horse bande in his retourne from the king had retyred himselfe to a strength, for avoydeing the encounter of

---

[117] This episode remains mysterious. However, there was considerable illicit contact between Essex's men and English Catholic exiles based in Flanders: BL, Lansdowne MS 68, fos 145r–8r, 149r–51r; P.E.J. Hammer, 'A Welshman abroad: Captain Peter Wynn of Jamestown', *Parergon*, new series, 16 (1998), pp. 69–71.

[118] Rennes.

[119] Henri de Bourbon-Vendôme, Prince of Dombes, Henri IV's commander in Brittany.

[120] St Brieuc.

[121] 'nihill [...] boni': 'nothing good from there'. This wild story reflected the report of a Captain Jonas. Sir John Norris subsequently informed Burghley that it was almost entirely untrue: PRO, SP 78/25, fos 318r–321r: Norris to Burghley, 16 September 1591.

[122] This second parenthesis missing in MS.

[123] This letter seems to be missing.

[124] Sir John Hawkins (1532–1595), treasurer of the navy.

the enemie, who is gotten between him and Deipe with 1000[125] horse and 2000 foote, haveing had intilligence of his being to come backe. For succor wherof, all the English armie is gonne towardes him, of which God send the issue more fortunate then the occasion is heer judged to have bynn given with discretion.[126] The queen seemeth so offended with this journey and adventure as shee, in height of passion, wisheth him to pay for yt, so that her troupes *[fo. 18v]* may not miscarry.[127] But what shee would doe uppon better advice, to your lordshipp's judgement I referr yt, who knoweth best her princely disposition to the earle and what yt would bee also to have her generall so overtaken. I hope well of the matter yf our rawe troupes bee well conducted and that the very same parties hasten him not (before the rescue come) to some over hazardous offer[128] of escape, which were, in my conscience, the cheife ringleaders of him into the journey to the king without the queen's privity or without great cause. It is pitty that the common cause receiveth prejudice by the queen's[129] displeasure against the generall, which, though I doubt not but in her gratious nature to him in particuler may receive qualification. Yet is yt so used as, in the meane time, yt is the instrumentall cause wheron her Majestie groundeth her denyalls of theire demandes. This shalbee more particularly knowen by the queen's embassador, who stayeth a shipp of purpose to send advertizement of the further particularities of his estate and of his fore-comeing towardes him. The reisters were within 2 dayes' journey of Paris. And thus, with my humble duty, I take my leave. From my lodging neer the court att Tichfeilde this 3 of November [2 or 3 September] 1591.

Your lordshipp's humbly to command
R.C.

[fo. 19r]
I feare hee hath bynn betrayed by some of his company.

The queen saith your lordshipp is one that hath ever cockered the earle and would not suffer her to chasten him. Because shee saide yt I am boalde to write yt, knowing to whom yt is now delivered.

---

[125] 'retyred himselfe [...] 1000' underlined.

[126] Bostock initially sent a despatch to this effect. Burghley received it by 2 September (*UC*, p. 60, where Burghley's letter to Unton is wrongly dated 6 September. For the correct date, see Unton's reply of 7 September: *ibid.*, pp. 65–66). This letter suggests that Bostock himself arrived at court very shortly afterwards.

[127] 'towardes him of which God [...] miscarry' underlined.

[128] 'I hope well [...] offer' underlined.

[129] 'It is pitty [...] queen's' underlined.

The governor of Deipe[130] is gonn with him with two companies of his French old souldiers, for our men att first, yf they bee discomfitted, will streyne who shall runne fastest, who after one or two dayes' of experience (as yt is saide) grow very hardy.[131]

Letter 12: Sir Robert Cecil to Lord Chancellor Hatton, 3 or 4 September 1591
[fo. 17r–v]

My most humble dutie remembred unto your lordshipp. This night her Majestie arrived att Southampton well and merrie (praysed bee God), with which newse I first begin as with that I best know your lordshipp affectes the most carefully to heare and, for the rest, as I have them, your lordshipp shall understand them, though often times they are not so certaine but that the next lettres may alwayes repeale greate partes of the first, which I hope your lordshipp will pardon. For I write as hither is advertized, alwayes though ever with this provisoe, that I will forfeyte nothing yf, upon the windes' change, the wordes that are written over doe alter.

The newse of my lord of Essex's danger, which in my lettre yesternighte I towched, are untrue in parte, for my lord is safe att Ponte de Larche and, being come from the king, hath sent to Deipe to have the governor of the towne and Sir Thomas Baskervyle,[132] with the queen's forces, to come to him within 4 miles of Roan, wher hee attempteth a passage kept by the Leaguers, which being cleered will make approach more safe to the seige of Roan. This hath the queen's embassador written to her Majestie and therfore yt is to bee beleeved.[133]

Hee writeth also that the reisters are yett in the hither partes of Lorraine, which makes mee ashamed of them that write that they were within 3 dayes' march of Paris. In Lorraine they spoile so much the duke de Lorraine's[134] townes and villages as his lettres are intercepted,

---

[130] Aymar, Mons. de la Chatte. This news was reported in PRO, SP 78/25, fo. 248r: Edward Yorke to Burghley, 31 August 1591.

[131] Unlike similar instances, these sentences on fo. 19r are not explicitly marked as being a postscript. This may be a slip by the copyist or (perhaps) an indication that this information was annexed to the letter in some other way, possibly as a separate ticket folded in with the letter.

[132] Sir Thomas Baskerville (d. 1597), serjeant-major of the foot in Essex's army.

[133] PRO, SP 78/25, fos 244r–245r; *UC*, pp. 52–55: Unton to Burghley, 31 August 1591. This letter was carried across the Channel by John [or Jean] de Vignes, who was paid £6 13s 4d for his service by a warrant from Burghley dated at Southampton, 5 September 1591 (PRO, E 351/542, m. 158d).

[134] Charles de Lorraine, Duke of Guise, a leader of the Catholic League.

wherin hee hath written to the duke of Parma[135] eyther directly to
hasten his succour, or else that hee will make upp his owne peace with
the king. More from Deipe is not yet advertized but yt is very *[fo. 17v]*
much merveyled that the generall, being att leasure and haveing
comoditie to send to Deipe to his marshall,[136] would not also remember
to write wher hee ought most dutie and satisfaction. But in the mean
time, for the jestes of the counsaile's replycation, by the queen's
comandment, and the minutes of the instruction for the lettres addressed
to the earle, what will come of yt I leave to your lordshipp's wisdome,
whose experience cann best censure the eventes which my rawe
judgement cannot deeplie looke into. I doe therfore (leaveing other
reportes of court to my freind Mr Morgan's relation) most humbly take
my leave and, from my heart, beseech God to blesse your life and
make my happe as fortunate as my minde desireous to doe your
lordshipp honor and service. From the court this second [3rd or 4th] of
September 1591.

Your lordshipp's most humbly att your commandment
R.C.

Letter 13: Sir Robert Cecil to Lord Chancellor Hatton, 4 September 1591
[fos 19r–21r]

My humble dutie remembred to your lordshipp. The comeing of
Monsieur de Reiux hath much displeased her Majestie in respecte of
the small satisfaction hee hath yeilded for the protraction by the king
used in the begining of the seige of Roan, which was the cheifest cause
of her Majeste's consentinge to lende her men, to spend her monies,
munitions and other chargeable furniture of warr in a time when shee
is circumvented with doubts of preparations offensive, even against her
att her owne doores. And now, instead of answering theise her Majeste's
materiall objections, is this man come with new demaundes of more
time for their stay, of more munition, yea, and of libertie to bee given
for the *[fo. 19v]* transferring her forces according to the occasion the
king shall have to use them elsewhere, so as, when the queen expected
her forces, adjoyned to his, should have bynn a moneth since before
Roan, according to which ground the substance of the contracte was
ratified, now is yt by his new demaundes made doubtfull wher hee will

---

[135] Alexander Farnese, Duke and Prince of Parma, Governor-General of the Spanish
Netherlands.
[136] Baskerville, who assumed command of Essex's infantry while the Earl and Williams
travelled to meet Henri IV.

beginn or when. So as the queen's forces must bee made serveantes to diverse humours without regard of employment in the partes wherin her Majestie is particularly interessed, who, haveing sent into Brittanie, sent her embassador into Germany[137] and spent hir[138] mony in the leavies there, did little suspect eyther this alteration or this slender satisfaction and therfore, as Mr Ashley cann well deliver, who was present att the consultation and sent to the embassador since,[139] her Majestie will in noe wise yeeld to have her troupes thus wander and bee employed uppon petty townes and fortresses, ther to bee consumed and wasted, holding yt noe prudent resolution so much to tender her neighbours as to forgett her owne saftie.

I assure your lordshipp I doe not looke, of all her 4000 in Normandie or 3000 in Brettany, to see retourne one parte of 3, and yet nothing of importance donn. *[fo. 20r]* Her Majestie hath written very sharpely to my lord of Essex,[140] reproveing his negligence in advertizing and his loosenes in being more plyable to a strange king's demaunds then to his soveraigne's instructions, and this withall, that shee will send shipping for her men to come home att the 2 moneths' end, which wilbee the 3 October, unless the king sitt downe before Roan really, which donne, shee wilbee pleased to lycence her companies to tarry out a 3 moneths, so as the king doe pay them, which otherwise shee will not consent unto. Surely, sir, yt is hardly donne of Sir Roger Williams to presume in his lettres to assure the queen that the king was 17 thowsand foote and 5000 horse,[141] when now the embassador himselfe confesseth hee is not, with our men to, not so many, but in hope to bee. These men that dare so loosely to assure their prince will not sticke to miscarry her leiutenant with inconstant projectes yf shee wilbee lead by them.

This I have as succinctly as I could (for feare to trouble your lordshipp with long lettres) towched, as I cann remember, the particulars of the embassador's negotiation. The summe of the jestes I sent your

---

[137] For Horatio Palavicino's dealings with the German princes in support of Henri IV, see Wernham, *After the Armada*, pp. 193–197, 265–268; L. Stone, *An Elizabethan: Sir Horatio Palavicino* (Oxford, 1956), pp. 156ff.

[138] 'his' in MS.

[139] De Reau delivered letters from Henri IV and presented a copy of his diplomatic instructions to the Privy Council at Southwick on 1 September (*L&A, 1591–1592*, p. 83, doc. TP 4). He also 'delivered [...] a long declaration of the causes why the French kyng cold not come to Roan' (BL, Cotton MS Titus B VI, fo. 34v). Ashley served as the duty clerk for this council meeting. He reported the Queen's verbal response to de Reau (who had by then travelled to Portsmouth) between 8 p.m. and 9 p.m. that same evening (*L& A, 1591–1592*, p. 334, §563). On 4 September Ashley delivered the Queen's written response to de Reau (still at Portsmouth), in the form of a letter to Henri IV (BL, Cotton MS Titus B VI, fo. 34v). There is no copy of Elizabeth's letter in PRO, SP 78 or *UC*.

[140] No copy of this letter seems to survive.

[141] See Letter 6.

lordshipp I will not give my worde for doen.[142] Now her Majestie is determined, without possibility of change, to goe to the Isle of Weight to bedd on Munday night[143] with very few in a pynnace of her owne and to dyne *[fo. 20v]* att Cawshott,[144] which is x miles by sea and from thence after dynner to the landing place called Cowes and so to bedd att the castle[145] and to tarry ther but a night. The answer her Majestie[146] made your lordshipp, to the tune, shee saith, of your baggpipe, today shee read to mee and told mee withall how strange your lordshipp would finde yt that yow had taken such a journey. The embassador, to whom her Majestie had written to Deipe in way of comforting him in his sicknes, hath written (I doe assure your lordshipp) a very fine answere to my lord[147] in token of his dutifull acceptation of the queen's favor, which, when I read to her Majestie today, did very deeply imprint in her royall hearte a feeling conceipte of his minde's true worth and valewe to serve her, which hee doth most honorably and diligently, with very great judgement what and when to write, which is not the least point of his discretion. I am required (my most noble lord) humbly, but foolishly, to recommend the affectionate service of my life's companyon,[148] who wisheth your lordshipp all honor health and long life, according to her plaine woomanish fashion, which your lordshipp is well acquainted *[fo. 21r]* with, as your favor hath long suffered her, in which shee is noe changling. With which idle matter I presume no longer to hold your lordshipp, but doe heer humbly take my leave, beinge comaunded by my lord my father most heartily to recommend to your lordshipp his true and unfeyned love, with wishes of better health then his soare foote keepes him in, for all hee beare yt out with continewall traveile. From Southampton this 4th of Sept. 1591.

Your lordshipp's most bounde att your comandement

R.C.

[142] This word is uncertain, but seems to be 'done' (ie finished). These 'gestes' were plans for the Queen's future itinerary constructed in the form of lists of lodgings: Dovey, *Elizabethan Progress*, 4.

[143] i.e. 6 September.

[144] Calshot Castle, Hampshire.

[145] Carisbrooke Castle, residence of governors of the Isle of Wight.

[146] 'Majestie' interlined.

[147] PRO, SP 78/25, fos 244r–245r; *UC*, pp. 52–55: Unton to Burghley, 31 August 1591. Cecil was apparently unaware that Unton had enclosed a copy of this letter with the letter which he wrote to Hatton on the same date (*UC*, pp. 51–52).

[148] Followed by 'which your lordshipp is well acquainted with', struck through. Here, as elsewhere, the copyist has clearly skipped a line ahead when transcribing Cecil's original letter. This error probably explains the abbreviated Latin scrawl which appears in the margin beside it. The words in the margin (written in the same hand as the text) seem to be 'stulsto loc. sim. p. summa'.

Letter 14: Sir Robert Cecil to Lord Chancellor Hatton, 6 September 1591
[fos 27r–28r]

My dutie humbly remembred to your lordshipp. I find so small matter of worth to trouble your lordshipp withall as I am halfe ashamed to write unto your lordshipp toyes and untruthes, hopeing your lordshipp, that best knoweth courtly alterations, will accept my lettres as they are ment, which are only to bee their master's messengers of the dutie and honor hee beareth your lordshipp, as hee hath good cause. This was the day appointed and sett downe for the queen to goe to the Ilande,[149] and so continewed firmly till yesterday night att 6 of the clocke, that Sir George Carye came hither, who expressed the length of the journey and the uncertainty of the winde, which must for her Majestie's purpose bee one way going and another comeinge, for else might shee have stayed longer then shee would. By this and other like circumstances, her Majeste's purpose is altered and homewarde. According to my last jestes sent your lordshipp, shee doth tomorrow take her journey, not finding herselfe very well disposed and troubled with a cold.

[fo. 27v] Out of Spaine daylie advertizementes are brought of great preparation for nexte yeare hither to bee employed, yf hee cann once gett footeinge firmely in Brettany, to bring downe his shipping and his men, which will, I feare mee, weary us out even with alarumes, till they bee soundly and compleatly fitt for a directe invasion to assayle us.

From Deipe is only knowen what her Majestie's embassador carefully advertizeth, but what is become of the general, what her Majestie's forces doe, or how or when they are to be imployed, surely, by all apparaunces yt may bee well said which Tully remembred to his forgetfull freind, that the queen is ever advertized *quasi tota Gallia clausa esset.*[150] Ther is some error, whersover yt lightes, but I hope yt wilbee amended, wherof, when I heare or see anything, I will according to my duty advertize[151] yt because I know your lordshipp wilbee glad to heare that every man should doe as they ought, espetially in the chardges which her Majestie comendeth to any man's care.[152] In the meane *[fo. 28r]* time her treasure consumes, the yeare spendeth and nothing is donne, into all which your lordshipp's judgement cann best penetrate, to whom I leave yt, with my true wishes of your life and

---

[149] Isle of Wight.

[150] 'From Deipe is only knowen [...] esset' underlined. Quasi [...] esset: 'as if the whole of France were shut off'. Tully is Marcus Tullius Cicero (106–43 BC).

[151] A word which appears to be 'calde' marginated here.

[152] Marginal annotation here: 'Se 18'. This is apparently a cross-reference to fo. 18r, where the Queen's anger at Essex journeying to see Henri IV is mentioned.

health, to the queen's greatest contentment and the countrie's good, for which yow were borne and in which your lordshipp is worthily placed a capitall member,[153] wherof God send yow happy and honorable continewance, for in my poore observation (some few excepted) wee cannot bragg of great plentie of such in this iron age to bee our rulers, wherin consisteth all people's true blessednes.[154] From my poore lodgeing in Southampton neer the court this 6th of November [September] 1591.

> Your lordshipp's humbly att comaunde,
> seconde to none in all loveinge dutie
> Robert Cecyll

Letter 15: Sir Robert Cecil to Lord Chancellor Hatton, 7 September 1591

[fo. 26r–v]

May yt please your lordshipp. This very day ther is newse come from my Lord Thomas Howarde[155] that, the 2nd of August last, hee was in very good state for victuall, health of his men and of himselfe.[156] Hee hath taken a very good price of sugar and cochinele comeing from the East Indies, wherin was one Lewis de Castiglia,[157] a man of very great accounte. Hee understandeth of the viceroy of Perue comeing home from the Indies, for which hee meaneth to attend very carefully and, by this man, doth hee understande that the fleete is to come downe shortly by the Ilandes,[158] wher he meaneth to ride yt out[159] and doubteth

---

[153] 'lightes, but I hope yt wilbee [...] member' underlined.

[154] 'my poore observation [...] blessednes' underlined.

[155] Lord Thomas Howard (1561–1626), second son of Thomas Howard, fourth Duke of Norfolk (1536–1572), and distant cousin of the Lord Admiral. Howard served as a naval commander during the 1580s and '90s, seeking to repair the damage done to his family's fortunes by his father's execution for treason and the condemnation of his older brother Philip Howard, Earl of Arundel (1557–1595) for the same offence in 1589 (having already been imprisoned in 1585). Howard's letter has not survived.

[156] 'was in very good state [...] himselfe' underlined.

[157] Don Luis de Castilla or Castillon, who is described as 'governor of the island of Gemeira', was taken on 29 July when the *St Thomas* was captured by Howard's fleet. He was subsequently sent back to England (BL, Landsdowne MS 67, fos 150r, 169r, 172v).

[158] The Azores.

[159] 'meaneth to ride yt out' underlined.

nothing of his owne strength yf hee encounter them.[160] *[fo. 26v]* Wattes[161] the merchant hath now brought 3 very rich shippes to Plimouth from the very face of the porte of the Avanna,[162] laden with cochinelle, silver and great stoare of pearle and bullion. This was noe badd newse to my lord admyrall when hee awaked this morneing. I would yt were as good to your lordshipp.

Of France nothing is yet written but the queen's resolution is firme for my lord of Essex his revocation yf the 2 monethes were once ended. And for her companies, yf the king cann pay them, they shall continew longer, of which ther is great likelyhood, for those of Caen have promised him a good contribution.

Out of Brettany likewise nothing is advertized. This is all my lord[163] could deliver mee for your lordshipp to understand, wherwith I humbly take my leave. This 7 of November [September] 1591, from Southampton.

Your lordshipp's most bound att command

R. Cecyll

Letter 16: Sir Robert Cecil to Lord Chancellor Hatton, 9 September 1591

[fos 25v–26r]

May yt please your lordshipp. Ther are not come any lettres from my lord of Essex yet, but by Sir Henry Unton is advertized[164] that hee will

---

[160] Howard's optimism proved misplaced. Unknown to him, the Spanish were about to despatch a very powerful fleet to escort the treasure fleet home from the Azores. Howard's attempt to intercept the treasure ships was thwarted and the *Revenge* was lost on 30 August in an epic battle made famous by Sir Walter Ralegh's *A Report of the Truth of the Fight About the Iles of the Acores* (*STC* 20651, London, 1591).

[161] *Mattes* in MS. For these prizes taken by John Watts (c.1550–1616), merchant of London (Lord Mayor in 1606–1607), see BL, Lansdowne MS 67, fos 139r, 141r, 145r, 148r, 159r, 165r; A. Latham and J. Youings (eds), *The Letters of Sir Walter Ralegh*, (Exeter, 1999), pp. 57–59. Watts invested so frequently and successfully in privateering voyages that he was later described as 'the greatest pirate that has ever been in this kingdom'; K.R. Andrews, *Elizabethan Privateering: English Privateering During the Spanish War, 1585–1603* (Cambridge, 1964), pp. 104ff.

[162] Havana, Cuba.

[163] i.e. Lord Burghley, Cecil's father.

[164] PRO, SP 78/25, fo. 273r–v; *UC*, pp. 65–67: Unton to Burghley, Dieppe, 7 September 1591. This letter was carried by the pursuivant Robert Cooke, who was paid £6 13s 4d for his service by a warrant from Burghley dated 10 September 1591, 'at the courte' (PRO, E 351/542, m. 158d).

send over Mr Francis Darcy[165] with full accompte of his actions, who, I assure your lordshipp, will deserve his thankes yf hee yeeld her Majestie any satisfaction, from which hee seemeth the further off every day and hower, both in regard of his so perpetuall silence and because hee tarryed so long from his charge. Till the arrival of Mr Darcy noe newse are expected, by which time, yf your poore frindes bee not so happy as to see yow wher the queen earnestly expecteth your lordshipp, att my lord of Hartford's,[166] your lordshipp shall from your poore intilligencer bee informed of as much as his slender conceipt apprehendeth.

That your lordshipp may see how Bothwell standes in Scotlande, I have sent yow a coppy of his lettre to the king which Colonell Stewart delivered and was committed for his presumption. The humour of the lettre is worth the well noteing. [167] *[fo. 26r]* More att this time I have not to trouble your lordshipp, but with my humble duty which shall never dye while my spirit liveth. And so I humbly take my leave. From the court att Abersone[168] this 9th of November [September].

Your lordshipp's most bounden at command
R. Cecyll

[*Marginated*] Postscript
My lord of Essex hath had some fitt of an ague.

---

[165] Francis Darcy (d. 1641). Darcy's departure for England was delayed by Essex's ill-health on 6 September and the death of Walter Devereux on 8 September. He finally left Dieppe on 9 September, carrying letters from Essex and Unton (*UC*, pp. 59, 61–62; Berkshire Record Office, TA 13/2). For his arrival at court, see Letter 18. Darcy was knighted by Essex near Rouen on 8 Oct. (Poole, 'Journal', p. 536)

[166] Elvetham, a house owned by Edward Seymour, first Earl of Hertford (1537–1621). For the entertainment staged there by Hertford, 20–23 September; see Wilson, *Entertainments*, pp. 96–118; C. Breight, 'Realpolitik and Elizabethan ceremony: the Earl of Hertford's entertainment of Elizabeth at Elvetham, 1591', *Renaissance Quarterly*, 45 (1992), pp. 20–48. An account of the visit was published in London with lightning speed (within a week of the Queen's departure!) as *The Honorable Entertainement Gieven to the Queene's Majestie at Elvetham* (*STC* 7583).

[167] Robert Bowes, Elizabeth's resident ambassador in Scotland, enclosed a copy of Bothwell's letter to James VI in his own letter to Burghley of 2 September 1591 (*CSPSc.*, X, pp. 567–568). Colonel William Stewart had delivered this letter to James at Stirling at the request of the Countess of Bothwell (*ibid.*, p. 566: Bowes to Burghley, 27 August 1591).

[168] Abbotstone, Hampshire. This property was owned by the Marquess of Winchester (*VCH, Hampshire*, IV, pp. 193–194).

Letter 17: Sir Robert Cecil to Lord Chancellor Hatton, 10 September 1591

[fos 29r–30r]

May yt please your lordshipp. I may not dissemble my feeling comfort of your most noble favor, wherin I doe myselfe most right when I profess both a publique dutie and particuler true and unfeyned devotion, for which happy occasion I wish daylie not my lettres to trouble you, but by honest endeavours to serve yow.

Though I am not glad that your lordshipp (to doe mee favor by useing your owne hande) hath bynn so much trobled in time of your lordshipp's indisposition, yet I protest to your lordshipp yt doth so much please my heart to see this your extraordinary grace as yf therby I had received a great benefitt (wherin such is your absolute possession of mee) as I have strictly performed your favorable salutations, which bred mee some suspicion of worse *[fo. 29v]* matter by the comforte I founde the partie[169] received, in that her blood begann to come to her cheeks so suddainely. But now, my lord, that I have obeyed yow, I take yt not that I am bounde to keep promise with her who would have so much love, honor and dutie retourned and I should blush as fast to write, though I perceave her hearte is hardened.

I assure your lordshipp I am now so farr to seeke for matter to trouble yow which, as I thinke, France, Spaine and Ireland have forgotten us, but, yf I should cumber your lordshipp with my silly conjectures, this calme will prove to a storme, for out of Brittanie ther cann bee noe possibilitie of any good tydinges and belike out of France nothinge must come till the wynneing of the castle bee certified betweene Roan and Pont de Larche. Out of Ireland ther cometh daylie advertizementes that the cheife justice of the Common Place is in pryson for treason and yet doth the deputie[170] neyther write of the matter nor circumstances. His name is Robert Dyllon,[171] a knight, accused now by one Nugent, who marryed the baron of Deluyn's sister.[172] The queen is much offended with *[fo. 30r]* the deputie's silence,

---

[169] Presumably a reference to Cecil's wife.

[170] Sir William Fitzwilliam (1526–1599), who was serving his second term as Lord Deputy (he had previously been Deputy in Ireland, 1572–1575). A client and relative of Burghley, Fitzwilliam was a bitter enemy of Sir John Perrot, his predecessor as Lord Deputy.

[171] Sir Robert Dillon (d. 1597), Chief Justice of Ireland since 1581.

[172] William Nugent (d. 1625), brother of Christopher Nugent, third Baron Delvin (c.1540–1602). Nugent and Delvin claimed that Dillon had been corruptly using charges of treason to pursue vendettas and to extort benefits from the accused. The Nugents were bitter enemies of Dillon and the Lord Deputy claimed that these accusations were motivated by a family feud, stemming from the judicial murder of Nicholas Nugent at the urging of Sir Robert and Sir Lucas Dillon in 1582. Nugent's charges plagued Dillon

the action being of weight and worth the wryteinge. Hee was committed the 7 of August and lettres are come both of the 15, 20 and 27th, and without any mention.

Of removes my freind Mr Morgan can well certifie your lordshipp, though, for myne owne parte, I will advise your lordshipp once sawcylie not to build much uppon anything hee saith therof to your lordshipp. And yet, in other counsel, I will peradventure bee bounde for his honestie, yf hee want so badd a suertie.

I see your lordshipp so nobly to interprete my boald humours of writeinge as yt shall make mee little scrupulous still to write of somewhat, though never forgettful, I trust, to reserve an honest minde frawghte with so much dutie and true reverence that yt shall not appeare that nimia familiaritas parit contemptum[173]

I doe not beleeve that Mr Darcy will so soone write as is expected, till which time little cann be judged of their proceedinges. And therfore heer I most humbly take my leave. From my lodgeing neer Aberstone this X No. [September] 1591.

Your lordshipp's most humbly to command
R. Cecyll

Letter 18: Sir Robert Cecil to Lord Chancellor Hatton, 11 September 1591

[fos 28v–29r]

Even now, sir, your lordshipp may bee pleased to understand that Mr Darcy is come and that Mr Devereux,[174] within 4 miles of Roan, in an unnecessary light skyrmish, is slaine with a muskett shott in the face. It was in noe great service, but even a meere braverie.

My lord hath written[175] very largly that the king went to meete the reisters uppon good groundes, the particularitie [you] shall understand by my nexte. Only this, my lord, is his resolution: the king will send parte of his reysters to Brytannye and the rest with himselfe shall come to Roan, wher hee maketh noe doubte to bee the xxv[th] of this moneth

---

until he was finally cleared in November 1593 and re-appointed as Chief Justice in 1594. The reference to Nugent's marriage probably recalls his notorious abduction and marriage of Janet Marward, heiress to the barony of Skyrne and ward of his uncle, Nicholas Nugent, in 1573.

[173] 'nimia [...] contemptum': 'too much familiarity breeds contempt'.

[174] Walter Devereux (1569–1591), younger brother of the Earl of Essex. For his death, see Poole, 'Journal', 530; *L&A, 1591–1592*, pp. 204–205, §276; *HMCS*, IV, p. 140. His body was recovered for burial at Carmarthen.

[175] PRO, SP 78/25, fos 254r–255v; Devereux, I, pp. 225–229: Essex to Privy Council, Pont de l'Arche, 2 September 1591.

and, being joyned to the Marshall Byron's troupes and the Duke Montpensier's[176] with the queen's forces, they meane to sitt downe resolutely before Roane.

In the meane time the marshiall and my lord doe make the trenches ready and blocke upp all passadges to the towne, which (to use his lordshipp's owne wordes) they hope to wynn in 8 dayes, not because the towne need so quickly to yeeld, but because the people, beeinge [fo. 29r] assured of a furious battrye, will rather yeeld then hazard a sacke, which in Paris a lingering seidge did not so certeynly threaten.[177] But, of this, the issue is left to God and the judgement of the probabilitie, with all dutie, I leave to your lordshipp's grave wisdome, and so most humbly take my leave. This xi[th] of November [September] 1591.

Your lordshipp's most obedient att command
R Cecyll

Letter 19: Sir Robert Cecil to Lord Chancellor Hatton, 13 September 1591
[fos 30v–32v]

Eiusdem[178]

My dutie humbly remembred to your lordshipp. In some letters from my lord embassador att Deipe, I heare of your lordshipp's vouchsafeing [fo. 31r] to accepte of my poore services, for now hee writes that your lordshipp so expresseth yt to him. Surely, sir, I know superfluitie agrees neither with your mind nor quallitie and therfore doe I forbeare with words to cumber yow. Only this, my good lord: seeing I have noe more to offer but my service and love, and seeing your lordshipp deserveth noe less then both, I beseech yow accept of both as of that which your lordshipp hath purchased with your favor and kindnes, and which (if I bee of any price) may bee an ornament to your greatnes.

I have sent your lordshipp the coppy of the earle's lettre by way of apologie of the king's actions.[179] It is to bee thought that the king's martiall experience teacheth him to doe what is best for himselfe. Marry, my lord hath only to answere and give accounte for his goeing without leave, tarryinge without lymitation and hazard (as her Majestie saith) of him and her forces not uppon soundest discretion. These

[176] François de Bourbon-Vendôme, Duke of Montpensier, Henri IV's governor of Normandy and father of the Prince of Dombes.
[177] For Henri IV's failed attempt to capture Paris in 1590, see Wernham, *After the Armada*, pp. 182–186.
[178] 'Eiusdem': 'of the same man'.
[179] i.e. Essex's letter of 2 September, summarized in Letter 18.

points (shee, like herself) princely insisteth uppon and addes to the errors this misfortune and evill befalling his brother, which att first was kept from her, but, being declared, her Majestie digested yt loine fortune de guerre.[180]

Her resolution is to have the earle home and her forces also revoaked, but of the last her counsaile doe not so well tast, not because the king hath not wronged her Majeste in hastening her forces and now abandoning so long the attempt of Roan, but because *[fo. 31v]* her Majestie cannot leave him but shee must danger the cause, and therfore doe they humbly move her Majestie to suspend the revocation of her forces yf their pay may be assured and that is now, for all their suits, but thus answered (which I would to God your lordshipp had bynn heer to have furthered for the common cause sake with your counsell)[181] that, if the king cann pay them, some of them shall tarry, but not all. And for him that governeth absolutely,[182] her Majestie will not lett him longer abide. To this purpose even now are lettres[183] directed and, except God turne her Majestie's mind, none heer dare move reason for yt, but for the matter yf her Majeste's troupes might tarry, which are the countenance of the king's strenth against the enemie and even in a manner his guarde. For the matter who should bee longer generall, to God and her pleasure yt is to bee left, for that yf one man bee not fitt for yt, another may bee found. But yf this occasion overpass, halfe a million next yeare will not so much helpe him, for, togeather with her Majestie's withdrawinge, all this parte will grow cold and desperate. But this am I able to shew yow but as in a glass and therfore to your lordshipp's wisdome I referr yt onely because I said in my last lettre I would doe so. I doe send your lordshipp that wherby yow may see their arguments and also doe write your lordshipp heerwith such of her Majeste's resolutions as *[fo. 32r]* att this dispatche I understand. There hath bynn great care today in counsaile for the safe tradeinge to Burdeauxe,[184] which is more now looked into because yt is advertized that fower gallies of Spaine are come to Brehac in Brittanie, wher Sir John Norris[185] first landed, of whom ther is no certainty advertized but

---

[180] 'loine fortune de guerre': 'distant fortune of war'.

[181] This second parenthesis missing in MS.

[182] i.e. the Earl of Essex.

[183] PRO, SP 78/25, fos 307r–311r; *UC*, pp. 72–76: Privy Council to Essex, Unton and Leighton, from Farleigh [Wallop], 13 September 1591.

[184] For the Privy Council's orders for convoying ships to Bordeaux, see *APC*, XXI, pp. 442–445. The clerk has assigned these orders to a meeting at Basing, but has failed to specify the exact date. Cecil's letter indicates that the meeting actually took place at Farleigh Wallop. Since the council meeting was clearly held on 13 September, the confusion was probably caused by the court's removal to Basing later on the same day.

[185] Sir John Norris (c.1547–1597), commander of English forces in Brittany. For his career, see J. Nolan, *Sir John Norreys and the Elizabethan Military World* (Exeter, 1997).

a rumour by a letter from Sarcy[186] that the Prince and hee have overthrowne 500 Spaniards.

I humbly crave your lordshipp's pardon and desire God to send yow as much honor and as long life as I wish to any to whom eyther nature or dutie hath bounde mee. From the court att Farley[187] this 19th November [13 September] 1591.

Your lordshipp's most bounden and therfore att command,
R. Cecill

[*Marginated*] Postscript:
I beleeve the gallys next remove wilbe to New Haven.[188]

[*Marginated*] Postscript:
One the 3 of 8tobre the 2 moneths end and because shipping requireth tyme for victualling and manninge, her Majestie hath this day given order to have the hoyes taken upp, which will cost mony and therfore her Majeste's resolution is firme, except second cogitation breed with time change before that day.

The embassador hath att Deipe reasoned uppon the pointe of the king's meanes to pay, which are the contribution of Caen, who to have Roan beseiged doe offer 50000 crownes, [*fo. 32v*] 50000ˡⁱ in corne and have given 10000 to the Marishall Byron underhand[189] to urge yt. But this doth hee onlie advertize and wisely assureth nothing, of which now the queen sends to know an assured confirmation.

Letter 20: Sir Robert Cecil to Lord Chancellor Hatton, 16 September 1591
[*fo. 30v*]

My dutie humbly remembred to your lordshipp. It pleased the queen's Majestie, att my entreateing for leave for a day or two to come to London, expressly to charge mee to waite uppon your lordshipp, wheresover your lordshipp was, and to comende her most gratiouslie unto yow, with some more particularities which I will not tonight

[186] Nicolas de Harlay, Seigneur de Sancy. This may be a garbled account of the inconclusive clash at St Meen on 28–29 August (*L&A, 1591–1592*, pp. 281–283, §445–448).

[187] Farleigh Wallop, Hampshire, house of Sir Henry Wallop (c.1531–1599), who spent most of his career as a government official in Ireland.

[188] Le Havre.

[189] 'understand' in MS. For the correction of this scribal error and the source of Cecil's information, see PRO, SP 78/25, fo. 285r: Unton to Burghley, 8 September 1591. This letter is not in *UC* because Unton 'wrote to the lord threasurer by Mr Darcye but I could not, for haste, reserve a coppie thereof' (*UC*, p. 59).

trouble your lordshipp with. I heard your lordshipp was att Drayton[190] and, beinge very neere your howse, understoode the contrary. I came out very late today before dynner, which made mee come more unseasonably heer then stood with good manners to have cumbred your lordshipp. In which regard I am bold to crave pardon tonight and therfore doe presume to deferr my attendance till tomorrow att your lordshipp's better leysure. In the meane time, I humbly take my leave. From my owne poore howse att 8 of the clocke this night the xvi[th] of No. [September] 1591.

Your lordshipp's most assuredly att command,

R. Cecyll

Letter 21: Sir Robert Cecil to Lord Chancellor Hatton, [19 September] 1591

[fos 32v–35r]

May yt please your lordshipp. I came to Odiam on Satturday night[191] att 6 of the clocke, wher I found the queen warmed with the lettres which Smith, my lord of Essex his man, had newly brought.[192] They conteyned matter of excuse, but by way of apologie of his owne actions, which hee justifieth to have bynn don uppon good ground with assent of all of judgment about him and by procurement of the king that hee should come. This doth no[t] please, although his lettres to her Majestie expresseth his greife for her Majeste's mislike, his passion att his first apprehension of her Majeste's indignation, his weaknes of body growne by his troubled an[d] afflicted thoughtes and his resolution, yf her Majeste's absolute authority now calls him home, to betake himselfe to a life answerable to his miserable fortune, which hee forseeth yf his honor be thus ruined *[fo. 33r]* by her Majeste's dealeing with him heer, who was sent to beseige a towne from which, now when hee is ready for yt, hee is called backe with all disgrace that may bee. To tell your lordshipp what shee will doe uppon this my capacity comprehendeth not, but what now her Majestie doth say shee will doe is that, yf his honor were never so dear to him, yet her Majeste's owne is dearer to herselfe and therfore will shee be noe longer deluded by the king's protractions nor have the world to see herselfe to continew a generall

---

[190] West Drayton, Middlesex. The manor and rectory had been seized by the crown upon the attainder of Thomas Lord Paget and were leased to Hatton for life in July 1587: PRO, C 66/1288, mm. 6–7.

[191] i.e. 18 September.

[192] BL, Additional MS 74286, fos 15r–16r; Devereux, I, 235–237: Essex to Elizabeth, 12 September 1591; PRO, SP 78/25, fos 299r–300r: Essex to Burghley, Arques, 13 September 1591.

there who, as her Majestie saith, so much forgetteth himself and her service. This for the action, to us that bee pecora lanigre,[193] her Majestie vehemently expresseth. But what after her second bethinkinge, with consultation of her counsailers of wisdome and experience, her Highnes may doe in the cause and what shee will doe out of comiseration of his estate of bodie and mind (which both her embassador and Mr Killigrew[194] pathettically describe in their lettres)[195] that must time discover and to your lordshipp's grave judgment doe I leave yt, who best doe looke into the necessity of the affaire ytselfe in question and truliest know her Majeste's inwarde gracious and favorable proceedings with those that shee hath favored when the bitterness att first is a little digested. With one voice every man speakes for the matter. Sir Henry Unton writt a very discreet lettre both in shewing the perill of the whole French king's cause, yf by this soddaine hee bee weakened and so his tickle partie discouraged and also in setting forth my lord's sorrow. Hee affirmeth that in his life hee never saw man so worne and changed. [fo. 33v] Mr Killigrew describes the manner of his passion to bee such as that hee sounded att the readinge[196] of the queen's lettre thrise and that, imediately being laid on his bedd, his bodie so swelled as his buttons broke from his dublett.[197]

Now that I have particularly declared what termes as yet things stand in for this matter, I will speake of that which, by your lordshipp's comaundment, I had to deliver to the queen.

I told her Majestie wher I found your lordshipp in the morneinge, busied with such things as the Citty had acquainted your lordshipp withall, upon the death of the maior.[198]

I did lett the queen know that your lordshipp most humbly accepted her Majeste's favors in sending to see yow, which yow tooke most comfort in as a signe her Majestie remembred yow, who never lived so longe devided body from the mind as since this progress your

---

[193] 'pecora lanigre': these two words are enclosed in parentheses in the MS, perhaps because their meaning was obscure even to the copyist. It is perhaps possible that this is a corruption of the Latin for 'wool-bearing animals' (i.e. sheep).

[194] Henry Killigrew (c.1528–1603), a long-serving royal servant and diplomat who had been sent to France as an adviser to Essex. See A.C. Miller, *Sir Henry Killigrew: Elizabethan Soldier and Diplomat* (Leicester, 1963).

[195] PRO, SP 78/25, fos 292r–294r, 297r–298r; *UC*, pp. 68–70: respectively, Killigrew and Unton to Burghley, Dieppe, 12 and 13 September 1591.

[196] 'describes the manner [...] readinge' underlined.

[197] According to Killigrew, Essex felt 'suche an extreme agony and passion that he sownded often and did so swell that, castyng hemselfe upon his bed, all his bottons of his doblett brake away as thoth they had ben cut with a kneffe' (PRO, SP 78/25, fo. 294r).

[198] John Allott (d. 17 September 1591), fishmonger. Sir Rowland Hayward (senior alderman and previously Lord Mayor in 1570–1571) served the remainder of Allott's term.

lordshipp had donne, which had made your life so melancholy and so fedd yow with solitary conceipts as yow should esteeme your life but a death untill yow came to her presence, of whose good health, lookes and disposition of body, I told her Majeste, yow very particularly enquired, being very glad to heare mee confirme what yow had to your greatest comfort understood by your owne messengers of the protection of that wherwith yow were so well acquainted by your lordshipp's dayly contemplation of the same, which was the greater cause *[fo. 34r]* of your greater feeleing now of that want because, since your journey to Spaine,[199] yow had not bynn from her Majestie so long and therfore, although her Majestie did now forbid your attendance to Elvetam, yet did I lett her Majestie know yow were so impatient of seeing her as yow did underhand enquire of mee whether ther were not some likelyhood of some longer stay from Otlandes. For, yf ther were, noe comandment should longer hold yow, although your lordshipp did indeed find some more access of your indisposition then yow had a good while.

I am ashamed to have marred your lordshipp's matter as much have her Majestie looked for of mee from yow.[200] For shee begann, before I could deliver halfe my message, to speake of your lordshipp's passion for being so long absent from her and withall sware that never any man loved her trulier then yow did and that yf shee should forgett her swete lyddes.[201] God must forgett her and therfore, saith shee, sirra, tell mee truly, for I am sure yow were a welcome messenger to him and to yow hee would say his mind. To which I answered, truly, madam, yf I should for his favorable opinion of mee belye his lordshipp in not telling truly as much as I cann remember what I found in him towards your Majestie, I should not bee worthy to bee sent by yow nor trusted by him. This made mee, my good lord, the larger with her and, yf I would have spoken longer, shee would have bynn pleased with the longer heareing of yt. The jewell then (with the best wordes of excuseing the *[fo. 34v]* unworthiness of yt) I did deliver and withall the suite yow made that to the distressed earle yt might be sent, affirmeing that your lordshipp was so well acquainted with the greifes that such as hee conceaved, yf her Majestie were displeased, as both for the cause and

[199] This reference (which is very clear in the MS) is perplexing because Hatton is not known to have visited Spain. It is undoubtedly a scribal error, in which 'Spa' has erroneously been expanded to 'Spaine'. Despite the Queen's misgivings, Hatton travelled to Spa to recover his health on 3 June 1573 and apparently remained abroad until the autumn of that year: Nicolas, *Memoirs of Hatton*, pp. 24–31.

[200] This sentence is obviously missing several words, but the sense (and Cecil's exaggerated self-deprecation) seems clear.

[201] 'Lids' (as in eyelids) was Elizabeth's pet name for Hatton. She also called him her 'mutton' (see Letter 9).

the person, your lordshipp did beseech her Majestie to shew her gratious disposition in comforting of him. I am little able and not worthy to judge of her Majeste's inward thoughtes but shee fell into so great prayse of your nature, your faith and constancy as, to deale plainely with your lordshipp, yf shee send him any comfort, in myne opinion, this hath exceedingly sett yt forward, which I confess, in my poorest interest in this publike action, I should bee glad to see yow well onward. And for her particuler disposition of him, I wish him all good, but for that herselfe knowes best her time and with time, mee thinketh, yt should not long bee ecclipsed for all this storme.

I was bold (not thinkeing yt an ill office) to lett Mr Smith know what I had to say[202] of my lord his master to the queen from your lordshipp and how much hee was beholding to yow, of my particuler knowledg in his absence.[203]

My lord writes[204] that the Marishall Byron would have him beginn with Gourney neer Roan, which is the place that may annoy the king in the seidge and may [fo. 35r] best from Abbevill releeve the Duke of Perma yf hee come in to rayse the king from Roan. Yt is some 5 leagues from Roan and easily wonn, as hee writeth, but yet dareth hee not attempt yt without hir Majeste's leave. Only hee and the embassador are gonn to speake with him and have removed the company from Deipe and Arques by reason of the infection. Thus all things stand yett in a stay and thus have I tediously tyred your lordshipp. Let my duty excuse my folly and then shall your favor make mee thinke myselfe happy to be protected with your grave judgment. From Odiam this Sunday morneing att 9 of the clocke.

> Your lordshipp's most humbly
> [no signature added]

Letter 22: Sir Robert Cecil to Lord Chancellor Hatton, 24 [September] 1591
[fo. 4r–v]

May yt please your lordshipp. Divers letters are come tonight of the

---

[202] Followed by 'lett', struck through.

[203] There is a marginal annotation against this paragraph which is written in a different hand from that of the copyist: 'what to be shewed at hafle lightes to know a great point of discretion'. Comparison of the hand suggests that this is a note by William Drake.

[204] PRO, SP 78/25, fos 299r–300r: Essex to Burghley, 13 September 1591.

good forwardnes of the French action.[205] Gourney is beseiged by the marishall and there are our troupes. By letters which my lord of Essex writes to the counsaile[206] your lordshipp may perceive that which my lord my father doth now send your lordshipp. The embassender may pray for his lordshipp's retourne, for although hee writes as warily as any man lyveing and cannot for dutie's sake but doe what hee doth, yet, I assure your lordshipp, yf in his writeinges her Majeste perceave the least justification (yea, or almost tolleration) straight hee is coupled with Sir Thomas Leighton and Mr Killegrew in lettres of reprehension, so as yt is very hard for the embassendor (whiles my lord is there) to avoid her Majestie's blame, except hee doe eyther pull my lord on his head or not deliver his minde for the cause, though his heart thinketh yt. This letter to the counsaile[207] and Sir Thomas Leighton's[208] will reporte the whole proceedinges to your lordshipp, of which what your lordshipp may judge I presume not to censure. But I assure your lordshipp that her Majestie nothing tasteth them, though, to my poore understanding, ther cannot bee better likelyhood then these purposes promise and yet, for all this, her Majestie writeth directly for my lord to come away. Hee contrarily to her Majestie writeth[209] peremptorily for leave for 6 weekes[210] att the least *[fo. 4v]* (though the troupes retourne), wherof her Majestie collecteth his so small desire to see her as shee doth requite[211] him accordingly with crossing him in his most earnest desire, wherin (as one that wisheth him all honorable fortune) I pray God to put in his minde to make her Majestie's absolute will his perfectest reasone[212] and to frame his actions to her Majeste's likeinge. And thus for this time doe I humbly take my leave, hopeing your lordshipp's counsaile will yet keepe the cause from perill and, for my lord to make his peace, I leave him to her Majeste's grace when

[205] PRO, SP 78/25, fos 334r–335r, 336r–v, 338r, 340r–v; *UC*, pp. 78–81, 81–83: respectively, Unton, Killigrew and Leighton to the Privy Council, Unton to Burghley, Essex to Burghley, Killigrew to Burghley, all dated 18 September 1591. These letters were brought over by James Painter, who was paid £10 for this service by a warrant from Burghley dated at Farnham, 24 September 1591 (PRO, E 351/542, m. 158d). Burghley noted the arrival of these letters in his campaign journal: BL, Cotton MS Titus B VI, fo. 35v. Painter's packet also apparently included at least one letter from Essex to the Queen (see below).

[206] *HMCS*, IV, pp. 139–141: Essex to the Privy Council, c. 18 September 1591.

[207] PRO, SP 78/25, fos 334r–335r; *UC*, pp. 78–81: Unton, Killigrew and Leighton to the Privy Council (noted above).

[208] Presumably, PRO, SP 78/25, fo. 290r–v: Leighton and Killigrew to Burghley, 13 September 1591.

[209] BL, Additional MS 74286, fo. 21r; Devereux, I, pp. 241–242: Essex to Elizabeth, [September 1591].

[210] 'which what your lordshipp may judge [...] weekes' underlined.

[211] 'collecteth [...] requite' underlined.

[212] 'I pray God [...] reasone' underlined.

hee is once att home, who is as ready to forgive as apte to reprove, yf good meanes bee taken, which in truth her royall absolute estate ought to challenge as dutie. From Farnham the 24 of [September] 1591

Your lordshipp's humbly att commande
[no signature added]

Letter 23: Sir Robert Cecil to Lord Chancellor Hatton, 24 September 1591

[fo. 5r]

My dutie remembered to your lordshipp. By this my lord willeth mee to lett your lordshipp see what is sent in satisfaction of her Majeste's former objections,[213] but all cannot stay her Majeste's resolution to revoake my lord and all hers, both in regard of the wrong already donne her by the kinge and the disobedience (as her Majesty termeth yt) of my lord. Yf yt please your lordshipp to peruse them and, att your pleasure, the next day to send them, yow shall perceave fully the disposition ther and, till your lordshipp come to joyne your helpe, his lordshipp cannot but doubt the continewance still of her Majeste's offence, which, yf yt were not like to prejudice the cause, the rest would not prove deadly: nam nullum violentum est perpetuum.[214] Heerwith my lord commend[s] him hartily to your lordshipp and I most humbly take my leave. This 24th of September 1591.

The dispatch[215] for the earle's revocation and as many as the shipps cann bring is now gonne.[216]

Your lordshipp's most humbly
[no signature added]

---

[213] 'remembred to your [...] objections' underlined. The letter sent to Hatton may be Essex's letter to the Privy Council of c.18 September (see above) or BL, Additional MS 74286, fos 15r–16r; Devereux, I, pp. 235–237: Essex to Elizabeth, 12 September 1591, in reply to her letter (now lost) of 3 September.

[214] 'Nam [...] perpetuum': 'for nothing fierce can last forever'.

[215] APC, XXI, pp. 461–465 (dated 23 September 1591). Further letters were sent on 26 September (ibid., pp. 466–467).

[216] 'The dispatch for [...] gonne' underlined.

Letter 24: Sir Robert Cecil to Lord Chancellor Hatton, c.28 September 1591

[fos 21r–22v]

My dutie humbly remembred to your lordshipp. I troubled yow not by Mr Morgan because I could have wished to have had a better subject. Her Majestie groweth much more stiffe in this matter of France then before and, where Mr Smith[217] did hope to carry his lord some comfort, her Majestie now dispatched away Mr Francis Darcy[218] to assure my lord that in noe wise shee would have him thinke of any stay[219] and, for her forces residing there, shee saw noe reason, considering his reisters being come downe, and that, yf shee would stay them uppon his promise of paying them, shee knew that her people should have *[fo. 21v]* nothing but parrolls.[220] True yt is her Majestie writt to my lord,[221] but I cann assure your lordshipp (for shee vouchsaffed to read yt), more then for her gratious contentation now to use her owne hand and for her grave and serious admonition, ther was little matter wherof might bee derived to him in this action any matter of consolation. Shee hath also written to Sir Thomas Leighton sharpely because hee wrote now a lettre in the earle's defence, wherin somewhat to much hee inserted, for hee expostulated with her Majestie that hee knew no manner of cause to make her Majestie mislike my lord's actions. But that which more I am sorry for, because her embassador did write plentifully in setting forth the necessity of her Majestie's secondinge the king att this time and that yt would bee a great perill to the whole cause yf by her the king in the eye of his partie were disgraced now. Although of my lord of Essex hee did write very temperately, yet hath shee, for company, caused my lord to write to him that shee little thought hee would have followed the rest, and espetially goe to the Marshall Byron before hee was presented to the king as her Majestie's embassador. All this was but to accumulate more uppon my lord of Essex and yet to him, that is not used to her Majestie's disposition (meaneing so well as hee *[fo. 22r]* did), may yt bee some trouble. I have therfore a little advised

---

[217] Smith left for France on 26 September (see above).

[218] Burghley noted the date of Darcy's departure for France as 20 September (BL, Cotton MS Titus B VI, fo. 35v). This seems too early because he did not arrive at Essex's camp outside Rouen until 5 October (Nichols, 'Journal by Coningsby', p. 24). Cecil's letter also suggests that Darcy was despatched after Smith. A departure date of 27–28 September seems more probable. Darcy had left court by the time Robert Carey arrived on 1 October.

[219] Followed by 'them uppon his promise of paying', struck through.

[220] i.e. 'paroles': fine words or promises.

[221] PRO, SP 78/25, fos 354r–355r; *UC*, pp. 94–96: Queen to Unton and Leighton, 25 September 1591.

him,[222] because I was a hearer of her manner of reprehension, not to
thinke yt more then a venial sinne, for when my lord my father
answered, by God, madam, I would have written as hee did and so
donne, except yow meant to make him stand for a cypher, shee
answered, well, I will have him knowe his error and, yf yow doe yt
not, I will, and, when my lord chancelor comes, hee shall doe so too.
Donne yt is and by this time all is paste, but this will not bee the last
which hee shall have before his time bee expired, which hee hath witt
to judge of and patience to indure and, yf hee had heard how infinitely
her Majestie praysed him for the same lettre not an hower before
and for his carriage of himselfe, hee would have thought of Ovid's
Metamorphosis.[223] When I may bee so happy as to see your lordshipp,
I will tell your lordshipp more. In the meane time, I humbly take my
leave and, for your jewell, I doe not finde that her Majestie is willing
to parte with yt yet. But I have written to him[224] as truly as I had cause
that, in his absence, your lordshipp as any[225] occasion hath bynn
presented, have honerably stood to his lordshipp and, yf I shall not lye
to yow, I have a shrewde gess that your fresh favor to yt will, att your
comeing, mende the matter, *[fo. 22v]* which I wish may prove to the
good of that cause which wee are bound to defende. And thus, from
my Elvetia,[226] I humbly take my leave. From my lodging neer the court
this 20th [c.28th] of September 1591.

Your lordshipp's humbly att [commandment]
[no signature added]

Letter 25: Sir Robert Cecil to Lord Chancellor Hatton, 8 October 1591

[fos 22v–23v]

My humble dutie remembred to your lordshipp. When my lord went
on Munday to Theobalds, I came hither,[227] wher I have mett with
nothing worthy your lordshipp's trouble. The queen hath taken a great
cold which doth much troble her and with yt shee seemeth, to us that
att any time shee vouchsafeth to speake withall, very melancholy and

---

[222] *UC*, pp. 93–94: Cecil to Unton, 24 September 1591.

[223] The *Metamorphoses*, written by Publius Ovidius Naso (43 BC–18 AD), which consist
of fifteen books of poetry telling stories of miraculous and mythical transformations.

[224] This letter from Cecil to Essex has not survived. Cecil's letter was presumably a
reply to PRO, SP 78/25, fo. 290r–v: Essex to Cecil, c.13 September 1591.

[225] 'my' in MS.

[226] Helvetia (i.e. Switzerland).

[227] Richmond.

indisposed. Ther came lettres from Mr Killigrewe[228] that Monsieur d'O,[229] the king's treasurer, and Sir Roger Williams were come to Deipe to take order for mony for her Majestie's souldiers. Neyther was Mr Darcy nor Smith then gonn to my lord and therfore, yf any longer stay were made by them for want of conveyes to the campe, yt is then to bee thought that both they and Mr Cary[230] will arive togeather, the one with bona nova, the other[231] catina.[232] The queen wisheth yt otherwise because this last, donne with the olive branch, might bee the more welcome [fo. 23r] when the other former messengers have delivered their unwelcome message.[233] Mr Cary was dispatched on Munday the 4th and Mr Killigrewe's lettres were of the 3, wherin hee writt that, within a day or two, those messengers should bee able to goe to the earle, which without a convey they could not, so as the times being distinguished, the difference will not bee very greate. Her Majestie had by them commanded the embassador to forbeare going to the king till hee came to Roan, but hee, following his former instructions originally and being ignorant of this caution, accidentally is gonne to the king.[234] But yt is not spoken of to the queen, but when shee shall know yt, he may bee justly excused and yet, as the queen is pleased to use yt yf other thinges succeed not well, this will likewise by her Majestie bee misconstrued. And therfore is yt thought good by my lord[235] to lett yt fall out heerafter, when with yt some other pleaseing matter may bee

---

[228] This letter from Killigrew of 3 September has apparently not survived. Heneage had previously written to Burghley on 29 September that d'O and Williams were expected at Dieppe very shortly: PRO, SP 78/25, fos 380r–381v.

[229] François d'O (or d'Au), surintendant des finances.

[230] Robert Carey (?1560–1639), youngest son of Lord Hunsdon (see above). He had been sent over from France by Essex to report the capture of Gournay, leaving Dieppe on 27 September. He received an icy initial reception from the Queen, but ultimately managed to convince her to send Essex a conciliatory message. Leaving Oatlands on 4 October, he returned to Dieppe with all possible speed, but arrived two hours too late. Upon landing, he discovered that Essex had already sailed for England late on 8 October, obeying the Queen's peremptory summons which Darcy had delivered. Carey was knighted by Essex immediately after the Earl's return to Dieppe on 16 October (Mares, *Memoirs of Robert Carey*, pp. 15–18; Nichols, 'Journal by Coningsby', pp. 24, 28; Poole, 'Journal', p. 537).

[231] Followed by 'with', struck through.

[232] 'bona nova': 'good news'; 'catina': catena, 'a chain'.

[233] Carey carried a letter granting Essex and his army an extra month in the field, instead of their immediate recall: HMCS, IV, pp. 143–144: Elizabeth to Essex, 4 October 1591.

[234] Unton decided to go to meet Henri IV on 1 October (BRO, TA 13/2; UC, pp. 102–103: Unton to Burghley, from near Gournay, 1 October 1591). However, it was not until the morning of 22 October that Unton finally managed to speak with the King (PRO, SP 78/26, fos 85r–86r, 84r; UC, pp. 119–121: Unton to Elizabeth, from Noyon, 28 October 1591).

[235] i.e. Lord Burghley.

delivered, for I find that att some time good is badd and, another time, worse not so ill taken. Her Majestie's displeasure against the French king appeareth in her suspence of his embassador's audience,[236] whose being att Mr Vice-chamberlaine's marriage her Majestie much misliked in Mr Vice-chamberlaine,[237] *[fo. 23v]* as I may privately to your lordshipp write yt, who I know and find ar pleased with whatever I say or doe to use for my good, which, as I account a principle ornament to my poore fortune to live in so noble a protection, so will I make yt one of my hearte's most greedy desires by all love and honor to bee worthy of your lordshipp's undeserved favor, which noe man's affections shall more challenge whiles my life lasteth, though my meanes may come shorte of other men's powers. And so I humbly take my leave. From the court this 8th of October 1591.

> Your lordshipp's most humbly att commandment
> [no signature added]

Letter 26: Sir Robert Cecil to Lord Chancellor Hatton, 21 October 1591

[fos 24v–25r]

My humble dutie remembred to your lordshipp. I have forborne to trouble your lordshipp with my lettres these few dayes because I knew I could not sooner advertize your lordshipp of any thing then yourselfe had yt att loud. The lettres are first brought to my lord and then sent hither, in which interim I doubt not but my advertizementes would bee stale. Yesterday the duke of Sax[ony][238] his death troubled, as ther is good cause. Today the newse[239] of Cawdbeck's[240] being taken pleaseth but, in the meane time, her Majeste's people wast, her treasures

---

[236] Despite this delay, Beauvoir la Nocle had an audience with Elizabeth before 15 October (*UC*, pp. 110–111).

[237] The reference here to the vice-chamberlain, Sir Thomas Heneage, must reflect a scribal error. Heneage's wife was alive in August 1593 and died at the end of November 1593 (*HMCS*, IV, pp. 348, 423). He did not remarry until 2 May 1594. His only child, a daughter, had been married since c.1573.

[238] Christian I, Elector and Duke of Saxony (d. 15 September 1591). A key ally of Henri IV, his support helped to ensure that German troops could be recruited for the King. His death not only threatened to undermine the international coalition which was supporting Henri against Spain and the Catholic League, but also made it likely that the German troops would abandon Henri if he could not immediately give them their full pay (*HMCS*, IV, p. 151: Burghley to Essex, 22 October 1591. Cf. *UC*, pp. 112–114: Elizabeth to the Prince of Anhalt, 23 October 1591).

[239] PRO, SP 78/26, fos 48r–49v, 50r, 52r, 54r–55r, 56r, 58r, 60r: letters to Burghley from Essex, Williams, Leighton, Killigrew and Maurice Kiffin, all dated 18 October 1591.

[240] Caudebec.

consume and, yf the takeing of Roan bee not effected, ther is none of
these petty places worth the haveing.

[fo. 25r] Of the king's comeing towardes Roan uncertaintie, my lord of
Essex writes,[241] but hee hath sent Sir Roger Williams to the king, from
whom in 6 daies hee expecteth particularity and certainty. The bruite
is that hee should bee att Senlys[242] and wilbee att Roan in 5 daies.

The queen is well (God be thanked) and that, I know, is to your
lordshipp the welcomest newse. Wherfore I will heer humbly take my
leave, haveing only donne this to lett your lordshipp know by my
remembring yt to your lordshipp (for other tryall I cannot give you),
that yf I were in anything worthy your comandmentes they should bee
as welcome to mee as to any creature liveing. From the court this 21
October 1591.

> Your lordshipp's humbly to doe yow service
> [no signature added]

The earle plyes the queen with much kind writeing but, yf I shall tell
your lordshipp my poore conceipte, his favor is much in the waine.
Heer is an earle of N[243] well used.

Of the imbassador[244] nothing is heard since his goeing towardes the
king, the passages are so stopped.

Letter 27: Sir Robert Cecil to Lord Chancellor Hatton, 27 October 1591

[fo. 24r–v]

My humble dutie remembred to your lordshipp. I could not conveniently offer your lordshipp's bill to her Majestie till yesterday att 4
of the clocke. Her Majeste's answere was that att this I should bring yt
to her againe. Although to your lordshipp this bee asmuch as if I had
written nothinge, yet, in discharge of my dutie to my minde, yt is
somethinge that I may not bee held, by my silence, to your lordshipp
unmindfull of your comandments, who shall ever dispose of my service
next myne owne father without exception. I know yt a small addition

---

[241] PRO, SP 78/26, fos 48r–49v: Essex to Burghley, 18 October 1591.

[242] Senlis.

[243] Presumably Henry Percy, eighth Earl of Northumberland (1564–1631). In late July, Northumberland had requested that Elizabeth visit his house at Petworth, Sussex, during her forthcoming progress. However, it seems that this could not be accommodated in the Queen's schedule (W.D. Cooper, 'Queen Elizabeth's visits to Sussex', *Sussex Archaeological Collections*, 5 (1852), pp. 196–197; *HMC, Seventh Report, Appendix* (London, 1879), pp. 649–650.

[244] i.e. Unton.

to your greatnes which my love cann yeild yow but yet is yt that which I have vowed out of dutie to your lordshipp and that which mine owne heart shall never bee negligent to performe while I have breath.

The newse[245] of the king's approach towardes Roan with 10000 foote and 7000 horse may pascifie the queen's displeasure towardes the king but the makeing of knightes hath ministred her just cause to speake her pleasure of the earle.[246] Yt was told her the last day in the afternoone by Sir W. Rawleigh, after your lordshipp had taken *[fo. 24v]* your leave, since which time her Highness hath not forgotten yt, I can assure your lordshipp. I humbly crave pardon for this trouble to your lordshipp, and with my best wishes of honor, health and long life, I take my leave. From the court this 27 October 1591

Your lordshipp's humbly att command
[no signature added]

---

[245] The source of this information is uncertain.

[246] For Essex's mass dubbing of twenty-four knights 'upon a faire grene in the sighte of' Rouen and its inhabitants, see Nichols, 'Journal by Coningsby', p. 27; Poole, 'Journal', pp. 536–537. Essex also subsequently dubbed at least three more knights, including Sir Robert Carey (see above). Burghley warned Essex about his knightings in a letter of 22 October: 'your lordship so liberall bestowing of knighthoods is here commonly evil censured, and when her Majesty shall know it, which yet she doth not, I fear she will be highly offended, considering she would have had that authority left out of your commission if I had not supplied it with a cautelous instruction. But quod factum est, infectum esse non potest ['what has been done cannot be undone'] and hereby you have increased the state of ladies present and future' (*HMCS*, IV, p. 151). For details of the men knighted, see Tenison, *Elizabethan England*, VIII, pp. 524–527.

INDEX